Where the Domino Fell

America and Vietnam,
1945–2006

Fifth Edition

Where the Domino Fell

America and Vietnam
1945–2006
Fifth Edition

James S. Olson
Randy Roberts

Brandywine Press • Maplecrest, New York

Cover photo courtesy *AP/Wide World Photos*

Contents

Preface

The earliest Rambo movie could almost be taken as an antiwar film. Sylvester Stallone's John Rambo in *First Blood* is a troubled Vietnam veteran hunted by backwater police and gun wielders of a type ordinarily identified with blood-hungry patriotism. If that is the message, the producers of the Rambo movies apparently later changed their focus. In his return to the screen, Rambo is a vehicle for hyperpatriotic fantasies, a muscled and fearless avenger of freedom against Vietnamese Communists, Soviet invaders of Vietnam, and surely any other enemies of the American Way. The introspection that makes its tentative, half-articulate presence in *First Blood* gives way to a dreamscope of retaliation and triumph.

John Rambo as Stallone plays him is a contradictory symbol of what Americans frustrated by their country's failure in Vietnam think should have been done there. The more massive deployment of force that they are convinced could have achieved victory would be technological. But Rambo pits brain and sinew against the superior fire-power of his enemies; he is our Vietcong guerrilla. That confusion of image, coupled with the half-start in *First Blood* toward a quite different sensibility about the Vietnam experience, suggests the difficulty that Americans have had in getting a clear grasp not only of the war itself but of their feelings about it.

That, so we hope to show throughout this book, had been the trouble from the beginning. War is, above all else, a political event. Wars are won only when political goals are achieved. Troops and weapons are—like diplomacy and money—essentially tools to achieve political objectives. The United States went into Indochina after World War II with muddled political objectives. It departed in 1975 after a thirty-year effort with political perceptions as blurred as they had been in the beginning. The war was unwinnable because the United States never decided what it was trying to achieve politically.

We are grateful to the reference librarians at Sam Houston State University and Purdue University for their assistance. We appreciate the help of Louise Waller and Lynnette Blevins. We would also like to thank these reviewers who offered useful comments: Truman R Clark,

Tomball College; Anthony O. Edmonds, Ball State University; Ben F. Fordney, James Madison University; Katherine K. Reist, University of Pittsburgh at Johnstown; and Clifford H. Scott, Indiana University— Purdue University at Fort Wayne. We are indebted to the hundreds of students in our Vietnam War classes who have helped us shape our own ideas about the war.

James S. Olson
Randy Roberts

Prologue: LBJ and Vietnam

On November 22, 1963, as his plane taxied down the runway at Andrews Air Force Base, President Lyndon B. Johnson could have counted up the days in his head. President John F. Kennedy had died only a few hours before. The assassination fulfilled Johnson's lifelong dream to become president of the United States, but in his heart sadness competed with ambition. The presidential election of 1964 was less than a year away, and the Twenty-Second Amendment allowed him to run in his own right, legitimize his presidency, and then seek re-election in 1968. If he astutely shuffled the deck of Washington politics, he could live in the White House until January 21, 1973, not quite the thirteen-year reign of Franklin D. Roosevelt, but long enough to distinguish him in history. Lest he appear inappropriately political, Johnson kept a low profile while the nation mourned Camelot.

On January 1, 1964, however, Johnson greeted the new year with relief and confidence, or perhaps hubris, possessed only by anyone out to change the world. With JFK interred at Arlington National Cemetery, the eternal flame already burning over his grave, and the horrific events of November 1963 receding somewhat into the past, the president finally could think, and talk, about the future. Desperate for approval and obsessed with his place in history, he yearned to join the ranks of George Washington, Abraham Lincoln, and Franklin D. Roosevelt, whom historians universally regarded as the nation's greatest presidents. On the foundation of Roosevelt's New Deal and Truman's Fair Deal, he intended to build the Great Society, where prosperity replaced poverty and tolerance quenched the fires of racism. He began mulling around what would become the War on Poverty, the Civil Rights Act of 1964, and the Voting Rights Act of 1965. Had Vietnam not spun out of control, Johnson might have joined the pantheon of greatness, but Indochina and its miseries would steadily crowd out any good he achieved.

Early in February 1964, just three months in office, the president ordered the withdrawal from Vietnam of all American dependents. The Vietcong threatened Americans there, and the country was not secure. The United States had nearly 15,000 troops in South Vietnam, but the

Vietcong, or "Charlie" as they became to be known, controlled the country-side and the night. Worse is that North Vietnamese regular soldiers were infiltrating South Vietnam. In Saigon, rebellions and coups created a musical-chairs government providing abundant fodder for political satirists and ambitious Republicans.

Already worrying that foreign affairs, in which Johnson had little interest, were distracting Americans from more important tasks, the president turned to his closest advisors. On March 2, 1964, after another coup d'etat in Saigon, Johnson met in the Oval Office with his aide McGeorge Bundy. "There may be another coup, but I don't know what we can do," the president complained. "If there is, I guess that we just . . . what alternatives do we have then? We're not going to send our troops there, are we?" Two months later, Johnson learned that 20,000 Vietnamese, many of them civilian victims of American firepower, had died in 1963, compared to 5,000 in 1962. Calling on Secretary of Defense Robert McNamara, he asked whether he should go public with the news. "I do think, Mr. President," McNamara replied, "that it would be wise for you to say as little as possible [about the war]. The frank answer is we don't know what's going on out there." In subsequent weeks, the president's concern deepened. "I stayed awake last night thinking of this thing," he told Bundy in May. "It looks to me like we're getting into another Korea . . . . I don't think we can fight them 10,000 miles away from home. . . . I don't think it's worth fighting for. . . . It's just the biggest damned mess I ever saw." Although the secretary of defense admitted that he did "not know [what was] going on over there" and the president did not consider Vietnam "worth fighting for," both behaved as if the future of the republic were at stake, investing hundreds of billions of dollars and the soul of a generation. Between 1964 and 1975, Vietnam consumed the lives of more than 58,000 American soldiers and upwards of three million Vietnamese. Today, in 2006, Vietnam stands as a relic of the Cold War, one of a handful of countries still wedded to Marx, Lenin, and May 1st renditions of the Communist *Internationale*. If anything, the war made Vietnam *more* dedicated to Communism, not less.

Forty years after admitting complete ignorance of Vietnam, Robert McNamara released his memoirs, a book "I [had] planned never to write," he admitted. No wonder. In a warning to future presidents and policymakers, he confessed to monumental arrogance. "We viewed . . . South Vietnam in terms of our own experience," he wrote. "We saw in them a thirst for—and a determination to fight for freedom and democracy. . . . We totally misjudged the political forces in the country . . . We underestimated the power of nationalism to motivate a people. . . . [We exhibited] a profound ignorance of the history, culture, and politics of . . . the area . . . We failed to recognize the limits of modern, high-technology military equipment. . . . We [forgot] that U.S. military action—other than direct threats to our own security—should be carried out only in conjunction with multinational force supported fully . . . by the international community. . . . External military force cannot substitute for the political order and stability that must be forged *by* a people *for* themselves. . . . The consequences of large-scale military operations . . . are inherently difficult to predict and to control. . . . These are the lessons of Vietnam. Pray God we learn them."

The one war in three decades in which the United States had probably done far more good than harm turned unpopular simply because it was not easy enough. The Vietnam syndrome had never left and the Iraq War (2003–) seems unlikely to vanquish it.

Indochina, 1995. *Inset:* A comparison in size between Vietnam and United States.

Eternal War:
The Vietnamese Heritage

Vietnam is nobody's dog.

—Nguyen Co Thach, 1978.

He was a wisp of a man, thin and gaunt, frail and seemingly vulnerable, his stringy goatee elongating an already long face. After seventy-six years of world wandering, hiding, and escaping, he was finally declining, wrinkled brown skin now only translucently covering his bones. Over the years his rivals might easily have failed fully to recognize the fire that possessed him. In 1966 Ho Chi Minh was ill, and he calmly waited for eternal rest from a life of boundless striving. It was his peculiar lot that two enemy nations had drawn his very qualified admiration. A lover of much of French culture, he had led Vietnam in a war of national liberation against France at one point adopting, in a vain hope to get American support, a close version of the American Declaration of Independence. Now that country was his antagonist.

Late in 1966, when the war in Vietnam approached its peak, Ho remarked to Jean Sainteny, an old French diplomat and friend: "The Americans . . . can wipe out all the principal towns of Tonkin [northern Vietnam]. . . . We expect it, and, besides, we are prepared for it. But that does not weaken our determination to fight to the very end. You know, we've already had the experience, and you have seen how that conflict ended." It was only a matter of time before the Americans went the same way as the Chinese, Japanese, and French. Vietnam was for the Vietnamese, not for anyone else, and that passion had driven Ho Chi Minh throughout his life.

That key to Ho's passion is the fundamental theme of Vietnamese history. Long ago a Chinese historian remarked, "The people of Vietnam do not like the past." No wonder. Vietnam developed in the shadow of Chinese imperialism. In 208 B.C. the Han dynasty expanded into southern China and Vietnam, declaring the region a new Chinese province—Giao Chi. Its informal name for the region was Nam Viet, which meant "land of the southern Viets." Over the centuries the Chinese brought to Vietnam their mandarin administrative system, along with their technology, writing, and Confucian social philosophy. But control did not translate into assimilation. Intensely ethnocentric, the Vietnamese, while welcoming many Chinese institutions, refused to accept a Chinese identity. The historian Frances FitzGerald describes that dilemma in Vietnamese history: "The Vietnamese leaders assumed Chinese political culture while rejecting . . . Chinese political domination."

Periodically, the Vietnamese violently resisted, giving Vietnam such national heroes as the Trung sisters, who led an anti-Chinese insurrection in A.D. 40; Trieu Au, the Vietnamese Joan of Arc who led a rebellion in A.D. 248; and Ngo Quyen, the military leader of Vietnam's successful revolution in 938. An old Vietnamese proverb captures the region's history: "Vietnam is too close to China, too far from heaven." Even after they achieved independence in 938, the Vietnamese had to deal periodically with Chinese or Mongol expansionism. Vietnam fought major wars against invaders from the north in 1257, the 1280s, 1406–1428, and 1788. Tran Hung Dao, the great thirteenth-century Vietnamese general, defeated the enemy after having all his soldiers tattoo the inscription "Kill the Mongols" on their right arms. He wrote: "We have seen the enemy's ambassadors stroll about in our streets with conceit. . . . They have demanded precious stones and embroidered silks to satisfy their boundless appetite. . . . They have extracted silver and gold from our limited treasures. It is really not different from bringing meat to feed hungry tigers."

In the centuries-long struggle against China, Vietnam developed a hero cult that elevated martial qualities as primary virtues. Vietnamese art glorified the sword-wielding, armor-bearing soldiers riding horses or elephants into battle. War, not peace, was woven into the cloth of Vietnamese history. The historian William Turley writes that out of this experience the Vietnamese fashioned a myth of national indomitability. . . . The Vietnamese forged a strong collective identity . . . long before the Europeans appeared off their shores." Vietnam's enemies learned that lesson the hard way.

But there was also a patience to Vietnamese militarism, an unwillingness to be intimidated, a conviction that a small country could prevail against an empire if it bided its time and waited for its moment. Between 1406 and 1428, led by the great Le Loi, the Vietnamese attacked the Chinese through hit-and-run guerrilla warfare, letting rugged mountains and thick rain forests do much of their work for them, wearing down the enemy, sapping its spirit, confusing its objectives, finally delivering a death blow, a strategic offensive to drive the Chinese back across the border. That story became legendary in Vietnamese military history.

Anti-Chinese resistance became the cutting edge of Vietnamese identity. A prominent eighteenth-century Chinese emperor lamented the stubbornness of the Vietnamese. They are not, he said, "a reliable people. An occupation does not last very long before they raise their arms against us and expel us from their country." Suspicion of the Chinese permeated Vietnamese history. In 1945, for example, with the French ready to return to Vietnam and Chinese troops occupying much of northern Vietnam, Ho Chi Minh agreed to cooperate temporarily with France. When some of his colleagues protested, Ho remarked that it "is better to sniff French shit for a while than to eat Chinese shit all our lives."

For Ho Chi Minh, the "French shit" was still bad enough. France had come to Vietnam in two stages, first in the seventeenth century and again in the nineteenth. Father Alexandre de Rhodes, a French Jesuit, traveled to Hanoi in 1627, converted thousands of Vietnamese to Roman Catholicism, and created a Latin alphabet for the Vietnamese language. Although suspicious Vietnamese leaders expelled de Rhodes in 1630 and again in 1645, he planted the seeds of the French empire. The French returned in force to Vietnam in 1847 when a naval expedition arrived at Tourane (later called Danang) and, within a few weeks, fought a pitched battle with local Vietnamese. Two more French warships fought another battle at Tourane in 1856. A French fleet captured Tourane in 1858 and conquered Saigon in 1859. Vietnamese resistance drove the French out, but in 1861 they returned to Saigon to stay. After signing a treaty with Siam (now Thailand) in 1863, France established a protectorate over Cambodia. France extended its control over southern Vietnam, or Cochin China, during the rest of the decade. France then turned north, and in 1883 a naval expedition reached the mouth of the Perfume River, just outside Hue. When the French fleet shelled the city, a Vietnamese leader gave France a protectorate over Annam (central Vietnam) and Tonkin (northern Vietnam), although it took France years to assert its control in those regions. To provide uniform government over the colonies, France established the French Union in 1887. After securing a protectorate over Laos by signing another treaty with Siam in 1893, France had five regions in the Union: Cochin China, Annam, Tonkin, Cambodia, and Laos.

The Vietnamese were no more satisfied with French domination than with Chinese. The most resentful Vietnamese lived in Nghe An Province, located in Annam in central Vietnam, a low coastal plain bordered by the Annamese mountains. Nghe An and the surrounding provinces were the most densely populated areas of Vietnam, and by far the poorest. The soil was leached and dry, the weather alternating between torrential monsoon rains and hot summer winds.

The French called the Nghe Annese the "Buffaloes of Nghe An" because of their reputation for stubbornness. The Vietnamese referred to them as the "People of the Wooden Fish." The Vietnamese love a special sauce known as *nuoc mam*. They alternate layers of fish and layers of salt in a barrel and let the brew ferment in the heat several weeks. The fish decompose into a mush and the fluid into a salty brine. *Nuoc mam* is to Vietnamese fish what catsup is to American french fries. The Nghe Annese were too poor to afford fish, the proverb says, so they carried a wooden fish in their pockets to dip into *nuoc mam* at restaurants. Nghe Annese, the jesters claimed, licked the wooden fish until they were kicked out, only to repeat the culinary charade somewhere else.

But Nghe An, with its neighboring Ha Tinh Province, was not known only for its poverty. Year after year the prizewinning poets, musicians, and scholars at the imperial court at Hue came from Nghe An and Ha Tinh. They were thinkers and tinkerers, creative people who looked at life from unique perspectives, refused to believe what they were told, and insisted on having things proven to them. Their skepticism bred unhappiness. By the 1800s the best schools at Hue no longer accepted applicants from Nghe An and Ha Tinh, no matter how high their scores. Central Vietnamese, "the people of the wooden fish," were troublemakers, dreaming of a better world.

Born in 1890 as Nguyen Sinh Cung, Ho Chi Minh grew up in Nghe An. Near his birthplace was the *den,* a monument to Le Loi. The Vietnamese believe that the spirit of an honored individual lives on in a *den.* Ho Chi Minh visited the *den* as a child and listened to tales of how Le Loi had expelled the hated Chinese. His father, Nguyen Sinh Sac, was the son of peasants who became a scholar and a ferocious anti-French nationalist. His sister was a renowned balladeer, and her folk songs railed at China and France. Sac passed the mandarin examinations and found a job at the imperial palace at Hue, but the imperial court was full of pro-French Vietnamese sycophants or tradition-bound mandarins. "The French," said Phan Boi Chau, an early twentieth-century nationalist, "used honeyed words and great rewards to entice the Vietnamese. They offered high government positions and benefits of all sorts to make some of us into their hunting dogs."

For a while in the late 1890s and early 1900s Nguyen Sinh Sac was a minor government official in Hue. Ho Chi Minh's mother died in 1900, and Sac, along with his two sons and a daughter, lived in a tiny, dingy one-room apartment facing the opulent splendor of the Palais de la Censure where the Vietnamese emperor and the mandarin court ruled Vietnam. Ho bore the brunt of ridicule from the children of the court mandarins, and he developed a spontaneous dislike for intellectual snobbery. Throughout his life, he frequently quoted the poet Tuy Vien: "Nothing is more contemptible than to seek honors through literature."

Although the Vietnamese had thrown off the Chinese yoke in 938, over the centuries they gradually adopted the Chinese mandarin system to govern the nation. Eventually, mandarin teachers and bureaucrats became a self-conscious elite. To pass the civil service examinations and secure the best jobs, Vietnamese scholars immersed themselves in the Chinese language and Confucian values, which gradually distanced them from Vietnamese peasants. The mandarins also adopted many Chinese institutions—a centralized tax system, a judicial hierarchy, and the royal palace architecture complete with gates, moats, bridges, and pools. Confucianism promoted rule by a paternalistic elite committed to morality and fairness, and it demanded unswerving obedience from the governed. The essence of personal behavior is obedience, submissiveness, and peaceful acquiescence in the social hierarchy.

The mandarin system was also conservative to a fault. Mandarins were suspicious of all change. They opposed science, technology, industrialization, and democracy, any one of which might dislodge them from their positions of privilege. A popular late nineteenth-century Vietnamese poem reflected the growing resentment of the mandarin class:

> Becoming a mandarin you treat your servants as dirt,
> And steal every bit of money the people have.
> Although you scoop in who knows how much money,
> Do the people get any help from you?

On top of the mandarin elite, the French imposed the colonial bureaucracy. They ruled Vietnam through local clients—French-speaking Roman Catholic Vietnamese, who soon became a new elite, competing with the mandarins for influence. Eventually, the French abolished the mandarin examinations, prohibited the teaching of Chinese, and displaced the mandarins as power brokers. Except for the French bureaucrats themselves, the Francophile Vietnamese enjoyed the finest homes, the best jobs, the fanciest clothes—the good life.

The French viewed the Vietnamese as children at best and savages at worst. They refused to learn the Vietnamese language, and in 1878 they declared French and *quoc ngu,* the Latin alphabet Father Alexandre de Rhodes had developed, the official languages of the colony. They replaced the local legal code with their own version of Roman law. Convinced that the word "Vietnam" was symbolic of protest, the French outlawed it, insisting that "French Indochina" was the proper term. Centuries-old Buddhist pagodas were often bulldozed when prime land was needed to construct Roman Catholic churches.

The imposition of the French language and French law accelerated the alienation of peasant land. There were widespread poverty and millions of landless peasants in Vietnam before the French, but most peasants owned at least a small plot, and historically the emperor had discouraged the development of large estates. But between 1880 and 1930 the French changed landholding patterns. Many peasants lost their property because they could not pay high French taxes, could not contest claims against the land in French courts, or fell into debt to French or Vietnamese creditors who foreclosed on their property. The number of landless peasants, tenant farmers, and debt peons rose. In Tonkin nine percent of the population came to own 52 percent of cultivated land, and 250 people owned 20 percent. They included French settlers and wealthy Vietnamese. It was the same in Cochin China. Tenant farmers paid up to 70 percent of their harvest to the landlord, and farmers borrowing money to finance production on their own land paid interest rates of 100 percent. French companies had monopolies on the production of alcohol, opium, and salt, robbing peasant farmers of another source of income.

With imported rubber trees, the French created a new industry. By 1940 there were more than six hundred rubber plantations in Vietnam, but a handful of French companies controlled them. Poverty forced thousands of Vietnamese peasants to leave home for years to work the French plantations. The taxes imposed by the top-heavy French bureaucracy added to the poverty. "French imperialism," Ho Chi Minh declared in 1920, "conquered our country with bayonets. Since then we have not only been oppressed and exploited shamelessly, but also tortured and poisoned pitilessly. . . . Prisons outnumber schools and are always overcrowded. . . . Thousands of Vietnamese have been led to a slow death or massacred." Though not so eloquent, millions of Vietnamese felt the same way. To them France was a nation of police, soldiers, pimps, tax collectors, and labor recruiters.

Almost as bad was the Vietnamese elite who did the French bidding. For any Vietnamese to succeed in the French colony, he or she had to be a French-speaking Roman Catholic who carried out the edicts of the empire. If these Vietnamese were not mandarins in their educational background, they were just as elitist, just as hierarchical, and just as conservative. They got the best government posts, the finest homes, and the largest estates. Ho Chi Minh referred to them as *colonis indigeniae* [indigenous colonists]: "If you take the largest and strongest member of the herd and fasten a bright substance to its neck, a gold coin or a cross, it becomes completely docile. . . . This weird . . . animal goes by the name of *colonis indigeniae,* but depending on its habitat it is referred to as Annamese, Madagascan, Algerian, Indian."

Nguyen Sinh Sac's job at the imperial court had given him a living but no dignity. Indeed, he came to view the post as a dishonor. "Being a mandarin," he said many times, "is the ultimate form of slavery." Sac refused to let Ho Chi Minh even study for the examinations. He refused to speak French, arguing that doing so "would corrupt my Vietnamese," and openly advocated the abolition of the mandarin class and the disintegration of the French empire. Nguyen Sinh Sac was one of Nghe An's most troublesome children. The French fired him.

The father passed on those passions to his children. His daughter Nguyen Thanh worked in Vinh supervising a French military mess hall and smuggled rifles and ammunition to the De Tham guerrillas, a group already fighting against the French. When French police convicted her of treason, the mandarin judge gave her a life sentence and an epitaph: "Other women bring forth children, you bring forth rifles." Her brother Nguyen Khiem was just as militant. He repeatedly wrote eloquent letters to French officials protesting Vietnamese poverty and calling for freedom. But it was the other son—Nguyen Sinh Cung, later known as Ho Chi Minh—who realized Sac's dream.

At five years old, Ho was running messages back and forth to members of the anti-French underground. The house was a beehive of political talk, always around the theme of Vietnamese independence. A frequent visitor, and occasional fugitive, was Phan Boi Chau, the most prominent of Vietnam's early nationalists. Among other acqaintances of Nguyen Sinh Sac was Phan Chu Trinh, the constitutionalist who wanted to overthrow the mandarin bureaucracy.

The Nguyen Sinh Sac family was also a "brown canvas" household. The traditional dress of the Vietnamese was the *ao dai,* the *non,* and the *quoc.* For women, the *ao dai* was a long dress worn over black or white trousers that fit loosely around the legs. A rectangular piece of material formed a panel reaching down from the waist in the front and the back. For men the dress was only knee length. The embroidery on the cloth indicated the station in life of the wearer. Gold brocade was reserved for the imperial family. High-ranking mandarins used purple embroidery, and low-ranking mandarins used blue. Peasants could have only the plainest cloth. The *non* was the ubiquitous conical hat made of latania leaves, and the *quoc* were the wooden shoes. Radicals adopted brown canvas clothes as a symbolic protest against mandarin authority and a gesture to blur class lines. By the late 1880s large numbers of men in Nghe An wore brown canvas, in spite of mandarin edicts to the contrary. For much of his life Ho Chi Minh wore brown canvas clothes except at the most formal occasions.

Long before Ho Chi Minh ever heard of Karl Marx and communism, he viewed society through the lens of class conflict, a philosophical inheritance from an egalitarian family. Years later, *The Communist Manifesto* resonated with Ho Chi Minh, fitting nicely into an intellectual schema decades in the making. When the time came for Ho Chi Minh to become a communist, he played the role enthusiastically.

Phan Boi Chau, a nationalist whose ideas formed much of the discussion in the household, had been born in Nghe An in 1867. His father, though passing the mandarin examinations, refused to work for the government, becoming a teacher in a small village. Phan Boi Chau joined the Scholars' Revolt in 1885, a resistance movement of Vietnam's emperor Ham Nghi and a number of mandarin officials against French rule. In 1893 he participated in Phan Dinh Phung's unsuccessful Nghe Tinh uprising against the French.

By the early 1900s Phan Boi Chau was convinced that Vietnam could enter the modern world only if the French were expelled from Indochina. For a teenaged Ho Chi Minh, Phan Boi Chau must have been an imposing figure. Phan Boi Chau's round face and wire-rimmed spectacles gave him a scholarly, almost mandarin look, as did the full goatee. But he was no simple scholar. He was a man of intense passion and commitment. "The French," he said, "treat our people like garbage. . . . The meek are made into slaves, the strong-minded are thrown into jail. The physically powerful are forced into the army, while the old and weak are left to die. . . . The land is splashed with blood." There was also an ascetic look to Phan Boi Chau, as if he had transcended mundane pursuits for a grander cause. If Vietnam was to flower, France must fall.

In 1907, a few years after visiting with the family of Nguyen Sinh Sac, Phan Boi Chau led the abortive Poison Plot, in which low-ranking Vietnamese soldiers tried to poison French officers in Hanoi. The conspiracy was uncovered before it took too large a toll, but Phan Boi Chau became known as the first violent revolutionary in modern Vietnam. He spent years moving about in Japan, China, and Siam, with French police always on his trail. The Chinese arrested him in Shanghai in 1913. He was released from prison in 1917 and spent the rest of his life in China. He died there in 1940.

As a nationalist, Phan Boi Chau was rivaled only by Phan Chu Trinh, another Nghe Annese. Born to a well-to-do family in 1872, Phan Chu Trinh passed the mandarin examinations. A meeting in 1903 with Phan Boi Chau changed his life. Phan Chu Trinh resigned his government post two years later, convinced that the Vietnamese emperor and his mandarin "lackeys" would doom Vietnam to oblivion. But he parted company with Phan Boi Chau on two accounts; Phan Chu Trinh did not believe in radical violence, and he was convinced that the imperial court and mandarin bureaucracy, not the French empire, should be destroyed first. He wanted to work with the French in replacing the mandarins with a modern, democratic political and educational system.

Although neither Phan Boi Chau nor Phan Chu Trinh was able to implement his ideas in the early 1900s, they left a rich legacy. From Phan Boi Chau came the conviction that only revolutionary violence would dislodge the French, and from Phan Chu Trinh came the certainty that the mandarin system was rotten, corrupted by its elitism and its hostility to the modern world and its technology. Ho Chi Minh would eventually have to decide which to destroy first—the French empire or the mandarin court—but by the time he was a young man he already knew his destiny. Nghe An had produced yet another radical.

Ho Chi Minh left Nghe An Province at the end of 1910. He spent nearly a year in Phan Thiet teaching at a school financed by *a nuoc mam* factory. Late in 1911 he headed south to Saigon, where he enrolled in a vocational school, but he was unhappy learning a trade that the French would use only to exploit him. He left school early in 1912, signed up as a mess boy on a French ocean liner, and left Saigon for the other side of the world. Traveling under the alias of "Van Ba," Ho Chi Minh got a glimpse of much of the world in the next several years. In North Africa he saw what France was doing to the Algerians; in South Africa he noted what the English and the Boers were doing to the blacks; and in other ports of call he observed the imperial rule of the English, French, Dutch, and Portuguese. He worked in New York City, whetting his curiosity about American democracy, and on the eve of World War I, Ho was in London working as a cook at the Carlton Hotel.

Ho Chi Minh moved to Paris in 1918 and quickly immersed himself in anticolonial politics. There were 100,000 Vietnamese in Paris, and Ho found good restaurants in which to eat his favorite dishes. He met the exiled Phan Chu Trinh and listened to him preach against the evils of the Vietnamese imperial court at Hue and the virtues of democracy and industrialization. Ho Chi Minh met frequently with French socialists, pressing them on the question of empire, trying to discern whether they really wanted to change the world. He supported himself by touching up photographs and writing newspaper articles, adopting the name "Nguyen Ai Quoc" (Nguyen the Patriot) or "Nguyen O Phap" (Nguyen Who Hates the French). In the Vietnamese community, Ho became a leading nationalist, and the French secret police kept track of him.

But then overnight, Ho Chi Minh became a genuine hero. At the Paris Peace Conference negotiating the end of World War I, Ho electrified Vietnamese nationalists when he submitted an eight-point set of demands that included Vietnamese representation in the French parliament; freedom of speech, press, and association; release of all political prisoners; and full equality under the law for the Vietnamese in Indochina. If France would not meet those demands, the empire was morally bankrupt and would surely be destroyed. Looking back on that moment in 1919, the Vietnamese student Bui Lam would remember: "It was like a flash of lightning. . . . Here was a Vietnamese insisting that his people be accorded their rights. . . . No two Vietnamese residing in France could meet, after this, without mentioning the name of Nguyen Ai Quoc."

Ho Chi Minh was soon the soul of the expatriate Vietnamese community. The Vietnamese sought him out, no longer looking to Phan Chu Trinh as their leader. Ho was a charismatic figure. Perhaps it was his combination of revolutionary soul and Confucian personality. His hatred of the French empire knew no bounds, nor did his love for his country. But at the same time Ho Chi Minh was a man of the *luc duc,* the six virtues Confucianism demanded of all leaders: *Tri* (wisdom), *Nhan* (benevolence), *Tin* (sincerity), *Nghia* (righteousness), *Trung* (moderation), and *Hoa* (harmony). He seemed unassuming, a "brown canvas" man from Nghe An.

Paris solidified Ho's political philosophy. For several years he had been a member of the French Socialist party, but he grew weary of its unwillingness to do anything more than sympathize on the "colonial question." Ho Chi Minh decided the socialists were "capitalist souls in syndicalist bodies," too given to parliamentary debate, political compromise, and intellectual moderation to help the Vietnamese. His decision in 1920 to part company with the socialists left him with the problem of finding the real key to Vietnamese liberation. Along with a large faction of French socialists, he decided in 1920 to convert the organization into a French Communist party. His conversion came when a French communist gave him a copy of Vladimir Lenin's "Thesis on the National and Colonial Questions." Lenin argued that imperialism was the natural consequence of capitalism. Industrial monopolies, to secure new sources of raw materials and new markets, expand into the underdeveloped world and exploit colonial peoples. The imperial powers enrich themselves by pushing the colonies into poverty. But alongside Western imperialists, Lenin named another enemy: Asian feudalists. A tiny minority of Asian natives, protected by European technology, controlled enormous economic assets, intensifying the suffering of peasants and workers. Revolution was the answer. Throw off the imperial yoke and redistribute property to the peasant masses.

Ho's introduction to Leninism was electrifying. "What emotion, enthusiasm, clear-sightedness and confidence it instilled in me! I was overjoyed. Though sitting alone in my room I shouted aloud as if addressing large crowds: 'Dear martyrs, compatriots! This is what we need, this is our path to liberation.'" Here was the solution to the long debate between Phan Boi Chau and Phan Chu Trinh. In the name of Phan Boi Chau, the people of Vietnam must destroy the French colonial apparatus, and in the name of Phan Chu Trinh they must promote revolution in Vietnam, wiping out the last vestiges of mandarin elitism and stripping wealthy, Francophile Vietnamese of their huge estates.

After years of searching, Ho Chi Minh had an ideology to match his passion. In later years, people would debate which was his true love, nationalism or communism? In the United States, anticommunists would see only his communism, arguing that nationalism was just a subterfuge. Antiwar critics, on the other hand, claimed that deep down Ho was a nationalist, that communism was simply the most effective tool for bringing about independence. Ho hated the French empire for what it had done to his country, but he also hated the French-speaking Vietnamese Catholics who enriched themselves at the expense of poor peasants. Ho Chi Minh was a devout communist because in communism he saw the resolution of both evils. Communism fit the hand of Nghe Annese radicalism like a glove.

Ho Chi Minh's conversion to communism transformed his life. He was a founding member of the French Communist party, and in 1921 he established the Intercolonial Union, a communist-front group to work against imperialism. He spent 1923 and 1924 in Moscow. Late in 1924 the Soviet leadership asked him to go to Canton as an adviser to the

Soviet envoy. There Ho discovered a large Vietnamese expatriate community coalescing around Phan Boi Chau, the old family friend. But the joy of the reunion was short-lived. Ho Chi Minh talked at length about revolution, but Phan Boi Chau's commitment stopped at talk. Perhaps he was just too old—the fire had dimmed. Ho also found him conservative, willing to get rid of the French but not the Vietnamese elite in a genuine revolution.

Young Vietnamese nationalists in Canton gravitated to Ho Chi Minh's leadership. One of them was Pham Van Dong. Born in Quang Nam Province of central Vietnam in 1906 to a mandarin family, Dong had studied at the French lycée in Hue. His father was exiled to the French colony of Reunion in 1915 for fomenting rebellion among the Vietnamese troops recruited to fight in World War I. As a student, Pham Van Dong became intensely anti-French, and he moved to Canton to escape the secret police. He was captivated by Ho Chi Minh's "shining simplicity." Nguyen Luong Bang, another young nationalist born in Hai Hung Province in 1904, met Ho in Canton and saw him "healthy-looking, extremely bright-eyed . . . with an engagingly gentle way of speaking." With Pham Van Dong, Nguyen Luong Bang, and several other young Vietnamese, Ho Chi Minh founded the Revolutionary Youth League of Vietnam in 1925. It was the first purely Marxist organization among the Indochinese.

French secret agents and Chinese police went after the rebels, and Ho Chi Minh urged his associates to return to Vietnam and organize anti-French communist cells. He went to Moscow in 1927, attended conferences in Europe later in the year, and in 1928 lived in Bangkok as a Buddhist monk organizing the Vietnamese emigrant community. In Moscow, he temporarily ran afoul of Soviet Premier Joseph Stalin, who worried that Ho's sense of nationalism ran deeper than his commitment to communism. Stalin always suspected nationalists because their devotion to country or ethnic group often transcended their devotion to the class struggle. In Moscow, Ho was too much of a nationalist and not enough of a communist to suit Stalin.

Ho traveled to Hong Kong in 1929 and met Le Duc Tho, another Vietnamese nationalist. Tho, who was born in Nam Ha Province in 1910 to a mandarin family, had become an anti-French nationalist while attending school. With Le Duc Tho, Pham Van Dong, Nguyen Luong Bang, and several other Vietnamese in Hong Kong, Ho Chi Minh established the Indochinese Communist party in June 1929. Its leaders wanted to "overthrow French imperialism, feudalism and the reactionary Vietnamese capitalist class." Another young Vietnamese nationalist soon joined them. Vo Nguyen Giap, born in Quang Binh Province in 1912, came from a well-to-do family. He earned a law degree at Hanoi University. By the time he was a teenager, Giap hated the French.

Although he had never met Ho Chi Minh, Giap was familiar with his revolutionary nationalism and joined the Indochinese Communist party.

In northern Vietnam, not the south, the revolution began. There the population was denser, the rice yields lower, the landholdings smaller. All this evoked a more intense sense of community than prevailed in the south. Religions contributed to the differences. Buddhism came to Vietnam from two different sources. To the south, from India came Theravada Buddhism, viewing salvation as a future state distinct from the present; individuals find nirvana by transcending the present and detaching themselves from earthly cares. In the north, Mahayana Buddhism from China was progressive. It is in acts of love and charity directed to the problems of the moment, in which devotees put off their own salvation until others achieve it, that salvation is to be found. Mahayana Buddhism reinforced the communal spirit that social and economic conditions fostered in the north. When the time came to resist the French and the Japanese, that spirit supplied the conditions for political organization.

It started in Nghe An. The Great Depression depressed rice prices, eroding peasant income and creating an epidemic of economic misery and political discontent. Widespread tax revolts erupted spontaneously throughout central Vietnam, and more sporadic eruptions took place in the Mekong Delta. But in Nghe An, radicals organized peasants into Red Soviets—local councils demanding an end to rents, seeking massive tax cuts, and in conformity with communism, striving for land redistribution.

On September 12, 1930, more than 6,000 Nghe An peasants marched on Vinh, the provincial capital. Although the march began as a peaceful demonstration, the French called in an air strike, killing more than 174 people. Later in the day, when relatives drifted in to claim the bodies, aircraft killed another fifteen people. A French journalist called the second attack "an awkward error which had a bad effect." Bad effect, indeed! The repression of the Nghe An Revolt was a seminal event, proof that France would stop at nothing to keep the empire. For the French, the revolt was sobering testimony to the power of Vietnamese peasants if anyone organized them. For the mandarins, the revolt signaled their downfall if communists ever took over. The "Vietnamese reactionary class," as Ho described them, would lose everything.

But the collapse of the Nghe An Revolt taught Ho Chi Minh and his followers another lesson. Nobody would overthrow the French empire without first creating a broad-based political organization reaching all the way down to the peasant masses. As far back as 1924, Ho had said that in "all the French colonies . . . conditions have combined to further an uprising of the peasants. Here and there they have rebelled, but their rebellions have been drowned in blood. If the peasants remain pacific today it is because they lack organization and a leader." Revolution de-

September 1945—Ho Chi Minh, right, poses with Vo Nguyen Giap, minister of the Interior in Ho Chi Minh's provisional government. Giap led the Vietminh and North Vietnamese military through the fall of Saigon. (*Courtesy, AP / Wide World Photos.*)

pended on the support of millions of peasants. Success in Vietnam would be more a political than a military question.

After the suppression of the Nghe An Revolt, the French went after all revolutionary nationalists. Pham Van Dong was arrested in 1930 and sent to the dreaded "tiger cages" at Con Son Island, where he spent the next eight years. Nguyen Luong Bang held out for a year, but he was put in a French prison in 1931. Tho spent years in hiding and in French jails during the 1930s. Vo Nguyen Giap went into exile in 1939, but the French arrested his wife and baby. Both died in prison in 1941, giving Vo Nguyen Giap a vendetta to accompany his nationalism. The French tried Ho in absentia, convicted him of treason, and sentenced him to death. Under pressure from the French, British authorities imprisoned him in Hong Kong. Rumors quickly spread that he had died there, a story both the French and the Soviet Union believed.

But late in 1932 some British contacts smuggled Ho Chi Minh out of Hong Kong and drove him to Shanghai, where he met with Soviet officials who helped him get to Moscow in 1933. Five years later, Ho Chi

Minh returned to China, and the next year he met Vo Nguyen Giap for the first time. Pham Van Dong made it out of the French prison in 1939 and headed for China as well. There the three planned their next move, hoping that the turmoil in the world would provide them with an opportunity. It came in June 1940 when Germany conquered France. Nazi successes fit in well with Japan's designs for Asia. Indochina seemed like a ripe plum, and Japan picked it. In September 1940 Japanese troops moved south out of China into Tonkin. They occupied the rest of Annam and Cochin China by July 1941. Ho now faced another foreign power. He quietly left China and returned to Vietnam. His thirty-year odyssey was over.

When Ho Chi Minh and his followers took up refuge in a limestone cave near Pac Bo in the mountains of Cao Bang Province, he was beginning one more in a long series of anti-imperialist uprisings. The Can Vuong movement of the late 1800s had demanded restoration of Vietnamese royalty, but in doing so it did not address the resentments of the peasant masses for the mandarin elite. Phan Boi Chau and Phan Chu Trinh tried but failed; their isolated, poorly planned uprisings were easy prey for the efficient French colonial administrators. Phan Boi Chau's close associate Hoang Hoa Tham organized the De Tham war against the French in a poorly structured effort that ended with Hoang Hoa Tham's assassination in 1913. Nguyen Thai Hoc established the Viet Nam Quoc Dan Dang, or Vietnam Nationalist party, in 1929 and launched an abortive uprising against the French at Yen Bay, but the movement, composed exclusively of middle- and upper-class Vietnamese, disintegrated. Nguyen Thai Hoc died at the guillotine in 1930.

After 1910, urban nationalists had appeared in the cities. Such groups as Bui Quang Chieu's Constitutional party and Nguyen An Ninh's Hopes of Youth were influenced by Western values. They wanted reform, not revolution, and definitely not any sort of violence. They failed to capture the mantle of Vietnamese nationalism because they were isolated from peasants, not just in their use of the French language but in their abandonment of Confucian symbols. The leaders were primarily intellectuals, given to endless ideological squabbles. It was also easy for French authorities to keep track of urban nationalists. A different approach had to be taken that would absorb Vietnamese from all classes.

Ho Chi Minh remembered Lenin's advice that Asian communists should form alliances with each nationalist organization while keeping their independence from all of them. Ho downplayed communism, not wanting to give his French critics anything to use against him. The organization to liberate Vietnam had to be based on nationalism, not revolution, at least in the beginning. Only then was there any hope of bringing together large numbers of Vietnamese in a resistance movement. In May 1941, outside the cave in Cao Bang Province, Ho established the political organization for implementing his dream: the Viet

Nam Doc Lap Dong Minh, or Vietminh—the League for Vietnamese Independence. Ho Chi Minh declared: "Our people suffer under a double yoke: they serve not only as buffaloes and horses to the French invaders but also as slaves to the Japanese plunderers. . . . Rich people, soldiers, workers, peasants, intellectuals, employees, traders, youth, and women who warmly love your country. . . . Let us unite together!"

Like George Washington, whose towering presence held together competing interests in the fledgling United States of the 1790s, Ho became an iconic figure, a charismatic presence whose personality and image attracted Vietnamese nationalists of every sort. To make sure that he kept the loyalties of middle-class and upper-class Vietnamese nationalists, he soft-peddled his Communist credentials, prompting many Americans to conclude that he was more nationalist than communist. Ho Chi Minh was both, devoting fervor to each.

The Vietminh were about to inherit the mantle of Vietnamese nationalism. They built a coalition of urban intellectuals and peasants. French-educated Vietnamese intellectuals found in Marxism a scientific, anti-imperialist ideology that explained history and provided, in its moralistic fervor, a neo-religion to replace the void they felt in rejecting Confucian traditionalism. Peasants saw in the Vietminh a passionate movement dedicated to providing them with economic relief. Above all else, the Vietminh enjoyed the charisma of Ho Chi Minh.

Shortly after the formation of the Vietminh, Ho Chi Minh went back to China to seek assistance from Jiang Jieshi in fighting the Japanese. Just before leaving, Ho Chi Minh announced to his closest associates that he was changing his name from Nguyen Ai Quoc, by which he had been known among Vietnamese nationalists for more than thirty years, to "Ho Chi Minh" (He Who Enlightens). In China, Jiang Jieshi had Ho arrested, and he spent more than a year in prison, almost dying from the conditions. He was released late in 1943 when some Chinese leaders decided he might be useful after all in fighting Japan. Ho Chi Minh returned to Cao Bang Province.

The treachery he experienced at the hands of Jieng Jieshi sent Ho Chi Minh directly into the embrace of Mao Zedong and the Chinese Communist Party. Even though the Soviet Union, in order to expedite its war in East Asia against Japan, tried to exploit rivalries between Chinese Nationalists and Chinese Communists, Ho negotiated an independent course, making sure to offend neither Mao or Stalin.

By that time Ho Chi Minh was ready to look toward a new source for assistance. Ever since his visit to New York City in 1913, he had a bemused curiosity about the United States. Although American capitalism created classes and exploited the poor, there was nevertheless a powerful sense of opportunity there. The Americans had, after all, been the first colony to revolt successfully against a European imperial power, and their Declaration of Independence was eloquent in its proclamation of human equality. American imperialism was even more intriguing. The United States had acquired the Philippines in 1898 and then fought a bloody war against Filipino insurrectionists who had no interest in replacing their Spanish yoke with an American one. American troops crushed the rebellion, but not before a guerrilla war took thousands of lives. But afterwards the Americans made good on their promise. The Tydings-McDuffie Act of 1934 launched the Philippines on the road to independence, with a twelve-year timetable before the American withdrawal. Maybe the Americans were as good as their Declaration of Independence proclaimed?

Ho Chi Minh had no illusions about why the Americans might be willing to help him. They opposed Japan's expansion into Indochina in 1940 and 1941 not because of any sympathy with the national aspirations of the Vietnamese. Instead, the United States had been worried about its own access to the French rubber plantations, about British and Dutch oil reserves in Malaya and the East Indies, about the future of the Philippine Islands, and about the fate of the Open Door policy in China. But Ho thought that perhaps the Americans might be willing, if not to liberate Vietnam from the French, at least to help expel the Japanese invaders.

So Ho Chi Minh sought American assistance. The Office of Strategic Services (OSS), forerunner of the Central Intelligence Agency, wanted to develop good intelligence sources in Southeast Asia. Ho made himself available, promising to return downed American fliers and escaped prisoners of war as well as provide information on Japanese troop movements. He wanted arms shipments, first to fight the Japanese and then the French. After securing a promise that the weapons would be used against the Japanese and not the French, the OSS airlifted 5,000 guns to the Vietminh. The OSS agent who brought the guns found Ho Chi Minh "an awfully sweet old guy. If I had to pick out one quality about that little old man sitting on his hill in the jungle, it was his sweetness."

Steely resolve undergirded the sweetness, and Ho Chi Minh's associates shared it. Vo Nguyen Giap, the lawyer and history teacher turned revolutionary, emerged as a brilliant military tactician, and from that mountain cave he expanded Vietminh power into the other northern provinces. By 1945 the Vietminh exercised widespread authority in Cao Bang, Phong Tho, Ha Giang, Yen Bay, Tuyen Quang, and Bac Kan provinces. Ho, not France or Japan, ran those provinces. Pham Van Dong led the effort to recruit more peasant soldiers into the Vietminh, and on several occasions whole garrisons deserted the French and came over.

By the spring of 1945, Giap was itching for a large-scale military effort. Ho Chi Minh, gifted with an uncanny sense of timing, was more cautious, not wanting to see a repeat of the Nghe An slaughter of 1930. The Vietminh should stay with their guerrilla tactics, attacking French and Japanese forces only when victory was certain, not taking unneces-sary risks. The Vietminh should be, Ho said, "like the elephant and the tiger. When the elephant is strong and rested . . . we will retreat. And if the tiger ever pauses, the elephant will impale him on his mighty tusks. But the tiger will not pause and the elephant will die of exhaustion and loss of blood."

Ho Chi Minh persuaded Giap to continue to fight like a tiger, not like an elephant. A large-scale military confrontation was probably unneces-sary anyway. By 1945 the Americans were pounding the last nails into the Nazi coffin in Europe, and they were preparing an invasion of Japan. With the Japanese empire collapsing and the French empire still in limbo, Ho believed that "we will not even need to seize power since there will be no power to seize." Why waste men and resources in a military esca-lation when victory was at hand?

Suddenly, in August 1945, after the Americans dropped nuclear weapons on Hiroshima and Nagasaki, the war was over. Bao Dai, the last Vietnamese emperor whom Japan recognized as a puppet head of state, tried to assert himself as the leader of the new nation. But on August 17, 1945, when Bao Dai supporters held a rally in Hanoi, 150,000 people showed up, many of them waving Vietminh flags. Soon the Vietminh leaders had the crowd marching through the streets of Hanoi, leaving the court mandarins sitting alone on an empty dais. In Vinh, Hue, Saigon, Haiphong, Danang, and Nha Trang, the Vietminh staged similar people's rallies.

Two days later, a few thousand Vietminh soldiers took control of Ha-noi. Emperor Bao Dai, ensconced in the imperial palace at Hue, sent a message to the French warning them that their return to Vietnam would be doubtful at best in face of "the desire for independence that has been smoldering in the bottom of all hearts." If the French colonial apparatus is reconstructed, he said, "it will no longer be obeyed; each village would be a nest of resistance, every enemy a former friend." When Bao Dai pro-posed a coalition government with the Vietminh, he was roundly re-jected. On August 25, 1945, Bao Dai abdicated the Vietnamese throne. Ho entered Hanoi the same day, wearing a brown canvas shirt, short pants, and a brown pith helmet. A week later, on September 2, he announced the creation of the Democratic Republic of Vietnam with a simple mes-sage:

> We hold these truths that all men are created equal, that they are endowed by their Creator with certain unalienable Rights, among these are Life, Liberty and the pursuit of Happiness. . . .
> The French have fled, the Japanese have capitulated, Emperor Bao Dai has abdicated; our people have broken down the fetters which for over a century have tied us down; our people have at the same time overthrown

the monarchic constitution that reigned supreme for so many centuries and instead have established the present Republican government.

At independence celebrations later that day, United States military officials were invited guests. A Vietminh band played "The Star-Spangled Banner." Washington was a friend. Vietnam was free. Or so Ho Chi Minh—perhaps tentatively—thought.

2

The First Indochina War, 1945–1954

In war, a great disaster always indicates a great culprit.
—Napoleon, 1813

As artillery shells burst relentlessly on the base at Dienbienphu, Colonel Charles Piroth, the French artillery commander, sank into a deep depression. He had lost his left arm to German shrapnel during World War II, but his commitment to soldiering was so intense that his superiors allowed him to continue in the military. For months Piroth bragged that the end was near for the Vietminh, that they would not be able to go toe to toe with his "big guns." But on March 15, 1954, Piroth realized the truth. He apologized to his comrades, claiming that "it is all my fault," lay down on the cot, held a grenade with his hand, and pulled the pin with his teeth.

Ten years earlier, President Franklin D. Roosevelt could have predicted a Dienbienphu of some sort. He believed World War II would destroy European colonialism. In March 1943 Roosevelt suggested to the British foreign secretary, Anthony Eden, that when the war was over Indochina should be placed under international trusteeship. In a private conversation with Secretary of State Cordell Hull in 1944, the president remarked, "France has had the country—thirty million inhabitants—for nearly one hundred years, and the people are worse off than they were at the beginning. . . . The people of Indochina are entitled to something better than that." Eventually, Roosevelt backed down, primarily because of intense British and French opposition.

Roosevelt died on April 12, 1945, and the new president did not share his concern. Southeast Asia was another world to Harry Truman. Born and reared in Missouri, Truman had the traditional strengths—and a few of the weaknesses—of the Midwest. Decent, honest, hard working, he took a man at his word and the world as he found it.

Harry's father, who had a speculator's optimism, had been prone to economic failures, and by the time Truman graduated from high school there was no money for college. He worked in a bank for a while, then he farmed a full section of land. When President Woodrow Wilson asked for a declaration of war against Germany in 1917, Truman left the plow and picked up a rifle. The war took him to France, where as a captain he successfully commanded troops in battle.

Peace returned Truman to his childhood love, and the newlyweds moved to Kansas City, where he opened a haberdashery. The store went bankrupt in 1922, and for the next twenty years—almost to the time he became president—Truman was strapped for money. And so he turned to politics. There he discovered his métier. Equipped with valuable political assets—honesty, dedication, and a likeable personality—Truman rose through the Kansas City political machine. In 1934 he won a seat in the United States Senate, where he was a loyal if undistinguished party man. In 1944 the Democratic party turned to the well-liked but obscure Truman for the vice-presidential nomination; he seemed the candidate least likely to hurt FDR in the election. The American electorate responded with an amazed "Who's Truman?" Even John Bricker, the Republican vice-presidential candidate, remarked in a press conference, "Truman—that's his name, isn't it? I never can remember that name." On April 12, 1945, people started remembering the name.

Grave matters greeted the new president. Germany was in flames but not yet defeated. Japan was losing the war but refused to entertain the fact. There were troubles in Palestine, a meeting was scheduled with Joseph Stalin, and, of course, there was the entire question of the bomb. Truman faced difficult and momentous decisions. Indochina was not one of them. At the Potsdam Conference in July 1945, the Allied governments quickly worked out a plan for the Japanese surrender in Indochina. The Chinese would accept the surrender of Japanese forces north of the sixteenth parallel, and the British troops would land in Saigon and deal with the Japanese south of the line. What Truman and the Allies did not understand is that they would have to come to terms with Ho Chi Minh.

Whatever hopes Ho had for securing American assistance died in anticommunist paranoia. After the defeat of Germany and Japan, President Truman and American policymakers began looking at the Soviet Union as a successor to the Axis powers in threatening world peace. They wanted to rebuild Western Europe and thereby create an economic and military barrier to Soviet expansion: The fulcrum of a stable Western Europe was France. But the French were still irritated over Roosevelt's position on Indochina. The State Department urged Truman to repair the rift by assuring France that the United States would not prevent a French return to Indochina. Truman acquiesced in the revival of the empire. In the summer of 1945 he told Charles de Gaulle that the United States would not undermine the French there. And as the French economy staggered and the communist party there gained strength, moderate French politicians warned that even the most benign discussions of colonial independence played into the hands of the communists.

Ho Chi Minh was prepared to go it alone if necessary. World War II had created an unprecedented opportunity for him. When the Vietnamese saw Japanese troops defeating French soldiers, the myth of French superiority vanished. The service that the French bureaucracy and military in Vietnam thereupon did for Japan deepened popular hatred of France. In 1943 Japan ordered French soldiers to seize the Vietnamese rice harvest for export to Japan and for fuel in Vietnamese factories. Small farmers went bankrupt the first year and starved to death in 1944. Somewhere between 500,000 and two million Vietnamese men, women, and children died in the famine. Ho used the suffering to build his movement. His guerrillas attacked granaries and distributed rice to peasants. They assassinated local landlords along with Vietnamese officials working for the French and the Japanese. Vietminh political organizers spread out into central and south Vietnam preaching nationalism. At the war's end, more than 500,000 people in Vietnam considered themselves loyal to Ho. The Vietminh ruled whole sections of the country as a quasi-government. By the end of the 1945, Ho would have 70,000 followers under arms.

On September 13, 1945, the British under General Douglas D. Gracey entered Saigon with 2,000 Indian troops, most of them famed Gurkha soldiers. Another 18,000 were scheduled to arrive soon. General Lu Han left southern China with 200,000 soldiers and entered Tonkin on September 20. Most of the Chinese troops were barefoot and starving. When they reached the shops in Tonkin, they ate everything in sight, including bars of soap and wrapped packages, which they had never seen before and mistook for food. Sporadic fighting broke out between the ancient enemies. A month before, Ho had marched triumphantly into Hanoi, convinced that independence was imminent. Now he faced 20,000 British troops, 200,000 Chinese and several thousand unarmed French.

Ho Chi Minh's dream of independence was quickly fading. General Gracey had no sympathy for the Vietminh. Two weeks before arriving in Saigon, he announced that "civil and military control by the French is only a question of weeks." Gracey rearmed French troops so they could protect French citizens from the Vietminh. On September 22, the French rioted in Saigon, attacking police stations, stores, and private homes, and mugging or shooting Vietnamese civilians on the streets. On September 24, the Vietminh declared a general strike. Water and electricity went off in Saigon, trams stalled in their tracks, rickshaws disappeared, and Vietminh roadblocks paralyzed commercial traffic. Vietminh agents went into a French suburb and murdered 150 people. Gracey rearmed Japanese soldiers, and the combined force of Japanese, Gurkha, and French troops went after the Vietminh.

There was a small American contingent in Saigon. Prime within it was A. Peter Dewey, who had parachuted into Tonkin in 1945 to harass the Japanese, and as head of the OSS team in Saigon he soon developed a close relationship with Ho Chi Minh. An outspoken opponent of French imperialism, Dewey clashed repeatedly with Gracey. Their personal battle came to a head late in September when Gracey would not let Dewey fly the American flag on the fender of his OSS jeep. On the way to Tan Son Nhut airport in Saigon on September 26, 1945, Vietminh soldiers fired on the flagless jeep, killing Dewey instantly. Just before leaving for the airport, Dewey had written, "Cochin China is burning, the French and British are finished here, and we ought to clear out of Southeast Asia." When he learned of Dewey's death, Ho Chi Minh formally apologized. Gracey, to the contrary, remarked that Dewey "got what he deserved." A. Peter Dewey was the first United States soldier to die in Vietnam.

The Vietminh were also on the run in Tonkin, where Chinese troops removed the Vietminh from power and replaced them with a group favorable to the anticommunist Chinese leader Jiang Jieshi and wanting Vietnamese independence without communism. By the end of September, while British, French, and Japanese troops hounded the Vietminh in southern Vietnam, the Chinese reduced Vietminh-controlled territory in Tonkin. In just a month, Ho found himself dealing with all of Vietnam's enemies—the Chinese, French, and Japanese—as well as the British.

Although Great Britain was officially neutral about the French return to Indochina, most British officials were worried about their own empire. Insurgent nationalists were active in Malaya and Burma, and Mohandas Gandhi was steadily gaining power in India. When their responsibility for disarming Japanese troops ended in December 1945, the British withdrew from southern Vietnam. Each departing group of British-Indian troops was replaced by French soldiers wearing American fatigues, helmets, boots, and ammunition belts, carrying M-1 carbines, and driving Jeeps and Ford trucks. In Tonkin, the Chinese and French reached a formal agreement in February 1946: China would withdraw from Tonkin, and France would surrender the commercial concessions a Franco-Chinese treaty had granted in the 1890s. The last Chinese troops were out of Vietnam in October.

The French were back, and while most of Ho Chi Minh's colleagues opposed rapprochement, his political instincts dictated compromise. General Jacques Philippe Leclerc, temporary head of French military forces in Vietnam, also favored compromise. Even though he had 35,000 soldiers at his disposal, Leclerc had no enthusiasm for fighting an open-ended war against the Vietminh. Late in January, he toured the Mekong Delta and the Iron Triangle, a Vietminh stronghold twenty miles northwest of Saigon. "Fighting the Viet Minh," Leclerc decided, "will be like ridding a dog of its fleas. We can pick them, drown them, and poison them, but they will be back in a few days." On February 5, 1946, Leclerc remarked, "France is no longer in a position to control by arms an entity of 24 million people."

January 12, 1947—Some of the 8,000 French troops aboard the *Ile de France* prior to departure from Toulon Harbor for duty in Indochina. (*Courtesy, AP/Wide World Photos.*)

On March 6, 1946, the French and Vietminh negotiated the Franco-Vietminh Accords. France extended diplomatic recognition to Ho Chi Minh's regime—calling it a "free state . . . within the French Union"— and promised to hold free elections in the "near future" to determine whether Cochin China, as the southern part of Vietnamese territory had been called, would come under Ho's control. Ho agreed to have 25,000 French troops replace Chinese soldiers north of the sixteenth parallel and stay until 1951. Both sides consented to have a Vietminh delegation travel to Paris later in the year to work out details of the agreement. But when Ho Chi Minh went to Paris in the summer of 1946, he was in for a big surprise. Georges Thierry d'Argenlieu was the culprit.

After graduating from the French Naval Academy, d'Argenlieu had taken vows in the Carmelite Order in 1920 but then returned to active naval duty in 1940. In 1943 he became commander in chief of the Free French Naval Forces. D'Argenlieu was a devout Roman Catholic, a man who lived permanently in the past. D'Argenlieu believed that Adolf

Hitler's victory over the French had been a fluke, a brief pause in the reign of France as the premier nation on earth. Buoyed by the Allied victory in 1945, d'Argenlieu expected France to return to its former splendor. With that vision, he became high commissioner for Indochina in August 1945.

On June 1, 1946, the day after Ho Chi Minh sailed for Paris, d'Argenlieu created the Republic of Cochin China, a new, separate colony in the French Union. Ho Chi Minh felt "raped." Unification was as important to him as independence. In fact, the two were for him inseparable, not only because his nationalism extended to include a larger Vietnam but because northern Vietnam was overpopulated and poor, unable to feed itself, while the nutrient-rich Mekong Delta produced rice surpluses. To keep Ho Chi Minh away from the Vietnamese émigré community, French officials moved him out to Biarritz in southwest France. The conference was held out of the press limelight at the isolated Fontainebleau Palace. For eight weeks Ho tried to get France to recognize Vietnamese independence, but the French preferred total control over French colonies. Desperate for assistance, Ho contacted the United States embassy, promising to open up Vietnam to American investment and lease a naval base at Cam Ranh Bay in return for help in keeping the French out. Rebuffed, he remarked to an American reporter, "We . . . stand quite alone; we shall have to depend on ourselves." Before returning to Hanoi in mid-September, Ho Chi Minh signed a document in which France agreed to a unification referendum in Cochin China in 1947, but he had few illusions about France's real intentions. During his last meeting with Georges Bidault, the French prime minister, on September 14, 1946, Ho warned: "If we must fight, we will fight. You will kill ten of our men, and we will kill one of yours. Yet, in the end, it is you who will tire."

In October Ho was back in Tonkin. The battle for Vietnam began a month later over the collection of customs duties in Haiphong. The French insisted it was their right; the Vietminh insisted it was not. When gunfire erupted between Vietminh and French soldiers, d'Argenlieu decided to "teach the Viets a lesson." On November 23, after giving the Vietminh two hours to evacuate Haiphong, the French attacked guerrilla hideouts in the city. French infantry and armored units swept through Haiphong; French aircraft provided tactical air support; and the French cruiser *Suffren* unloaded a sustained artillery bombardment. When the day was over, much of Haiphong was rubble. Six thousand people, including a few Vietminh, were dead.

Four weeks later, the Vietminh retaliated in Hanoi, destroying the city's electrical power plant and assassinating several French officials. Ho Chi Minh fled the city and established new Vietminh headquarters in the jungle sixty miles from Hanoi, where he controlled several provinces with 40,000 Vietminh troops. General Etienne Valluy, who replaced Leclerc, announced that if "those gooks want a fight, they'll get it." General Vo Nguyen Giap was obliging: "I order all soldiers and militia in the center, south, and north, to stand together, go into battle, destroy the invaders, and save the nation." The war was on.

Firmly in control of Tonkin's major cities, the French high command knew it would have to conquer the Red and Mekong River Deltas to deprive the guerrillas of their rice supplies and the mountains near the Laotian and Chinese borders to strip them of their sanctuaries. General d'Argenlieu's strategic approach seemed logical: Build isolated military outposts that the French termed hedgehogs, man them with crack troops, and roam into the countryside seeking out and destroying the Vietminh. Eventually, d'Argenlieu assumed, the Vietminh would run out of hiding places and be forced into a conventional set-piece battle, where superior French firepower could annihilate them. The French hoped to conclude a quick victory; otherwise, the war would be expensive, both politically and financially.

Among the greatest challenges facing French soldiers, and later their American counterparts, was the climate, especially in southern Vietnam. Beginning in September, monsoon winds hit central Vietnam from the northeast, blowing across the South China Sea, picking up enormous amounts of water, and dropping them on the countryside until early February. Rainfall averages 100 to 200 inches a year there. Meteorologists classify it as tropical monsoon, but French troops dubbed it "wet hell." Farther south, in the region of Saigon and the Mekong Delta, a tropical savanna climate prevails. Summers receive large amounts of rainfall, with temperatures and humidity hovering in the nineties. French soldiers on summer patrols, especially if they were working their way through swamps and wetlands, often joked that they could not tell where the waterline stopped and the air began. A remark in the mid-1940s by Jean Dubé, a French soldier stationed in Cochin China in the late 1940s, sums up the experience: "I know what those GIs are going through. It really didn't matter if we were wading through swamps or grasslands. We sweat so much we got just as wet in either place." The Vietnamese were not going to give the French a quick victory.

Ho Chi Minh and Vo Nguyen Giap prepared for guerrilla war. They assumed that France would not have the resources to stay for the long haul. French politics was already a quagmire, and socialists as well as communists were calling for an end to the war. A bloody guerrilla conflict of ambushes, booby traps, and assassinations, with high casualties but no set-piece battles—at least not yet—was Giap's strategy. While the French saw the war in military terms—defeating the Vietminh on the battlefield—Ho Chi Minh saw it in political terms: destroying the French will to continue.

Throughout 1948 and 1949 the French established their hedgehogs on Route 3 from Bac Ninh to Cao Bang, Route 18 from Bac Ninh to Haiphong, Route 5 from Hanoi to Haiphong, Route 1 from Hanoi to Lang

Son, and Route 4 from Cao Bang to Lang Son. In the Mekong Delta, they sought out the guerrillas in search-and-destroy missions. On the political front, the French had Bao Dai, whom they restored to the throne in 1946, sign the Elysée Agreement on March 8, 1949, which created the State of Vietnam as an independent nation but placed France in control of defense, finance, and diplomacy. France promised elections to incorporate Cochin China into a unified Vietnam and held them one month later. Convinced the elections were a sham, the Vietminh boycotted them. Only 1,700 people showed up at the polls, and they voted overwhelmingly to join the State of Vietnam. D'Argenlieu proclaimed that democracy had prevailed.

But in 1949 the war became part of a much larger global struggle between the United States and the Soviet Union. From 1945 to 1948, anticommunist rhetoric had grown shrill in Washington. President Truman announced the Truman Doctrine in 1947 to provide $400 million in military and economic assistance to Greece and Turkey in the fight against leftist-backed guerrillas. The fall of Greece and Turkey, Truman argued, would threaten all the eastern Mediterranean and the Mideast. To save Western Europe, Truman launched the Marshall Plan in 1948, a $12.6 billion program of American economic assistance.

Three events in 1949 elevated anticommunism in the United States from fear to paranoia. In 1948, hoping to starve West Berlin into surrender, the Soviet Union had blocked the highway from West Germany to West Berlin. Truman responded with the Berlin Airlift, an unprecedented daily resupply of a city of two million people. Tension escalated well into 1949 until Moscow backed down. When the Soviet Union detonated an atomic bomb in 1949, a wave of fear swept throughout the United States. Finally, at the end of 1949, Mao Zedong and the Chinese communists drove Jiang Jieshi and the Chinese nationalists off the mainland out to the island of Taiwan.

Many Americans were convinced that an international communist conspiracy was set to take over the world from Moscow. Whenever communists caused any trouble anywhere, the Truman administration blamed Moscow. Late in 1948 the Republican Congressman Richard M. Nixon of California accused Alger Hiss, a Democrat and former State Department official, of being a communist. The trial, which resulted in Hiss's conviction for perjury, generated headlines throughout much of 1949. Early in 1950 Senator Joseph McCarthy, a Republican from Wisconsin, charged that 205 communists were working in the State Department. Congress passed the Internal Security Act in September 1950 requiring registration of communist and communist-front organizations. Communist subversives seemed to be everywhere.

Ever since President Franklin D. Roosevelt's pronouncements on the inherent problems of French imperialism, prominent Americans had at least been able to recognize the existence of Vietnamese nationalism.

But as the fear of communism increased, they subsumed the country's nationalism under Ho Chi Minh's communism, which they believed tied him inextricably to the Soviet conspiracy. They had no idea of the extent of Ho's political independence.

A few people expressed a different point of view. In Paris, General Leclerc repeated his conviction that "anti-communism will be a useless tool unless the problem of nationalism is resolved." Raymond Fosdick, a State Department expert on Asia, claimed that whether "the French like it or not, independence is coming to Indochina. Why, therefore, do we tie ourselves to the tail of their battered kite?" But Leclerc and Fosdick were lonely voices. Far more typical was Dean Acheson, Truman's secretary of state. In 1949 Acheson remarked that whether "Ho Chi Minh is as much nationalist as Commie is irrelevant. . . . All Stalinists in colonial areas are nationalists."

Out of that fear of Indochinese communism emerged the "domino theory," the belief that the fall of one country to communism would topple the next, as though in a row of dominos. For a time in the 1950s and early 1960s, it was central to the way Americans interpreted the world. It appeared as if the whole free world depended on the survival of French Indochina. If Ho Chi Minh succeeded in conquering Tonkin, Annam, and Cochin China, Laos and Cambodia would succumb; then Thailand and Burma, Pakistan and India. Afghanistan, Iran, and the rest of the Middle East were sure to follow. Next communism would infect North Africa and the entire Mediterranean.

The dominos could fall in either direction. On September 20, 1951, during a visit to Washington, General Jean de Lattre de Tassigny, the commander in chief of French Indochina, described a chain of dominoes reaching from Tonkin to Europe: "Once Tonkging [sic] is lost, there is really no barrier before Suez. . . . The loss of Asia would mean the end of Islam, which has two-thirds of its faithful in Asia. The fall of Islam would mean upheavals in North Africa jeopardizing strategic defense bases situated there." American leaders preferred to describe a row of dominoes in the other direction. Secretary of State John Foster Dulles warned in 1953 that if "Indo-China should be lost, there would be a chain reaction throughout the Far East and South Asia," posing a "grave threat to Malaya, Thailand, Indonesia, the Philippines, Australia and New Zealand." Thomas Dewey, the Republican governor of New York, claimed that the "French are holding Indo-China, without which we would lose Japan and the Pacific." In 1965 Senator Thomas J. Dodd of Connecticut carried the domino theory to its extreme: "If we fail to draw the line in Vietnam we may find ourselves compelled to draw a defense line as far back as Seattle and Alaska, with Hawaii as a solitary outpost."

As Andrew Rotter and Gabriel Kolko along with other historians have pointed out, there was more to the domino theory than anti-Soviet rhetoric and anticommunist paranoia. Communist expansion was no idle threat. The Philippines were already dealing with communist guerrillas, and in Malaya and Burma the British government faced similar threats. Radical insurgents in Indonesia were undermining the Dutch colonial regime. Political leaders in Australia and New Zealand were genuinely concerned about the prospects of a communist victory in Vietnam. The fall of Vietnam might topple Malaya, the Philippines, and Indonesia, and once Indonesia fell, so would Australia and New Zealand.

In strategic and economic terms, Southeast Asia was also thought to be critical to American interests. The fall of Southeast Asia would threaten the island chain stretching from Japan to the Philippines, cutting off American air routes to India and South Asia and eliminating the first line of defense in the Pacific. Australia and New Zealand could be isolated. The region was loaded with important natural and strategic resources, including tin, rubber, rice, copra, iron ore, copper, tungsten, and oil. Not only would the United States be cut off from those resources, but huge potential markets for American products were threatened.

The United States was particularly concerned about the relationship between Southeast Asia and Japan. Japan was notoriously poor in resources, and with China now in communist hands, one reliable source of raw materials for the Japanese economy was gone. If the Japanese economy stagnated, the nation's communists might gain power. One way to preserve the economic integrity of Japan was to effect an economic integration of Japan and Southeast Asia. But if Southeast Asia fell to communism, such an integration would be impossible, or so policy makers feared. A 1952 National Security Council memo specifically stated that concern: "In the long run the loss of Southeast Asia, especially Malaya and Indonesia, could result in such economic and political pressures in Japan as to make it extremely difficult to prevent Japan's eventual accommodation to the Soviet Bloc."

Washington even detected a connection between Southeast Asia and the survival of Western Europe. In 1949 Great Britain was still in the economic doldrums and dangerously low in dollar reserves. Recovery required huge capital investments, and the entire British empire needed to increase its exports to the United States. Southeast Asia was critical to that process. Before World War II a vigorous triangular trade had existed between Great Britain, the United States, and British Malaya, which had valuable rubber and tin assets. That trade needed to be revived. Nor could the French economy be restored to health as long as the war in Indochina was such a financial drain.

Throughout 1950 political events in Asia seemed to confirm American fears. Early in 1950, the Soviet Union and China extended diplomatic recognition to Hanoi, which for Dean Acheson revealed "Ho in his true colors as the mortal enemy of native independence in Indochina." The

United States responded quickly, confirming the Elysée Agreement by recognizing Bao Dai's State of Vietnam as an "independent part of the French Union." In February the National Security Council declared "that the threat of communist aggression against Indochina is only one phase of anticipated communist plans to seize all of Southeast Asia." On May 15, 1950, President Harry Truman announced his decision to supply $15 million in military assistance to France to fight the Vietminh.

At the time, Mao Zedong had decided to contest Joseph Stalin's status as leader of the communist world by fashioning his own image of the "Stalin of the East," the de facto leader of all communist parties in East Asia, South Asia, and Southeast Asia. Vietnam provided the first opportunity to upstage Stalin and the Soviet Union. United States policymakers would not really appreciate the reality of the Chinese-Soviet split until the mid-1960s, but it first emerged in the early 1950s when the Soviet Union and the Chinese competed to win the loyalty of Ho Chi Minh.

In the race to keep the Vietnamese, armed, clothed, and fed, Mao enjoyed a distinct geographic advantage, one he began to exploit almost as soon as American aid started flowing to Vietnam. For Russians to send massive volumes of supplies, the goods would have to travel by sea. Goods from the heavily industrialized Soviet west had to be shipped by rail either to Vladivostok or the Black Sea and loaded on supply ships. From Vladivostok, the ships would make their way through the Sea of Japan and Straits of Molucca to the South China sea and the northern Vietnamese port city of Haiphong. From the Black Sea, Soviet ships bound for Vietnam had to sail west through the Bosporous and the Dardanelles straits into the Mediterranean, then through the Suez Canal to the Indian Ocean and from there to the South China sea and Haiphong. To give China the upper hand, Mao constructed multiple railroad lines connecting Guangxi and Guangdong provinces in southern China with trunk lines in northern Tonkin. The railroads allowed for massive shipments of supplies to the Vietminh.

When North Korea invaded South Korea in June 1950, the Truman administration became all the more convinced that the Soviet Union wanted all of Asia. Led by the United States, the United Nations pledged to defend South Korea. Besides sending troops to Korea, Truman increased the American commitment to France, sending more than $133 million in Indochina aid at the end of the year. He extended another $50 million for economic and technical assistance. A contingent of DC-3 Dakota aircraft landed in Saigon in June. Waiting on the runway with paintbrushes, the French enraged American pilots when they replaced the aircrafts' white star markings with the French tricolor insignia. Late in November, Chinese troops joined the Korean War, killing thousands of UN troops. To most Americans, the international communist conspiracy was well under way.

In Hanoi, Vo Nguyen Giap was not thinking about any international communist conspiracy. From Mao Zedong's writings on revolutionary warfare, Giap developed a three-stage formula for defeating the French. Beyond that, he had no passionate interest in the spread of communism.

During the first stage that the Vietminh strategist projected, the insurrectionists would just survive, avoiding confrontations until they built up their reserves. If they could achieve surprise and complete superiority, they would strike, but otherwise the Vietminh bided their time. Giap's fear of premature battle was not sentimental. He possessed a unique philosophy about death. "Every minute," he remarked to a French reporter, "hundreds of thousands of people die on this earth. The life or death of a hundred, a thousand, tens of thousands of human beings, even our compatriots, means little." What Giap did not want was an engagement that destroyed his fledgling army. Stage one characterized Vietminh operations in 1946 and 1947.

The second stage employed guerrilla tactics—ambushes, road destruction, hit-and-run attacks, and assassinations. At night the Vietminh placed booby traps along French patrol routes. Their favorite ones were sharpened bamboo "punji stakes" dipped in human feces or poison and driven into holes or rice paddies, or attached to bent saplings; hollowed-out coconuts filled with gunpowder and triggered by a trip wire; walk bridges with ropes almost cut away so they would collapse when someone tried to cross; a buried bamboo stub with a bullet on its tip, activated when someone stepped on it; the "Malay whip log," attached to two trees by a rope and triggered by a trip wire; boards studded with iron barbs and buried in stream beds and rice paddies. In 1948 and 1949 Vo Nguyen Giap's second stage was under way.

By 1949 Giap thought he was almost ready for the third stage. He wanted a real fight with the French Expeditionary Corps. Between 1945 and 1947, he had built the People's Army from a ragtag group of 5,000 to more than 100,000, most of them irregular troops but also including thousands of highly disciplined, well-trained Vietminh soldiers. Events in 1949 made the general offensive even more inviting. Mao Zedong's victory gave Giap a sanctuary at his rear. Vietnamese peasants constructed four roads from the Chinese border to staging areas, and Chinese and Soviet supplies began to arrive. By 1950 the Vietminh had five fully equipped infantry divisions, along with an artillery and engineering division. It was time for what Giap termed the "general counter-offensive."

Giap set his sights on the French outpost at Dong Khe. The hedgehog sat astride Route 4, a road the French considered the Vietminh "jugular vein" in northern Tonkin. They reasoned that control of Route 4 would cut Vietminh supply lines from China and stall their troop movements. French truck convoys supplied Dong Khe on a daily basis, but in early 1950 Giap blocked all shipments to the garrison. On May 26, 1950, with monsoon rains drenching the land and Vietminh infantry surrounding the outpost, he began the artillery bombardment. Two days later, thousands of Vietminh soldiers stormed the garrison. It fell on May 28. French paratroopers retook Dong Khe a few days later, but the Vietminh successfully attacked again on September 18. Early in October, they took Cao Bang, the northernmost city on Route 4, and over the next several months the French abandoned Lang Son, their southern outpost on Route 4, and Thai Nguyen, the city on Route 3 between Hanoi and Cao Bang. Vo Nguyen Giap killed or captured 6,000 French troops and eliminated the French presence all along the Chinese border.

The events at Dong Khe left French military planners with the wrong impression. In their final assault, the Vietminh had attacked in massive human wave assaults, infantry troops literally running into and overrunning the French barricades. The Vietminh sustained staggering casualties, but Giap was less concerned with the number of soldiers lost than with their success in achieving the military objective. From the battle of Dong Khe, the French erroneously concluded that in the future, the Vietminh would again employ human wave infantry assaults, as if that was tactical doctrine. That presumption rested on quicksand. In the future, the Vietminh would prove to be quite flexible in attacking fixed French positions.

Heads rolled in Hanoi and Saigon. France fired most senior officials and conferred joint military and political command on General Jean de Lattre de Tassigny, who in December 1950 became high commissioner and commander in chief of Indochina. A hero of both world wars, de Lattre had an ability matched by his ego. Handsome, confident, and obsessed with victory, he rebuilt French outposts in the Red River Valley, betting that Vo Nguyen Giap, flushed with success, would push too far.

De Lattre was right. Giap wanted to drive the French back into Hanoi, so he decided to attack Vinh Yen, a reinforced garrison thirty miles northwest of the capital. De Lattre was ready. The Vietminh attacked but failed to overrun the base. Giap tried an attack up the Day River southeast of Hanoi but was repulsed again. He threw the Vietminh against Nam Dinh, a French garrison twenty miles south of Haiphong. Bernard de Lattre, the general's son, had orders to hold Nam Dinh at all costs. He died obeying his father. By the end of May 1951, 6,000 were dead and Vo Nguyen Giap retreated from Vinh Yen. The general returned to stage two.

De Lattre was barely able to savor the victories. He was terminally ill with stomach cancer and died seven months later in Paris. General Raoul Salan replaced him, but he was little more than a caretaker. De Lattre had created the Vietnamese National Army, on paper a 115,000-man force, to make it appear at least that Bao Dai's government was really fighting the communists. In the meantime, Giap replenished his divisions. At the end of May 1953 Salan was relieved of his command.

By that time the war was a bottomless pit. Since 1945 the war had cost France 3 dead generals, 8 colonels, 18 lieutenant colonels, 69 majors, 341 captains, 1,140 lieutenants, 9,691 enlisted men, and 12,109 French Legionnaires, along with 20,000 missing in action and 100,000 wounded. Saint-Cyr, the French military academy, was not graduating officers fast enough to replace the dead in Indochina. The military situation was even worse. From the Chinese border in northern Vietnam to the Ca Mau Peninsula on the South China Sea, the Vietminh controlled two-thirds of the country. Their army, including regular and irregular troops, numbered in the hundreds of thousands, and in the words of the journalist Theodore White, "has become a modern army, increasingly skillful, armed with artillery, organized into divisions." French control had been reduced to enclaves around Hanoi, Haiphong, and Saigon, as well as a strip of land along the Cambodian border.

Salan's replacement was Henri Navarre, a veteran of both world wars who believed French forces could bring the Vietminh to their knees within a year. Navarre had joined the French infantry in 1916 after graduating from Saint-Cyr as a cavalry officer. Except for duty in North Africa during World War II, his career was in army intelligence. Supremely self-confident, dictatorial, and righteously committed, Navarre was an instant celebrity in the French social circuits of Hanoi and Saigon. In both cities he outfitted himself with air-conditioned command posts complete with the best in French wine and cuisine. When he arrived in Saigon to assume his command, Navarre predicted an early end to the war: "Now we can see it clearly—like light at the end of a tunnel."

Navarre decided that French strategy needed an overhaul. After eight years of fighting, the French were no closer to winning than they had been back in 1946. The Vietminh were steadily growing, and Vo Nguyen Giap was preparing to widen the war into Laos. Navarre believed that France was wasting men and resources fighting scattered guerrillas in a conflict that had no end. The key to victory was conventional war. He would seduce the Vietminh into a major engagement where French firepower could annihilate them.

What became known as the Navarre Plan was actually an elaborate military scheme devised in Washington and Paris. Because American troops were tied down in Western Europe and Korea, the United States insisted that France, with massive financial and matériel assistance, take care of Indochina itself. The plan called for a large increase in the size of the Vietnamese National Army and nine new French battalions. Navarre proposed removing his troops from isolated outposts, combining them with the new French troops, and taking the offensive. He hoped to be able to use the Vietnamese National Army elsewhere in Vietnam.

In its first formulation, the Navarre Plan contemplated the Red River Valley as the setting for the massive battle. But in the fall of 1953, Vo Nguyen Giap countered with increased guerrilla attacks throughout the

February 1954—General Henri Navarre *(left)*, commander of French forces in Indochina, reviews the troops at an inspection of the camp Dienbienphu with Colonel Christian de Castries *(center)*, commander of the camp and General René Cogny *(right)*, commander of forces in North Vietnam. (*Courtesy, AP/Wide World Photos.*)

Red River Delta as well as an invasion of central and southern Laos. He also readied three Vietminh divisions for northern Laos. Already at the limits of their economic and military commitment, the French became obsessed with keeping the Vietminh out of Laos, where the Pathet Lao, a guerrilla force backed by the communists, was already causing enough trouble. Navarre began considering a new option—going after the Vietminh in western Tonkin along the Laotian border.

Navarre scoured the map looking for the perfect place and found it near Laos at the village of Dienbienphu. There Navarre would establish a "mooring point," a center of operations from which French patrols could go out into the hills in search of the Vietminh. A large French garrison at Dienbienphu would make it more difficult for Giap to ship supplies through Laos to southern Vietnam or invade Laos. Finally, Dienbienphu, was the center of Vietminh opium production; revenues from the drug traffic financed weapons purchases. Suppressing opium production, Navarre hoped, would cut Vietminh revenues.

Navarre was convinced that Ho Chi Minh would not be able to abide the French presence at Dienbienphu. In order to push ahead with his plans for domination of Indochina, Ho would have to destroy the French garrison. Anticipating massive, human-wave assaults like the attack the Chinese had launched in Korea and the Vietminh at Dong Khe and Vinh Yen, Navarre planted the base in the center of the valley, with vast stretches of flat territory separating it from the neighboring mountains, where dozens of howitzers were aimed. Colonel Charles Piroth, the one-armed commander of French artillery, predicted that "no Vietminh cannon will be able to fire three rounds before being destroyed by my artillery." If the Vietminh attacked, they had to cross thousands of yards of open fields where French tanks, machine guns, and tactical aircraft would cut them to pieces. With complete air superiority, the French built an airstrip and thought they could hold out indefinitely, resupplying themselves by air from Hanoi.

Navarre wanted to double the size of the Vietnamese National Army to relieve the French Expeditionary Corps of its obligations to fight a nonstop war against Vietminh guerrillas. French advisers would remain in the countryside to work with the Vietnamese National Army in suppressing the guerrillas. At the same time, Navarre assembled a new, powerful army corps to occupy Dienbienphu and engage the Vietminh in battle.

But where would Navarre find the men and the money? In France the Indochina War was increasingly unpopular, swallowing men and matériel with no victory in sight. Conscription was out of the question; there was no way the government could get the necessary legislation through the French National Assembly. Public debate was already at a fever pitch. Instead, Navarre turned to the other colonies, putting together a polyglot army of French Legionnaires and volunteers from France, Lebanon, Syria, Chad, Guadeloupe, and Madagascar. For money Navarre looked to the United States. Ever since 1950, when Congress appropriated the first $15 million, American assistance had steadily increased. Navarre wanted even more, and the administration of Dwight Eisenhower was quick to agree. By the end of 1953 the United States was supplying Navarre with 10,000 tons of equipment a month, at an annual cost of $500 million. That amount increased to $1.1 billion in 1954, nearly 78 percent of France's war expenses. Navarre had money and men.

Navarre placed Colonel Christian de Castries in command of Dienbienphu. The aristocrat, horseman, and athlete Castries had won several European high jump and long jump championships in the mid-1930s. During World War II he made the transition from cavalry to armor and was wounded several times. The Germans captured him in 1941, but he escaped in 1944 and rejoined French fighting forces. Known to show off at parties by chewing glass, Castries declared that life was sweet if a man "had a horse to ride, an enemy to kill, and a woman in his bed."

Beginning in November 1953, Castries supervised the construction of the base at Dienbienphu. He was immediately identifiable by his red cap, flaming red scarf, and riding crop in his hand. He put the main base at the center of the valley and then set up three major artillery bases: one three miles to the south, which he designated Isabelle; another, Béatrice, about a mile to the northeast; and a third nearly two miles to the north, which he called Gabrielle. Castries was supporting three mistresses by these names, and he wanted to immortalize them. Castries named other firebases and French posts after earlier conquests: Anne Marie, Francoise, Dominique, Eliane, Claudine, and Huguette. Castries manned the base with 13,200 paratroopers. In a radio broadcast on January 1, 1954, General Navarre announced that he expected "total victory after six more months of hard fighting."

Navarre's commander of the Tonkin theater was not so sanguine. René Cogny came from humble stock, but with scholarships he had graduated from Saint-Cyr in artillery and then earned degrees in political science and law. The Germans captured him in 1940, but he escaped in 1941, only to be captured again in 1943. He spent the rest of the war at the Buchenwald concentration camp, where torture left him with a permanent limp. In the eight years after his release, Cogny enjoyed a spectacular rise through the ranks of the officer corps, from captain to major general. He feared the Navarre Plan. He wanted to avoid battles in the highlands, except for minor skirmishes; maintain a permanent offensive against the Vietminh in the Red River Delta; and frequently raid enemy supply lines and infiltration routes. When he first heard about the plan from Navarre, Cogny remarked to his chief of staff: "Dienbienphu will become, whether we like it or not, a drain on manpower . . . as soon as it is pinned down by a single regiment. . . . The consequences of such a decision may be very serious."

From his post in the mountains above Dienbienphu, Vo Nguyen Giap was dumbfounded. The Navarre Plan represented a significant shift in French strategy, and he was in a quandary at first about how to deal with the change. His philosophy about such confrontations with the French had always been consistent: "Strike to win, strike only when success is certain. If it is not, then do not strike." Giap's biggest mistake, trying to overrun the French base at Vinh Yen in 1951, had made him more prudent and deliberate, more willing to wait until victory was certain. But he could not understand why the French had picked Dienbienphu. The roads were narrow and exposed; the Vietminh would never let supply trucks reach the valley; and Vietminh artillery would prevent supply aircraft from landing at the hastily constructed airfield. The valley was a wet bottomland of the Nam Yum River. After heavy rains the valley turned into mud and drained very slowly. French tanks would be immobilized. Any competent engineer or hydrologist could have taken a look at Dienbienphu and concluded that tank warfare would be difficult at best. Even in dry weather the ground was covered with heavy, vined brush that would clog tank tracks. The French had also assumed that the Vietminh did not have any decent artillery pieces and that even if they did they would not be able to place them in the mountains above Dienbienphu. There were no roads up there for trucks to make deliveries. That was a gross misjudgment on the part of the French.

When Vo Nguyen Giap calculated the deficiencies of the French position, he concluded that Vietminh victory was certain. The terrain would destroy armor mobility; tanks would become stationary artillery pieces. By assaulting Gabrielle, Isabelle, and Béatrice in sequence, Giap could eliminate French artillery. He was also counting on his own artillery. In Korea the Chinese had captured hundreds of 105-mm howitzers and 120-mm potbellied mortars built by the Americans, and they were on their way. Giap intended to destroy the airfield and put Dienbienphu under siege. Nor was he worried about the vast open spaces between the mountain slopes and the French perimeter. He would dig hundreds of miles of tunnels and trenches from the mountain slopes toward the base, eliminating the French tactical advantage.

For years the French had waited for the set-piece battle in which their firepower would prevail, assuming, of course, that they would win such a contest. Jean de Lattre de Tassigny, Raoul Salan, and Henri Navarre all prayed for the confrontation. Castries put it best in January 1954: "If he [the Vietminh] comes down, we've got him. It may be a tough fight, but we shall halt him. And we shall at last have what we have always lacked: a concentrated target that we can smash." The French were convinced that if Vo Nguyen Giap attacked Dienbienphu, the Vietminh would suffer a decisive defeat.

Navarre had completely underestimated Giap's ability to relocate the Vietminh. Slowly and steadily he did the impossible—he put four Vietminh divisions into the mountains surrounding Dienbienphu. Even though most of them had only cut-up rubber tires for shoes, he got twenty to fifty miles a day out of them, each carrying a rifle, a large bag of rice, clothing, a shovel, and a water bottle. When French aircraft bombed the small roads heading for Dienbienphu, Giap repaired them. Along Routes 13B and 41, he had 10,000 workers who restored roads within an hour of the attack.

By early March 1954 Vo Nguyen Giap had 50,000 combat-hardened Vietminh troops and another 50,000 support troops in place, along with 100,000 Vietnamese porters carrying supplies on their backs. General Navarre was confident that Giap would not be able to bring heavy artillery into battle, that French artillery and tactical air support would put him at a tremendous firepower disadvantage. Suddenly 105-mm shells began to rain on the airstrip at Dienbienphu, pockmarking it with craters and rendering it unsafe for supply landings. The French had expected Giap to move the artillery into place the way they did—on large trucks over visible roads. But he had disassembled each artillery piece, organized thousands of porters to carry the elements to Dien-bienphu, and then reassembled the artillery there.

The shelling on March 12 was just a preview. The main feature started at 5:00 p.m. the next day when Vietminh artillery exploded all over the French artillery bases. By midnight Vietminh troops had seized outpost Béatrice. The bombardment of Gabrielle began at dusk the next day. Nine hours later Gabrielle fell. The Vietminh sustained thousands of casualties, but in less than fifteen hours Castries had lost most of his artillery. Isabelle was so far south of the main base that in order to protect it Castries had to move a large troop contingent there. Instead of attacking, Giap left Isabelle alone, rendering useless the French troops there. The next day the Vietminh bombardment became so heavy that aircraft could no longer land. French soldiers could be supplied only by air, and on March 17, 1954, American and French pilots began flying C-119s and C-47s over Dienbienphu, dropping food, weapons, and ammunition to the besieged soldiers. That same day armed Montagnard tribesmen, allied with the French, realized their plight and fled Dien-bienphu. France needed help.

On March 20, General Paul Ely, chief of staff of the French armed forces, flew to Washington for a meeting with President Dwight Eisen-hower, Secretary of State John Foster Dulles, and Admiral Arthur Radford, chairman of the joint chiefs of staff. A member of the West Point class of 1915—called the "Class on Which the Stars Fell" because 59 of its 164 graduates rose to the rank of brigadier general or higher—Ike was perhaps the best of the group. As commander of the European operations in World War II, he had earned a reputation for decisiveness, energy, intelligence, and skill in handling temperamental and egotistical individuals. Said FDR's press secretary of Ike: "To acquire these characteristics he worked constantly, sleeping only five hours a day . . . and laboring seven days a week and holidays. Chain smoking cigarettes, he had an inexhaustible supply of nervous energy." Once in the presidency, Eisenhower seemed more subdued. White House reporters recall not his energy and precise thinking but rather his mangled syntax and his fondness for golfing and bridge—a very intellectual game: Ike could remember all the cards of each suit as a game was played. But behind the mild facade Ike was still in charge. In foreign affairs, he made all the important decisions. Intellectuals and English teachers could fault his syntax, but as Fred I. Greenstein notes, Eisenhower "had geometric precision in stating the basic conditions shaping a problem, deducing their implications, and weighing the costs and benefits of alternative possible responses." As Ely talked, the geometry of Ike's mind was calculating.

The French general wanted to make sure that American assistance would continue under Eisenhower. Although he did not know how the communists could "continue to suffer the losses they have been taking . . . I don't know how they can stay in the battle," Ely readily admitted that Dienbienphu was finished. He made no specific request for anything more than continued American financial support. When the meeting concluded, Eisenhower asked Radford to see whether the United States could offer some more assistance to the French. Without the knowledge of Eisenhower, Dulles, or even other joint chiefs, Radford with the assistance of American and French officers in Saigon was hatching a rescue plan.

Radford, a graduate of the Naval Academy in Annapolis, had commanded aircraft carriers in the Pacific during World War II. In May 1953, when President Eisenhower toured the Pacific and East Asia to assess the Korean situation, Radford was commander of naval forces in the Pacific. He spent some time with Eisenhower during the tour and impressed the president with his grasp of Asian affairs. Eisenhower named Radford chief of naval operations in 1953 and chairman of the Joint Chiefs of Staff. By that time Radford was a saber-rattling darling of the Republican right. A zealous convert to complicated weapons technology and air power, Radford had endeared himself to a number of conservative politicians during World War II when he said the only approach to the Japanese was "to kill the bastards scientifically." Infantry combat "was messy and wasted personnel." Strategic and tactical bombing was "precise and clean." Radford was convinced that Asia, not Europe, would be central to American foreign policy for the rest of the twentieth century. Late in 1953, when the president expressed concern about the defense budget, Radford became the author of the "New Look." Radford urged, and Eisenhower and Dulles accepted, the notion that instead of planning for a variety of military contingencies—strategic nuclear war, conventional war, limited nuclear war, and guerrilla war—the United States should plan for a war in which nuclear weapons would be used whenever they were strategically advantageous. Such an approach would be less expensive than a more comprehensive response system. Secretary of State John Foster Dulles used Radford's logic in his famous "massive retaliation" speech of January 12, 1954, when he threatened to use strategic nuclear weapons whenever and wherever the Soviet Union fomented rebellion.

When Radford learned of the desperate situation at Dienbienphu, he was eager to use air power. It was the perfect place, he thought, to try out the Eisenhower administration's "New Look" defense policy. He proposed Operation Vulture: the use of B-29s, based in the Philippines and accompanied by aircraft from the carriers USS *Essex* and USS *Boxer*, to knock out Vietminh artillery. Without artillery the Vietminh could not destroy the outpost. The airstrip could be repaired, and a full-scale resupply resumed. "We could have helped the French with air strikes," Radford's memoirs declare. "Whether these alone would have been successful in breaking the siege of Dien Bien Phu is debatable. If we had used atomic weapons, we probably would have been successful."

The proposal triggered an intense debate. The other chiefs of staff, especially General Matthew Ridgway of the army, were opposed. Fresh from his command of United Nations forces in Korea, Ridgway felt sure the bombing would fail to lift the siege and that only ground troops— seven to ten full divisions—could rescue Dienbienphu. The Korean War had already proven how difficult Asian land wars could be, and the terrain of Indochina was far worse, the stuff of which bloody, endless guerrilla wars are made. Eisenhower listened carefully to Ridgway; the two infantry commanders understood each other. Vice President Richard Nixon supported Operation Vulture. On March 13, the day the Vietminh overran Gabrielle, Nixon announced, "We have adopted a new principle. Rather than let the communists nibble us to death all over the world in little wars, we will rely in the future on massive, mobile retaliatory forces." In a press conference Nixon declared that there "is no reason why the French forces should not remain in Indo-China and win. They have greater manpower, and a tremendous advantage over their adversaries, particularly air power." Like Radford, Nixon was prepared to use atomic bombs to lift the siege.

Eisenhower listened to Radford. He listened to Ridgway and Nixon. Never threatened by conflicting viewpoints, Ike believed in the value of good advice and well-reasoned arguments. As Walter Bedell Smith, Eisenhower's World War II chief of staff and close friend, described him: "One of his most successful methods in dealing with individuals is to assume that he himself is lacking in detailed knowledge and liable to make an error. . . . This was by no means a pose, because he . . . values the recommendations . . . he receives, although his own better . . . judgment might cause them to be disregarded." And so Eisenhower listened to opinions bold and cautious—and then he made his decision. He knew from experience that wars are seldom as neat as they seem in strategic papers, and that the "fog of battle" confounds the best laid plans. And the politics of the issue brought conflicting perils. The Republican right wing was making enormous political capital out of the claim that the Democrats had lost China, and he was not prepared to be blamed for losing Indochina. But at the same time, he perceived public skepticism about American involvement in Vietnam. The Korean armistice was just a few months old. Most Americans did not want another war in Asia. Eisenhower was intrigued with Radford's plan. He would not, however, go forward without the support of Congress and the British.

Congress was the president's first target. On April 3 he had Dulles and Radford try to sell the idea to a congressional delegation that included Senators William Knowland and Lyndon Johnson and Congressmen Joseph Martin and John McCormack.

Eisenhower was not asking for an immediate air strike. He was more cautious than that. What he wanted to know was whether the delegation would give him the discretionary authority to use American forces if a Vietminh victory at Dienbienphu would lead to the fall of Indochina. The legislators were skeptical. They worried about what would happen if the bombing failed. Would ground troops be committed? They also were concerned about Washington's taking unilateral action. Why not coordinate an international effort to save Dienbienphu? The legislators did have one unequivocal answer for Ike: no more Koreas, where the United States had supplied 90 percent of the combat troops. John F. Kennedy added on the floor of the Senate: "No amount of military assistance in Indo-China can conquer an enemy that is everywhere and at the same time nowhere, 'an enemy of the people' which at the same time has the support of the people."

The debate in the administration and the reservations within Congress persuaded Eisenhower that American intervention would have to be contingent on securing cooperation from other North Atlantic Treaty Organization powers, and getting France to make plans for granting independence for its Indochinese colonies. That was going to take some time, time Dienbienphu did not have. Convinced that Operation Vulture was the only way of saving Dienbienphu, the French asked Eisenhower for an immediate air strike, leaving the question of joint allied military operations for later discussions. He summarily rejected the request, chastising Radford for misleading the French but agreeing to explore the possibility of subsequent American intervention if European allies would cooperate. Eisenhower asked Dulles to go to Europe and secure NATO support. Dulles set out to achieve what he called "United Action."

Dulles and Eisenhower made an odd couple. Compared to the warm, friendly president, the secretary of state seemed cold and distant. In fact, compared to almost anyone Dulles was cold and distant. The nation called Eisenhower "Ike," but no one called Dulles "Jack." The historian Townsend Hoopes describes Dulles as a "solid tree trunk of a man gnarled and durable . . . a rectangular brow and aquiline nose, a thin and drooping mouth, a strong jaw, the whole creating an effect of ultimate seriousness and at the same time of ultimate plainness." Proud of the history of foreign service in his family—a grandfather as secretary of state for Benjamin Harrison and an uncle in the same position for Woodrow Wilson—Dulles had been part of the Versailles peace mission in 1919, a Wall Street lawyer with clients across the globe, a delegate to the United Nations, and a lifelong student of foreign relations. As Eisenhower told reporters, there is "only one man I know who has seen *more* of the world and talked with more people and *knows* more than Dulles does—and that's me." Dulles, described as a "card carrying Christian," equated communism with all the sins of atheism. Once on hearing Jiang Jieshi and Syngman Rhee spoken of in unflattering terms, Dulles responded heatedly, "No matter what you say about them, those two gentlemen are modern-day equivalents of the founders of the church. They are Christian gentlemen who have suffered for their faith."

Travel was as much a part of John Foster Dulles's life as diplomacy and breathing. He used airplanes as other men used cabs. Now he began a dizzying round of shuttle diplomacy, traveling back and forth between Europe and the United States trying to line up allies. Back home the president tried to drum up public support for intervention, using the domino theory in an April 7 press conference: "You have a row of dominoes set up and you knock over the first one, and what will happen to the last one is the certainty that it will go over very quickly. . . . The loss of Indochina will cause the fall of Southeast Asia like a set of dominoes." But while Eisenhower and Dulles were trying to line up the allies, General Ridgway torpedoed the idea. He was furious with Radford. Ridgway was convinced that Ike would not use atomic weapons; in 1945 he had advised Truman against employing them on the Japanese. Ridgway was right. At a meeting of the National Security Council in late April, when the issue came up again, the president finally interrupted a discussion with a frustrated outburst: "You boys must be crazy. We can't use those awful things against Asians for the second time in less than ten years. My God!" Ridgway also believed that conventional air strikes would not lift the siege. Intervention with ground troops would be inevitable. In a memo to President Eisenhower, Ridgway shared his misgivings: "How deep was the water over the bar at Saigon? What are the harbor and dock facilities? Where could we store the . . . supplies we would need? How good was the road network—how could supplies be transported as the fighting forces moved inland, and in what tonnages? What of the climate? The rainfall? What tropical diseases would attack the combat soldier?" Eisenhower understood. The next day Dulles informed Henri Bonnet, the French ambassador to the United States, that American intervention might not be forthcoming.

Operation Vulture and the larger proposal for United Action were compromised also by French intransigence. During the discussions with the French, Eisenhower became more and more frustrated. He complained that the French "want us to come in as junior partners and provide materials, etc., while they themselves retain authority in that region." In the previous months they had balked at the notion of United Action, fearing that French power would be subordinated in a multinational force. Nor were the French willing even to talk of independence for Vietnam. That, too, bothered Eisenhower, who wrote to a friend that France had employed "weasel words in promising independence . . . and through this reason . . . have suffered reverses that have been inexcusable." The French would not even cooperate with the Military Assistance and Advisory Group, an American mission sent to Vietnam in 1950 to coordinate United States economic and military aid. France wanted American money, not American advice.

Britain as well doomed United Action. The British thought Ho Chi Minh was a highly independent communist who would not let the Chinese, any more than the French, take over his country. When Dulles predicted the apocalypse if Dienbienphu fell, the British calmly replied that the United States was viewing the situation through ideological blinders. Foreign Minister Anthony Eden predicted that India, Burma, Pakistan, Thailand, Malaya, Indonesia, the Philippines, and Japan would survive even if Ho Chi Minh took over Vietnam. Dulles left London empty-handed on April 14. Prime Minister Winston Churchill was relieved to see Dulles go. In his judgment, "Dulles is the only case of a bull I know who carries his china closet around with him."

Everything also went wrong at Dienbienphu. Navarre's plans to increase the size of the Vietnamese National Army failed miserably. The government of Bao Dai sent 94,000 draft orders late in 1953, but only 5,400 new soldiers reported for duty. The Vietnamese National Army never exceeded the 115,000 level, and by early 1954 the desertion rate reached nearly 4,000 men a month. In a country where nationalism, communist and noncommunist, ran very deep, the French plan to develop a highly effective army of colonial troops was incredibly naive. The idea of turning the war over to the Vietnamese was no closer to reality in 1954 than it had been in 1951 when General de Lattre created the Vietnamese National Army. Monsoon rains immobilized French tanks in the heavy mud and prevented resupply from Hanoi. French troops rationed food and water. The shovels Vietminh soldiers carried into Dienbienphu were as useful as their rifles. They dug trenches and tunnels. Twenty-four hours a day, day after day, antlike, tens of thousands of Vietminh extended the trenches, inching their way toward the French outpost, steadily reducing the French perimeter, eliminating the stretches of open space the French had relied on. By the end of April, the Vietminh outnumbered the French ten to one, and the French perimeter, which once had a circumference of fifteen miles, was reduced to a thousand-yard square.

As Vo Nguyen Giap closed the circle on Dienbienphu, the Geneva Conference convened in Switzerland. Conflicts of interest and personality abounded. John Foster Dulles did not want to be there at all and was committed to making sure that the Geneva Accords resulting from the conference did "not give one inch of territory to the Communists." At Geneva he behaved badly, "like a puritan in a house of ill repute," according to his biographer. Pham Van Dong, representing the Vietminh, wanted a complete political settlement leading to the withdrawal of French forces and establishment of a new, independent government under Ho Chi Minh. France only wanted a military ceasefire. Georges Bidault, who headed the French delegation, recognized that the fall of Dienbienphu would banish the French from the north, but he hoped to regroup in Cochin China and maintain the empire. Laos and Cambodia sided with Bidault. They were already dealing with internal communist rebellions and assumed that French withdrawal, combined with a Vietminh triumph, would destroy the French Union and condemn Indochina to communism. Zhou Enlai and the Chinese wanted to partition Vietnam. They did not want a united Vietnam—French or Vietnamese—to the south. The Soviet Union was conciliatory. Joseph Stalin's death in 1953 had removed the most militant voice in Moscow, and the new Soviet chieftains did not want a confrontation with the United States, not over a faraway place like Indochina. Only they and the British, represented by Anthony Eden as foreign secretary, came to Geneva without a firm political agenda. The two emerged as the leaders of the conference.

The various delegations spent their first two weeks at Geneva on other questions before turning their attention to Indochina. On May 6, just when the talks began, Vo Nguyen Giap attacked the French fortress, hitting it with new Soviet Katyusha field rockets, which the French dubbed "Stalin's organs" because of their roar, and sending thousands of Vietminh out of the trenches, through the exploding shells, and into the base. On the afternoon of May 7, after bitter, hand-to-hand combat, Vietminh entered the French headquarters and struck the flag. In a final radio message, Castries cried: "Our resistance is going to be overwhelmed. The Viets are within a few meters of the radio transmitter where I am speaking. I have given orders to carry out maximum destruction. We will not surrender. We will fight to the end. . . . Long live France!" The Vietminh seized Castries moments later, along with more than 10,000 of his comrades. The French prisoners spent the next ten weeks in horrible prison camps before their repatriation began on July 20.

Vo Nguyen Giap's troops had sustained 22,900 casualties, 7,900 killed and 15,000 wounded, while the French buried 2,080 dead and treated 5,613 wounded. But Giap was the victor. He regrouped his four divisions at Dienbienphu and marched them east toward the Red River Delta and Hanoi. Certain that a general French defeat was near, General Navarre rearranged his troops in the Red River Delta and placed them around Hanoi and along Highways 5 and 18 between Hanoi and Haiphong, the last escape route out of Tonkin.

The defeat toppled the French government. Prime Minister Joseph Laniel resigned on June 12 and Pierre Mendes-France, a radical socialist, became prime minister. He stunned the French Chamber of Deputies announcing, "I promise to resign if, one month from now, on July 20, I have failed to obtain a cease-fire in Indochina." Mendes-France was committed to ending the war that had brought only humiliation to his country.

The Eisenhower administration realized that a settlement in Geneva was inevitable and that the communists would gain part of Indochina. On June 24 Dulles told congressional leaders that the United States would have to look beyond Geneva and try to salvage something in

Southeast Asia. In particular, he talked of assuming the responsibility for making sure that not another domino fell in Indochina. In order to "keep freedom alive," Dulles worked for a NATO-like regional alliance system in Southeast Asia. Nobody was farsighted enough to recognize that the United States was setting itself up for another Asian land war.

Mendes-France's promise and the change in the American position breathed new life into the Geneva talks. Anthony Eden began assuming a central role in the conference, as did Vyacheslav Molotov, the Soviet representative. Along with Zhou Enlai, they persuaded Pham Van Dong and the Vietminh to accept a temporary partitioning of Vietnam to be followed by reunification elections. The French and the Vietminh hotly debated the question of where to divide Vietnam and when to hold the elections. Bidault wanted the dividing line as far north and the elections as far into the future as possible. Pham Van Dong wanted the dividing line as far south and the elections as soon as possible. Unlike Dienbienphu, this battle went to the French. The Geneva Accords divided Vietnam at the seventeenth parallel into North Vietnam and South Vietnam. The accords imposed a ceasefire and provided for the withdrawal of French forces from North Vietnam and Vietminh forces from South Vietnam within the next three hundred days. Both the French and the Vietminh were to withdraw their troops from Laos and Cambodia. The accords provided for free elections in 1956, with the goal of reunifying the two Vietnams. An International Control Commission composed of representatives from India, Canada, and Poland was established to monitor compliance with the accords.

Ho's acquiescence in the partitioning of his country caught many Vietminh offguard. The victory at Dienbienphu should have let them dictate the diplomatic settlement at Geneva and secure outright independence. Ho Chi Minh, however, still hoped to work out a rapprochement with the United States, to restore some of the trust he had enjoyed during World War II. That the United States had granted the Philippines independence without a fight in 1946 left Ho with the conviction that many Americans must have been sympathetic with the aspirations of colonial peoples. He was also convinced that in 1956 he would win the election handily and see his country reunited without more bloodshed.

Signed on July 21, 1954, the Geneva Accords received a wholesale endorsement only from France, Great Britain, China, and the Soviet Union. Pham Van Dong signed the agreement for the Democratic Republic of Vietnam, but Vietminh leaders were privately bitter about the partitioning. The Geneva Accords accomplished little. Pham Van Dong left the conference expecting free elections in 1956 to bring about the long-awaited unification of Vietnam. But Georges Bidault and the French left hoping to maintain French authority in Saigon and the Mekong Delta. They dreamed of bringing Tonkin back into the French Union. Ngo Dinh Diem, the anticommunist Vietnamese nationalist who became prime minister of the State of Vietnam on July 7, refused to sign the accords. Secretary of State John Foster Dulles told the American delegation to leave the agreement unsigned. The first Indochina War was over, and the second was beginning.

Ho Chi Minh's prediction in 1946 that France would kill ten Vietnamese for every dead French soldier proved prophetic. When the mud dried around Dienbienphu, the eight years of war had resulted in the deaths of nearly 300,000 Vietminh and up to a million Vietnamese civilians. France counted 95,000 dead. But the war was not a body count, a simple military equation in which the party that piled up more kills emerged as victor. As Ho Chi Minh had believed all along, the first Indochina War was a political conflict in which the Vietminh outlasted the French. It was a lesson the United States would have to relearn.

3

The Making of a Quagmire, 1954–1960

There are profound differences between the Vietnamese and American people, in customs, outlook, political training, and philosophy. I hope we can find a bridge between Eastern and Western cultures.
—Ngo Dinh Diem, 1961

Intoxicated with his victory, convinced that he would win the elections in 1956 and take over South Vietnam, and now ready to live more fully his commitment to communism, in 1954 Ho Chi Minh set out on a savage campaign. With the French gone, he was determined to right the other great wrong in Vietnam: upper-class Vietnamese landlords who exploited peasants. Actually, few North Vietnamese peasants owned more than three or four acres, but Ho created Agricultural Reform Tribunals in every village to identify landlords. Accusations, lies, informants abounded as neighbor turned against neighbor. The tribunals had quotas of landlords to identify and kill, and their justice, if it could be called that, was as swift as it was capricious.

Ho behaved as if he had something to prove. Stalin was dead, but his legacy of viciousness and mass death lingered. Several million *kulak* peasants in the Ukraine had succumbed during his campaign of terror and land redistribution, and Mao's ruthlessness knew no bounds. Mao had repeatedly since 1949 employed mass terror as a blunt instrument of political control. The victory over the French at Dienbienphu had demonstrated the triumph of Ho's nationalism, while the Agricultural Reform Tribunals revived communist credentials.

With a year, thousands of landlords were dead and tens of thousands more were in labor camps for "reeducation." The whole process was a political disaster. By the summer of 1956, Ho decided the campaign had gone too far. On August 17, he wrote a public letter confessing that "all this has caused us to commit errors and meet with shortcomings carrying out land reform." Of the people who had been executed, Ho Chi Minh simply said, "One cannot wake the dead." In Nghe An Province, however, his apology did not satisfy his constituency. Early in November, farmers in Quynh Luu district, angry about the land reform program as well as the government's official anti-Catholicism, rioted and government troops were dispatched to restore order. The whole program, in Vo Nguyen Giap's description, was "an extraordinary error. . . . We did not emphasize the necessity for caution and for avoiding unjust punishment of honest people . . . [and] resorted to terror on a wide scale." With the end of the Agricultural Reform Tribunals, political life in North Vietnam settled down.

Not so in South Vietnam. In the Mekong Delta, formerly Cochin China, debt burdens and farm tenancy rates had risen in the last years of the war. The country depended on rice and rubber exports, as well as French money, to keep the economy going, and that source of funds was about to dry up. There was a wealth of peasant resentment of the French and the pro-French Vietnamese. Rural South Vietnam was ripe for rebellion. The region was also a bewildering caldron of competing ethnic, religious, economic, and political groups. Most of them were at least reasonably happy that the French were gone, but there was nothing approaching a consensus about who would fill the vacuum and rule the country. In Hanoi, there was only one power center in 1954. In South Vietnam there were many.

The least of the South Vietnamese power centers, the remains of the three-hundred-year-old Nguyen dynasty, was occupied in theory by Emperor Bao Dai. Born as Prince Nguyen Vinh Thuy in 1913, he had been tutored by French nannies and teachers from birth. Bao Dai was round faced with a high brow, husky and full but not fat, a face reflecting the cherubic complacency of a man who had never missed a meal. S. J. Perelman, who met him in Hanoi in 1946, has left a description: "Bao Dai was seated in a snug alcove surrounded by several hostesses. . . . The royal exile, a short, slippery-looking customer rather on the pudgy side and freshly dipped in Crisco, wore a fixed, oily grin that was vaguely reptilian."

In 1921, Bao Dai left Vietnam for Paris. When his father, Emperor Khai Dinh, died in 1925, he returned to Vietnam for the funeral, but the

December 8, 1950—Ex-emperor Bao Dai and General Marcel Carpentier, commander in chief of French forces in the Far East, enjoy refreshment in the presidential palace in Saigon after signing the French-Vietnam military pact creating a pro-French Vietnam army. (*Courtesy, Library of Congress.*)

French whisked him back to Paris. He did not return to Vietnam until 1932; by that time his French was better than his Vietnamese. In Paris, Bao Dai had learned more than French literature and history. He spent his spare time in high-class Paris brothels and cabarets, becoming more infatuated with sexual acrobatics and mirrored ceilings than he had ever been with Rousseau or Voltaire. Bao Dai was intelligent, but he suffered from a fatal political weakness. He was a "man who resisted nobody." He did attempt some modernization of imperial rule, and wanted for Vietnam as much independence as the French would allow, but he had no real ability to stand up to France. During the Japanese occupation of Indochina in World War II, Bao Dai served as the head of state for the Japanese. When Ho Chi Minh called for his abdication in 1945, Bao Dai was quick to agree, not wanting, in his own words, "to make the same mistake Louis XVI made." Later the French restored him, and once more he accepted a role that others demanded of him. Bao Dai was careful in public to wear the regal, gold-brocaded *ao dai,* speak Vietnamese, and conduct himself with regal reserve. In private, he preferred to wear double-breasted suits, speak French, and hunt, dance, eat, and enjoy women. Bao Dai was still on hand in 1954, but most Vietnamese held him in contempt.

Huynh Phu So, source of the effective Hoa Hao movement, was born in 1919 in the Mekong Delta village of that name. He had a sickly childhood accompanied by a mystical sensibility. In 1939 he entered a Buddhist monastery where, in his own words, he underwent a "vision and miraculous cure." An extraordinary speaker and gifted practitioner of herbal medicine and acupuncture, Huynh Phu So returned to the Mekong Delta and began preaching a curious mixture of Buddhism and nationalism. He believed people should pray four times a day to Buddha as well as such ancient Vietnamese heroes as the Trung sisters, Ly Bon, Tran Hung Dao, and Le Loi. The nationalist mystic, bitterly hostile to France, converted thousands of southern Vietnamese and earned from the French police the title the mad monk. They arrested Huynh Phu So in 1940 and placed him in a mental hospital, where he converted his psychiatrist and most of the staff.

Hoa Hao conversions skyrocketed during World War II. Enjoying the protection of the Japanese, Huynh Phu So raised a personal army of 15,000 troops in the Mekong Delta. In 1946 he established the Dan Xa, or Social Democratic party, to oppose the French. But in 1947 Ho Chi Minh, concerned about Huynh Phu So's growing power, ordered his death, and that year Vietminh assassins killed him. One of the new Hoa Hao leaders was a man named Ba Cut. A committed nationalist, Ba Cut sliced off the tip of his forefinger in 1947 to remind himself how much he hated the French. By the early 1950s the Hoa Hao had more than 1.5 million followers in South Vietnam. Most of them were anticommunists. Another powerful Buddhist sect in South Vietnam was the Cao Dai.

Ngo Van Chieu, born in Cholon in 1878, was deeply involved with spiritualism and seances. He was also infatuated with movies, which he watched in the theaters of Saigon. Claiming to have received a visit from the supreme power, the Cao Dai, Ngo Van Chieu established a religion fusing Buddhism, Christianity, and the movies. Cao Daists prayed to Buddha, Confucius, Jesus Christ, Joan of Arc, Victor Hugo, Charlie Chaplin, Laurel and Hardy, and a host of other religious, historical, and pop culture figures. Their pagodas were plastered with posters of the Cao Dai symbol, the huge, all-seeing eye. The Cao Dai faith spread rapidly in the Mekong Delta and frightened the French, who harassed its leaders. Centered around Tay Ninh, about sixty miles northwest of Saigon, the Cao Dai evolved into a semiautonomous state, eventually maintaining its own army. Van Chieu died in 1932. By the early 1950s, the Cao Dai under their new leader Pham Cong Tac had two million adherents and an army of 25,000 troops.

Regular Buddhist monks were another political force. Buddhist monks lived in nearly every village, maintaining pagodas, working in the fields, living side by side with peasants. Most of them were well educated, and they knew a great deal about philosophy, medicine, and astrology. Buddhist political activity functioned on a local level, trying to maintain balance and peace in the villages. The monks took little interest in Hanoi or Saigon unless either disrupted village life. They turned against the French for just that reason. In promoting Roman Catholicism and harassing Buddhist priests, the French committed the unforgivable sin: They brought dissonance to the villages. With the French gone, the monks returned to local concerns, but they were still capable of causing trouble.

No less important were the Binh Xuyen. Led by a ruthless cutthroat, Bay Vien, the Binh Xuyen were the Vietnamese Mafia. They were centered in Cholon, the Chinese suburb of Saigon. By the early 1950s they were a powerful political faction, complete with an army of 25,000 soldiers. Bay Vien's complex in Saigon was legendary. The Grande Monde was a huge gambling complex capable of taking two piasters from a Vietnamese drunk or a million francs from a wealthy French businessman. Down the block was the world's largest brothel, the infamous Hall of Mirrors, where a thousand "tricks" could be performed at once. Further down the block, an opium factory refined a high-grade product for distribution throughout Indochina. Bay Vien's opulent home was separated from his complex by a moat occupied by dozens of alligators. Outside his bedroom, on a very long chain, a full-grown leopard paced. Pythons slithered up the two posts on the front porch. A huge Siberian tiger lived in a cage; its door could be tripped open from inside the house. It was not uncommon to find bits of cloth and human bones inside the cage. Bao Dai accepted payoffs from the Binh Xuyen, and in return, with French consent, the emperor made Bay Vien a general in the South Vietnamese

army and head of the national police, with authority over casinos, prostitution, opium traffic, gold smuggling, and currency manipulation. Bay
Vien had little use for the communists.

The most troublesome political group were the Vietminh. At the time
of the French surrender at Dienbienphu, there were more than 100,000
Vietminh soldiers in South Vietnam, most of them native southerners.
They controlled a third of the country and were especially powerful in
the Ca Mau Peninsula and along the Cambodian border. When the Geneva Accords were signed, Ho ordered most Vietminh to move to North
Vietnam until after the 1956 elections. About 10,000 stayed behind with
orders to return to their villages, work in the fields, and organize the
peasants for the elections. The Vietminh had no doubt they would win
a free election. But if the elections were postponed or canceled, the
Vietminh were to become the heart of a new guerrilla movement. They
were revolutionary nationalists. They hated the French and the Chinese
as well as the Vietnamese emperor and his upper-class mandarins.

Among the ethnic minorities that further divided Vietnam were the
Chinese. In 1954 there were almost 1 million in South Vietnam, most of
them in the Saigon suburb of Cholon. The Vietnamese nurtured an intense dislike for the Chinese, not just for China's periodic invasions of
Indochina but for their control of business and commerce. The Chinese
were hardly bent on gaining political power. On the contrary, they were
economic opportunists ready to work with whatever regime came to
power, as long as goods moved and profits flowed. What the Chinese did
have was an intense anticommunism. The French, the mandarins, the
Nguyen emperors, even the Japanese—anybody, as far as the Chinese
were concerned—would be better for business than the communists.

The second-largest ethnic minority were the Khmer, the ethnic Cambodians. Totaling more than 600,000 people, the Khmer were concen-
trated northwest of Saigon around Tay Ninh, southwest of Saigon near
Phu Vinh, and throughout An Xuyen Province in the Mekong Delta.
They hated the French for conquering Cambodia, but they also despised
the Vietnamese. Hundreds of years ago, the Khmer had controlled the
Mekong Delta, but beginning in the eleventh century the Vietnamese
expanded slowly out of Tonkin, down the spine of Annam, and into the
Mekong Delta, crushing the Khmer and pushing them up the Mekong
River into present-day Cambodia. The Vietnamese looked down upon the
Khmer as backward, ignorant people, and the Khmer returned the dis-
like. After World War II, Khmer guerrillas, known as the Khmer Kampuchea Krom, began fighting the French, hoping to bring the Mekong
Delta back under Cambodian sovereignty. Periodically, the Krom also
fought the Vietminh and the Vietnamese National Army. When the
French surrendered at Dienbienphu, the Krom launched a small-scale
guerrilla war against the Vietnamese.

Still another of the ethnic minorities were the Montagnard, or Mountain People: more than forty tribes of hunters and foragers in the Central Highlands. They hated the Vietnamese because of the annual tribute payment the emperors collected, and they had little use for the French, who also taxed them heavily. In 1946 Giap claimed that "to seize and control the highlands is to solve the whole problem of South Vietnam." The rugged mountains of the Central Highlands were perfect hiding places for guerrillas, and the Montagnard were perfect guides. The French tried to buy Montagnard support and occasionally succeeded. One French sergeant remarked that he had "the Sedangs as allies. They are great big good-looking fellows with nothing on except paint and tattooing and magic charms." More often than not, the Montagnard sided with the Vietminh. In the late 1940s, Ho Chi Minh brought thousands of Montagnard to Vietminh schools in Tonkin for training as teachers, nurses, and political agents. He promised them that once the French were gone and the imperial court at Hue was destroyed, there would be no more tribute payments.

In South Vietnam Roman Catholics, successors to Vietnamese converted by French missionaries in the eighteenth and nineteenth centuries, numbered 600,000 people in 1954. They were a privileged minority who had worked for the French and received the benefits of land, education, and place. Graduates of the French lycées in Hue and Saigon, many received postgraduate training at military schools and universities in France. In South Vietnam they dominated the professions, colleges, civil service, and military. Among most Vietnamese Buddhists, the Roman Catholics were despised, a community tied to foreigners. Ho had targeted them long ago. Once the French were gone, the South Vietnamese elite had to go as well. But in the 1950s and 1960s, South Vietnam was not to be ruled by the Hoa Hao, Cao Dai, Binh Xuyen, Buddhists, Vietminh, Chinese, Khmer, or Montagnards. Power went to Roman Catholics, and at the center of that elite was the Ngo family.

The Ngo had formed a short-lived political dynasty in the tenth century and then served in the mandarinate at the imperial court for centuries. Early in the 1700s they converted to Catholicism. They were deeply religious. In the 1880s Buddhist monks led anti-Catholic riots that nearly destroyed the Ngo family. A Buddhist mob attacked the parish church at Dai Phong during mass. More than one hundred of the Ngo family were burned at the stake later that day.

One family member was not there. Ngo Dinh Kha was in Malaya studying for the priesthood. When he received news that his parents, grandparents, brothers, sisters, aunts, uncles, and cousins were dead, Ngo Dinh Kha returned to Hue and tried to rebuild. He passed the mandarin examinations and, fluent in French, moved quickly up the civil service ladder. Ngo's first wife died soon after their marriage, but his second wife had nine children. The third of them was Jean Baptiste Ngo Dinh Diem, born on January 3, 1901.

Ngo Dinh Diem grew up Confucian and Catholic. Every morning at 6:00, seven days a week, the family put on their best robes and attended mass, and nearly every day their father spoke to them about duty, fidelity, and loyalty: in effect, the Confucian virtues. Diem attended the French lycée in Hue and became thoroughly engrossed in French history, language, and literature.

Of all the Ngo children, Diem was the most religious. He did not play with other children, and as soon as he could read he spent hours each day by himself studying catechisms and religious histories. At the age of fifteen he entered a Catholic seminary in Hue to begin studying for the priesthood. His older brother, Ngo Dinh Thuc, was doing the same thing. But it soon became apparent that Diem was not meant to be a priest. Thuc urged him to leave the seminary, arguing that he "was too unworldly for the church." Another friend put it more clearly: "A priest at least learns of the world through the confessional. Diem is a monk living behind stone walls. He knows nothing." Diem left the seminary but took with him his vow of celibacy, which he kept throughout his life. He attended the French College for Administration in Hanoi and graduated at the top of his class in 1921. Back in Hue, Diem rose through the civil service ranks, becoming a district chief and then a provincial administrator, coming to the attention of the French in 1929 when he uncovered plans for a communist-inspired uprising. There were no distractions in Diem's life, no women or movies or gambling, only work and prayer. In 1933 Bao Dai appointed him minister of the interior. At the

1961—Ngo Dinh Diem, president of South Vietnam, rides through the streets of Saigon. (*Courtesy, National Archives.*)

age of thirty-two, Ngo Dinh Diem seemed destined to become prime minister.

Like so many other Vietnamese, Diem longed for the day when France would leave Vietnam. In Bao Dai's cabinet, he realized that the French, while talking about Vietnamese autonomy, restricted the imperial court, transforming the emperor and his civil servants into mere puppets. Late in 1933 he resigned from the cabinet in protest.

Diem retired to the family home in Hue, where he spent his days reading, praying, horseback riding, hunting, working in a rose garden, attending mass, and talking with his mother. Except for an abortive attempt to become prime minister in the Japanese puppet regime, Diem for years remained distant from public life. But his relatives believed he was born for greatness, and they supported him financially until an opportunity should come. To his family Diem wrote, "We must continue the search for the Kingdom of God and Justice. All else will come of itself."

Although a nationalist, Diem kept faith in the Confucian virtues: loyalty, acquiescence, and social place. He wanted the French out, but he did not want the social structure turned upside down. After 1945 Diem's opposition to communism was intensely personal. His older brother Ngo Dinh Khoi, a former governor of Quang Ngai Province, was anti-French but also anticommunist. The Vietminh arrested him and his young son, convicted them in a kangaroo court, and executed them by burying them alive. Ngo Dinh Diem never forgave the Vietminh. The Vietminh caught up with Diem in Tuy Hoa. They moved him to the highlands of North Vietnam, where he remained in custody for several months, and sent him to Hanoi in January 1946. Ho Chi Minh, interested in gaining the support of Vietnam's leading Catholic layman, offered Diem a cabinet position. Diem refused, calling Ho an "accomplice and a criminal" in Khoi's death. Diem was released in March 1946 as part of the Franco-Vietminh Accords.

During the next nine years Diem traveled around the world, staying away from home to avoid the Vietminh. He spent more than three years in the United States, living at the Maryknoll Seminary in Lakewood, New Jersey. At the time the United States was assisting France against the Vietminh but also hoping to find an anticommunist Vietnamese leader around whom a stable government could be built. Diem appeared to be that leader. Wesley Fishel, professor of political science at Michigan State University, met Diem in Japan and spoke at length with him about Indochina. Diem seemed perfect. He was a well-educated Roman Catholic who wanted an anticommunist, independent Vietnam. That Diem was not a believer in democracy mattered little to Fishel. "The people of Southeast Asia are not," Fishel said, "sufficiently sophisticated to understand . . . democracy."

Fishel saw to it that Diem met a number of prominent Americans, including Francis Cardinal Spellman, the Roman Catholic archbishop of New York; Senators John F. Kennedy of Massachusetts, Mike Mansfield of Montana, and Lyndon B. Johnson of Texas; and Supreme Court Justice William O. Douglas. In 1953 Douglas called Diem "a hero . . . revered by the Vietnamese because he is honest and independent and stood firm against the French influence." These men became the core of what was called the Vietnam Lobby, or the American Friends of Vietnam, who incessantly promoted Ngo Dinh Diem in 1953 and 1954. When the Geneva Accords divided Vietnam in 1954, Diem had strong supporters in the United States. On June 18, 1954, destiny called. Bao Dai invited Diem to serve as prime minister in a new government.

Although Ngo Dinh Diem seemed a candidate fit to build an anticommunist South Vietnam, official Washington debated the issue in 1954 and 1955. The French were dead set against Diem. They hoped to stay in South Vietnam and keep their empire, and they knew that he was too much of a nationalist to allow France to remain. They could manipulate Bao Dai, but not Diem. The French reservations concerned President Eisenhower. It was nothing profound, just an uneasiness about Diem's penchant for a solitary life and his extraordinary commitment to his family. Eisenhower also worried whether so devout a Roman Catholic could really rule a large Buddhist majority. But the real debate in American policy-making circles raged around the views of Diem expressed by two Americans living in South Vietnam in 1954 and 1955: J. Lawton Collins and Edward G. Lansdale.

Nicknamed "Lightning Joe" by his army troops, Collins had commanded the Twenty-fifth Infantry Division at Guadalcanal and then the VII Corps at the D-Day invasion of Europe. After the war Collins served as army chief of staff before President Dwight Eisenhower sent him to Saigon in 1954 as a special envoy to train the South Vietnamese. Collins despised Diem—his political base was too narrow and his sense of destiny too broad. "Lightning Joe" was convinced that Diem would self-destruct and create a political vacuum, which Ho Chi Minh could fill. Collins strongly advised Washington to shift support away from Diem. Diem hated Collins, whom he viewed as a self-righteous American given to pompous advice. Diem wanted American money, not American advice. Collins represented both. In private Diem could be quite animated and often put on a mime act for family members in which he pretended to be Collins, waving his finger in people's faces and talking loudly about what to do and how to do it. Much more to Ngo Dinh Diem's liking was Edward G. Lansdale.

Lansdale, an air force officer and former intelligence agent, came to Saigon in 1954 as CIA station chief. He had already helped the Philippines crush the communist-backed Huk Rebellion. Assigned to conduct CIA paramilitary operations against North Vietnam, Lansdale spread rumors and leaflets about Ho Chi Minh, littered North Vietnam with counterfeit currency, warned northern Catholics that communists would persecute them, and destroyed weapons supplies north of the seventeenth parallel. He arranged for several hundred South Vietnamese soldiers to dress up as civilians, infiltrate North Vietnam, and spread rumors that the Vietminh wanted Chinese soldiers to come and rape Vietnamese women. This ploy backfired. The troops went into North Vietnam but did not return, at least not until a few years later, when they came back as guerrillas loyal to Ho Chi Minh. Lansdale became a close friend of Diem, one of the few confidants Diem had outside his family. To Lansdale, Diem was "a man with a terrible burden to carry and in need of friends, and I tried to be an honest friend." Lansdale thought Diem a dedicated nationalist who loved Vietnam, hated communism, and wanted the best for his people. There was no other individual capable of governing South Vietnam. John Foster Dulles agreed. Dulles's brother Allen, head of the CIA, told the secretary of state that Lansdale was an astute judge of character and that Diem could be trusted. John Foster Dulles, desperate for a South Vietnamese leader with enough mettle to pull the country together, passed the advice on to Eisenhower, who remained skeptical about Diem's ability.

South Vietnam preoccupied Dulles. In July 1954, the National Security Council committed the United States to "maintain a friendly noncommunist South Vietnam and to prevent a Communist victory through all-Vietnam elections." In September 1954 Dulles established the Southeast Asia Treaty Organization (SEATO), a regional security alliance signed by the United States, Great Britain, France, Australia, New Zealand, Thailand, the Philippines, and Pakistan. South Vietnam, Laos, and Cambodia were forbidden by the Geneva Accords from joining, but a subsequent protocol to the treaty stated that if any one of them fell to communism, it would pose a threat to the alliance and justify a military response.

A few people were doubtful. Secretary of Defense Charles E. Wilson urged Eisenhower to get out as soon as possible. The most eloquent dissent was Graham Greene's novel *The Quiet American*, published in 1955. "It was a first warning to me," wrote Gloria Emerson, who read the novel in 1956 and later recalled "but I dismissed the book as brilliant but cynical, until it came back to haunt me." It is a novel of good intentions, idealism, lack of insight, and dangerous innocence. The quiet American is Alden Pyle, a character based on Edward Lansdale. Pyle believes in a coldly passionate way in abstractions—democracy, freedom, monolithic communism, falling dominoes, and the love of God. The novel is written from the viewpoint of Thomas Fowler, a British journalist who is as committed to reality as Pyle is to abstraction. Trying to convince Pyle of the error of his theories, Fowler observes:

> I know the record. Siam goes. Malaya goes. Indonesia goes. What does 'go' mean? If I believed in your God and another life, I'd bet my future harp against your golden crown that in five hundred years there may be no New

York or London, but they'll be growing paddy in these fields. . . . Thought's a luxury. Do you think the peasant sits and thinks of God and Democracy when he gets inside his mud hut at night? . . . Isms and ocracies. Give me facts."

Of course Pyle is impervious to Fowler's logic. He continues with the best intentions to ruin lives and kill innocent people. When one of his plans goes awry and several innocent Vietnamese are killed, Pyle observes: "They were only war casualties . . . it was a pity but you can't always hit your target. Anyway they died in the right cause. . . . In a way you could say they died for democracy."

Greene intended his novel to expose the absence of a moral vision in American policy in Vietnam. Stationed in Saigon as a war correspondent in the early 1950s, Greene witnessed the transference of power from France to the United States. He watched the arrival of fresh Pyles—men with crew cuts and "wide campus gazes" who seemed "incapable of harm" and were determined to do good "not to any individual person but to a country, a continent, a world." But harm was implicit in a mission that framed good and evil in universal abstract terms. Yet Americans were not prepared to listen. In 1977, after the war was over, Michael Herr would observe in his brilliant book *Dispatches,* "Maybe it was already over for us in Indochina when Alden Pyle's body washed up under the bridge at Dakao, his lungs full of mud."

Robert Gorham Davis, reviewing *The Quiet American* for the *New York Times Book Review,* declared that Greene's work was anti-American: "Pyle . . . does not remind Fowler of the thousands of individuals who make desperate escapes from Communist countries every week in order to live as humans." For Americans in the mid-1950s this was the crux of the matter: Vietnam was fighting communism and communism was a threat to humanity. That confidence kept the United States in Vietnam and wedded to Ngo Dinh Diem. In October 1954 the Eisenhower administration decided to channel economic and military assistance directly to Diem rather than through the French mission in Saigon. Late in 1954 the CIA foiled several coup attempts against Diem. On the shoulders of Ngo Dinh Diem rested American hopes to save Southeast Asia, strengthen the Japanese economy, rebuild Europe, and preserve the American defensive picket line in the western Pacific.

It would have taken a political genius to control the centrifugal interests of Catholics and Buddhists, Hoa Hao and Cao Dai, Montagnard and Khmer, Chinese and Binh Xuyen. Ngo Dinh Diem was not a politician; he was a Confucian mandarin who expected to rule with "the mandate of heaven," to preside over a people who looked to him as their father and behaved obediently. The word "compromise" was not in Diem's vocabulary. Nor was "democracy." In Diem's words: "Our political system has been based not on the concept of management of the public affairs by the people or their representatives, but rather by an enlightened sovereign." His sister-in-law, Madame Ngo Dinh Nhu, stated it more symbolically: "If we open the window not only sunlight but many bad things will fly in also." Diem, writes the historian William Turley, was "heir to a dying tradition, member of an elite that had been superbly prepared by birth, training, and experience to lead a Vietnam which no longer existed." Instead of opening the window, Diem tried to shut out every ray of sunlight. He brooked no opposition and expected total obedience, nothing less.

Diem began against an opponent who deserved to be shut out. In April 1955 he asked Bay Vien and the Binh Xuyen to lay down their arms and close the opium dens and brothels. Bay Vien refused and dared Diem to come into Cholon. Diem called his bluff and invaded Cholon with tanks. As the Binh Xuyen retreated, they set fire to hundreds of homes and buildings. French authorities in Saigon, hoping Diem would fall, assisted the Binh Xuyen. It was civil war in Cholon. Bay Vien escaped to the jungles northwest of Saigon and from there to Paris. By that time thousands of people were dead, most of them Chinese civilians. Diem crushed the Binh Xuyen but in the process earned the enmity of the Chinese. Thousands of Binh Xuyen soldiers fled into the Mekong Delta and Central Highlands, where they vowed to continue the fight against Diem.

The crushing of the Binh Xuyen resolved the dispute between Edward Lansdale and J. Lawton Collins. Diem had exercised brutal power, but successfully. American praise was quick in coming. John Foster Dulles cabled the French: "Diem is the only means U.S. sees to save South Vietnam and counteract the revolutionary movement. . . . U.S. sees no one else who can. Whatever U.S. view has been in the past, today U.S. must support Diem wholeheartedly."

Flush with victories in Saigon and Washington, Diem in his determination to consolidate his power turned next on Bao Dai. He considered Bao Dai a morally bankrupt whoremonger whose ties to the Binh Xuyen were unforgivable: Imagine—the Nguyen emperor, the symbol of a dynasty that had ruled Vietnam for centuries, taking kickbacks from pimps and drug dealers! In 1955 Diem called for the abdication of Bao Dai. He set up a national referendum to decide the question. In an election in which 605,000 of Saigon's 405,000 registered voters cast ballots, Diem received 98.2 percent. On October 23, 1955, he proclaimed the Republic of Vietnam, with himself as president.

Late in 1955 Diem sent troops into the Mekong Delta to destroy another obstacle to absolute power, the Hoa Hao army. The Hoa Hao fought a bloody guerrilla war against the Army of the Republic of Vietnam (ARVN), but in April 1956 Ba Cut was arrested. He had a curious look about him. The short finger still reminded him of the French, but when he heard news of the partitioning of Vietnam in 1954, he had vowed not to cut his hair until the country was reunited. Uncombed and unwashed, the hair tangled down his shoulders. To the sharkskin-suited Diem, Ba Cut was disgusting and dangerous. In July 1956 Diem sent him to the guillotine. Surviving Hoa Hao soldiers scattered throughout the countryside.

There was also the Cao Dai to dispose of. Diem bought off some Cao Dai leaders. It took $1 million to get General Trinh Minh The to change sides. ARVN troops invaded Tay Ninh Province late in 1955 to disarm the Cao Dai army. The Cao Dai fought for a time, but they knew of Diem's ruthlessness and did not want to go the way of the Binh Xuyen and Hoa Hao. In February 1956 Pham Cong Tac, the Cao Dai leader, escaped into Cambodia. Most Cao Dai soldiers surrendered their arms, but others escaped into the Mekong Delta.

With Bao Dai in France, the Binh Xuyen crushed, and the sects in disarray, Diem was able to fulfill his nationalist dream. In a speech on January 19, 1956, he announced, "The presence of foreign troops, no matter how friendly . . . [is] incompatible with Vietnam's concept of full independence." He told the French to leave. The French empire in Vietnam finally died on April 10, 1956, when the last of 10,000 French troops left Saigon.

The Khmer Kampuchea Krom remained as a challenge to Diem's rule. Krom troops were powerful in An Xuyen Province, and early in 1956 ARVN troops moved against them. Dressed in the distinctive button-down jacket and skirts with the lower end brought between the legs and tucked in at the waist, Krom soldiers were indistinguishable from Khmer peasants working the rice paddies. ARVN troops, indiscriminate at best, killed thousands of Khmer civilians in their operations against the Krom. In return the Krom launched their own guerrilla war against Diem.

Ngo Dinh Diem soon had the Khmer even angrier at him, along with the Buddhists and the Montagnards.

As soon as the Geneva Accords divided the country, Diem, Lansdale, and CIA operatives had encouraged northern Catholics to move south, warning that the communists would persecute them if they stayed where they were. Agents sent messages that the Virgin Mary was living in Saigon. More than 600,000 Catholics moved to South Vietnam. Another 300,000 North Vietnamese—former soldiers in the Vietnamese National Army, colonial administrators, and businessmen afraid of what the communists would do to them—also left. They emigrated in complete village units, led by the parish priest, with nothing but what they could carry. Once in South Vietnam these people increased the Roman Catholic population to 1.5 million people. Those with good educations moved into the South Vietnamese civil service. For others the government established 319 villages, giving the immigrants land and financial support until they could establish an economic foothold. More than

400,000 settled in the Mekong Delta, most of them on land that had traditionally been worked by the Khmer. The Khmer sense of alienation strengthened. Diem also placed nearly 100,000 immigrant Catholics in the Central Highlands, giving them Montagnard land. Diem believed the Montagnard should learn to speak Vietnamese, leave the mountains, study a useful trade, and adopt Vietnamese values. He approached the Montagnard much as Americans had treated the Indians in the seventeenth to nineteenth centuries. The South Vietnamese developed programs to relocate the Montagnard and provided them with schools, all the while giving their land to other Vietnamese. The expulsion gave the Vietminh the opportunity to promise the Montagnard that once the Diem government was eliminated their land would be returned.

Northern Catholics were intensely anti-Buddhist. Led by Father Hoang Quynh, they joined the Luc Luong Dai Doan Ket, or Greater Unity Force, which demanded the conversion of all of South Vietnam. Quynh asked Diem to promote Catholics over Buddhists and destroy infidelity. Diem's personal inclinations were less militant, but northern Catholics were his strongest supporters. Large numbers of Buddhists as well as Montagnard and Khmer saw their land go to Catholic refugees. And taking land from well-to-do South Vietnamese for redistribution to the landless and the expelled would rob Diem of a loyal constituency. By 1960, in the Mekong Delta, nearly half of cultivated land was owned by two percent of the people.

Finally, to reinforce his power in the countryside, Diem abolished local elections and appointed his supporters to official village posts. For centuries, even under the Nguyen imperial court and the French, local politics had been governed by the ancient slogan, "The empire stops at the village gates." Peasants elected their own officials to govern local affairs, and neither the emperor nor the French interfered. Diem destroyed the only democratic institution functioning in South Vietnam.

Diem then turned on the national elections that the Geneva Accords had guaranteed for 1956. The CIA chief Allen Dulles sent a memo to President Eisenhower in 1956 predicting an overwhelming victory by Ho Chi Minh in both North and South Vietnam. The Vietminh had assumed that France would stay in South Vietnam, honor the accords, and supervise the elections. But the French were gone. South Vietnam was an independent nation wallowing in American money. The United States was the new Western power in Vietnam, and its entire foreign policy revolved around anticommunism. The United States wanted an anticommunist government in Saigon—democratic or not. In 1955 Diem canceled the scheduled elections. Ho Chi Minh denounced the decision, but there was little he could do about it since the United States had no intention of forcing Diem to keep an agreement he had never signed.

Diem ruled South Vietnam as close to an absolute monarch as he could come. But he was always worried, with good reason, about conspiracy, revolution, and assassination. He led a monklike existence inside the presidential palace, sleeping on a narrow cot, covered by a mosquito net, and cooled by a slow-moving ceiling fan. Diem got up early, went to pray in a private chapel near his room, and breakfasted on a soup of noodles and pork. He visited with staff members after breakfast and then underwent a medical examination every morning. On his desk was a crucifix and a picture of the Virgin Mary. Diem received visitors in the afternoon, but the Saigon diplomatic corps dreaded his summons, knowing that it meant listening to a monologue of anywhere from three to ten hours. He worked all day and much of the night, falling asleep at 1:00 or 2:00 a.m., with documents on his lap. And since he could trust nobody outside his immediate family, Ngo Dinh Diem created a family dynasty.

Ngo Dinh Thuc, the oldest surviving brother, was a relaxed man blessed with congeniality and a fine sense of humor. With great political skills as well as a genuinely spiritual nature, he had risen steadily in the Roman Catholic hierarchy, becoming a monsignor during World War II and then bishop of Vinh Long. In 1957 Pope Pius XII named Thuc the archbishop of Hue, the Roman Catholic primate for all of Vietnam. Diem's younger brother, Ngo Dinh Luyen, was international spokesman for the family. Born in Hue in 1909 and educated at the French lycée there, Luyen was bright and articulate. In 1956, Diem named Luyen ambassador to Great Britain and roving ambassador to the rest of the world. Luyen preached a single message: Survival of the Republic of Vietnam was essential to the future of Asia.

The next youngest brother was Ngo Dinh Can. Unlike the others, Can was poorly educated and had never traveled abroad. He lived a simple, reclusive life in Hue with his mother, and although he held no official position in the Diem regime, he was warlord of central Vietnam, absolute ruler of the region between Phan Thiet Province and the seventeenth parallel. Protected by his own secret police and private army, Can was autonomous, the law in the northern half of South Vietnam. Diem deferred to him in all matters concerning that region.

Diem's youngest brother, Ngo Dinh Nhu, was his closest associate as well as the political boss of South Vietnam from Phan Thiet Province to the Ca Mau Peninsula. Nicknamed "Smiley" by Americans because of a permanent smile fixed on his face, Nhu was privately contemptuous of the United States. Americans had too much power, too much money, and too little humility. Nhu was short on humility himself. A devout Roman Catholic educated at the École de Chartres in Paris, Nhu hated the Buddhists and wanted to "put the monks in their places." He was commander of the Vietnamese Special Forces and transformed them into his own personal army of henchmen, hit men, and spies. Nhu, a heavy opium user and a chain smoker, admired Adolf Hitler. Next to Diem, Nhu was the most powerful man in South Vietnam.

Because of Diem's vow of celibacy, it fell to Nhu's wife, Tran Le Xuan,

May 9, 1963—Ngo Dinh Nhu, brother and advisor to South Vietnamese President Ngo Dinh Diem, sits in front of a map of Southeast Asia in his study in the presidential palace in Saigon. (*Courtesy, AP / Wide World Photo.*)

to serve as first lady or, in the words of her critics, the "Queen of Saigon." She was completely Gallicized. Educated at private Catholic schools in France, she was more comfortable speaking French than using Vietnamese. Arrogant, intolerant, insensitive, and prudish, fancying herself a reincarnation of the ancient Trung sisters, she led public campaigns

Madame Ngo Dinh Nhu, wife of Ngo Dinh Nhu, brother and close advisor to President Diem. She was officially the first lady of Vietnam and an active leader in anti-Buddhist government actions. (*Courtesy, AP / Wide World Photo.*)

against card playing, adultery, blue movies, gambling, horse racing, fortune telling, boxing, divorce, prostitution, dancing, and beauty contests. She wanted to outlaw the use of "falsies" in women's bras but gave up on the idea when she realized it would be impossible to enforce. Using her own private police force, Madame Nhu had people arrested for wearing loud clothing and boots or bizarre hairstyles. Her father, Tran Van Chuong, was a major landowner and during World War II had been foreign minister for the Japanese regime. He was minister of state for Diem and then ambassador to the United States.

Ensconced in power, the Ngo family then turned on its last real rival in South Vietnam—the Vietminh. Fewer than 10,000 Vietminh remained in South Vietnam after the Geneva Accords; the other 100,000 or so withdrew to North Vietnam to wait for the elections. Diem refused to call them Vietminh, preferring the derogatory term "Vietcong," or "Vietnamese Communist." Diem launched a violent campaign against the Vietcong late in 1955, using ARVN soldiers and village officials to expose them. His slogan: "Let us go mercilessly to wipe out the Vietcong, no longer considering them human beings."

And that is just what Diem tried to do. Between late 1955 and early 1960, ARVN soldiers arrested more than 100,000 people accused of being Vietminh, even though at the most there were only 10,000 Vietminh in South Vietnam. Executions took place near the homes of the accused, so their bodies could be found and the village intimidated. Somewhere between 20,000 and 75,000 South Vietnamese were killed and another 100,000 sent to concentration camps for "reeducation." Diem also desecrated Vietminh war memorials and cemeteries, an unforgivable insult in a culture practicing ancestor worship and family obedience. Though the terrorism successfully reduced the number of Vietminh in South Vietnam from 10,000 people in 1955 to only 3,000 in 1958, it inspired surviving Vietminh leaders to conduct a dedicated guerrilla war against the Diem government. Because most of Diem's victims were simple peasants, the terrorism drove a greater wedge between the Vietnamese people and the government.

The Vietminh leader in South Vietnam was Le Duan, born in Quang Tri Province in 1908. As a student, Duan had become an anti-French nationalist. He spent most of the years between 1931 and 1945 in the French prison on Con Son Island. After World War II, he stayed in southern Vietnam. Convinced that the French were just trying to preserve their empire, Duan opposed the Geneva Accords of 1954—better to destroy French troops in the south just as the Vietminh had destroyed the French at Dienbienphu. The Flame of the South, so called for his commitment to reunification, Le Duan went along with Ho Chi Minh's decision to sign the Geneva Accords, but when Ho called the Vietminh back to North Vietnam in 1954, Duan stayed behind. Between 1954 and 1956, the year reunification elections were supposed to take place, Vietcong activities had been primarily political: working with peasants, helping plant and harvest crops, delivering rice to markets, improving community buildings and peasant homes, and providing drugs and basic medical care. Diem's decision to cancel the elections precipitated a bitter debate in North Vietnam. Most party members in North Vietnam were cautious about reigniting the armed struggle in the south. They were busy consolidating their power, and they wanted to avoid a confrontation with the United States. But most Vietminh who pulled out of South Vietnam after the Geneva Accords were native southerners who resented the division of Vietnam. The old ethnic rivalry between northern and southern Vietnamese was revived within the Vietcong. Southerners accused northerners of abandoning them, of enjoying the fruits of power in the north while southerners suffered under the oppression of Ngo Dinh Diem. While circumspect in his proposals, Le Duan represented that southern point of view. As early as 1956 Duan urged Ho Chi Minh to overthrow the Diem regime, but Ho was cautious, preferring political to military action. Duan was obedient and worked hard to keep southerners in line, but he knew their patience was running out. In December 1956 North Vietnamese leaders compromised, agreeing that firming up the revolution in North Vietnam was their priority while southerners should work to destabilize the Diem regime politically and defend themselves if necessary.

In mid-1957 the Vietcong launched their campaign against Diem. In 1958 they assassinated more than 1,100 village officials in South Vietnam, and they increased that number in 1959. Minh instructed the Vietcong not to engage in military operations; that would lead to defeat. Do not take land from a peasant. Emphasize nationalism rather than communism. Do not antagonize anyone if you can avoid it. Be selective in your violence. If an assassination is necessary, use a knife, not a rifle or grenade. It is too easy to kill innocent bystanders with guns and bombs, and accidental killings of the innocent will alienate peasants from the revolution. Once an assassination has taken place, make sure peasants know why the killing occurred. Vietcong assassins went after the most corrupt village officials first, those who stole from the peasants or raped women. Regardless of political affiliation, peasants were glad to see those officials dead. Where Diem had appointed Roman Catholics to preside over Buddhist villages, the Vietcong assassinated the Catholics, earning silent praise from local monks. And to strike terror into village leaders, to let everyone know that nobody was safe, the Vietcong sometimes targeted the best, most efficient officials for assassination. The Vietcong often decapitated their victims. Vietnamese spiritualism held that people who lost their heads were destined to an eternity of restless wandering in the world of spirits. Ho Chi Minh told the Vietcong that the quickest way to the heart of a peasant was land. The Vietcong seized the land from absentee landlords, gave it to poor farmers, and spread the word that the Vietcong robbed from the rich to give to the poor.

Diem responded to the deteriorating political situation in the only way he knew how—increasing the use of force, which played into the hands of the Vietcong. To keep peasants from being converted by Vietcong propaganda, Diem launched the Agroville Program, relocating peasants into hastily constructed villages placed along Vietcong infiltration routes. The villages were heavily defended and surrounded by barbed wire. It was difficult for the Vietcong to get in, but to the peasants the new villages looked like prisons. People were rounded up into forced labor gangs to build the camps and then were forcibly moved there, far from ancestral villages. Since Vietnamese peasants looked upon their family land with deep reverence, relocation was a spiritual and physical crisis. The resettlement enraged peasants. Diem had the National Assembly pass Law 10/59 in May 1959. Designed to wipe out the Vietcong, it created special military tribunals to arrest any individual "who commits or intends to commit crimes . . . against the State." Equipped with portable guillotines, the tribunals rendered one of three verdicts: innocent, life in prison, and death. The ensuing trials were kangaroo courts. Nhu's secret police took part in the trials, sometimes carrying out the guillotining of convicted "traitors." For the moment, the campaign was effective. Diem's terrorism was so widespread and capricious that innocent peasants were afraid even to be seen with suspected Vietcong. Large numbers of Vietcong either quit the party or were killed. Communist party membership in South Vietnam shrank to 3,000 in 1959. But the 10/59 campaign also terrorized thousands of innocent peasants who came to hate the Ngo family.

Finally, the regime corrupted the 1959 National Assembly elections. Although there were opposition candidates, the government prohibited newspapers from publishing their names or printing campaign literature. Opposition posters were not allowed to be displayed, nor could candidates opposed to Diem speak to gatherings of more than five people. In the southern part of the country, Nhu's secret police worked as election officials, handing out ballots and watching how people voted. In the northern provinces, Can's secret police performed the same functions. When it appeared that large numbers of people might not vote, the government passed an ordinance requiring them to carry a voter identification card that had been punched at the polls. When the election turned out to be a resounding victory for the Ngo family, Diem announced, "The people have spoken."

In 1959 Diem's increasing consolidation of power, along with the decline of the Vietcong, brought about a change in Communist party policy. Recognizing that it would probably take an armed struggle to overthrow South Vietnam, Ho Chi Minh gave in to Le Duan's urgings and began infiltrating cadres into South Vietnam. At first they were southern-born Vietminh who had relocated to North Vietnam. After five years away from his family, one Vietminh remarked, "I was joyous to learn of my assignment to go south. I was eager to see my home village, to see my family, to get in contact with my wife." Another decision was to prepare for a more protracted military struggle throughout Indochina. In May 1959 the North Vietnamese military established Group 559 to develop a means of moving people and supplies from North Vietnam to South Vietnam through Laos and Cambodia. Group 759, established in July, was to develop techniques for infiltrating South Vietnam by sea. Another project was to establish Indochina as a single strategic entity. In order to bring about the reunification of North and South Vietnam, the communists had to prevent the United States from securing control of Laos and Cambodia. In 1958 and 1959, with United States assistance, right-wing forces in Laos ousted the neutral government of Prince Souvanna Phouma and tightened their power. The Royal Army then attacked strongholds of the Pathet Lao, the Laotian communist guerrillas. The civil war in Laos worried North Vietnam. If the Royal Army succeeded in expelling the Pathet Lao from their mountain strongholds, Group 559 would be hard-pressed to get people and supplies into South Vietnam, since the Laotian mountains were the vital communication link. In September 1959 North Vietnam established Group 959 to provide supplies to Pathet Lao guerrillas and urged Vietnamese soldiers to join the fight. In 1960 North Vietnamese and Pathet Lao troops defeated the Royal Army along the border and secured the corridor Hanoi needed into South Vietnam. When the time was right, North Vietnam would begin moving large numbers of cadres, supplies, and eventually soldiers down that Laotian corridor into South Vietnam. It became known as the Ho Chi Minh Trail.

The United States and South Vietnam were preparing for a different type of invasion. Washington aimed to build ARVN into a reliable fighting force. American policymakers wanted to reduce it from a ragtag army of 250,000 poorly equipped, demoralized troops to a streamlined, efficient army of 150,000 dedicated soldiers. The United States also wanted a reliable, 40,000-man local militia. The training unit was the Military Assistance and Advisory Group (MAAG), commanded by General Samuel ("Hanging Sam") Williams. Fresh from duty in Korea, where he had witnessed the North Korean and Chinese invasions, Williams was convinced that the assault on South Vietnam would come by way of a large-scale sweep southward by North Vietnamese and perhaps Chinese troops across the seventeenth parallel. Along with seven hundred American military advisers, Williams trained the South Vietnamese army in the art of conventional warfare—how to use artillery, air support, and armor to repel an invasion. He placed ARVN soldiers in static positions along the borders with Laos and North Vietnam. When ARVN troops moved, they depended on armored personnel carriers and trucks, and they rarely ventured off the main roads. Off the main roads was, of course, exactly where the Vietcong were operating. In what can be considered an extraordinary example of naiveté, Williams remarked in 1957: "We have exactly 342 men, the number allowed by the Geneva Armistice Conference. It would be a breeze if we had more."

Few people in South Vietnam, however, had any sense of patriotic nationalism; their country was a diplomatic creation just a few years old. Asking men and women to die for their country is one thing; asking them to die for someone else's country is quite another. There was no identity between the army and the nation. The other problem MAAG faced was the traditional Vietnamese suspicion of foreigners. One American said that MAAG's greatest challenge was "assuring the Vietnamese that the United States is not a colonial power—an assurance that must be renewed on an individual basis by each new adviser." Still, the United States supplied $1.65 billion to South Vietnam between 1956 and 1961, and nearly 80 percent of the money went into military equipment and personnel. The United States and ARVN thought they were ready for the invasion.

But Le Duan was training the Vietcong for a very different kind of war. For them the real issue was political, not military. They wanted to secure the allegiance of the peasants and destroy the credibility of the Diem regime. With peasant support they would enjoy food, protection, and recruits, and through selective terrorism they would prove that Diem could not provide security. "Establish yourselves in the Central Highlands," Giap told the Vietcong. "Like the French before them, the Americans and their puppet Diem will stay in the cities. Then extend your influence into the lowland jungles and the villages of the Mekong Delta. Assault on the cities will be only the last stage of the conflict." Le Duan's instructions to the guerrillas were known as the Xuan Mai: "When the enemy masses we disperse. When the enemy passes we harass. When the enemy withdraws we advance. When the enemy disperses, we mass." Instead of coming across the seventeenth parallel by the thousands, former Vietminh came a few at a time down the Ho Chi Minh Trail, through the jungles and mountains of the North Vietnam panhandle into Laos and then into South Vietnam. It was an arduous trip—one to two months of hard marching. When the guerrillas arrived in South Vietnam, they joined with Vietcong already there. They brought weapons with them or dug up weapons and ammunition they had buried in 1954.

The nature of the political uprising in South Vietnam has caused considerable debate in the United States. Antiwar activists claimed that it was spontaneous, purely a civil war and popular rebellion against a repressive government that North Vietnam had ignored until American intervention forced Hanoi to react. Supporters of the war in the United States saw it purely as a matter of communist aggression from North

Vietnam against South Vietnam. The truth, of course, embraces both perceptions. The historian William Duiker noted "genuine revolt based in the South . . . organized and directed from the North." Diem created a wealth of hostility and resentment, which North Vietnam exploited through superb organization and extraordinary willpower.

Alienated from the government of Ngo Dinh Diem as well as frightened by the threat of Vietcong violence, South Vietnamese peasants vacillated for a while but eventually sided with the people in power at the local level. Whether they truly believed in the Vietcong cause or were simply intimidated matters little. When guerrillas controlled a region, the peasants went along. By late 1960, with reinforcements from North Vietnam and new recruits from South Vietnam, the number of armed Vietcong had increased to 10,000, and they were expanding out from their strongholds in the mountains of Quang Ngai Province, the U Minh Forest in Kien Giang and An Xuyen Provinces, the Plain of Reeds along the Cambodian border, and the swamps of southeastern Vietnam. They began to launch lightning guerrilla strikes against ARVN forces near the major cities.

Government soldiers, trained in conventional warfare, were no match for the guerrillas. Diem and Nhu packed the ARVN officer corps with Roman Catholics. Loyalty to the Ngo family, not leadership ability or tactical skill, was the prerequisite for appointment. Soldiers distrusted the competence of their superiors and resented their religion. Morale was poor and commitment weak. Diem viewed ARVN as a military force whose primary responsibility was keeping the Ngo family in power, not destroying the communists. Diem and Nhu discouraged offensive operations for fear that heavy government casualties would lead to popular discontent and political uprisings.

In 1959 and 1960 the political situation deteriorated rapidly. The number of assassinations and kidnappings was up, as were terrorist assaults on government offices, military bases, American transport convoys, and hotels and bars catering to the handful of GI servicemen. On July 8, 1959, Vietcong commandos infiltrated the American base at Bien Hoa and killed two air force personnel, Major Dale Buis of Imperial Beach, California, and Sergeant Chester Ovnand of Copperas Cove, Texas. The Americans were amazed at the audacity of the Vietcong, or "Charlie" as they came to call them. "Vietnam," announced Diem, "is a nation at war." For American troops, a new saying became common: "The daytime is ours, but the night belongs to Charlie."

In 1960 there were nearly nine hundred American advisers in South Vietnam carrying out the "Hanging Sam" training program, but they could not undo the damage of Diem's regime. On November 11, 1960, just a week after John F. Kennedy defeated Vice President Richard Nixon for president, South Vietnamese paratroopers under the command of Colonel Vuong Van Dong launched a coup against Diem, surrounding the presidential palace in Saigon and demanding his resignation. The coup collapsed when loyal ARVN marines and infantry attacked the paratroopers, but the event sent chills throughout the Saigon diplomatic community. Diem arrested thousands of people.

The crumbling political situation fueled the communist drive for reunification. In September 1960 the Third Congress of the Lao Dong party, the political group that had assumed power from the Vietminh in 1951 and became the ruling force in North Vietnam, called for the "liberation" of South Vietnam and reunification. Vietcong recruiting efforts were increasingly successful in the south, since Ngo Dinh Diem's regime was creating thousands of disaffected people. On December 20, 1960, at a secret location in South Vietnam, North Vietnam established the National Liberation Front to give political direction to the Vietcong guerrillas.

At that very moment, John F. Kennedy was meeting with Dwight Eisenhower, planning the transition to the new administration. International tensions were running high. During the same month that North Vietnamese leaders decided to push toward reunification with South Vietnam, President-elect John F. Kennedy was finishing his plans for taking office. Suddenly issues that he had debated in the abstract during the campaign, offering the free and easy opinions of a politician who did not have to implement policy, had become his issues. Eisenhower's burdens of office would in less than a month become his burdens.

On December 6, 1960, the two men met in the White House. They had met face-to-face only once before, though Ike had forgotten the occasion. And during the eight years Ike was President of the United States and JFK was a U.S. Senator, the two had never met. In an odd sort of way, it was like two different centuries meeting. Eisenhower, born in the nineteenth century, was at the time the oldest man ever elected president. Now, weakened by heart problems and illnesses, he was seventy-one. Kennedy, born in the twentieth century, was the youngest man ever elected president. Although he also had severe health problems, at forty-three he appeared young and vigorous, especially as he swiftly stepped out of his limousine at the North Portico entrance of the White House and bounded up the steps to shake hands with Eisenhower. Hatless, tan, smiling, and energetic, John Kennedy was the very face of a new, optimistic, confident generation.

There was no great closeness between the two men. In private, Eisenhower called the Kennedy "that younger man" or "Little Boy Blue." JFK sometimes referred to Ike as "that old asshole." Nor did the meeting draw them any closer. They talked largely about the decisionmaking process. As fitting America's greatest general, Eisenhower followed a chain-of-command approach. The only issues that reached his desk were important ones. "No easy matters will ever come to you as President," he told JFK. "If they are easy, they will be settled at a lower level." Kennedy listened politely but Eisenhower could tell that his words were not penetrating very deeply. Kennedy clearly intended to be involved in decisions large and small. He wanted his hands in the making of every pie.

Eisenhower saw himself as the top of a flow chart. Kennedy regarded himself as the center of the action. Same job, different approaches. But the two men did develop a grudging respect for each other as they talked about the foreign policy issues that confronted America. They discussed Berlin and the Soviet Union, defense communities and hot spots. But neither ever considered conversing about Vietnam. A year later Kennedy ruefully recalled, "You know, Eisenhower never mentioned it, never uttered the word, Vietnam."

Vietnam, showing 1954 North/South division, and routes of invasions and
evacuations, 1945 to 1975.

4

The New Frontier in Vietnam, 1961–1963

We are going to win in Vietnam. We will remain here until we do win.

—Robert F. Kennedy, 1962

When the 1960s dawned, the United States was ready to embark on the salvation of the world: more specifically, to save it from communism. The most popular novel of the time bearing on the Cold War criticized Americans not for being fixated on communism but for their failure to make the effort that the struggle demanded. William J. Lederer and Eugene Burdick's *The Ugly American,* written as a response to *The Quiet American* and published in 1958, stayed on the bestseller list for seventy-eight weeks and was made into a successful motion picture starring Marlon Brando. Set in Sarkhan, a fictionalized Saigon, the novel has a character based on Colonel Lansdale. Unlike Greene's Pyle, however, Colonel Hillandale is an example of the type of American the country needs more of overseas.

The primary target of *The Ugly American* is the foreign service. Chosen for their "personal wealth, political loyalty, and the ability to stay out of trouble," most of the nation's ambassadors cannot even understand the languages of the countries to which they are assigned. They hear only what their interpreters want them to hear and obtain from newspapers only what their readers want them to obtain. Isolated in the cities, they and their spoiled staff spend their days entertaining visiting American VIPs, socializing with other Western diplomats, and occasionally meeting with members of the local elite. They ignore the masses who live in rural poverty. They have no knowledge of their enemy. They have not read the works of Mao Zedong, Karl Marx, or Vladimir Lenin. While the communists speak the native languages and work closely with the peasants, building loyalties and political support, the Americans drift along on the belief that dollars will win the Cold War. In short, the novel argues, "We have been losing—not only in Asia, but everywhere." *The Ugly American* was a tale of woe but also a call for action. The United States was losing the fight against communism in the Third World, but it could still win. The United States needs hardworking, well-trained professionals: "They must speak the language of the land of their assignment, and they must be more expert in its problems than are the natives." The ugly American himself is one of the few admirable characters. He is a plain, honest engineer, his unvarnished features a symbolic contrast to the slick good looks of the pampered foreign-service staff, and he and his wife labor with villagers on practical projects that will make life a bit more livable. (The subsequent use of the phrase "ugly American" to describe Americans who show their country's worst face misses the content of the novel but is true to its intentions.) *The Ugly American* ends with a challenge and a warning: "If the only price we are willing to pay is the dollar price, then we might as well pull out before we're thrown out. If we are not prepared to pay the human price, we had better retreat to our shores, build Fortress America, learn to live without international trade and communications, and accept the mediocrity, the low standard of living, and the loom of world Communism which would accompany such a move."

President John F. Kennedy was to become the embodiment of this call to action. "Let the word go forth from this time and place, to friend and foe alike," he declared at his inauguration in 1961, "that the torch has been passed to a new generation of Americans—born in this century, tempered by war, disciplined by a hard and bitter peace, proud of our ancient heritage." The words contained pride and arrogance, promise and warning: "Let every nation know, whether it wishes us well or ill, that we shall pay any price, bear any burden, meet any hardship, support any friend, oppose any foe to assure the survival and success of liberty." Kennedy promised that his administration would never allow one form of colonialism to be replaced by another, for "those who foolishly sought power by riding the back of the tiger ended up inside." He asked for the commitment of all Americans, but he offered greatness in return: "In the long history of the world, only a few generations have been granted the role of defending freedom in its hour of maximum danger. I do not shrink from this responsibility—I welcome it. . . . The energy, the faith, the devotion which we bring to this endeavor will light our country and all who serve it—and the glow from that fire can truly light the world."

The speech was a tour de force. Only later—years later—would critics ask what it meant and, since it was largely written by the president's adviser Theodore Sorensen, whether it represented Kennedy's own views. No nation can limitlessly pay, bear, meet, support, and oppose. Yet Kennedy promised just that; he pledged to remove limits, to go beyond the possible to achieve immortality for his nation. Actually, 1961 was not a particularly dangerous moment for the United States and for the world. But Kennedy believed, as his *Profiles in Courage* had declared six years earlier, that "great crises produce great men" coveting greatness, he was determined to produce at least the illusion of a crisis.

About John Kennedy there was an air of romance and courage, a hint

he was born for greatness. He had been a sickly child reared in a family
of great wealth. Joe Kennedy, his domineering father, expected his sons
to show courage, drive, and manliness. They played sports, battled
among themselves, and competed for their father's love. Jack never used
his physical troubles as an excuse; he played as hard as his brothers.
The main difference between him and his brothers, perhaps since he
spent so much time in a sickbed, is that he loved to read. The tales of
King Arthur, Scottish chiefs, James Fenimore Cooper, and Marlborough
intrigued him. Stories of greatness and acts of courage molded his character. Sickliness was an enemy to be overcome, a call to inner strength.

Kennedy's education furthered his progress to greatness. His father
was rich, but that was not enough to gain a Boston Irish Catholic an
entry to the Anglo-American establishment. Therefore he sent his sons
not to Catholic institutions—to Holy Cross or Notre Dame—but to
establishment schools and universities. Jack followed Joe, Jr., to Choate,
an elite, Protestant prep school dedicated to producing Christian gentlemen who understood duty and obligation and believed that leadership
was their rightful heritage. From Choate Jack went to Harvard, where he
continued to mix and compete with the Protestant elite. The immigrant
family's rage to succeed burned in him. But he learned to conceal the
fire beneath a cool facade. Years later, when he was president, he twitted
one of his aides for refusing to resign from a prestigious Washington,
D.C., club that did not encourage Jewish or black membership. The aide
remarked that Kennedy belonged to the equally elitist and equally
restrictive Links in New York. "Jews and Negroes," Kennedy laughed.
"Hell, they don't even allow Catholics!" But a Kennedy—Boston Irish,
wealthy, and Catholic—had kicked down the door.

World War II allowed Joe, Jr., and Jack to show their father and their
country their mettle. Jack enlisted in the navy, and on the night of August 1, 1943, in waters near the Solomon Islands, a Japanese destroyer
cut his PT-109 in half. Two men died, and Kennedy saved the life of another badly burned crew member. It was all very courageous—the stuff
of his childhood reading. And it was fully covered by the American press.
Not to be outdone, Joe, Jr., volunteered for a near suicidal bombing mission. Just before his takeoff, he told a friend, "I'm about to go into my
act, and if I don't come back tell my dad . . . that I love him very much."
He did not come back. He was the one his father had groomed for politics. Now that Joe, Jr., was gone, Jack was the one: "He demanded it," so
Kennedy said of his father's desire that he enter politics.

On 1946 Kennedy ran for Congress from Cambridge, Massachusetts.
Running as a "fighting conservative," he was easily elected. In 1952 he
won a Senate seat from Massachusetts and set his sight on the presidency, the ultimate prize. Between 1952 and 1960, he attacked tasks
that enhanced his national reputation. Most important was that in an
era suspicious of ideology, Kennedy had a voting record that was cer-

tainly not liberal and not exactly conservative. He did not want to alienate potential presidential support with an unwise Senate vote.

If any philosophy guided Kennedy's actions, it was a belief in the need to demonstrate courage. He lived in pain. Addison's disease struck him in the late 1940s, and this adrenal deficiency made him susceptible to infections. In 1954 and again in 1955 he underwent serious spinal operations. There were also bouts with anemia, allergies, and various other illnesses. "At least one-half of the days that he spent on this earth were days of intense physical pain," according to his brother Bobby. But Jack seldom complained and tried not to allow a fragile body to circumscribe his life. In fact, he reacted to physical limitations by emphasizing the need to live a physically challenging life. To impress Kennedy, one associate learned, you had to "show raw guts, fall on your face now and then. Smash into the house once in a while going after a pass. Laugh off twisted ankles or a big hole torn in your best suit." As president, Kennedy was determined to show raw guts. Robert Frost, the poet, described Kennedy as "young ambition eager to be tried."

Along with courage, Kennedy adopted a locker-room sense of manliness. He enjoyed the company of men, the talk of politics, power, and women. Women—like wars—were things to be won. Like his father, Kennedy regarded sexual conquests as a sign of manhood. During his Washington years he moved from one affair to the next. He did not even bother to learn the names of his one-night stands, referring to them by the

Walt W. Rostow, a member of the Kennedy and Johnson administrations, was one of the "best and brightest" who led the United States into the Vietnam War. (*Courtesy, Library of Congress*)

generic names of "Kiddo" or "Sweetie." One woman found him to be "as compulsive as Mussolini. Up against the wall, Signora, if you have five minutes, that sort of thing. He was not a cozy, touching sort of man. In fact he'd been sick for so long that he was sort of touch-me-not." Another woman recalled that for Kennedy, "Sex was something to have done, not to be doing."

The people who came to Washington to join the administration personified the Kennedy mystique: money, power, courage, sensuality, and brains. The first American Kennedys were lace-curtain Irish who despised the origins of the Brahmin elite but in later generations aped its trappings. Critics quipped that if you cut them, the Kennedys would bleed "Irish green." What Joe Kennedy struggled for all his life was acceptance, and, with John in the White House, the family had it. The Kennedys surrounded themselves with glamorous, talented people—athletes and astronauts, Silver Star and Congressional Medal of Honor winners, Rhodes scholars, Nobel laureates, all-stars, and prizewinning writers. The Kennedys made winning—in bed, in battle, and in boardrooms—a way of life.

For secretary of state, Kennedy turned to David Dean Rusk. Cherokee County, Georgia, was a world away from the rocky beaches of Cape Cod. The Rusks were redneck dirt farmers. Dean was, in their own words, "quick"—smart but not a "smart-aleck," soft-spoken but blessed with the tenacity of a pit bull. They wanted him to go to school, perhaps to be a teacher or a country lawyer. Fate rescued Rusk. During his senior year at Davidson College in North Carolina he won a Rhodes scholarship to study at Oxford University. From the vantage point of the State Department, Rusk watched Hitler run over Europe and he vowed never to commit the sin of "appeasement." Rusk joined the army in 1942 and served under "Vinegar" Joe Stillwell in the China-Burma theater. With his combat experience in Asia and the prestige of the Rhodes scholarship, Rusk was named an assistant secretary of state in 1950, a post he kept until 1952, when he became president of the Rockefeller Foundation. Bearing names like Rhodes, Stillwell, and Rockefeller on his resume, Rusk attracted the attention of the Kennedys.

From the very beginning Rusk had no doubts about Ho Chi Minh or the war. It was part of a global communist conspiracy, not a civil war. Known as "Buddha" because of his reticence to speak out in general meetings, Rusk was the hardest of the hard-liners, and even in retirement he was unrepentant. The American commitment in Vietnam had been "honorable and necessary. Our only mistake was withdrawing when we did."

Equally hard-line was Walt W. Rostow. A renowned economist at the Massachusetts Institute of Technology, Rostow began advising Kennedy on foreign affairs in 1958. Two years later his book *The Stages of Economic Growth* made him the premier expert on Third World modernization. The Kennedys doted on intellectuals with well-received books, and in 1961 the new president appointed Rostow as deputy special assistant for national security affairs. Rostow believed that modernization creates economic and social dislocations that can render a developing country vulnerable to communist insurgency. He suggested for South Vietnam a dual strategy. The United States should use military force to cut off the Vietcong from their supply sources in North Vietnam, China, and the Soviet Union. Rostow was an early advocate of large-scale bombing of North Vietnam. And at the same time the United States should help accelerate modernization, to push South Vietnam through the stages of development until a modern economy emerged. Communism would then have no appeal.

Six years later Rostow was still in his ivory tower. At a 1967 briefing with John Paul Vann, a retired lieutenant colonel and Vietnam veteran who was heading up the army's pacification program, Rostow asked Vann whether he agreed that the "war would be over in six months." Privately a critic of Rostow, Vann laughingly replied, "Oh hell no, Mr. Rostow. I'm a born optimist. I think we can hold out longer than that." Rostow was not amused. The briefing ended. For the rest of his life Rostow remained convinced that the United States had failed in Vietnam only because not enough firepower was applied.

No less confident was Robert S. McNamara, Kennedy's secretary of defense. With a degree from Berkeley and a Harvard MBA, McNamara was one of the famous "whiz kids," moving rapidly through management ranks at Ford Motor Company, where he became president in 1960 at the age of forty-four. Possessing a keen, analytical mind and unbounded faith in technology, computers, and systems management, McNamara thought there was no way that a fourth-rate country like North Vietnam could stand up against the American miracle. On his first trip to South Vietnam in 1961, McNamara made up his mind quickly when he could not find a cold drink. Vietnam was a primitive, place. "North Vietnam will never beat us," he said. "They can't even make ice cubes."

McNamara assumed both logistical and operational control over the war, establishing strategic goals and objectives, selecting technologies, and, with an army of programmers, accountants, and statisticians measuring progress. Death and victory were matters of calculus. McNamara did not have the ideological fervor of Rusk or the intellectual paraphernalia of Rostow, but he had their faith in American power—it was only a matter of time before the "superior system prevails." During that 1961 visit to Saigon, McNamara revealed his faith to Frederick Nolting, the American ambassador to South Vietnam. "Fred," he said, "anything you want in the way of instruments, gadgets, or material, we can provide. . . . Don't hesitate to ask for it."

General Maxwell Taylor, another hawk in the administration, was a Missouri native who had graduated from West Point in 1922. Taylor was the father of airborne warfare. He was with the 82nd Airborne Division in North Africa and Sicily and parachuted into France in command of the 101st Airborne Division on D-Day. Between 1945 and 1949 Taylor was the commandant of West Point, and when the Korean War broke out he took over the Eighth Army. He became chief of staff of the army and remained there until his retirement in 1959. But he was a frustrated chief of staff. The New Look military was good for the air force and navy, which could deliver nuclear warheads, but bad for the army, which became a military stepchild. The New Look, for Taylor at least, was pure folly, forcing the United States to resort to nuclear terror every time a political or military crisis developed somewhere in the world. Instead, Taylor pushed a military policy he defined as "flexible-response." Nuclear weapons should be available for reacting to a nuclear attack, but a strong, well-equipped army and Marine Corps should be available for conventional threats. The president should also have a counterinsurgency option to respond to guerrilla wars and political uprisings where conventional forces were inappropriate.

Taylor's theory became a best-seller in his 1959 book *The Uncertain Trumpet.* Here was a general with a well-received book—perfect for the Kennedys. The president in 1961 appointed Taylor as his military adviser and in 1962 named him chairman of the joint chiefs of staff. The Kennedys found Taylor brilliant and reassuring, a fount of military wisdom who could be trusted to make wise, tough decisions. Attorney General Robert Kennedy named his second son Robert Maxwell Taylor Kennedy.

Finally, there was McGeorge Bundy. A descendant of the aristocratic Lowell family of Massachusetts on his mother's side, Bundy was born in Boston in 1919. Brilliant, caustic, and intolerant of lesser minds, Bundy graduated from Yale in 1940, and the Yale yearbook commented, "This week passed without Mahatma Bundy making a speech." After spending World War II in the army as a planner, Bundy returned to Harvard as a Junior Fellow. Without a Ph.D. or ever having taken a graduate-level political science course, Bundy was given tenure as a Harvard government professor. In 1953, at the age of thirty-four, he became the dean of arts and sciences at Harvard. Bundy was the lone Republican in his family, but he had earned Kennedy's respect in the late 1950s for his sheer brilliance. Of Bundy, Kennedy once said, "You can't beat brains." When Kennedy offered him the position of deputy undersecretary of state for administration, Bundy turned it down, refusing, he said, to leave Cambridge where he was a dean to go to Washington to be a dean. Bundy then turned down the appointment of assistant secretary of defense for international security affairs. Thereupon the president asked Bundy to come to the White House as special assistant to the president for national security affairs. Bundy accepted.

The Kennedy administration was caught up in a postwar assertive-

ness that intoxicated American culture. Kennedy's advisers represented
the essence of American power: the foundations, universities, corpora-
tions, and military. They had gotten their first taste of leadership in
World War II—the great triumph of American money, technology, organization, and will. They remembered the malaise of the Great Depression
and contrasted it to the euphoria of the war, with its missionary zeal,
national unity, unprecedented prosperity, and overpowering sense of virtue. During World War II the good guys fought the bad guys and the
good guys won. The United States became the leading economic and
military force in the world. There seemed nothing that American power
could not achieve. Communists, not fascists, were the new embodiment
of evil. The United States would provide the money, the leadership, and
the technology to defeat the threat.

Back in the late 1940s and early 1950s the United States had been
drawn to Indochina by the fear of monolithic communism as well as by
a concrete economic need to preserve Southeast Asia as a capitalist bas-
tion. But during the Kennedy presidency those concrete economic and
strategic interests acquired a new ideology of tough optimism. There was
one answer for world problems: Let American virtue define the moral issues and let American power resolve them. The United States should in-
vest resources and apply power until the Vietnamese communists reached
their breaking point, just as Hitler, Mussolini, and Tojo had reached theirs.

Yet confidence of this kind was not universal within the administration. Debate over Vietnam started soon after the inauguration. Hard-
liners wanted victory. General Lyman L. Lemnitzer, chairman of the
Joint Chiefs of Staff in 1961, urged Kennedy to "grind up the Vietcong
with 40,000 American ground troops . . . grab'em by the balls and their
hearts and minds will follow." McGeorge Bundy was just as adamant.
He urged Kennedy to attack the Vietcong—and if necessary North Vietnam—with an array of conventional weapons, including ground troops
and strategic bombing. Rostow believed in Taylor's concept of flexible
response and wanted to try it out: "It is somehow wrong to be developing these capabilities but not applying them in a crucial theater," he told
Kennedy, "in Knute Rockne's old phrase, we are not saving them for the
junior prom." George Ball, on the other hand, counseled caution. The
new undersecretary of state for economic affairs, Ball had undergradu-
ate and law degrees from Northwestern. After spending World War II in
the Lend-Lease Program, he had become director of the United States
Strategic Bombing Survey in London. Ball concluded that massive bombing of Germany had only marginally affected economic production while
stiffening German resistance. In the early 1950s Ball was counsel to the
French embassy in Washington, and he listened to the French debate
about Indochina. From the beginning of his tenure at the State Department, Ball argued that the Diem regime was corrupt, that a land war in
Asia was not in the interests of the United States, and that the objective

of creating a viable, democratic South Vietnam was impossible. Bundy could barely tolerate Ball, referring to him as the "Theologian." At a 1961 meeting with Kennedy, Ball predicted that the introduction of American troops would create its own momentum; within "five years there will be 300,000 American soldiers fighting in Vietnam." Kennedy laughed, "George, you're crazier than hell."

The deliberations over the introduction of United States combat troops in Vietnam took place within the context of a major strategic debate on the joint chiefs of staff. Curtis LeMay, air force chief of staff, believed in air power as the most effective military asset in the modern world. Like Admiral Arthur Radford, who chaired the joint chiefs during the early 1950s, and promoted the "New Look" defense policy, LeMay remained convinced that strategic air power had played the key role in defeating the Axis powers during World War II. He ridiculed the findings of George Ball and the United States Strategic Bombing Survey and insisted that an effective strategic bombing campaign in Vietnam would bring Ho to his knees. Maxwell Taylor, chairman of the joint chiefs, disagreed. During the 1950s, Taylor had opposed Radford's single-minded faith in air power and accepted the conclusions of the Bombing Survey and believed instead in "flexible response." According to Ball, Radford and LeMay missed the point. They disagreed on how to employ military assets in Vietnam, but both believed in the merits of a military solution there— that American technology and military power would inevitably prevail. It was inconceivable to them that Vietnam could succeed against the same American military machine that had crushed Germany and Japan. Ball correctly perceived that the complex political problems in Vietnam transcended a military solution. The United States, he feared, would funnel its military resources into a political black hole.

The president was caught in the middle. In McGeorge Bundy's description of the first few months of the Kennedy administration, "At this point we were like the Harlem Globetrotters, passing forward, behind, sidewise, and underneath. But nobody has made a basket yet." In April the CIA invasion of Cuba at the Bay of Pigs ended in disaster. Fidel Castro easily captured the exile army and enjoyed a propaganda orgy. The incident sent Kennedy into a depression, even though the invasion plan had been put together in the Eisenhower years. Great presidents deal toughly with crises like wars and depressions; they do not conduct botched invasions. Kennedy was also afraid that the Soviet Union would misread the Bay of Pigs and decide that he could be bluffed. He needed more information about South Vietnam, but in the meantime Kennedy decided in May 1961 to send another five hundred American advisers. That brought the American contingent to 1,400 men. But Kennedy also knew that five hundred more Americans in South Vietnam were not going to resolve the crisis. He decided to send Vice President Lyndon B. Johnson on a fact-finding mission.

Johnson arrived in Saigon on May 10, 1961. Tall, loud, and gregarious, Johnson could not have been more different from the short, reserved, and soft-spoken Ngo Dinh Diem. Johnson was raised in the democracy of central Texas, where politicians sold their souls for votes; Diem was a mandarin who expected deference from constituents. But the two men hit it off. Johnson stayed in Saigon four days and treated it like a Texas political campaign, full of official breakfasts, lunches, dinners, press conferences, meetings, speeches, and "pressing the flesh" events. The Vietnamese did not know what to make of Johnson. At six feet, four inches, he towered over them, and the muggy heat turned him into a fountain of sweat. In the back seat of the limousine, Johnson had three dozen pressed white shirts. He would come to a stop and plunge into the crowd, grabbing the "praying palms" of onlookers, who were using the traditional greeting of pressed palms and a bow. Johnson kept wanting to know, "Who the hell are they praying to?" By the time he finished shaking hands, he was drenched in sweat and would jump back into the limousine and change shirts, only to start all over again at the next stop.

The crowds warmed to this sweaty American giant; they laughed when he hovered over them, dripping sweat and shaking their hands. Spectators who had managed to shake his hand formed Shake the Hand of Lyndon Johnson Clubs. Johnson liked the Vietnamese, too, even though he had a hard time pronouncing their names. At a luncheon where Vietnamese guests were wearing name tags, Johnson kept mispronouncing the most common surname "Nguyen," calling people Mr. or Mrs. "Nu-gu-yen." When an aide told him the name was pronounced "Win," Johnson remarked, "We'll never lose the war. Everyone in the whole goddamn country is named 'win.'" At a farewell banquet, Johnson reiterated American support and remarked to Diem, "Your people, Mr. President, returned you to office for a second term with 91 percent of the votes. You are not only the George Washington, the Father of your country, but the Franklin D. Roosevelt as well." Privately, Johnson was much more pragmatic. To the journalist Stanley Karnow he remarked, "Shit, man, he's the only boy we got out there." He told Kennedy that the United States should continue its military support and launch a "New Deal for South Vietnam" so that economic development could undercut the appeal of the Vietcong.

Johnson's trip to Saigon launched Kennedy on one of his most persistent and frustrating problems: the contradictory reports he received about South Vietnam.

The Saigon press corps kept reporting a steady decline in support for Diem and steady increases in Vietcong strength. David Halberstam (who supported the war until 1965) of the *New York Times,* Neil Sheehan of UPI, Nick Turner of Reuters, Peter Arnett of the Associated Press, Bernard Kalb and Peter Kalisher of CBS, James Robinson of NBC, Charles Mohr of *Time,* Francois Sully of *Newsweek,* Pepper Martin of U.S. *News*

& *World Report,* and Stanley Karnow of *Time* consistently argued that
the Diem regime was isolated and paranoid, that a stable democracy
would never develop as long as the Ngo family held power. In short, the
United States and South Vietnam were losing.

In June 1961 the Department of Defense sent Eugene Staley of Stanford University to Saigon to study the situation. In August, Staley told
Kennedy that American policy must have three objectives: provide military protection from the Vietcong to peasants; convince Diem that "military operations will not achieve lasting results unless economic and
social programs are continued and accelerated"; and create a self-sus-
taining economy in South Vietnam. Only then would the war be winnable. But no sooner had Kennedy received Staley's report than Theodore H. White, a prominent journalist and fellow Bostonian, wrote from
Saigon with a different story. White, a highly respected Asian expert
who was then finishing his Pulitzer Prize–winning book *The Making of
a President, 1960,* which Kennedy had read in draft form and heartily
enjoyed, claimed: "The situation gets steadily worse almost week by
week. . . . Guerrillas now control almost all of the Southern delta—so
much so that I could find no American who would drive me outside
Saigon in his car even by day without military convoy. . . . What per-
plexes the hell out of me is that the Commies, on their side, seem to be
able to find people willing to die for their cause."

For a straight answer, Kennedy sent Taylor and Rostow to South
Vietnam in October. Rostow argued that to build a loyalty among South
Vietnamese, the United States should finance the construction of an infrastructure of schools, hospitals, roads, bridges, land development, farm
cooperatives, communications systems, and a stable currency. Rostow's
ideas reflected his book on the stages of economic growth—which critics
dubbed the "TV-in-every-thatched-hut" theory—and he wanted to push
the country rapidly toward modernization. At the same time Taylor's
theories about flexible response were coming to fruition. He criticized
the training efforts of the Eisenhower administration, which had focused
on conventional tactics, how to fight a war of fixed battles and territorial acquisition in a country where the population was friendly. For
Taylor, South Vietnam was not that place. It was a tropical jungle of hit-
and-run guerrilla attacks where the local population was neutral at
best. American training should teach ARVN how to fight a war of attrition against a guerrilla enemy. Rostow and Taylor called for the deployment of 8,000 regular United States ground troops and a 5,000-man
combat engineering group. Between 1955 and 1961 the United States
had poured $1.65 billion into South Vietnam, and ARVN troops were
still not ready. While counterinsurgency was giving stability to Diem
and training to ARVN to take over the war, Kennedy would have to increase the number of American troops until the Vietcong lost the will or
the ability to fight. Rostow added that Kennedy should consider large-

scale bombing of North Vietnam and the infiltration routes, which earned him his new nickname, the "Air Marshal."

Kennedy was worried, however, about committing combat troops. He suspected that 13,000 soldiers would put up a good fight against the Vietcong, but he was unsure of what North Vietnam would do, how many troops could be sent south, and what role the Chinese communists would take. In a comment to Arthur M. Schlesinger, Jr., a Harvard historian and one of his advisers, Kennedy remarked: "They want a force of American troops. . . . But it will be just like Berlin. The troops will march in; the bands will play; the crowds will cheer; and in four days everyone will have forgotten. Then we will be told we have to send more troops. It's like taking a drink. The effect wears off, and you have to have another." Years later Taylor remarked that Kennedy "just didn't want to be convinced that this was the right thing to do. . . . It was really the President's personal conviction that U.S. ground troops shouldn't go in."

Kennedy found an ally in General Douglas MacArthur. Feeling heat from conservative Republicans complaining about the administration's softness on Asian communism, Kennedy sponsored a congressional luncheon with MacArthur as the guest speaker. The general did not disappoint him. He argued that "we would be foolish to fight on the Asiatic continent" and that "the future of Southeast Asia should be determined at the diplomatic table." Maxwell Taylor saw that the speech had "made a hell of an impression on the President . . . whenever he'd get this military advice . . . he'd say, 'Well, now, you gentlemen, you go back and convince General MacArthur, then I'll be convinced.' But none of us undertook the task."

For the time being Kennedy preferred a middle road—no ground troops but enough American expertise and firepower to get the job done. If Vietnam fell, Kennedy could expect political crucifixion at the hands of the China Lobby in the Republican party. Kennedy planned on running for reelection in 1964, and he was not anxious to give the Republicans a moralistic campaign issue. "I can't take a 1954 defeat today," he told Rostow, meaning that his campaign could not withstand a defeat like that at Dienbienphu. But at the same time Kennedy did not want the war to get out of control. It was primarily a South Vietnamese affair; the United States should provide only technical advice and economic support. American pilots in South Vietnam were never to go up in the air without a Vietnamese trainee along (or, if no pilot trainee was available, at least some Vietnamese pilot who could pretend was a trainee). American advisers with ARVN were never to engage the Vietcong directly; and no American soldier wounded in action was allowed to receive a Purple Heart.

John Kennedy was a pragmatist, a man comfortable with compromise. Between the caution of George Ball and the rush to escalate that Lemnitzer, Rostow, and Bundy wanted he could try a moderate, steady increase of economic and military resources, nothing dramatic and attention getting, but enough to be effective. The trouble, of course, was that moderation meant escalation. When Kennedy took office in early 1961, there were nine hundred United States military advisers in South Vietnam. At the end of 1961 there were more than 3,200 advisers.

While the Kennedy administration debated the future of Vietnam, a crisis erupted in Laos. A mountainous country of two million people, Laos shared much with Vietnam. In 1945 the French had returned to Laos along with Vietnam, and two half-brothers vied for control of the government. Prince Souphanouvong hated the French and had a passionate respect for Ho Chi Minh. In the 1950s he emerged as the leader of the Pathet Lao, a group of guerrillas bent on expelling the French and reforming Laotian society. Farther to the right was Souvanna Phouma, who rejected the revolutionary rhetoric of Souphanouvong but shared his passion for independence. After the Geneva Accords of 1954, which gave independence to Laos, the two formed a coalition government. But as the cold war intensified, John Foster Dulles became more opposed to the coalition and intent on ousting Souphanouvong and the Pathet Lao. Between 1954 and 1959 the CIA spent $300 million fighting the Pathet Lao in a secret war. The CIA spent enormous sums to see to it that General Phoumi Nosovan, a hopelessly corrupt right-winger and former lackey of the French, took control of Laos as head of the so-called Committee for the Defense of the National Interests. By 1960 it looked as if the first domino in Indochina was about to fall. Souvanna Phouma and Souphanouvong joined forces in a guerrilla war against Phoumi Nosovan and the CIA. Just before he left office, Eisenhower made the American commitment clear: "We cannot let Laos fall to the Communists even if we have to fight," which meant propping up the Nosovan government. But Nosovan could not be saved. He was just too corrupt and too alienated from the Laotian people. Souvanna Phouma and Souphanouvong made steady headway. It seemed only a matter of time before Laos fell.

In March 1961 Kennedy stationed 5,000 American troops in eastern Thailand, hoping the show of force would provide some encouragement to Nosovan. But it was too late. The Defense Department offered a proposal for airlifting American troops into Laos, but Kennedy was skeptical. Laos was landlocked, and it would have been logistically impossible to support the troops. The Bay of Pigs mess had left Kennedy suspicious of his military and CIA advisers. The president decided on a diplomatic settlement. In May 1961 the United States participated in the Geneva Conference on Laos. W. Averell Harriman, heir to the great railroad fortune and former ambassador to the Soviet Union, headed the American delegation. The agreement, signed in July 1962, created a neutral Laos with Souvanna Phouma at the head of a coalition government including Souphanouvong and the Pathet Lao, called for an end to CIA activities in Laos, and insisted on the withdrawal of Vietminh troops from the northeastern border. The CIA, the Pathet Lao, and the Vietcong had no intention, of course, of keeping the agreement. The CIA had already commissioned Air America, the CIA commercial airliner, to begin dropping supplies to Meo (Hmong) tribesmen, a 9,000-member Laotian mercenary army hired to fight the Pathet Lao and attack North Vietnam supply routes.

While the Geneva Agreement gave Kennedy some breathing space on Laos, it rigidified his approach to South Vietnam. Harriman urged a diplomatic settlement for Vietnam, arguing that the Diem regime was "repressive, dictatorial and unpopular." Chester Bowles, an undersecretary of state, told the president that by committing support to Diem the United States was "headed full blast up a dead end street." Both advisers wanted the president to consider a comprehensive diplomatic settlement followed by an American withdrawal. But after failing at the Bay of Pigs and then allowing the Pathet Lao some power in a neutralist Laotian government, Kennedy was worried about appearing weak. As a result, the administration did not take seriously any proposals for a diplomatic solution, a coalition government in Saigon composed of the Vietcong and Diem supporters, or a unilateral withdrawal. Nikita Khrushchev, head of the Soviet Union, did not help much. In January 1961 he had publicly announced Soviet support for "wars of national liberation" around the globe, and Kennedy took that threat as given seriously. Instead of a negotiated settlement, the Kennedy administration opted for a political and military alternative—counterinsurgency.

Maxwell Taylor's counterinsurgency proposals seemed perfect for South Vietnam. Kennedy had been intrigued with the idea ever since reading *The Uncertain Trumpet.* What he needed was someone he could trust as a counterinsurgency adviser. Kennedy picked Victor ("Brute") Krulak. At five feet, four inches and 134 pounds, Krulak had talked his way into the Naval Academy in 1930 when he was only sixteen. The other midshipmen called him "Brute," and the nickname stuck. But what Krulak lacked in size, he made up for in imagination. He graduated in 1934, went into the Marine Corps, and in 1937 designed the standard landing craft used in the Pacific during World War II. Eleven years later Krulak was ahead of his time in seeing the tactical advantages of the newly invented helicopter, and he wrote the Marine Corps manual describing helicopter tactics. During World War II, Krulak won the Navy Cross in the Solomon Islands. During an amphibious raid on Choiseul in 1943, his landing craft hit a coral reef and began to sink under Japanese fire. John F. Kennedy pulled his PT boat beside the landing craft and rescued the marines. Krulak thanked Kennedy and promised him a bottle of fine Scotch. In the confusion of battle, Krulak did not get the bottle sent, but in 1961 he remembered and shipped a bottle of Three Feathers to the White House. Kennedy remembered. In 1962 he named Krulak, then a major general, as counterinsurgency specialist to the Joint Chiefs of Staff.

Kennedy, Krulak, and Taylor did not have to create a counterinsurgency strategy. They brought to the task American experience fighting the Huk Rebellion in the Philippines and the successful British campaign against the Malayan communists. Soon after gaining independence in 1946, the Philippines had faced a communist-led radical movement with more than a million followers on Luzon. The CIA sent Edward Lansdale to build a counterinsurgency movement, and Lansdale selected Ramon Magsaysay, secretary of defense for the Philippines, as a principal leader. Together they reformed the Filipino army, improving pay and discipline and firing incompetent, politically appointed officers. Army treatment of civilians improved; election laws were enforced; tenant farmers gained the right to sue landlords. Magsaysay and Lansdale offered the Huk rebels amnesty or death. By 1953 the rebellion was over. The British had similar success in Malaya. Early in the 1950s, communist insurgents threatened the British colony. British officials launched a large-scale counterinsurgency effort under the direction of Robert Thompson. Thompson concentrated on winning over the ordinary Malayans by providing them with military security, land reform, and economic development. Although it took ten years to put down the insurgency, Malaya was secure by 1960.

Edward Lansdale went to South Vietnam to head the CIA effort. In 1961 Thompson arrived in Saigon as head of the British liaison mission, where he could provide technical expertise to the counterinsurgency program. In Washington, Roger Hilsman began working on counterinsurgency. Hilsman, a Texas native with a Yale Ph.D. in international relations, had spent the 1950s with the CIA before becoming director of intelligence for the State Department in 1961. He warned repeatedly in 1961 and 1962 that military action alone could not solve guerrilla wars; popular support gained through economic development and political reform, proven in the Philippines and Malaya, was indispensable. Krulak, Hilsman, Lansdale, and Thompson hatched what became the Strategic Hamlet Program, a project for drawing peasants into secured centers where they could benefit from economic and social reform as well as protection from insurgents.

What none of these experts realized was that the model programs that had worked in the Philippines and Malaya did so for reasons specific to each. In the Philippines the insurgents were not nationalist leaders. The United States had granted the Philippines independence in 1946. Many Filipinos spoke English and even more lusted after the American consumer culture. The two countries were allies during World War II, and Douglas MacArthur was a Filipino hero. Filipino Independence Day was the Fourth of July. When Lansdale launched the CIA counterinsurgency program on Luzon, he represented a country and a culture widely admired by Filipinos. In Malaya the British were still colonialists in the 1950s, but independence was palpable. Most Malayans expected the British to do what they had already done in India and Pakistan. Britain was the government in Malaya and did not have to work through client politicians and military officials. The British counterinsurgency effort was efficient and disciplined. Ethnic reality simplified the British task. The communists were ethnic Chinese, a minority group in Malaya greatly resented by the native population. There was little chance the communists could launch a broad-based peasant uprising. Few Malayans would die for Chinese revolutionaries.

The Kennedy administration also faced a communist insurgency in Indonesia. In the former Dutch East Indies, nationalists had proclaimed the independence of Indonesia in 1945, but the Dutch did not recognize sovereignty there until 1949. A period of liberal democracy ensued until 1957, when Sukarno proclaimed martial law and imposed a virtual dictatorship. The Communist Party of Indonesia launched an insurgent movement aimed at overthrowing Sukarno and proclaiming a communist state. Financial chaos and gross corruption in the capital of Jakarta provided fertile ground for communist recruitment among Indonesian peasants, and the communists steadily increased in power. Because of its vast oil deposits, Indonesia dwarfed Vietnam and Laos in economic significance. Early in the 1960s, when it appeared that the communists might come to power in Indonesia, the Kennedy administration flirted with the idea of military intervention, but decided against such action. With its huge population scattered across thousands of islands, Indonesia was six times larger in area than South Vietnam and equally rugged in terrain. Convinced that Indonesia would become a military quagmire, Kennedy decided against the introduction of American ground troops. South Vietnam would become the testing place for military intervention in Southeast Asia.

Compared to South Vietnam, the Philippines and Malaya had been easy. Communism and nationalism fused in the minds of millions of Vietnamese, northern and southern, and Ho Chi Minh wore the mantle of independence. The Diem government was corrupt and isolated, its Roman Catholicism alien in a Buddhist society. The Vietcong and the South Vietnamese were the same people ethnically and culturally, which made it almost impossible to identify the enemy. The Military Assistance and Advisory Group (MAAG) spent eight years trying to prepare ARVN for conventional war, but the Vietcong were getting bolder and better. ARVN still needed more flexible military training. The United States would have to buy the time.

On February 12, 1962, Kennedy made the first purchase when he established the Military Assistance Command, Vietnam or "Macvee," to direct the United States military effort in South Vietnam. Maxwell Taylor personally selected "one of my boys" to command MACV—General Paul Harkins.

A 1929 graduate of West Point, Harkins had earned the nickname "Ramrod" during World War II because of the ruthlessness with which he implemented every whim of General George S. Patton, whom he served as deputy chief of staff. When Patton died in 1945, Harkins attached himself to Taylor, who as a commander of the Eighth Army in Korea was a rising star. Harkins knew that military careers are built on successful efficiency reports, and immediately after arriving in Saigon in February 1962 he started issuing a daily "Headway Report" showing the steady progress being made against the Vietcong. There was a common theme in all the Headway Reports: The war was going well, but Harkins needed the "3Ms—more men, more money, more matériel." It was not long before the Saigon press corps dubbed him "General Blimp" for his inflated success reports. Among American younger officers, the phrase "pulling a Harkins" became synonymous with bonehead decisions and bureaucratic foul-ups. But Harkins got his 3Ms. At the end of 1962 there were 11,300 American military personnel in South Vietnam, and the United States was spending $500 million a year to keep the war going. By mid-1962 huge Globemaster transport planes were arriving hourly at the Tan Son Nhut airbase delivering military equipment. Francois Sully, a veteran reporter on Indochina, had seen it all before when French troops poured into Indochina in 1953. He remarked to an American journalist that it "was *déjà vu*. The American planes bringing American equipment and confident young soldiers dressed in American green fatigues. It looks like 1953 all over again."

As the number of military advisers exceeded 11,000, more and more troops came down with local diseases or suffered from accidents and combat wounds. To meet these medical needs, the army's 8th Field Hospital deployed to Nha Trang in 1962; the unit included dozens of army nurses, most of whom were women. As the responsibilities of the embassy staff expanded during the Kennedy administration, several hundred female employees of the State Department were transferred to Saigon. All of the service branches, as well as the Central Intelligence Agency, had women employees in South Vietnam during the early 1960s. American women with the United States Army, the Agency for International Development, and the Peace Corps found themselves working in South Vietnam during the Kennedy years.

It "is fashionable in some quarters," observed General Earle Wheeler in November 1962, "to say that the problems in Southeast Asia are primarily political and economic rather than military. I do not agree. The essence of the problem is military." Harkins agreed. He placed American officers and noncommissioned officers at every level in ARVN, where they planned and provided tactical advice for military operations. At the battalion level, advisers accompanied ARVN in the field.

In February 1962 two Vietnamese pilots attacked the Norodom Palace in strafing runs trying to kill Diem. He became so paranoid that he kept the best ARVN units near Saigon, where they could quickly suppress any uprising. But that left the countryside to the Vietcong. Harkins wanted ARVN to "take the war to the enemy," but Diem was terrified that losing battles or sustaining heavy casualties would create political discontent and undermine his regime. Nor was he much more enthusiastic about victories, which produced popular generals who might pose a political threat. Caution and conservatism infected ARVN at every level.

The military advisers on the ground, then, had much prodding and nagging to do. So did the 4400th created in April 1961 and nicknamed "Jungle Jim." Crew members trained Vietnamese pilots in tactical air support, dropped propaganda leaflets over Vietcong territory, and supplied ARVN outposts along the Cambodian and Laotian borders. When the Vietnamese pilots proved less than aggressive, American pilots began assuming greater initiative than had been allowed them at the beginning. By 1962 and 1963 they were flying combat missions on their own.

In 1961 the Marine Corps launched Operation Shufly. From bases at Soc Trang in the Mekong Delta and Danang along the northern coast of South Vietnam, marine helicopters carried ARVN troops into battle, while marine advisers instructed ARVN in amphibious assault tactics. But the real entrance of the navy and Marine Corps to Vietnam began with Victor Krulak's brainchild—Operation Plan 34-A, Oplan 34-A in Pentagonese.

For years the navy and marines had conducted clandestine "DeSoto Missions" against the Soviet Union, China, and North Korea—covert intelligence gathering by commando teams and naval vessels. Krulak thought that North Vietnam, with its long coastline, was perfect for even more aggressive activities. He wanted PT boats to attack radar sites in North Vietnam while Vietnamese, Chinese, Korean, and Filipino mercenaries blew up highways, bridges, and ammunition dumps, before being quickly extracted. The plan struck Kennedy's fancy: PT boats, commandos, blackened faces, frogmen, secrets, passwords, adventure. He approved Oplan 34-A on November 20, 1963, three days before his assassination. By mid-1963 the number of American military personnel in South Vietnam had approached 15,000 people.

The men, money, materiél, and training bore some fruit. By late 1962 ARVN forces totaled 210,000 troops augmented by 142,000 militia. Equipped with M-14 rifles and M113 armored personnel carriers, backed by tactical air support from Farmgate pilots, informed by good intelligence reports from the CIA and Special Forces, and enjoying MACV operational planning, some ARVN units—particularly the ARVN Airborne Division, the First Infantry, and the ARVN marines—began to attack the Vietcong. They even had some unexpected success in War Zone D north of Saigon, in the U Minh Forest on the Gulf of Thailand, and in the Plain of Reeds west of Saigon.

Harkins thought he was creating a killing machine, a mobile army force to do what George Patton's Third Army had done to the Germans in World War II. The word was "attrition," wearing down the Vietcong to the point at which they could not keep fighting. Harkins started adding up the numbers of combat operations, search-and-destroy missions, tactical air sorties (round-trip attacks run by one aircraft), bombing tonnages, weapons captured, ARVN troop increases, and weapons distributed to militia. By the end of 1962, the numbers looked good. "Every quantitative measurement we have shows we're winning this war," Robert McNamara assured the reporters at a press conference. The most important statistic of all was the "body count," the number of Vietcong killed. General Lyman Lemnitzer, chairman of the Joint Chiefs of Staff in 1960–1961, viewed the American mission as teaching ARVN "to kill Communists." One day in 1961 when Douglas Pike, a psychological operations officer with the United States Information Office in Saigon, remarked that the French had killed or wounded more than a million Vietminh, Lemnitzer had a simple answer: "Didn't kill enough then. We'll teach 'em to kill more."

Harkins also wanted to improve the morale of South Vietnamese peasants, strengthen their loyalty to Diem, and reduce their vulnerability to Vietcong recruiting. Counterinsurgency rested on two fundamental principles, both of which had evolved out of the experiences in the Philippines and Malaya and Rostow's theories about economic development. Peasants needed security against Vietcong attack; they needed to be able to go to sleep at night in peace. And when they awakened in the morning, they needed land, jobs, and schools with which they could build economic prosperity. People enjoying the good life would not fall prey to communistic rhetoric.

The American military arm of counterinsurgency in Vietnam was the Special Forces. During the 1950s the Michigan State University Advisory Group had launched economic development projects in South Vietnam, and the CIA formed local militias—Civilian Irregular Defense Groups among Montagnard tribesmen. Organized in 1952 to allow the army to fight covertly behind enemy lines, the First Special Forces Group had sent a few advisers into South Vietnam in 1957. But in 1961 they caught President Kennedy's fancy. An avid reader of Ian Fleming's "James Bond" novels, Kennedy was fascinated by the paraphernalia of espionage, covert action, double agents, and guerrilla war. Against the wishes of army brass, in 1961 he authorized the Special Forces to wear the Green Beret. He increased them from 2,500 to 10,000 men and sent the 5th and 7th Special Forces Groups to Vietnam. Late in 1962 the Green Berets took over CIDG training from the CIA.

While the Special Forces were replacing the CIDGs, and MACV was trying to get ARVN to fight its own war, Roger Hilsman and Robert Thompson were putting in motion the Strategic Hamlet Program. It was a new version of the older Agroville program. "Strategic hamlets" were peasant villages surrounded by barbed wire and mine fields. Inside the strategic hamlets there would be schools, a community center, a small hospital and pharmacy, and homes for the peasants. American pilots could then open fire on the Vietcong, who by definition were all the people outside the hamlets. Unable to hide, the Vietcong would be crushed by the killing machine. The job of building the strategic hamlets MACV turned over to Diem, who just as promptly turned it over to Nhu, who went about the construction process with a vengeance. By the end of the summer of 1962, Nhu claimed to have built 3,225 hamlets and placed 4.3 million peasants behind the barbed wire. Robert Thompson was appalled by Nhu's slipshod approach: "No attention was paid to their purpose. Their creation became the purpose itself."

Harkin's daily Headway Reports were contradicted by pessimistic dispatches from journalists in Saigon. For an independent look, Kennedy asked Senator Mike Mansfield of Montana to go to Saigon in December 1962. Mansfield, a devout Roman Catholic and former professor of Asian affairs, had been an early supporter of Ngo Dinh Diem. But in Saigon he received alarming information from the press corps, and he gave Kennedy a pessimistic report: "Vietnam, outside the cities, is still . . . run largely by the Vietcong. . . . Out of fear or indifference or hostility the peasants still withhold acquiescence, let alone approval of the [Saigon] government. . . . In short, it would be well to face the fact that we are once again at the beginning of the beginning." The report caught Kennedy off guard. He lashed out at Mansfield, accusing him of defeatism. When a reporter asked Kennedy whether Mansfield's opinion did not justify a withdrawal, Kennedy replied, "For us to withdraw would mean a collapse not only of South Vietnam but of Southeast Asia. So we are going to stay there." Mansfield was still gloomier with his congressional colleagues, to whom he declared that the war "could involve an expenditure of American lives and resources on a scale which would bear little relationship to the interests of the United States or, indeed, to the interests of the people of Vietnam."

Kennedy was growing more and more frustrated. He wanted out of Vietnam but did not know how. "I got angry with Mike for disagreeing with our policy so completely," he commented to one of his aides, "and I got angry with myself because I found myself agreeing with him." Still, he dreaded anything resembling the defeat at the Bay of Pigs. But he did not want the war to become a large-scale conflict. That was why Mansfield's report had been such a blow. The war was already costing a fortune, and, according to someone Kennedy trusted, the investment made no difference at all. Now, in 2006, we have the word of fifteen contemporaries that Kennedy hoped to withdraw after defeating the Republican Barry Goldwater in 1964.

Kennedy asked Roger Hilsman and Michael Forrestal, a White House Far Eastern affairs adviser, to evaluate the situation. They returned from Saigon in January 1963 with an optimistic report. Two weeks later Kennedy sent Victor Krulak and General Earle Wheeler, the army chief of staff, to Saigon. They castigated Mansfield and predicted early victory. All the heavy brass worried Harkins, so he issued his most optimistic prediction of all: Kennedy could withdraw 1,000 troops from South Vietnam at the end of 1963, and all the rest by the end of 1965.

But in 1963, as the general's statistical cloth began to unravel, North Vietnam brought nearly 13,000 infiltrators down the Ho Chi Minh Trail that bypassed the division between North and South Vietnam by going in Laos. In 1959 and 1960 it had sent 4,500 and in 1961 it added 6,300. From 3,000 people in 1960 to 10,000 in 1961 to 17,000 in 1962, the Main Force Vietcong now stood at 35,000. Most were former Vietminh, native southerners regrouped to North Vietnam after 1954. They were highly motivated, well trained, and anxious to go home. Secret intelligence reports indicated that the Vietcong were gaining strength, that they were fielding 600- to 700-man battalions supported by communications and engineering units, and that the 9th Vietcong Infantry Division would soon be ready for full deployment.

And they were well armed. Homemade shotguns and World War II vintage rifles were a thing of the past. Between early 1962 and mid-1963, MACV distributed more than 250,000 weapons to CIA and Special Forces irregular troops—M-14 carbines, shotguns, submachine guns, mortars, recoilless rifles, radios, and grenades. Most of them ended up with the Vietcong. Some ARVN outposts were particularly notorious for losing weapons. Americans called them "Vietcong PXs." The American cornucopia of death was so reliable that in mid-1963 Vietcong commanders relayed messages north that it was easier to capture American weapons than to bring Chinese and Soviet arms down the Ho Chi Minh Trail.

Nor were the Vietcong having any trouble finding recruits. The Strategic Hamlet Program was a bonanza for them. Within a matter of months the Diem regime herded millions of peasants into hastily constructed hamlets that were more concentration camps than villages. Peasants were forced to build the new hamlets, dig the huge, water-filled moats around them, string the barbed wire, and knock down their old homes. Millions of peasants left ancestral villages at gunpoint for the confinement of the strategic hamlets. The Vietcong used a simple response: "When the Diem regime falls and the Americans leave, you will be able to go home again." The peasants listened. The Vietcong also infiltrated the Strategic Hamlet Program. Nhu gave control of the program to Colonel Pham Ngoc Thao, who ruthlessly implemented it. What Nhu did not know was that Thao was a Vietcong agent. His instructions were to be brutal in building the strategic hamlets, to alienate as many peasants as possible. He was eminently successful. According to the historian Larry Cable, "The United States had about as much effective control over the . . . Strategic Hamlet Program, as a heroin addict has over his habit."

No less successful in lining up peasants behind the Vietcong was American air power. Between early 1961 and the end of 1962 air force personnel in South Vietnam increased from 250 to 2,000, and the number of monthly bombing sorties from 50 to more than 1,000. By the middle of 1963 the air force was conducting 1,500 sorties a month, dropping napalm, rockets, and heavy bombs and strafing the Vietcong. The problem, of course, was that air power was indiscriminate. Guerrillas died, to be sure, but so did peasants.

Between the bombing runs and the strategic hamlets, the Vietcong were able to recruit as many new soldiers as they could equip and supply. In 1960 main-force Vietcong soldiers had been supported by only 3,000 village and regional self-defense troops, but that number increased to more than 65,000 in late 1963. At the end of the year the communists had more than 100,000 troops—main force and militia—at their disposal.

More than anything else, the battle of Ap Bac in January 1963 exposed the limits of the American ability to control the fortunes of battle. Late in December 1962, two hundred troops from the Vietcong 514th Battalion dug in along a mile-long canal at the edge of the Plain of Reeds in Dinh Tuong Province, near the village of Ap Bac. Hidden by trees, shrubs, and tall grass, they had a clear view of the surrounding rice fields. When intelligence reports revealed the Vietcong, MACV felt it finally had an opportunity to engage the elusive enemy in a set-piece battle. More than 2,000 troops from the ARVN 7th Division, advised by Lieutenant Colonel John Paul Vann, went into battle. The operational plan was simple. Two ARVN battalions would approach from the north and south, while a company of M113 armored personnel carriers came in from the west. The eastern approaches would be left unguarded, so that if the Vietcong tried to escape, they would be destroyed by tactical air strikes and heavy artillery. In previous battles, the Vietcong had fled when they saw the M113s and CH-21 helicopters, but this time they held their positions. With small-arms fire they brought down five helicopters and nearly destroyed nine more, and they methodically killed the machine gunners on the M113s. ARVN troops refused to attack, and the ARVN command refused to reinforce them. The Vietcong escaped with twelve casualties, leaving behind two hundred dead or wounded ARVN troops and three dead American advisers.

The battle of Ap Bac had immediate repercussions. Neil Sheehan and David Halberstam were among the reporters who knew they had a story; after a year of Headway Reports, Ap Bac showed how the war was really going. The military tried, of course, to discredit the journalists. Admiral Harry Felt, commander of the United States Pacific fleet, went to Saigon after the battle and announced in a press conference: "I don't believe what I've been reading in the papers. As I understand it, it was a Vietnamese victory—not a defeat, as the papers say." Harkins nodded and agreed: "Yes, that's right. It was a Vietnamese victory. It certainly was." Robert McNamara's confident proclamation, "We have definitely turned the corner toward victory," was predictable. But the only people turning any corner were the Vietcong.

The eccentricities of Diem's coterie hastened the deterioration brought on by the Strategic Hamlet Program. The president's elder brother Ngo Dinh Thu, archbishop of Hue, used his political clout to augment church property. One critic charged that his requests for contributions "read like tax notices." He bought farms, businesses, urban real estate, rental property, and rubber plantations, and he employed ARVN troops on timber and construction concessions. Ngo Dinh Can, the dictator of Hue, accumulated a fortune as head of a smuggling syndicate that shipped huge loads of rice to Hanoi and large volumes of opium throughout Asia. Ngo Dinh Luyen, the South Vietnamese ambassador in London, became a multimillionaire speculating in piasters and pounds using insider information gleaned from his brothers in Saigon. More bizarre still were the antics of Ngo Dinh Nhu. By 1963 Nhu was smoking opium every day. His ambition had long since turned into a megalomania symbolized by the Personalist Labor Revolutionary party, or Can Lao—secret police known for torture and assassination. Can Lao troops, complete with Nazi-like goose-step marches and stiff-armed salutes, enforced Nhu's will. Madame Nhu had her own stormtroopers, a group known as the Women's Solidarity Movement and Paramilitary Girls, which worked at stamping out evil: dancing, card playing, prostitution, divorce, and gambling. The Nhus amassed a fortune running numbers and lottery rackets, manipulating currency, and extorting money from Saigon businesses, promising "protection" in exchange for contributions. After reading a CIA report on the shenanigans, President Kennedy slammed the document down on his desk and shouted, "Those damned sons of bitches."

President Diem's peculiarities were fast becoming derangements. He was addicted to eighteen-hour work days and then left paperwork at the side of his cot to attend to when he woke up in the night to go to the bathroom. His mind locked into its own private world, he was afraid to leave business to others and assumed more and more duties, even personally approving all visa requests and deciding which streets got traffic lights. He gave military orders as well, not just to divisions and battalions but to companies, often not keeping their commanding officers informed of his decisions. In discussions with foreign journalists and American officials, Diem offered mind-numbing monologues of five, six, even ten hours. Visitors could not get in a single comment. Charles Mohr saved his questions for when Diem was lighting another cigarette; those were the only occasions he stopped talking. As Robert Shaplen of

The New Yorker observed of those interviews, Diem's "face seemed to be focused on something beyond me. . . . The result was an eerie feeling that I was listening to a monologue delivered at some other time and in some other place—perhaps by a character in an allegorical play." South Vietnam was a dictatorship: Dissidents were imprisoned, tortured, or killed; elections were manipulated; the press, radio, and television were controlled; and universities were treated as vehicles for government propaganda.

The national holiday on October 26, 1962, celebrating the triumphant Diem elections in 1955, exposed the depth of Diem's isolation. He staged an elaborate military parade through Saigon. ARVN troops and armored personnel carriers left the field late in September to get ready for the parade, much to the dismay of American advisers fighting the Vietcong. Diem invited a few members of the press corps and some foreign diplomats to join him on the stand. The parade proceeded uneventfully, except for one bizarre fact: Diem sealed off from the public the entire parade route and several city blocks. The parade wound its way along the Saigon River with no spectators, only vacant sidewalks. ARVN troops and Nhu's secret police forced store owners to close up shop and leave their buildings. Diem wanted no contact with his people. For David Halberstam the parade was a surrealistic experience: "One felt as if he were watching a movie company filming a scene about an imaginary country."

Resentment had long smoldered among the Buddhists who saw power, land, government jobs, and money flow to the Roman Catholics. The Buddhist political movement was led by Thich Tri Quang, an intensely nationalist monk who headed the militant United Buddhist church. Although he was not a communist, Quang had cooperated with the Vietminh in fighting the French and the Japanese. What Thich Tri Quang was able to exploit, in the name of civil liberties, was a widespread popular desire in many parts of South Vietnam to overthrow Diem, expel the United States, and restore Vietnam to its traditional moral values.

Pent-up feelings exploded on May 8, 1963, the 2,587th birthday of Gautama Buddha. Diem prohibited Buddhists from flying their religious flags during the holiday. More than 1,000 Buddhist protesters gathered at the radio station in Hue demanding revocation of the order. When they refused to disperse, ARVN troops opened fire, killing eight people and wounding dozens more. The next day 10,000 Buddhists showed up demanding an apology, repudiation of the antiflag regulation, and payments to the families of the wounded and the dead. Buddhist hunger strikes spread throughout the country, and demonstrators walked the streets in Saigon. Late in May, Ngo Dinh Can imposed martial law on Hue and patrolled the streets with armored personnel carriers, tanks, and ARVN troops. In Saigon, Ngo Dinh Nhu's police assaulted Buddhist crowds with attack dogs and tear gas. Mandarin leaders expect obedience, not argument resolved by compromise.

On June 11, 1963, Thich Quang Duc, a seventy-three-year-old Buddhist monk, knelt on Pham Dinh Phung street in Saigon, surrounded by Buddhist monks, nuns, and invited journalists. A colleague doused him with five gallons of gasoline, and Duc lit a match and ignited himself, burning to death in protest of the Diem regime. The picture of his motionless body burning for ten minutes spread across the world wire services. A series of Buddhist torch suicides came in rapid succession. Madame Nhu remarked that she would be "willing to provide the gasoline for the next barbecue."

Throughout July, Ambassador Frederick Nolting pleaded with Diem to reach some accommodation with the Buddhists. Kennedy threatened to cut off economic and military assistance unless Diem acquiesced, but Diem, stiffened by Nhu's fanatical opposition to American pressure, became more intractable. Many noncommunist South Vietnamese resented the American presence in their country, and Diem had to be careful about appearing to cave in to American pressure. In Vietnamese history, appearing as a puppet to a foreign power was political suicide. If Diem backed down, he might lose what little political support he still had.

So the assault on the Buddhists continued. Late in July, Nhu's goon squads, many of them dressed in ARVN uniforms, placed barbed wire around hundreds of Buddhist pagodas and arrested Buddhist leaders. Two weeks later they invaded the pagodas and dispersed all meetings there. In Hue they killed thirty worshipers and wounded two hundred

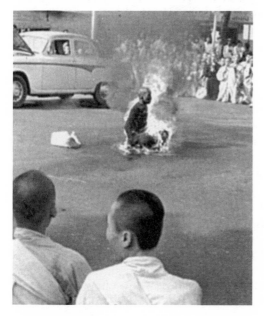

Quang Duc, an elderly Buddhist priest, immolates himself in protest against the Diem regime's religious persecution. (*Courtesy, National Archives.*)

more at the Dieu De Pagoda. Diem arrested children for carrying anti-government signs and closed schools. By mid-August he had jailed more than a thousand adolescents. Finally, on August 20 he imposed martial law throughout the country. The madness precipitated an intense debate in Washington. Harkins and Nolting insisted that the war was going well and that victory was still within reach. Maxwell Taylor, Robert McNamara, Walt Rostow, and Dean Rusk agreed. But Senator Mike Mansfield insisted that defeat, not victory, was just around the corner. At a meeting of the National Security Council on August 31, Paul Kattenburg, a State Department official who headed the Interdepartmental Working Group on Vietnam, suggested that the United States should "get out while the getting is good." Unfortunately for Kattenburg, his boss was at the meeting. "We will not," Dean Rusk insisted, "pull out until the war is won." Kattenburg kept his mouth shut, but his State Department career was over. Rusk posted him to Guyana.

It was clear to everyone in the administration, even the optimists, that it was time for a change. Frederick Nolting had to go. An aristocrat Virginian, Nolting sympathized with the Ngo family. But who would replace him? The new United States ambassador to South Vietnam needed Asian experience, but at the same time he had to be independent of the military. The inner circles at the White House discussed the matter at length during the summer of 1963, and Dean Rusk stunned everyone by suggesting Henry Cabot Lodge, Jr. The mere mention of Lodge's name was practically sacrilege. If the Kennedys bled Irish green, Lodge was the bluest of the blue bloods, a North Shore Yankee Republican of Massachusetts ancestry going back three hundred years. The Kennedys had long resented Boston Brahmins who disdained the famine-stricken Irish immigrants. Kennedy's defeat of Lodge for the Senate seat in 1952 had been gratifying, and in 1960 Lodge was Richard Nixon's running mate. On the night Lodge accepted the Republican vice-presidential nomination, Kennedy watched Nixon and Lodge raise their clenched hands on television. "That's the last Nixon will see of Lodge," he remarked to Kenny O'Donnell, his close friend and aide. "If Nixon ever tries to visit the Lodges at Beverly, they won't let him in the door."

The more Kennedy thought about Rusk's suggestion, the more he liked it. Fluent in French, Lodge had a Harvard education and a lifetime of experience. As a three-time United States senator and former ambassador to the United Nations, Lodge would not kowtow to anyone. And his gilt-edged Republican credentials might deflect some of the right-wing criticism of the administration. There was one final, mean little twist to the Lodge appointment, summed up in O'Donnell's later comment: "the idea of getting Lodge mixed up in such a hopeless mess as the one in Vietnam was irresistible."

It took Lodge a few days in Saigon to realize what a hopeless mess it was. In a cable of August 28 to President Kennedy, Lodge said that the United States was "launched on a course from which there is no respectable turning back: the overthrow of the Diem government. . . . There is no possibility that the war can be won under a Diem administration. The chance of bringing off a generals' coup depends on them to some extent. . . . We should proceed to make an all-out effort to get the generals to move promptly."

Kennedy wanted an independent assessment of how the war was going. On September 6 he asked Victor Krulak to take another look. He also sent Joseph Mendenhall, a career diplomat who had spent three years in Saigon. Both men made whirlwind trips, returning to the White House at about the same time on September 10. Krulak had met with Harkins and Lodge and a variety of MACV officials. Mendenhall spent his time with lower-echelon embassy officials and journalists. Krulak reported to Kennedy that the war was being won and that he could begin the promised withdrawal of 1,000 troops by the end of the year. Mendenhall announced that the Vietcong were getting stronger, that a religious civil war between Buddhists and Catholics was imminent, that the Diem regime had lost even the little credibility it once enjoyed, and that a communist victory was certain. Incredulous, Kennedy remarked at the end of their joint briefing, "You two did visit the same country, didn't you?"

Two weeks later, Kennedy sent Maxwell Taylor and Robert McNamara to Saigon. By that time peasants were leaving the strategic hamlets in droves, and the Vietcong were cutting up the barbed wire and using it in mines. The Vietcong were now fielding more than 35,000 troops and another 65,000 people in support services. Taylor and McNamara listened to Harkins and came back with the great promise "that the military campaign has made great progress and continues to progress" in spite of "serious political tensions in Saigon." By the end of 1965, they astonishingly said, "It should be possible to withdraw the bulk of U.S. personnel."

When he was in Saigon, Maxwell Taylor arranged a tennis match with General Duong Van Minh to feel him out about the possibilities of a coup. Taylor tried delicately to broach the issue, but a suspicious Minh kept his own counsel, preferring to talk only about forehands and backhands. But he had a view of the war, and it was glum: "more of the population on their side than has the GVN [Diem regime]" and the "heart of the Army is not in the war." Lodge distanced himself from Diem and Nhu, and it did not take long for them to realize that the United States was seeking their removal. South Vietnamese military leaders were worried that a frustrated United States might cut off military aid. General Tran Van Don, ARVN chief of staff, was aware of Maxwell Taylor's approach to Duong Van Minh, and he let Lucien Conein know that coup plans were under way. French-born but American-raised, Conein had spent World War II in France as an OSS agent. He was now a CIA agent in Saigon with powerful ARVN connections. He informed Tran Van Don that the United States wanted a new military government. The plotting started.

Diem and Nhu got wind of the plan and hatched a scheme of their own. Known as Operation Bravo, it involved staging a fake revolt in Saigon, complete with demonstrations, assassinations of prominent politicians—including Minh, Tran, Conein, and Lodge—orchestrated "revolutionary broadcasts" over Saigon radio, and the flight of Diem and Nhu to secret headquarters in the countryside. Once the chaos seemed at its peak, they would reenter Saigon with a column of ARVN troops commanded by their trusted military adviser General Ton That Dinh. They would then crush the "rebellion" and "save" South Vietnam. What they did not know was that Ton That Dinh was part of the conspiracy. On November 1, 1963, the two brothers realized that Operation Bravo was not to be, and they fled to Cholon. The brothers talked with several supporters and decided to give in. Diem telephoned staff headquarters and said that he was ready to surrender with "military honors." The surrender, the rebel leaders informed him, would be unconditional, but they promised him safety.

Minh dispatched two jeeps and an armored personnel carrier. Among the men on the mission was Minh's bodyguard, Captain Nhung, a professional assassin who notched his pistol after each killing. As the convoy set off, Minh gave Nhung a prearranged signal. In office or out, Diem and Nhu were powerful men whose craftiness and base of support commanded respect and honest fear. Such men, several rebels agreed, were best dead. "To kill weeds," one of them said, "you must pull them out by their roots." And Captain Nhung was an expert at this sort of gardening. Diem and Nhu surrendered, and rebels put them in the personnel carrier. Both men's hands were tied. The convoy then headed for the rebel headquarters. Captain Nhung rode with the brothers. When the vehicles arrived at Joint General Staff headquarters, Diem and Nhu were dead. Both had been shot. Nhu had also been stabbed several times, Nhung told Minh. Archbishop Ngo Dinh Thuc fled to Rome. Ngo Dinh Can was arrested in Hue and executed in Saigon. Madame Nhu escaped the bloodbath only because she was in the United States. When news of the assassinations became public, celebrations erupted in the streets of Saigon.

Although Lodge had not planned on the assassinations, they did not disturb him. The rebels told him that Nhu and Diem had died of "accidental suicide." To David Halberstam, Lodge remarked: "What would we have done with them had they lived? Every Colonel Blimp in the world would have made use of them." Minh was of like mind. "Diem could not be allowed to live because he was too much respected among simple, gullible people in the countryside, especially the Catholics and the refugees. We had to kill Nhu because he was so widely feared—and he had created organizations that were arms of his personal power."

When Kennedy got the news, he was profoundly disappointed. During his administration the United States had spent nearly $1 billion in South Vietnam, increased the number of American military advisers to more than 16,000, and had 108 United States soldiers killed there. But the Vietcong were stronger than ever. "Two weeks after the coup, Kennedy instructed Michael Forrestal to begin a "complete and very profound review of how we got into this country, what we thought we were doing, and what we now think we can do. . . . I even want to think about whether or not we should be there." Kennedy never got a chance to see the report. On November 22, 1963, he was assassinated in Dallas. Lyndon Johnson became president. A few days after the funeral, Johnson sent a memo to all State Department officials: "Before you go to bed at night I want you to do one thing for me: ask yourself this one question . . . what have I done for Vietnam today?"

Up to this point, almost the whole of the serious discussion of Vietnam had been within the administration. Few Americans had any idea of what their country was doing. In movies and television, combat was set in World War II: *12 O'Clock High,* a tale of an Army Air Corps bomber group in England; *The Wackiest Ship in the Army,* a comedy in a Pacific setting; *Combat,* which tells the story of a World War II army platoon; *Convoy,* which portrays the navy during the battle of the Atlantic; *Mr. Roberts,* featuring a naval officer; *McHale's Navy,* a slapstick comedy set in the South Pacific; *Hogan's Heroes,* a comedy set in a German prisoner-of-war camp. All of these, even the comedies, were extremely promilitary. The screwups of *McHale's Navy* and *Hogan's Heroes* can still outfight and outthink the enemy, even if in some highly unorthodox ways. When popular culture in the form of comic books did take note of Vietnam, it was even less helpful. In July 1962 Dell Publishing Company began producing its *Jungle War Stories.* Communist forces, inspired by the Soviet Union and Red China, are undermining the government of South Vietnam as part of a global conspiracy to conquer the world. The Vietcong are bloodthirsty sadists who torture and kill the innocent civilians of South Vietnam. The Green Berets are men of military prowess, humanitarianism, and leadership who help the South Vietnamese defend themselves against the communist juggernaut.

As yet, critics of the war had been few. A. J. Muste, one of the nation's veteran pacifists, headed the Fellowship of Reconciliation during the 1950s and early 1960s. Established in 1914 during World War I, FOR had long been the most influential pacifist group in Great Britain and the United States. Late in 1962 Muste began warning Americans about the war. The War Resisters League was even more active. Founded in 1923 as a secular pacifist organization, the WRL had opposed American involvement in World War II and the Korean War. By early 1963, under the leadership of David Dellinger, the WRL focused its protests on the expanding American military advisement effort in Vietnam. Except for these isolated voices, the Kennedy administration's Vietnam policy was virtually unopposed. Johnson was not to be so fortunate.

Planning a T
1963–1965

*It is fashionable in some (
in Southeast Asia are pri
rather than military. I do
problem is military.*

room and the shape of the
grandfather died at the
ancestor—the one who
San Jacinto. Johnso
arranged to have
dreds of copies
his biographe
only attem
ensure th
a riddl
is

Lyndon Baines Johnson was the Lon Chaney of American politics.
as Chaney, the man with a thousand faces, could play any film role, Johnson could play any political role. He could be all things to all people.
Always friendly, always ready to smile and flatter, never afraid to show
affection or to express his love, Johnson was almost irresistible. He believed that the intellectuals who criticized him simply did not understand him. He said they

> never take the time to think about what really goes on in these one-to-one
> sessions because they've never been involved in persuading anyone to do
> anything. They're just like a pack of nuns who've convinced themselves that
> sex is dirty and ugly and low-downed and forced because *they* never have it.
> And because they never have it, they see it all as rape instead of seduction
> and they miss the elaborate preparation that goes on before the act is
> finally done.

But who was the real Lyndon Johnson? Was he the conservative oil-
and-gas man? Certainly other conservative oil-and-gas men believed
that Lyndon was their boy in Washington, and they provided the dollars
that fueled his political career. Or was he a good Texas populist as his
father had been? Or perhaps he was a New Deal liberal Democrat. Perhaps he himself was not sure who he was. All his life he seemed bent on
creating a past for himself. He lied about his birth, his parents, his grandparents, his education, and his loves. He claimed that his great-great-
grandfather had died defending the Alamo. When a reporter pointed out
to him that none of his relatives had fought at the Alamo, Johnson ex-
claimed: "God damn it, why must all those journalists be such sticklers
for detail? Why, they'd hold you to an accurate description of the first
time you ever made love, expecting you to remember the color of the

indows. . . . The fact is that my great-great-
attle of San Jacinto, not the Alamo." But that
had not died at the Alamo—had also not died at
advised correspondents to burn his letters. He
information about his college years cut out of hun-
of the Southwest State Teachers College yearbooks. As
Robert A. Caro writes, "In a sense, Lyndon Johnson not
ted to create, and leave for history, his own legend, but to
at it could never be disproven." So the real Lyndon Johnson is

hnson was born in 1908 in the Texas Hill Country, a hot, impover-
ed section of the state. His family was poor, but his mother came from
a once-prosperous family that had been financially ruined by a bad investment. In her mind, at least, she remained above the world of dirty men and coarse women who populated the Hill Country. And she told Lyndon that he too was meant for better things, that unlike his father—who was very much at home among the unlettered folk of the Pedernales—he had culture in his blood. He grew up torn between the world of his mother and that of his father. His father cussed and talked politics; his mother read and dreamed of a better life. Lyndon embraced his father's world. He mastered the crude Texas metaphors, drank, trafficked in power politics, and expressed distrust of ideas, books, and lofty education if not outright contempt for them.

At Southwest Texas State Teachers College, Johnson showed that to achieve power he was willing, even eager, to work tirelessly at the most thankless task. Quick to recognize who had power, he attached himself to the powerful, shamelessly flattered them, made himself indispensable to them. It was a formula that Johnson was to repeat endlessly during his life. At San Marcos, he sought out the school's president, Cecil Evans. Within a year he was determining who got campus jobs, the life-blood of many poor students. Control of campus jobs translated into power. And Johnson used the power to control campus politics. Nicknamed "Bull" (short for "Bullshit") Johnson because he told so many lies, Lyndon nevertheless made the tiny school his fiefdom. The acquisition of power, he would often say, was necessary before he could do "good works." Perhaps his ends were noble, but so often it seemed that Johnson's only end was more power.

After a brief stint in teaching, Johnson went to Washington as a secretary to Congressman Richard Kleberg. It was 1931, a bleak year in the capital, but Johnson was euphoric. He moved into the Dodge Hotel, where seventy-five other legislative secretaries lived, and studied the conduits of power. He roamed the halls asking questions. He haunted the bathroom seeking knowledge. On his first night at the hotel he took four separate showers because he wanted to meet and talk to the other secretaries. The next morning he walked to the bathroom five times at ten-minute intervals so that he could meet more people. He extracted from each conversation knowledge about the workings of Washington that he mentally cataloged and filed away for future reference. He read the Washington newspapers as well as the *New York Times* and the *Wall Street Journal*. He talked with elevator operators, cooks, and janitors. And he courted the legislators. He was deferential, full of "Yes, sir" and "No, sir," and his flattery knew no bounds. One acquaintance called Johnson a "professional son." No father could wish for more respect and consideration and love from a son than Johnson seemed to give.

Johnson courted several power brokers on Capitol Hill. Most important is that he snuggled in close to Sam Rayburn, whose sharp eyes seemed to see through everyone. Rayburn liked Lyndon—perhaps even understood him—and became an unmatched patron. He helped Johnson get appointed as the Texas director of the National Youth Administration. He also aided Johnson's successful bid for a vacant congressional seat in 1937. No constituency was better served by an elected official. Johnson wrestled free the federal money needed to build great dams that produced electricity. Because of Johnson, electric light replaced candles and prosperity overcame poverty in the Hill Country.

Politically, Johnson kept rising. As a member of a three-man committee sent by President Franklin D. Roosevelt to observe the progress of the war in the Pacific, he received a Silver Star from General Douglas MacArthur, himself very much a politician, after a plane carrying the congressman came under a Japanese attack. Losing his first bid for the Senate, he won a seat in his second try in 1948. In 1951 he became the Democratic whip of the Senate; in 1953, the Senate minority leader; in 1955, the majority leader. Each new position meant more power and new challenges. Each Johnson mastered with the skill of a political artist. Nobody did it better. And, of course, Johnson loved the power that came with success. One night in 1958, a bit tight and in a good mood, he put an arm around two Texas congressmen and boasted, "I'm one powerful sonofabitch." It was an understatement. Johnson was the powerful sonofabitch, and everything he did demonstrated that power. This was true even to the smallest detail. The telephone, for example, had replaced the sword and the pen as the symbol of power, and Johnson made sure he was often photographed using the telephone. "No gunman," remarks one historian, "ever held a Colt .44 so easily" as Johnson handled a telephone.

Of his staff and cabinet Johnson demanded loyalty above honesty, sincerity, and good advice. Johnson once declared: "I don't want loyalty. I want *loyalty*. I want him to kiss my ass in Macy's window at high noon and tell me it smells like roses. I want his pecker in my pocket." For the sake of debate Johnson was willing to listen to the other side, but he listened with open ears and a closed mind. After the discussion ended, he expected everyone to agree with his previously formulated ideas. Whoever did not succumb to his flattery and reasoning and listening got exiled.

Raised in a region just emerging from frontier conditions, Johnson had a macho view of life. There were strong men and weak men. To show weakness was worse than cowardly—it was unmanly. Johnson said of the Kennedys that they vacationed at that "female island"—Martha's Vineyard—and spoke with affected accents. No country could afford to be unmanly, especially in the face of a bully. Remembering Munich— and considering its "lesson" as a universal truth—Johnson remarked, "If you let a bully come into your front yard one day, the next day he will be up on your porch and the day after that he will rape your wife in your own bed." The statement is pure Johnson, concrete and packed with sexual metaphor. It breathes an obsession with honor and bravery, the need to defend home and family. On a personal level Johnson was warm, friendly, humorous, and very hard to resist. Before a large group or a television camera, he lost his charm. His manner and language stiffened; his sense of humor fled.

Johnson the consummate politician considered foreign affairs above politics. During the years when his power was the greatest in the Senate, he seldom opposed President Eisenhower on foreign policy issues. In such matters he believed fully in bipartisanship. "I want to make absolutely sure," Johnson said in 1953, "that the Communists don't play one branch of government against the other, or one party against the other as happened in the Korean War. . . . If you're in an airplane, and you're flying somewhere, you don't run to the cockpit and attack the pilot." When bipartisanship died in the Vietnam War, Johnson reacted with anger and pain. "Don't [the American people] realize," he asked an aide, "I'm the only President they've got?" He could not explain to the people that he *was* their only pilot. Working in the small universe of the United States Senate, he had learned everyone's likes and dislikes. A president cannot do that.

When he took the oath of office after Kennedy's assassination, Johnson was a cold warrior. For Johnson the Truman Doctrine, the Marshall Plan, the Berlin Airlift, the Korean War, and the Cuban missile crisis were formative events in American history, bespeaking a commitment to keep the rest of the world from taking the road to communism. He was a true believer. There really was a monolithic communist conspiracy stirring up aggression around the world. In South Vietnam the threat was the Vietcong, who were pawns in the hands of North Vietnam, a puppet of Moscow and Beijing. The United States was in Vietnam, Johnson said, "to join in the defense and protection of freedom of a brave people who are under attack that is controlled . . . and directed from outside their country."

For a while, that was the consensus among policymakers. Debate concerned tactics, not morality, questions of how, not why. Which weapons were appropriate; which was the more effective, conventional or counterinsurgency warfare; what would be the best use of air power; should the United States destroy the dike system in North Vietnam; should the stress be on victory, negotiation, or a reform of Vietnamese politics and society: Such issues divided legislators and administrators who shared the mindset of the times concerning power, virtue, technology, and the domino theory. Even the most serious critics of United States policy in Vietnam were preoccupied with the management of the war, not with its moral or intellectual foundations. While he was attacking American military leaders for their conduct of the war, David Halberstam of the *New York Times* wrote early in 1965: "Vietnam is a strategic country in the area. It is perhaps one of only five or six nations that is truly vital to U.S. interests." And Vietnam, so believed Congress and the administration, was vital to American credibility. In order to maintain NATO, SEATO, and its other engagements abroad, the nation had to prove itself periodically. To flee Vietnam might raise questions about the strength of the American dedication to the world struggle against communism. In the mid-1960s war was raging in Laos, and in Cambodia Prince Norodom Sihanouk proclaimed his neutrality in the cold war. Chinese talk of fomenting wars of national liberation was as harsh as ever. Riots against the United States erupted in Panama, and Fidel Castro threatened to export revolution throughout the Western Hemisphere. For the nation to maintain its global commitment to anticommunism, South Vietnam had to be saved. If South Vietnam fell to the communists, declared Dean Rusk, "Our guarantees with regard to Berlin would lose their credibility." It was, he said, "part of the same struggle."

Despite those fears, Johnson remained cautious. There were political risks in rapid escalation. If the United States intervened on a massive scale in South Vietnam, there would be an outpouring of criticism abroad as well as the possibility of serious opposition at home. Johnson had an ambitious program of antipoverty and civil rights legislation planned, and he did not want to undermine his political base in Congress. If the United States entered the war on a large scale, moreover, ARVN forces might cease to fight altogether. Like John Kennedy before him, Lyndon Johnson sought a middle road. But the war slowly escalated.

On February 1, 1964, the navy implemented Oplan 34-A, Victor Krulak's plan for secret missions against North Vietnamese coastal installations. In case the time came to bomb or invade North Vietnam, the United States would need precise information about coastal radar, radio installations, and antiaircraft sites. Squads of South Vietnamese commandos in American-made patrol boats conducted covert raids along the coast in order to activate North Vietnamese radar. United States intelligence-gathering vessels in the South China Sea then collected the necessary information. By the summer of 1964 American military advisers in South Vietnam had reached 20,000 men.

Operation Farmgate was also expanding. Because American pilots found the Vietnamese too cautious, they assumed more and more responsibility. By mid-1964 more than one hundred air force pilots were flying regular combat missions to support ARVN operations. Farmgate flights did not come to light until May 1964, when Captain Edwin G. Shank was shot down in his T-28 fighter. Shank had written a letter to his wife, claiming: "They won't tell you people what we do over here. I'll bet you that anyone you talk to does not know that American pilots fight this war. . . . [The Vietnamese] are stupid, ignorant, sacrificial lambs, and I have no use for them. . . . They're a menace to have on board." Shank's wife released the letter to the press, and it was published nationwide through the wire services.

The air force was building up its sortie count through Operation Ranch Hand as well. American advisers had long complained about the ability of the Vietcong to melt back into the jungles where they could not be located. As early as 1961, Walt Rostow and Robert McNamara learned that army chemists had developed new herbicides; the most powerful was Agent Orange. Here was a technological solution. If the jungle kept advisers and pilots from locating the enemy, then eliminate the jungle. In January 1962 the Kennedy administration had Air Force C-123 aircraft dump defoliants on selected areas of the Ca Mau Peninsula. In 1964 Johnson increased the Ranch Hand sorties. Using the motto "Only you can prevent forests," Ranch Hand pilots turned more than 100,000 acres of jungle and rice paddies into mud.

By that time the debate between policymakers who saw the war primarily in diplomatic or political terms and others who saw it as a military venture was coming to an end in Washington, and the militarists had the upper hand. That new consensus reflected itself in a number of important personnel changes. Roger Hilsman was the first to go. At the time, he was an assistant secretary of state for Far Eastern affairs and an advocate of the political, "hearts-and-minds" war. President Johnson took an immediate dislike to Hilsman. His close relationship with Robert F. Kennedy, whom Johnson loathed, was one strike against him, and strike two was his opposition to the hard-line approach of Maxwell Taylor and Walt Rostow. Strike three came at a dinner party when Johnson overheard Hilsman insult General Lyman Lemnitzer for losing control of the Vietnam situation in 1960 and 1961. When Hilsman got word that Johnson was about to fire him, he resigned. The president replaced him with William Bundy. The president also exiled W. Averell Harriman. During the Kennedy administration the old diplomat had made himself useful, negotiating the Laotian settlement and shuttling back and forth with messages from Washington. Like everyone else, Harriman did not want to see South Vietnam fall to communism, but he did not think the solution was on the battlefield. The only permanent settlement was political and diplomatic, a position he advocated insistently, much to the anger of Rostow, Rusk, McNamara, and Taylor. And because of Harriman's close ties to the Kennedys, Johnson did not "trust him to take out my garbage." Early in 1964 the president relieved Harriman of his Asian duties and assigned him, in Harriman's own words, "to the oblivion of African affairs."

Hilsman and Harriman were gone, and Henry Cabot Lodge, Jr., joined them. By the spring of 1964 Lodge believed that he had completed his assignment in South Vietnam. Lodge was preoccupied with politics at home. A moderate Republican, he worried about the shrill voices of "Barry Goldwater and the Neanderthals" in the GOP's right wing. He wanted to get back home in time for the presidential primaries, in which, he hoped, he could deny Goldwater the nomination. Lodge even flirted with the idea of a dark-horse candidacy of his own.

After some indecision, Johnson asked Maxwell Taylor to step down as chairman of the joint chiefs and take over the embassy in Saigon. Taylor preached escalation—enough American advisers, money, and air power to win the war. He was convinced that the United States must make the war too expensive for Hanoi to pursue and so bloody for the Vietcong that they could not replace their casualties. The North Vietnamese saw what was happening—the full militarization of the dispute over the future of Vietnam, the dispatching of a major American general to take control of a difficult situation. Vo Nguyen Giap wrote that the "appointment of Taylor to South Vietnam reminds us of such top French generals as De Tassigny and Navarre going to Indochina every time the French Expeditionary Corps was in serious difficulty. Our compatriots in the South and the heroic southern liberation troops . . . will certainly reserve for Taylor . . . the fate our people reserved for the former defeated French generals." History would repeat itself.

To take the place of Taylor, Johnson appointed the army general Earle G. Wheeler chairman of the Joint Chiefs of Staff. Wheeler's career had been spent in planning and logistics rather than in infantry combat, but he was known as a superb organizer and manager. As deputy chief of the nation's European command and then as army chief of staff in the early 1960s, Wheeler listened to the debate over the war, but he had few doubts. It was simply a matter of military strength. The United States should crush the Vietcong and the North Vietnamese.

When Taylor went to Saigon in 1964, Paul Harkins came home. He retired from the army when he realized that Wheeler was going to get the chairmanship of the joint chiefs. Johnson held a special ceremony at the White House for Harkins and decorated him, but the name "General Blimp" and the phrase "pulling a Harkins" followed him everywhere. He had proclaimed success too many times. Instead of victory, he left behind a quagmire of confusion and bitterness. Harkins's successor was General William C. Westmoreland. Westmoreland who had punched all the right tickets—West Point graduation in 1936, World War II combat in North Africa, Sicily, France, and Germany, postwar command of the 101st Airborne Division, superintendent of West Point, and secretary to Maxwell Taylor and the joint chiefs. Coming from a distinguished family in Spartanburg, South Carolina, Westmoreland looked every bit the southern gentleman-turned-soldier. He was six feet tall, but his ramrod posture, dark eyebrows, and white hair made him seem taller. A century earlier in Confederate gray, Westmoreland would have been a perfect compatriot for Stonewall Jackson or Robert E. Lee.

Westmoreland disagreed with proposals to bomb North Vietnam in the absence of a sizable force of American ground troops. Air bases needed protection from Vietcong attacks, and ARVN troops could not be trusted with the job. And if ARVN was tied up defending American air bases, it would not be in the field fighting the Vietcong. It was already hard enough to get South Vietnamese troops out there. The need for defensive perimeters around places like Bien Hoa and Danang would give ARVN commanders another excuse for staying put. ARVN was so laced with corruption and incompetence that it would take years of serious training before it was ready to take on the Vietcong. By that time the United States, with the application of enough firepower, could wipe out the Vietcong as a fighting force, leaving no enemy for ARVN to worry about. As for hearts and minds, Westmoreland looked with contempt on "rice paddy peasants" and believed they would gravitate naturally to whatever government exercised power. With the Vietcong gone, Saigon would be the only nationwide power to which they could turn. What Westmoreland wanted was American ground troops, as many as 200,000 of them. He planned to fight a defensive war for a year or so until he could build the infrastructure to support a major military effort. Once that infrastructure was in place, Westmoreland would unleash the American military on the communists. Through what Westmoreland called "search-and-destroy" missions, American infantry could aggressively seek out the enemy while artillery, armor, bombers, and gunships cut the foe to pieces. According to William DePuy, Westmoreland's chief of operations, "We are going to stomp them to death."

A major policy decision was imminent in Washington. ARVN desertions had reached epidemic levels, exceeding 6,000 people a month in 1964. Politically the Vietcong controlled up to 40 percent of the territory of South Vietnam and more than 50 percent of the people. Early in 1963 the Vietcong had 23,000 troops organized into a hodgepodge of undermanned battalions, companies, platoons, and squads. They also had another 50,000 local self-defense militia troops. By late 1964 all that had changed. Those 23,000 soldiers became 60,000 men organized into seventy-three battalions of six hundred men each. Of those seventy-three battalions, sixty-six were full infantry units and seven were heavy weapons and antiaircraft machine gun battalions. The battalions were organized into regiments complete with communications and engineering units. And behind those 60,000 troops were 40,000 people engaged in full-time support services. Another 100,000 village self-defense forces rounded out the communist order of battle. Vietminh veterans trained the Vietcong well, creating highly motivated soldiers, real "sledge hammer battalions" in the words of Neil Sheehan. Westmoreland was convinced that ARVN would be completely unable to deal with them. "The VC," he argued, "are destroying battalions faster than they were planned to be organized under the build-up program. . . . The only possible US response is the aggressive employment of US troops together with Vietnamese general reserve forces to react against strong VC/DRV [Vietcong and North Vietnam] attacks." Only the vaunted American killing machine could handle the Vietcong.

Most American policymakers believed that the revolt in South Vietnam was directly connected to its support base in North Vietnam and that the United States would have to take the war to Hanoi to achieve a complete victory. Maxwell Taylor, along with Walt Rostow, McGeorge Bundy, and Robert McNamara, called for expansion of the war north of the seventeenth parallel through strategic bombing. The idea was simple: Raise the pain level to the point at which North Vietnam could stand it no longer.

The Johnson administration's understanding of the connection between the war in South Vietnam and support in North Vietnam was quite accurate. Throughout the late 1950s and early 1960s politicians in North Vietnam had debated the question of how much assistance to send south. The debate was inextricably connected to the larger competition between Moscow and Beijing. Under Nikita Khrushchev, the Soviet Union in the early 1960s preached the gospel of peaceful coexistence. North Vietnamese politicians who wanted to focus on building up their own country, as well as military officials worried about a confrontation with the United States, used the Soviet ideology to advocate caution. Their leader was Truong Chinh, a moderate who served as the Marxist theorist in the Lao Dong party and always favored caution and negotiation. But most of the North Vietnamese leadership lacked the prudence of the USSR. So did Mao Zedong, who called for wars of national liberation to overthrow United States influence in the Third World. The bitter anti-American posture of the Chinese encouraged General Tran Van Tra, commander of Vietcong military forces in South Vietnam, together with Le Duan and others in Hanoi's hierarchy. They wanted a total commitment to destruction of the South Vietnamese regime, expulsion of the United States, and reunification of the country, regardless of the cost. When the Central Committee of the Lao Dong party met in Hanoi in December 1963 to evaluate the situation, the debate continued. If North Vietnam increased its support of the revolution in South Vietnam, it might alienate the Soviet Union and place itself in the Chinese camp, which no Vietnamese politician wanted to do.

But if North Vietnam did not support the Vietcong, it might never be able to get the United States out of Indochina. The debate continued into the next year. Finally, in a meeting on March 27-28, 1964, Ho Chi Minh called for a unified effort and whatever sacrifice was necessary to bring the revolution in South Vietnam to a successful conclusion. A week later North Vietnam began training northern-born Vietnamese for deployment south.

Robert McNamara was convinced that "current trends . . . will lead to neutralization at best and more likely to a Communist-controlled state." He wanted a "tit-for-tat" policy in which the United States made Hanoi suffer for any damage done by the Vietcong. Privately, Johnson referred to the policy as the "titty program." Johnson's advisers drafted plans for attacking North Vietnam. A leading figure in the development of those plans was McGeorge Bundy's older brother William. After graduation from Yale and the Harvard Law School and a stint with the CIA, William Bundy had become a deputy assistant secretary of defense in the Kennedy administration. On March 1, 1964, he proposed bombing North Vietnam and mining Haiphong harbor both to stop infiltration of supplies to the Vietcong and to demonstrate that the United States possessed the will to win. Later in the month McGeorge Bundy produced what became known as National Security Adviser Memorandum (NSAM) 288, providing for gradually escalated bombing of military and economic targets in North Vietnam, particularly in response to Vietcong attacks in South Vietnam. NSAM 288 also committed the United States to the survival of an independent noncommunist government in Saigon. It argued that the United States would have to increase its level of military and economic assistance and South Vietnam must prepare for a full-scale war. McGeorge Bundy warned that such military measures "would normally require a declaration of war under the Constitution. But this seems a blunt instrument carrying heavy domestic overtones and above all not suited to the picture of punitive and selective action only." Bundy urged the president to consider seeking a special congressional resolution supporting limited military action.

During April and May, the National Security Council, the Joint Chiefs of Staff, and MACV in Saigon developed what became known as Operations Plan 37-64. Its objective was "to conduct graduated operations to eliminate or reduce to negligible proportions DRV [Democratic Republic of Vietnam] support of VC [Vietcong] insurgency in the Republic of Vietnam." The plan involved three projects: military action in Cambodia and Laos to eliminate Vietcong sanctuaries; increased levels of Oplan 34-A attacks on North Vietnamese coastal installations; and South Vietnamese and American strategic bombing of ninety-eight preselected targets in North Vietnam. In his White House office, Walt Rostow, the "Air Marshall," taped a large map of North Vietnam on the wall and, with the help of econometric models, selected targets for the bombing runs.

Johnson decided that to deal with the problem on a political level, he would seek a joint congressional resolution "supporting United States policy in Southeast Asia." Such a resolution would give the administration carte blanche in Indochina, allowing aerial bombardment, intervention in Cambodia and Laos, or any other "tit-for-tat" response that could bring North Vietnam to the negotiating table. It was, in effect, a preemptive declaration of war. William Bundy drafted the resolution, and the administration waited for the right time to submit it to Congress. It did not have to wait long.

On August 1, 1964, the USS *Maddox,* an American destroyer, was patrolling within a range of ten to twenty miles off the North Vietnamese coast, collecting electronic data on North Vietnamese radar signals and ship movements. The ship was also monitoring four South Vietnamese gunboats, which the night before had left Danang and attacked North Vietnamese coastal sites as part of Oplan 34-A. North Vietnamese patrol boats approached the *Maddox.* The *Maddox* opened fire, and the patrol boats launched several torpedoes. Jets from the USS *Ticonderoga* attacked the North Vietnamese ships, damaging all of them. The next day the *Maddox* was joined by another destroyer, the USS *C. Turner Joy.* President Johnson ordered the ships to continue their patrols.

More South Vietnamese gunboats left Danang for Oplan 34-A attacks. On August 4 the *Maddox* and the *C. Turner Joy* picked up radio traffic from confused and enraged North Vietnamese naval vessels. Tension was running high on both the *Maddox* and the *Turner Joy.* Men on both ships saw blips on the radar they believed represented PT boats, and the sonar man on the *Maddox* reported underwater noises that he thought to be the sounds of incoming torpedoes. Both ships commenced evasive actions and began firing into the dark at the direction of the radar blips, although they made no visual sightings of North Vietnam-

August 1964—The U.S. Navy destroyer U.S.S. *Maddox* was attacked by torpedoes and gunfire off Vietnam in the Gulf of Tonkin. (*Courtesy, Library of Congress.*)

ats. Several hours later, Captain John Herrick, head of the
ion on board the *Maddox,* concluded that there had proba-
attack, that rough seas and atmospheric conditions could
ated spurious radar blips, and that the evasive movements of
ad created torpedolike sonar sounds. In a cable to the Pentagon, ..errick reported that conclusion. By the time Herrick sent the
cable it was too late. The Pentagon and White House became hornets'
nests, and Admiral Ulysses S. Grant Sharp, Jr., the commander of American naval forces in the Pacific, confirmed to Robert McNamara that a
"bona fide ambush has occurred." The evidence at the time as to whether
an attack had really occurred was contradictory, but the Johnson administration decided nonetheless to retaliate. Late that afternoon, the USS
Ticonderoga and the USS *Constellation* sent aircraft to attack torpedo
boat bases and oil storage facilities in North Vietnam. While the attack
was going on, Johnson spoke live over all three television networks:
"Aggression by terror against peaceful villages of South Vietnam," he
said, "has now been joined by open aggression on the high seas against
the United States of America." He reassured the country: "We know,
although others appear to forget, the risks of spreading conflict. We seek
no wider war."

The next day Johnson met with congressional leaders to explain the
air strike and seek their support for the joint resolution William Bundy
had drafted. At the meeting Senator Mike Mansfield reminded Johnson
of his longstanding opposition to American military involvement in Indochina. Johnson asked Senator William Fulbright, an Arkansas Democrat,
to serve as floor manager for the resolution. An old friend and veteran of
many Senate battles, Fulbright agreed. Senator George Aiken, a Republican from Vermont, did not like the resolution and told Johnson, "By the
time you send it up, there won't be anything for us to do but support you."
He saw the measure as open-ended permission for Johnson to wage war
without a formal declaration. But Johnson gave Mansfield and Aiken
what other senators called the "full Johnson"— his arm tightly around
their shoulders, his face nose-to-nose with theirs, and his voice pleading,
cajoling, begging, whining, promising, and threatening. Before the meeting ended, they agreed to support the resolution.

At a joint session of the Senate Armed Services and Foreign Relations
committees, Senator Wayne Morse, the renegade Democrat from Oregon,
wanted to know whether the United States had provoked the North
Vietnamese patrol boat attack. Robert McNamara assured him that the
"navy played absolutely no part in, was not associated with, was not
aware of any South Vietnamese actions, if there were any. . . . This is the
fact." It was, of course, a bald-faced lie. On August 7 the administration
submitted to Congress the resolution Bundy had written. Its wording
was simple and direct, with enormous potential consequences:

The congress . . . supports the determination of the President . . . to take all necessary measures to repel any armed attack against the armed forces of the United States and to prevent further aggression. . . . The United States is, therefore, prepared, as the President determines, to take all necessary steps, including the use of armed force, to assist any member or protocol state of the Southeast Asia Collective Defense treaty requesting assistance in defense of its freedom.

The House of Representatives passed the resolution by voice vote, but a debate developed in the Senate. George McGovern of South Dakota declared that he did not wish his vote for the resolution "to be interpreted as an endorsement of our long-standing and apparently growing military involvement in Vietnam." Daniel Brewster of Maryland worried that the resolution might "authorize or recommend or approve the landing of American armies in Vietnam or in China." The strongest opposition came from Morse and Alaska's Ernest Gruening. Back in 1954, when John Foster Dulles tried to drum up support for the French, Morse had resisted, asking: "What is it we are going to fight for and to defend? I am a Senator and I don't know." Before the floor debate someone in the Pentagon tipped Morse off that DeSoto Missions and Oplan 34-A operations had probably inspired the first attack and that the report of a second attack was questionable. Morse argued that the place to settle the issue "is not by way of the proposed predated declaration of war, giving to the President the power to make war without a declaration of war." Gruening, a liberal Democrat, called the resolution "a predated declaration of war." In March he had warned on the Senate floor: "All Vietnam is not worth the life of a single American boy. . . . [The United States] is seeking vainly in this remote jungle to shore up self-serving corrupt dynasties or their self-imposed successors, and a people that has demonstrated that it has no will to save itself." But a chorus of approval drowned Morse and Gruening. The Senate passed the resolution eighty-eight to two. Later that day Morse predicted, "History will record that we have made a great mistake." When he heard of his congressional victory, Johnson laughed and told an aide that the wording of the resolution "was like Grandma's nightshirt. It covers everything."

The Gulf of Tonkin Resolution, in the short run at least, was a stroke of political genius. The president's standing in public opinion polls soared. More than anything else, the president wanted to be elected that year in his own right, to occupy the White House on his own merits, not on John F. Kennedy's. He wanted to project the image of a wise, thoughtful, and decisive leader, a balance between toughness and moderation. To most Americans, so it seems, the bombing raids on North Vietnam, followed by the president's stated willingness to go to the negotiating-table, so defined him. Later, when doubts mounted about what had actually happened in the Gulf of Tonkin, Johnson remarked to an associate, "Those dumb stupid sailors were probably shooting at flying fish."

Three weeks before the Gulf of Tonkin incident, the Republicans had nominated Senator Barry Goldwater of Arizona for president. In his acceptance speech, Goldwater announced that the nation should no longer "cringe before the bullying of Communism. . . . Failures cement the wall of shame in Berlin. Failures blot the sands of shame at the Bay of Pigs. Failures mark the slow death of freedom in Laos. Failures infest the jungles of Vietnam." Johnson's decision to bomb North Vietnam stole Goldwater's thunder, transforming a foreign policy liability for Johnson into a political asset.

Goldwater was a man of strong opinions and brutal honesty. Convinced that the United States was soft on communism abroad and drifting down the road to socialism at home, he preached against the welfare state, Social Security, the Nuclear Test Ban Treaty of 1963, the Laotian settlement of 1962, and any rapprochement with the Soviet Union and China. Johnson understood that Americans had vivid memories of the Great Depression and the New Deal and resented neither the welfare state nor Social Security. He also realized that most Americans feared nuclear weapons and that Goldwater's saber rattling scared them. In the presidential campaign, Johnson went after Goldwater's most vulnerable points. Proclaiming the coming of the "Great Society," the president campaigned for expansion of Social Security and Medicare, creation of job-training programs, a "War on Poverty," and civil rights legislation. Johnson's message had wide appeal: Every American deserved to be treated equally and to enjoy basic economic opportunity. Goldwater criticized government spending, large deficits, high taxes, and bureaucratic waste, but most Americans were not interested. On foreign policy, the Democrats ruthlessly attacked Goldwater, portraying Johnson as a wise, temperate leader and Goldwater as an extremist, an "unguided missile." In a late September rally in Eufaula, Oklahoma, Johnson on Vietnam struck what sounded like just the right course: "We don't want our American boys to do the fighting for Asian boys. . . . But we are not about to start another war and we're not about to run away from where we are." The Johnson campaign produced several nasty television commercials. The "Daisy Girl" spot showed a little girl plucking flower petals and counting them until a deep male voice smothers hers with a missile countdown, followed by detonation and the nuclear mushroom cloud, all of this with a promise that President Lyndon Johnson would not get the country involved in a nuclear war. Goldwater's slogan "In your heart you know he's right" the Democrats transformed to "In your heart you know he might."

But three developments were propelling the United States toward war: the instability of the South Vietnamese government, the increasing aggressiveness of the Vietcong, and the dramatic escalation of North Vietnamese transfers of troops and supplies into South Vietnam.

Nicknamed for his six-foot height, uncommon among Vietnamese, Duong Van ("Big") Minh was in control of the government after overseeing the assassination of Ngo Dinh Diem and Ngo Dinh Nhu. He had been trained in the French colonial army and was responsible for crushing the Binh Xuyen in 1955. Minh replaced the Diem government with a Military Revolutionary Council, of which he served as chairman. He repealed Madame Nhu's morality legislation and released most of Diem's political prisoners incarcerated at Poulo Condore. His closest associates on the council were Tran Van Don and Le Van Kim. Tran Van Don was born in France in 1917, served with the French army in World War II, and joined the Vietnamese National Army in 1951. He rose to become a commander of I Corps, the northern military district of South Vietnam. Le Van Kim, commandant of the National Military Academy, had spent years in Paris with the French police and came back home to join the Vietnamese National Army. Don and Kim were French citizens, and like Duong Van Minh they were Roman Catholics. From the very beginning, Minh, Don, and Kim faced repeated plots to overthrow them, some coming from their own military subordinates and others from the Buddhist majority. The change in rule was to initiate a series of governments by members of the old elite with French educations, hardly different from Diem, while Buddhist factions struggled for power, hostility between Catholics and Buddhists worsened, and student protest against political and social injustice grew.

On January 29, 1964, after only three months in office, the South Vietnamese government collapsed. Nguyen Khanh, a thirty-six-year-old ARVN officer whose baby fat appearance contrasted to a tiny goatee, carried out a bloodless coup that pleased the Johnson administration. Washington hoped that Khanh's strong-arm, one-man rule would be more decisive than Minh's rule by committee and that Khanh's Buddhist faith would mute the antigovernment movement among the Buddhist clergy. Johnson called Khanh "my American boy." Cursed with a paranoia matched only by that of Diem, Khanh inclined toward not government but intrigue. More than once he called for a "March to the North," a farfetched mass popular invasion of North Vietnam. When American bombers attacked North Vietnam after the Gulf of Tonkin incidents, Khanh was euphoric. Anticipating full war, he declared martial law on August 7 and banned freedom of speech, press, and assembly. Two weeks later Khanh issued the infamous Vung Tau Charter, a constitution he wrote overnight declaring himself president and dictator of the Republic of Vietnam. The reaction was swift. Buddhists and students took to the streets protesting Khanh's government. At one point an enraged mob surrounded Khanh on a Saigon street and forced him to climb up on a tank and shout "Down with dictatorships!" At the end of the month he backed down, losing face and credibility among the people he needed the most—his own generals.

The scheming and plotting commenced once again, and early in September, Khanh brought Big Minh back into power, along with Tran Thien Kheim, ARVN chief of staff. Together they ruled Vietnam as a triumvirate for two weeks until General Lam Van Phat overthrew Khanh. The United States managed to restore the triumvirate to power a few days later. At the end of October, Khanh established the High National Council, representing a variety of political groups, to draft a new constitution. It was ready on October 20, and Khanh voluntarily stepped down in favor of a civilian government headed by Phan Khac Suu, a devout Cao Daist who had opposed the French, the Vietminh, and Diem. For prime minister Suu appointed Tran Van Huong, a former schoolteacher and Vietminh soldier. Maxwell Taylor said he was "glad to get rid of that troublemaker Khanh."

The new civilian government was no more successful than its military predecessors. Plotting and conspiracies were endemic, and Nguyen Khanh yearned for power again. In December Khanh, supported by a number of young military officers including Nguyen Cao Ky and Nguyen Van Thieu, dissolved the High National Council and replaced it with the Armed Forces Council. Three weeks later the Armed Forces Council dissolved the civilian government, ousted Tran Van Huong, and ordered Khanh to form a new government. Khanh kept Phan Khac Suu as chief of state and named Nguyen Xuan Oanh as prime minister. George Ball called it the "Government of the Week Sideshow" in Saigon. The president was, as usual, the most blunt, telling anyone who would listen, "I'm sick and tired of this coup shit."

Vietcong tactics that were drawing the United States toward war, however, made Johnson sicker. Up to then, most American advisers killed had fallen in combat operations accompanying ARVN. Far more common were Vietcong tricks at American installations, which guerrillas infiltrated at night, leaving behind Vietcong flags or painting messages on the wall letting the Americans know that they were not safe. Still hoping that the United States would eventually see their side of the war, the Vietcong had been loath to alienate American policymakers by killing American soldiers. But after the Gulf of Tonkin and the American bombing raids on North Vietnam, Vietcong tactics changed. Intentional attacks on Americans increased steeply. On November 1, 1964, several sampans moved up a stream near the American air base at Bien Hoa and dropped off mortar-carrying guerrillas. They set up several 81-mm mortars and shelled the base, killing four Americans, wounding seventy-two more, and destroying or damaging thirteen B-57 light bombers. Almost as soon as the attack started it was over. The Vietcong got back on the sampans and drifted away downstream.

Maxwell Taylor recognized the attack for what it was, a dramatic shift in Vietcong tactics, and he believed that Ho Chi Minh was orchestrating it all. Taylor cabled Johnson that the assault "is a deliberate act of escalation and a change in the ground rules. . . . It should be met promptly by an appropriate act of reprisal against a DRV target. . . . The ultimate objective should be to convince Hanoi to cease aid to the VC (and not merely lay off us)." But with the presidential election just two days away, Johnson was being careful. He asked William Bundy to draft a policy response. On November 3, Johnson defeated Goldwater by a landslide, taking 61 percent of the popular vote and 486 of the 540 electoral votes. That same day Bundy offered three options to Johnson, including widespread bombing of North Vietnam, but the president ultimately decided to continue the existing policy of "tit-for-tat" in response to Vietcong and North Vietnamese attacks in South Vietnam.

Most Americans had not noticed the increased number of American military advisers being deployed to South Vietnam. Opposition to the war was still confined to vocal elements of the peace movement. David Dellinger and A. J. Muste, leaders of the War Resisters League (WRL), had been calling for de-escalation of the war in Vietnam since early 1963. In the pages of *Liberation,* an influential radical magazine supported by the WRL, they asked the American people to take a careful look at what was happening in Southeast Asia. In the spring of 1964, when President Johnson dispatched several thousand more military advisers to South Vietnam and modestly increased draft calls, the WRL began to organize a formal protest movement against the war. On May 16, it sponsored a demonstration in New York City in which twelve young men burned their draft cards. The event received widespread coverage in newspapers and television. The War Resisters League was highly skeptical of the administration's account of the Gulf of Tonkin incident, and vigorously opposed the subsequent bombing of North Vietnam. In December 1964, the WRL sponsored the first nationwide demonstrations against the Vietnam War. President Johnson disregarded the protest, comparing the War Registers League to "summer gnats in the hill country. They fly around a lot but never bite."

Some of Johnson's closest advisers suggested that only a sustained bombing of North Vietnam and Laos could stop the infiltration and demoralize the enemy. George Ball still opposed the scheme. He did not think bombing would break Hanoi's will, and he feared raising the ire of Moscow or the Chinese. "Once on the tiger's back," he said, "we cannot be sure of picking the place to dismount." But Ball was a minority of one in the inner circle. Early in January 1965 Maxwell Taylor cabled Johnson from Saigon: "We are faced here with a seriously deteriorating situation characterized by continued political turmoil, irresponsibility and division within the armed forces, lethargy in the pacification programs . . . and deepening discouragement and loss of morale. . . . The situation will continue to go downhill toward some form of political collapse unless new . . . elements can be introduced." For Taylor, Westmoreland, Rusk, the Bundys, Rostow, and McNamara, "new elements" meant massive bombing of North Vietnam. commitment of American troops, or both. Since ARVN was doing little to stem the growing power of the Vietcong, and the United States was not yet prepared to take over the war, bombing. North Vietnam became increasingly attractive. What stopped Johnson late in 1964 from adopting the proposal for large-scale bombing of North Vietnam was fear about reprisals. He did not think that if the communists escalated the war, South Vietnam would be able to handle it. "The political base in the South . . . was probably too shaky to withstand a major assault," he later observed.

When Johnson asked about bombing Vietcong targets in retaliation for the attack on Bien Hoa, the joint chiefs passed the question on to General Westmoreland in Saigon. Westmoreland found himself in a quandary. For months he had been requesting the deployment of more aircraft and pilots to MACV, but now he had to tell General Earle Wheeler that jungle cover, the problem of differentiating guerrillas from civilians, and the mobility of the enemy made it impossible to locate suitable Vietcong targets.

On Christmas Eve in Saigon, a Vietcong agent drove a car bomb into the basement parking lot of the Brinks Hotel, bachelor quarters for many American officers. The bomb exploded and blew out the entire bottom floor of the hotel, killing two Americans and wounding fifty-eight. Once again the president's advisers called for a retaliatory air strike against North Vietnam, but Johnson overruled them. Such a reaction during Christmas might offend much of the American public, and a massive air strike would be a disproportionately hostile response to the Brinks Hotel incident.

Johnson's caution disturbed his advisers, especially Robert McNamara and McGeorge Bundy. In a memo to the president on January 5, 1965, they wrote that they were utterly certain "that our current policy can lead only to a disastrous defeat. . . . What we are doing now, essentially, is to wait and hope for a stable government . . . but there is no real hope of success in this area unless and until our own policies and priorities change." The two argued that American indecisiveness was undermining the anticommunist effort in South Vietnam. "The Vietnamese see the enormous power of the United States withheld and they get little sense of firm and active U.S. policy." To bludgeon North Vietnam into submission and stabilize South Vietnamese politics, the United States should begin a concerted air war above the seventeenth parallel. Still Johnson hesitated.

Westmoreland's claim that MACV could locate no Vietcong targets worthy of air attack had a stunning confirmation on January 2, 1965, when Vietcong troops destroyed two companies of ARVN Rangers and tanks near Binh Gia, a village outside Saigon. More than two hundred ARVN troops died in the engagement, and five American helicopter pilots were wounded. One American officer, after praising the enemy's toughness, said that the "big question for me is how its troops, a thousand or more of them, could wander around the countryside so close to Saigon without being discovered." The Vietcong had the equivalent of three full divisions in the field, but MACV operational planners could not pick any bombing targets that could hurt the guerrillas.

Five weeks later the Vietcong struck again, this time at Camp Holloway outside of Pleiku, where the 52nd Combat Aviation Battalion was stationed. In the middle of the night on February 7, they rained mortar shells on the base and attacked a camp of 180 United States advisers about four miles away. In fifteen minutes seven Americans were dead and another hundred wounded. McGeorge Bundy was in Saigon on a fact-finding mission, and the next day he toured Camp Holloway with Westmoreland and Taylor. Deeply affected by the wounded men, Bundy wanted blood, prompting Westmoreland to think that, like so many civilians in positions of authority, Bundy "smelled a little gunpowder and . . . developed a field marshal psychosis." Still he joined Bundy in urging Johnson to retaliate. "Old Mac's really got himself stirred up," Johnson told George Ball. "Those poor wounded boys in the hospital sure as hell got to him." The attack on Pleiku stirred Johnson to action: "They're killing our men while they sleep in the night. I can't ask our American soldiers to continue to fight with one hand tied behind their back." On February 8, Johnson ordered American aircraft carriers to attack guerrilla bases in Dong Hoi, above the seventeenth parallel, while South Vietnamese pilots attacked similar sites at Vinh Linh and Chap Le. The air strike was known as Flaming Dart I. Johnson also ordered the evacuation of 1,800 American dependents from South Vietnam.

Three days later the Vietcong struck again, attacking the Viet Cuoung Hotel in Qui Nhon, which served as quarters for the American 104th Maintenance Detachment. While staging a brief firefight, the guerrillas planted two hundred pounds of plastic explosives around the foundation of the four-story hotel. When they were detonated, the building collapsed in rubble, burying forty-three American soldiers, only twenty-two of whom were dug out alive. President Johnson unleashed another air strike—Flaming Dart II. Within the next several days, the United States began Operation Rolling Thunder, the sustained bombing of North Vietnam that would last, off and on, until the end of 1968. When Vice President Hubert Humphrey wrote a memo opposing the raids, the president banned him from Vietnam planning sessions. Johnson's need for consensus, especially in a deteriorating situation, was becoming an obsession. At first the president kept tight control of the bombing, bragging that the pilots "can't even bomb an outhouse without my approval."

But in the early spring he relaxed that control, authorized the use of napalm, allowed pilots to drop their bomb loads on alternate targets without prior approval, and increased the frequency of the attacks. In April American and South Vietnamese pilots flew 3,600 sorties against North Vietnam.

In South Vietnam, political restlessness had continued. Buddhist monks organized hunger strikes, protest marches, and immolations; rumors of plots and coups were constant; and late in January 5,000 students destroyed the library of the United States Information Agency in Hue. Military confidence in Nguyen Khanh declined, especially among a group of younger officers on the Armed Forces Council. Led by Nguyen Van Thieu, the forty-one-year-old commander of the ARVN Fifth Division, and Nguyen Cao Ky, a thirty-four-year-old general in the Vietnamese Air Force, in February the "Young Turks" drove Khanh into peaceful exile as "roving ambassador." In fourteen months, the government of South Vietnam had changed hands seven times.

The bombing strikes were supposed to convince North Vietnam that its attempt to seize control of South Vietnam would be too expensive. But those assumptions came from a cold war mentality, the conviction that the war in Vietnam was just another example of communist aggression, and that if the United States brought its economic and political

Kim Phuc, who ripped off her burning clothes during a napalm raid, runs down the highway. At left is her younger brother who lost an eye in the attack and, at right, other members of her family. (*Courtesy, Library of Congress.*)

power to bear, the communists would back down. It had worked with the Truman Doctrine, the Marshall Plan, and at least in part the Korean War. From the American perspective, the struggle in Indochina was simply a case of external communist aggression. But from the perspective of the Vietcong and the North Vietnamese, it was a war to end foreign domination and reunite the two Vietnams. For most Americans, the war was a military struggle to be decided on a battlefield, but for Ho Chi Minh, it was a political struggle to be decided in the minds of the Vietnamese peasants. For the United States, Vietnam was a limited war to be escalated in carefully orchestrated stages until the communists broke. For Ho Chi Minh, it was a total war, the culmination of centuries of struggle, a cause worthy of risking complete annihilation. It "took us eight years of bitter fighting to defeat you French in Indochina," Ho Chi Minh had pointed out in an interview in 1962 with the French journalist Bernard Fall: "The Americans are stronger than the French. It might take ten years, but . . . I think the Americans greatly underestimate the determination of the Vietnamese people. The Vietnamese people have always shown great determination when faced with an invader."

Instead of intimidating or frightening the North Vietnamese, the American bombing raids of 1964 and early 1965 stiffened their resolve, convincing them that the United States was intent on their destruction. Whatever political opposition Ho Chi Minh faced at home disappeared. The flow of supplies and personnel into South Vietnam increased. Until the fall of 1964 the Vietcong had been an independent unit in South Vietnam, composed primarily of Vietminh regroupees born in the south and recruits from recently alienated peasants. They armed themselves with American weapons stolen or purchased from ARVN. By the end of 1964 North Vietnam was shipping Soviet and Chinese weapons down the Ho Chi Minh Trail, along with weapons specialists, trainers, and logistical experts from the People's Army of Vietnam: regular North Vietnamese troops. Hanoi had dispatched the first northern-born regulars in August 1964. Instead of dispersing them among the Vietcong as it had done with the regroupees, Hanoi let them operate as the independent 808th Battalion. The 95th Regiment reached South Vietnam in December, and by the spring of 1965 three more regiments were there—a total of 65,000 northern-born regular troops. The refrain "born in the North to die in the South" began to be heard in North Vietnam.

Early in 1965 the CIA reported that the Vietcong were stronger than ever before and were on the eve of a military victory in South Vietnam. The CIA and MACV also informed Johnson that the Vietcong posed a serious threat to American air bases. To make sure that South Vietnamese pilots participated in the air strikes, Taylor insisted that the air force pilots from Danang, not navy pilots from carriers, conduct the strikes against North Vietnam. That meant a sharp increase in the number of air force personnel, aircraft, and munitions. The buildup made Danang a primary Vietcong target, the perfect place to humiliate the American war machine. ARVN troops could not be trusted to defend Danang adequately.

On February 21, 1965, General Westmoreland asked for two marine battalions to protect Danang. He estimated that there were at least twelve Vietcong battalions with 6,000 troops in the area. The marines would improve security and permit ARVN troops to go out into the jungles after the Vietcong. Westmoreland routed his request through Maxwell Taylor, but the ambassador opposed the introduction of American ground troops. In a cable to President Johnson, Taylor argued: "Intervention with ground forces would at best buy time and would lead to ever increasing commitments until, like the French, we would be occupying an essentially hostile foreign country. . . . The white faced soldier . . . is not a suitable guerrilla fighter. . . . The French tried to adapt their forces to this mission and failed. I doubt that the U.S. forces could do much better." But Johnson was afraid of another Bien Hoa or Pleiku. American airmen at Danang needed security, and on February 26, 1965, he approved the request for two marine battalions.

Johnson's decisions stirred the souls of the Marine Corps. Out in Hawaii, where he had assumed command of the Fleet Marine Force, Pacific Command, General Victor Krulak ordered the 9th Marine Expeditionary Brigade to Danang. Plans were already under way to change the unit's name to the 3rd Marine Amphibious Force so that no comparisons would be made. On March 8, 3,500 troops stormed the beaches in full battle regalia, complete with M-14 rifles, landing craft, naval air support, amphibious tractors, helicopters, 105-mm howitzers, M48 tanks, and 106-mm recoilless rifles. But instead of a firefight, they encountered young South Vietnamese women waiting on the beaches with flowered leis to put around their necks. The smiling mayor of Danang welcomed the troops to his city. The marines clambered into trucks for the ride to the airbase, and all along the way waved at thousands of schoolchildren lining the highway and welcoming them.

When the news of the successful deployment of the marines reached Lyndon Johnson, he smiled broadly and remarked to an associate, "Now I have Ho Chi Minh's pecker in my pocket." The arrival of the marines created, in William Bundy's description, a mood of "disaster avoided or postponed. . . . But on the whole it was a period when no move seemed right, and the outcome remained wholly murky." George Ball, still playing devil's advocate, wrote that the presence of ground troops would make the American position "approach that of France in the 1950s. We would incur the opposition of elements in Viet-Nam otherwise friendly to us. Finally, we would find ourselves in *la guerre sale* with consequent heavy loss of American lives on the rice paddies and [in the] jungles." Events would soon vindicate George Ball.

6

Into the Abyss, 1965–1966

When the day comes for me to meet my Maker . . . the thing I
would be most humbly proud of was the fact that I fought
against . . . the carry-out of some . . . tactical schemes which
would have cost the lives of thousands of men. To that list of
tragic accidents that fortunately never happened I would add
the Indochina intervention.

—General Matthew Ridgway, 1956

Maxwell Taylor's prediction that "it will be very difficult to hold the line" came true sooner than he thought. The marines in Danang were there only three weeks when General William Westmoreland decided to establish another air base at Phu Bai south of Hue. In mid-April two more battalions arrived to establish and defend Phu Bai. That brought the marine contingent in I Corps to more than 8,600 troops. Deployed around Phu Bai and Danang, sitting in stationary placements, they itched for a fight. It was not going to be difficult to find one. The Vietcong were steadily gaining power. By the spring of 1965 no American could venture more than a few miles outside any major city without an armed convoy. The Vietcong were everywhere. When Nguyen Cao Ky called for an invasion of North Vietnam in 1965, John Paul Vann wrote, "The goddamn little fool can't even drive a mile outside Saigon without an armed convoy and he wants to liberate the North! How damned ridiculous can you get?"

Few Americans harbored any real hope of transforming ARVN into a reliable fighting force. ARVN suffered from desertion, absenteeism, cronyism, and nepotism. Too many officers were promoted because of political connections, not tactical abilities. Many officers capable of fighting a war were immobilized by fear of failure, which meant taking too many casualties, and by fear of success, which posed a political threat to their superiors. Doing nothing was the surest way to promotion. Corruption was rampant. In some ARVN units half the roster consisted of "potted-tree soldiers," men who had bribed their way out of active service. They were safe behind the lines, like a plant in its own pot. The government still sent monthly pay and allowance checks in their names, which ARVN officers pocketed. Peasant soldiers—underpaid, far from home, and commanded by officers on the take—deserted in record numbers. ARVN troop levels increased from 243,000 in late 1963 to 514,000 a year later, but they were paper troops. The desertion rate of 6,000 a month in 1964 increased to 11,000 in 1965. The desertion rate at ARVN draft induction centers reached 50 percent. Creating a disciplined, highly motivated army takes a generation, not a year. The United States had such an army, and so did the Vietcong and the North Vietnamese. South Vietnam did not.

Behind ARVN lay corruption, assassination, fraudulent elections, and constant political intrigue. The February 1965 coup of the Young Turks that brought Nguyen Cao Ky and Nguyen Van Thieu to power did nothing to change the situation.

Nguyen Cao Ky was born in Son Tay, a city near Hanoi, in 1930. When he was twenty, France drafted him into the Vietnamese National Army, and three years later the army sent him to pilot training. Ky rose quickly in the ranks, one of the few promoted for ability rather than connections. His personality was perfectly consistent with the stereotype of a jet pilot. Ky liked fancy jumpsuits and purple scarves, and he carried two pearl-handled revolvers in holsters. In 1961, when he was "just a colonel," Ky wanted to prove his flying skills to William Colby, the CIA station chief in Saigon. Ky got Colby into the cockpit and took him on a roller-coaster, mountain-hopping, wave-skimming flight from the Central Highlands to the South China Sea. Ky later laughed to another Vietnamese pilot that Colby was going to "have to go and clean the shit out of his pants." In 1962 Ngo Dinh Diem awarded him his general's star. Ky hated Nguyen Khanh. At one point in 1964, during a flight from Bien Hoa, he almost carried out an incendiary raid on Khanh's headquarters. The coup must have been doubly gratifying to him.

From left, U.S. Secretary of State Dean Rusk, South Vietnamese Prime Minister Nguyen Cao Ky, and U.S. Ambassador to Vietnam Henry Cabot Lodge meet in Saigon. (*Courtesy, National Archives.*)

For his first meeting with Maxwell Taylor after assuming power, Ky showed up wearing a white sharkskin dress jacket, tight silk black pants, bright red socks, and a purple scarf, prompting an American official to describe him as a "saxophone player in a second-rate night club." Ky was thoroughly Westernized. A well-trimmed mustache gave him an American look, and he walked with a swagger, imitating John Wayne, drinking Budweiser beer, and watching reruns of *Gunsmoke* and *Have Gun Will Travel* on armed forces television. William Bundy's later comment sums the administration's initial reaction to Ky: It "seemed to all of us the bottom of the barrel, absolutely the bottom of the barrel."

The chairman of the National Leadership Committee and the chief of state was Nguyen Van Thieu. Born in Ninh Thuan Province in 1923, Thieu had won a degree from the Vietnamese Military Academy in 1949 and distinguished himself fighting the Vietminh. After graduating from United States Command and General Staff College in 1957, Thieu commanded the ARVN Twenty-first, First, and Fifth Infantry Divisions. During the 1963 coup overthrowing Diem, Thieu led a brigade against the presidential guard. He was one of the Young Turks on the Armed Forces Council in 1964 who desired an end to Khanh's reign.

Except in his lust for power, Thieu was different from Ky. American military leaders appreciated his conservatism, proper dress, and political caution. Thieu seemed more astute than Ky, with little of Ky's hostility toward Buddhism. And he was ready to forge a political and military alliance with the Americans in order to defeat the communists. The Americans also found Thieu more circumspect. While Ky was talking about building luxury hotels along the coast once the Vietcong were destroyed, Thieu focused on more immediate problems—how to locate and attack the Vietcong, undermine their control over rural peasants, and intimidate the North Vietnamese.

But like Ky, Thieu was part of the corruption of Saigonese politics. American money created opportunities for graft at every level—sales of weapons, marketing of opium and heroin, kickbacks on military construction projects, licensing fees for American businesses operating in Saigon, and payments from thousands of potted-tree soldiers. Americans knew about the corruption. Between 1965 and 1972 the United States ambassador or MACV commander questioned Thieu more than a hundred times about official corruption in his government, but each time, after a warning, let him off. It was Ky's impulsiveness that most bothered Americans. They wanted to maneuver Thieu into the role of chief executive, with Ky switched to military czar, where his impetuousness could be controlled.

The corrupt, illegitimate government of South Vietnam, with its incompetent, ineffectual military, could not handle the Vietcong. The choice Lyndon Johnson faced was simple: Escalate American involvement and rescue Saigon or get out before the collapse. After a White House breakfast early in March 1965, the president told General Harold K. Johnson, "You get things bubbling, General." The general toured Vietnam a few days later and learned just how desperate the situation was. Two marine battalions guarding Danang were not going to make much difference. Westmoreland asked for two full divisions of American combat troops, one to go to the Central Highlands and the other for Saigon. In what the press corps regarded as the understatement of the year, General Johnson argued that "what the situation requires may exceed what the Vietnamese can . . . do."

On March 15 General Johnson recommended deploying an international force near the Demilitarized Zone (DMZ). Established at Geneva in 1954, the DMZ was a five-mile-wide buffer zone dividing North Vietnam from South Vietnam. It extended from the South China Sea to the Village of Bo Hu Su along the Ben Hai River, and from there due west to Laos along the seventeenth parallel. Westmoreland also proposed that to stop the infiltration of troops and supplies from North Vietnam, the United States send large numbers of ground troops. Engineering and logistical battalions should be set to preparing for their arrival. Finally, Westmoreland wanted a full infantry division to defend United States installations. Maxwell Taylor demurred. He worried that American troops were inadequately prepared for guerrilla warfare in Vietnamese jungles, that ARVN might do even less with more American soldiers around, and that even a few infantry troops would greatly alter the American mission in Vietnam. But Vietcong attacks undercut Taylor's caution. As if to confirm American fears, on March 30, 1965 two Vietcong agents drove a gray Renault up to the United States embassy in Saigon. When an embassy guard approached the car, another Vietcong agent on a motor scooter shot and killed him. In the trunk of the Renault were 300 pounds of plastic explosives connected to an American-made brass detonator. At 11:00 A.M. the bomb exploded, gutting the embassy's first three floors and wounding 52 Americans. The blast killed 20 Vietnamese and wounded 130 others in the street. President Johnson was at a dinner party when he heard the news. The next morning at an impromptu press briefing he proclaimed, "Outrages like this will only reinforce the determination of the American people . . . to strengthen their assistance and support for the people and government of Vietnam."

Johnson lied when he reassured the reporters that he knew of "no far-reaching strategy that is being suggested or promulgated." Before the attack Johnson had called Maxwell Taylor home for consultation. In meetings on April 1 and 2, the administration developed what became known as National Security Adviser Memorandum 328 authorizing deployment of 20,000 engineering and logistical troops to South Vietnam and the beginning of offensive operations against the Vietcong. John McCone, head of the CIA, reacted strongly to NSAM 328. Intelligence reports indicated that the Rolling Thunder air strikes "have not caused a change in the North Vietnamese policy of directing Vietcong insurgency, infiltrating cadres and supplying material. If anything, the strikes to date have hardened their attitude." McCone believed that without a significant escalation of the air war over North Vietnam, American ground troops would fail: "We will find ourselves mired down in combat in the jungle in a military effort that we cannot win. . . . If we are to change the mission of the ground forces, we must also change the ground rules for strikes against North Vietnam. We must hit them harder, more frequently, and inflict greater damage." Operation Rolling Thunder had to be escalated.

The president still hoped for another way out. In a speech on April 7 at Johns Hopkins University, he offered to hold "unconditional discussions" to end the conflict. He also offered billions of dollars of assistance to develop the Mekong River Delta once peace was achieved. Johnson viewed the proposal as his strongest enticement. The American labor leader George Meany "would jump at that offer in a minute," he told McGeorge Bundy. Early in May, Johnson launched Operation Mayflower, suspending the bombing raids over North Vietnam to see whether Ho Chi Minh was ready for talks, warning that if "this pause should be misunderstood . . . it would be necessary to demonstrate more clearly than ever, after the pause ended, that the United States is determined not to accept aggression without reply in Vietnam."

The bombing pause did not provoke the desired response. Ho Chi Minh insisted that peace would come only after all American troops left South Vietnam, the National Liberation Front participated fully in the government of South Vietnam, all bombing raids over North Vietnam stopped, and the two countries enjoyed a "peaceful reunification . . . without any foreign interference." The United States wanted a peace settlement based on the withdrawal of North Vietnamese forces from South Vietnam as well as the elimination of the National Liberation Front in South Vietnam. The impasse had not changed. Pham Van Dong had been through it all before: "We entered into negotiations with the French colonialists on many occasions, and concluded with them several agreements in an effort to preserve peace. To them, however, the signing of agreements was only designed to gain time to prepare . . . for furher aggression. . . . This is a clear lesson of history . . . which our people will never forget."

Both sides were prisoners of history. For American policymakers, the recollections of Munich—of Britain and France's giving in to Hitler's demands only to see him take over much of Europe—were overpowering. American policymakers saw Ho Chi Minh as just another bully, not a national hero, who would back down in the face of brute power as the Nazis might have done. But the North Vietnamese were in their own way just as blind. They saw the Americans as merely another foreign power, a later version of the Chinese and the French, intent on colonizing Vietnam. Nothing the Americans said could be trusted. There could be no negotiations. On May 18, 1965, the president ended Operation Mayflower and resumed the bombing.

A few weeks earlier, Johnson had dispatched Robert McNamara, Earle Wheeler, William Bundy, and Maxwell Taylor to Honolulu to meet with General Victor Krulak of the Marine Corps and Admiral Ulysses S. Grant Sharp, commander in chief of the United States Forces in the Pacific. They agreed to send another 40,000 marines and army infantry to South Vietnam. But they also decided to keep American troops out of the Central Highlands, confining most of them to the northern coast of I Corps. Johnson approved the decision. Early in May the 173d Airborne Brigade, the first army combat troops, arrived to protect the Bien Hoa air base. Another marine battalion went to Chu Lai. By the end of May 1965 there were nearly 50,000 American troops in South Vietnam.

But Johnson wanted the middle road, and he refused to give Westmoreland full rein. Instead he took up the advice of James Gavin, a retired army general. Gavin, a West Point graduate in 1929, had won a Silver Star during World War II. Before his retirement in 1960, he earned his third star as a lieutenant general. John Kennedy appointed Gavin ambassador to France in 1961. The French let Gavin know that the Vietnamese were a relentlessly militaristic people, that the United States would bog down in the jungles just as the French had. Gavin decided that if American ground troops were going to be introduced to South Vietnam, they should be used only to defend "coastal enclaves"— major cities along the South China Sea. Securing all of South Vietnam would take a million troops and an entire decade, bringing severe casualties and bitter political debate. Better to use fewer soldiers to hold coastal enclaves. Such a strategy would prove to North Vietnam that the United States was willing to stay indefinitely in South Vietnam and make Ho Chi Minh more willing to settle the dispute diplomatically. The enclave strategy would also minimize American casualties, leaving the real bloodletting to the ARVN. The American people were willing to tolerate large contingents of American troops stationed indefinitely overseas—twenty years in West Germany and fifteen years in South Korea had proved that. What they would not tolerate was a long-term commitment with mounting casualties.

For the moment, President Johnson held to the enclave strategy along with bombing attacks on North Vietnam. American combat troops were confined to the major American bases but could patrol to a fifty-mile radius. The president hoped that such an approach would stop short of a full-scale ground war while buying time for the South Vietnamese government to stabilize and for the bombing raids to push Hanoi toward the negotiating table. Still worried about the political fallout over a serious escalation, that "that bitch of a war" might destroy "the woman I really loved—the Great Society," Johnson did not truthfully explain his decision to the public. He said the troops were in South Vietnam to protect the bases. It was the perfect time to go to Congress to ask for more money. The GIs were already in the field, and the president insisted that they were there for self-defense. On May 4, 1965, Johnson asked Congress for another $700 million to support those troops, and the legislators quietly agreed. For the next three years President Johnson argued that in the Gulf of Tonkin Resolution of 1964 and the May 1965 funding vote, Congress had consented to the Vietnam War.

At this point the president tried to do what President Harry Truman had done in Korea—put together a multinational, "free world fighting force." But Vietnam was not Korea. The British Prime Minister Harold Wilson argued that the war was a dead end and that Johnson should stop the bombing and seek a negotiated settlement. Charles de Gaulle of France was more blunt. "The United States," he said, "cannot win this war. No matter how far they push it in the future, they will lose it." Australia, New Zealand, and the Philippines sent small contingents, and the South Koreans sent their vaunted Capital Division and a Marine Brigade to II Corps in October 1965 and the White Horse Division in September 1966. But that was all. It was going to be an American war.

Westmoreland came back with requests for more troops. The 23,000 military advisers, the 8,600 marines, the 20,000 engineering and logistical troops, and the promised 40,000 new combat troops would not be enough. "The enemy," General Westmoreland's memoirs note, "was destroying [ARVN] battalions faster than they could be reconstituted." General Earle Wheeler insisted that "the ground forces situation requires a substantial . . . build-up of U.S. and Allied forces in the RVN [Republic of Vietnam], at the most rapid rate feasible." The generals wanted an end to the enclave strategy and the beginning of full-scale offensive operations. Wheeler insisted that the United States "must take the fight to the enemy. No one ever won a battle sitting on his ass."

Westmoreland and Wheeler told Johnson in June 1965 that they needed another 150,000 troops. Dean Rusk was stunned by the request. Just a month before, the administration had been heatedly discussing whether to send 3,500 marines to protect Danang. Rusk asked Westmoreland whether there really was "a serious danger of complete military collapse within a relatively short period of time." Westmoreland was brutally honest. ARVN "cannot stand up to this pressure without substantial US combat support on the ground. . . . The only possible response is the aggressive deployment of US troops." As far as Westmoreland was concerned, it was time to get on with the war.

Not everyone was convinced. Johnson was frustrated that a "raggedy-ass, fourth-rate country like North Vietnam [could] be causing so much trouble," and he worried that the war might get out of control. George Ball wanted Johnson to stop listening to the generals, limit American ground troops to 100,000, and withdraw if South Vietnam proved unable to carry its fair share. But Johnson's half-measures were frustrating him. As his memoirs recall, he saw that the situation had "reached the desperate point. . . . We had tried everything . . . to get . . . to the peace table . . . from November 1963 to 1965. And we had not succeeded. And we either had to run in or run out."

Johnson's handling of the revolution in the Dominican Republic in the last week of April 1965 strengthened his resolve. A rebel movement led by Juan Bosch had overthrown the Dominican military government, and the CIA said communists were at work. Johnson sent 21,000 marines to seize control of the country, stabilize the government, and establish a regime favorable to Washington. The decision was popular with the public. Success in the Dominican Republic reassured Johnson and raised his hopes that enough soldiers could achieve similar success in South Vietnam.

But in Vietnam, enough was never enough. In General Earle Wheeler's retrospective judgment, by the summer of 1965 "it became amply clear that it wasn't a matter of whether the North Vietnamese were going to win the war; it was a question of when." At the same time Nguyen Cao Ky told Maxwell Taylor that more American ground troops were necessary if the country was going to survive the monsoon season. Johnson had approved a troop level of 95,000 in June, but Westmoreland and Wheeler wanted forty-four infantry battalions, another 100,000 troops. John McCone and Walt Rostow desired an escalation of the Rolling Thunder bombing raids. George Ball urged Johnson to find a way to get out before it was too late. On July 1, 1965, with his usual eloquence, Ball told Johnson he was facing a "protracted war involving an open-ended commitment of U.S. forces, mounting U.S. casualties, no assurances of a satisfactory solution, and a serious danger of escalation at the end of the road. . . . Once we suffer large casualties, we will have started a well-nigh irreversible process. Our involvement will be so great that we cannot—without national humiliation—stop short of achieving our complete objectives." Senate Majority Leader Mike Mansfield told Johnson, "There is not a government to speak of in Saigon." Maxwell Taylor, skeptical of what ground troops would be able to achieve, wanted Johnson to limit the troops to 95,000 men and stick to the enclave strategy.

Johnson sought the advice of Robert McNamara, whom he called "the smartest man I ever met." Early in July McNamara presented his analysis. Summing up the three options already given, he sided with Westmoreland, Wheeler, McCone, and Rostow—expand the military effort against the Vietcong and North Vietnam until they had to negotiate or be destroyed. He proposed giving Westmoreland his forty-four battalions, mining Haiphong harbor, sealing off North Vietnam from all external commerce, and bombing to destroy munitions, fuel supplies, railroads, bridges, airfields, surface-to-missile sites, and war industries.

He wanted to call up 225,000 army reservists to active duty. Short of nuclear weapons, McNamara wished to bring every ounce of American firepower to bear.

The proposal was so far reaching and involved such an alteration in the nature of American policy that McGeorge Bundy took exception. The commitment was too open ended, the outcome too blurred, to justify such an investment. "If we need 200,000 men now for these quite limited missions," Bundy wrote to McNamara at the end of June, "may we not need 400,000 later? Is this a rational course of action? . . . If US casualties go up sharply, what further actions do we propose to take or not to take?" What if the Chinese or the Soviet Union intervened? What if the bombing did not bring North Vietnamese diplomats to the table? What if the war went on for years without resolution? The terrible "ifs" multiplied.

Johnson turned for advice to the "Wise Men," a group of elder statesmen who represented the American foreign policy establishment. If the United States ever had an aristocracy, it was these men—Ivy Leaguers with a wealth of experience in wielding power. Included in the group were Dean Acheson; Robert Lovett, a Wall Street investment banker and former secretary of defense; and John McCloy, for a time head of the World Bank. Johnson called them to the White House on July 10 to evaluate McNamara's proposal. In a letter to Harry Truman after the meeting, Acheson recalled listening to Johnson "complain about how mean every-one was to him . . . (every course of action was wrong; he had no support from anyone at home or abroad; it interfered with all his programs, etc., etc.). . . . I blew my top and told him he was wholly right on Vietnam, that he had no choice except to press on. . . . With this lead my colleagues came thundering in like the charge of the Scots Grey at Waterloo."

Still Johnson searched for a middle course. For political reasons withdrawal was out of the question, especially for a Democratic president familiar with the attacks directed at Truman in 1949 for the fall of China. Johnson was certain that the loss of Vietnam would "shatter my Presidency, kill my administration, and damage our democracy" while compromising American credibility around the world and encouraging communists to launch more "wars of national liberation." But McNamara's proposal also threatened to be a political disaster. It placed the United States in a state of war emergency. To save his Great Society, Johnson had to appease both liberal critics of the war and conservative critics of the welfare state. So he accepted most of McNamara's advice but rejected the secretary's notion of a massive bombing campaign over North Vietnam and a call-up of reserves. Johnson listened to Dean Rusk, who argued that the United States "should deny to Hanoi success in South Vietnam without taking action on our side which would force the other side [China and the Soviet Union] to move to higher levels of conflict."

Rusk wanted to keep limits on Rolling Thunder. Johnson agreed. Although he increased the number of sorties from 3,600 in April to 4,800 in June, the president kept them below the twentieth parallel. At the end of July, in a low-key speech, he announced the deployment of another 50,000 troops. It was a lie, or at least a half-truth. The president had decided to send another 150,000 and to abandon the enclave strategy. Few American presidents have made such colossal miscalculations.

The first rule in strategic thinking is political, not military: War leaders must be certain of the nature of their enemy; only then can they apply the proper level of force and know just what constitutes a victory. The Johnson administration, like its predecessors, had difficulty precisely defining the real enemy in Vietnam. At times policymakers talked vaguely of communism, while at other times they identified the Chinese, the North Vietnamese, or the South Vietnamese guerrillas as the real culprits.

The second rule of strategic thinking is also political: Leaders must maintain support for the war at home so people will make the necessary sacrifices. But here, too, Johnson had to be careful. Although the break between Moscow and Beijing and, beginning in 1966, the Cultural Revolution in China probably precluded direct Soviet or Chinese intervention, the administration worried constantly about the prospect of another Korea, an influx of Chinese troops, which the public would not tolerate. The Vietnam War, then, was going to be a limited war, in which political issues dictated military constraints. That did not bother Johnson, at least not at first. He promised Senator George McGovern of South Dakota, "I'm going up old Ho Chi Minh's leg an inch at a time." Assuming that North Vietnam would cave in quickly to American firepower, the president thought the American people would tolerate heavy casualties in the short term if they saw victory and peace on the horizon. But when the North Vietnamese proved to be intransigent and long suffering, limited war became a horrendous political liability. The longer it went on, the more political support Johnson lost at home.

Yet another rule of strategic thinking that Johnson could not hold to is political: Leaders must remember that the military, like diplomacy, is simply a tool for achieving political objectives. The political objective was establishing a stable, democratic, noncommunist government in South Vietnam, but the United States was never able to correlate the use of military hardware with nation building. Saigonese politics were inherently undemocratic in the first place, and as the United States escalated the war and the volume of firepower, the war's sheer destructiveness inevitably alienated more and more people in South Vietnam. Even a clear military victory over North Vietnam would not necessarily translate into the creation of a stable democratic regime in South Vietnam.

Within that strategic fog, William Westmoreland tried to fight a war.

He was convinced that the United States should focus on destroying the enemy just as the Allies had done to Germany and Japan during World War II. The American economy was unmatched in its ability to produce and deliver military firepower, and Westmoreland planned to build, in the words of the journalist Neil Sheehan, a "killing machine," a huge army backed by the latest in technology and organization. Westmoreland projected a conflict in three stages. In 1965 and early 1966 he would build the infrastructure to support a large, modern army. He estimated it would take one soldier in a logistical support role to maintain each soldier in the field. The second stage would begin in late 1966. Westmoreland planned to establish a system of fortified firebases in South Vietnam, each with the capability of covering a large area in artillery fire. From those bases infantry patrols could go on search-and-destroy missions to locate the enemy. GIs would use the old technologies—aircraft surveillance and tracking dogs—as well as the latest: hand-carried radar, infrared spotting scopes, and urine-detection "people-sniffer" devices. IBM 1430 computers back in Saigon consumed huge amounts of CIA and MACV data, developed probability curves, and tried to predict when and where the enemy would attack. Operation Ranch Hand would be expanded. Westmoreland wanted to rely mostly on tactical firepower, directing artillery, helicopter gunships, fixed-wing gunships, and B-52 bombers on the enemy. In the final stage, ARVN was to move into the area for "clearing operations"—killing any enemy troops who survived the bombardment—and local militia would then maintain security.

The weak link in the strategy was ARVN together with the Regional Forces and Popular Forces, which American troops derisively termed "Ruff-Puffs." But Westmoreland was confident that even if they did not do their job of clearing and securing behind the killing machine, the North Vietnamese and the Vietcong could not long stand the heavy losses they would incur. "We'll just go on bleeding them," Westmoreland said, "until Hanoi wakes up to the fact that they have bled their country to the point of national disaster for generations."

Operation Starlight, for Westmoreland at least, proved his point. On August 18 at the Batangan Peninsula in northern South Vietnam, the 3rd Battalion of the 3rd Marine Division came ashore while the 2nd Battalion of the 4th Marine Division flew into landing zones to the west, chasing the 1st Vietcong Regiment. Fighting was heavy, and the marines called in artillery, naval bombardment, and tactical air support. More than 6,000 marines participated. Operation Starlight was the first large battle with Main Force Vietcong. When the battle of Chu Lai, as the marines called it, was over, the United States claimed 573 Vietcong dead, compared to 46 marines dead and another 204 wounded. Westmoreland's "boys" had inflicted death at the rate of twelve to one. The math was self-evident. How long could the enemy hold out?

Westmoreland wanted to invade across the seventeenth parallel and hold territory there, bringing the ground war home to North Vietnam. But at the White House memories of Korea, of crossing the thirty-eighth parallel only to be attacked by hordes of Chinese soldiers, were still vivid. Johnson did not wish to awaken the slumbering giant. He confined American troops south of the seventeenth parallel. Westmoreland also sought to invade Laos south of the seventeenth parallel to stop the infiltration along the Ho Chi Minh Trail, and cross into Cambodia to attack enemy staging areas along the border. But Johnson remained cautious and prudent, too prudent and too cautious for Westmoreland.

Logistical planners and strategic bombing experts told Westmoreland that cutting off the flow of supplies by bombing raids and military occupations of large amounts of territory would stretch American resources without achieving acceptable results. A much easier approach was to mine or blockade Haiphong harbor, the depot where most of the Soviet and Chinese supplies entered North Vietnam. Johnson balked because it increased the probability of a confrontation with Moscow. Westmoreland's memoirs record his opinion that "Washington's phobia that . . . mining the harbor would trigger Chinese Communist or Russian intervention was chimerical."

Westmoreland faced obstacles in the command structure as well. MACV was a "subordinate unified command." Though Westmoreland eventually directed 543,000 American troops fighting a land war in Asia, real authority over the war was in Honolulu with CINCPAC. During Westmoreland's four years with MACV, CINCPAC was Admiral Ulysses S. Grant Sharp. To get requests to the president and the joint chiefs or to receive decisions from them, Westmoreland had to go through CINCPAC. Command of air operations was even more complicated. Westmoreland controlled the air force sorties inside South Vietnam and on the southern parts of the Ho Chi Minh Trail in Laos, but CINCPAC controlled naval air strikes over North Vietnam and northern Laos.

The Marine Corps had misgivings about Westmoreland's strategy. Trained as assault troops, the marines at Danang found themselves holding static positions and defending territory. That had never been part of their historical mission. Their main purpose was to overrun the enemy, take heavy casualties, and evacuate, leaving army infantry to hold the positions. In instances that did involve holding territory for long periods, the Marine Corps was better at it than the army. For decades before World War II, marine detachments had occupied Central American and Caribbean countries, where they worked with local governments and emphasized pacification.

Prominent among the critics of Westmoreland's war was General Krulak, one of the few senior military officers convinced that the key to victory was political, not military. Big engagements between

Americans, ARVN, Main Force Vietcong, and the North Vietnamese, he declared, "could move to another planet today, and we would still not have won the war because the Vietnamese people are the prize." He wanted his marines together with the army to fight small-unit actions while investing most of their energies in pacification. Krulak proposed placing a marine rifle squad with a South Vietnamese local militia company in what he called a combined action platoon. The CAPs would provide security while pacification programs—health, education, economic development, and land reform—won over the peasants. But Westmoreland vetoed the plan; he was just going to solve the problem militarily.

While muddled strategic thinking bedeviled the American effort in Southeast Asia, North Vietnam had a simple political goal that enjoyed clear strategic expression: Expel the American military from Indochina, conquer South Vietnam, and reunify the two countries. The North Vietnamese knew they could not match American firepower. The war would be won or lost, Ho Chi Minh repeated over and over again, in the mind of the typical American citizen and the will of the typical South Vietnamese peasant.

Vo Nguyen Giap looked on the American buildup with incredulity— amazement at the wealth and technology but disbelief that such resources would be invested so poorly. In 1969, looking back on the first four years of the enlarged war, he remarked, "The United States has a strategy based on arithmetic. They question the computers, add and subtract, extract square roots, and then go into action. But arithmetical strategy doesn't work here. . . . If it did, they'd already have exterminated us. . . . When a whole people rises up, nothing can be done." Giap was right. Westmoreland measured progress by adding up the dead, the "body count," along with the numbers of prisoners taken, weapons captured, tonnages exploded, sorties flown, and "battalion days in the field." But those statistics did not measure commitment. Even the American bombing of North Vietnam, originally designed to break the people's will, only made them more angry and resentful, more willing to sacrifice everything on Ho Chi Minh's bold course. Ho estimated that rural South Vietnam and all of North Vietnam could produce 250,000 to 300,000 new military recruits a year. For a war of attrition to erode Vietnam's ability to stay with the war, Westmoreland would have to kill that many people every year. American leaders could not imagine Vietnam's making such a sacrifice. But Ho Chi Minh was willing.

Just as critical were the American people. Vietnam had already waged one war against Westerners who grew tired of it. Ho Chi Minh expected Americans to be no different. Vietnam was a little place a long way from Main Street. Once the boys started coming home in body bags, the American people would insist on a settlement. While Westmoreland planned a war of military attrition, Ho Chi Minh waged a war of political attrition. When his generals pushed for more aggressiveness, Ho Chi Minh reassured them: "Don't worry. I've been to America. I know Americans. They are an impatient people. They will leave."

Vo Nguyen Giap, though still an influential member of the Politburo in Hanoi, no longer controlled war strategy. Those decisions were firmly in the hands of Le Duan, the militant advocate of reunification who was now general secretary of the Lao Dong party. Late in 1964 Duan named Nguyen Chi Thanh head of the Central Office for South Vietnam, which controlled the Vietcong effort in South Vietnam. He argued that the North Vietnamese should engage the United States in big-unit, conventional battles before American firepower reached its peak. If the North Vietnamese inflicted heavy losses on the American army early in the war, Lyndon Johnson would stop the buildup. Giap countered that the North Vietnamese should not get into a slugging match with the American heavyweight. For a brief period, Thanh prevailed.

The battle of the Batangan Peninsula in August 1965 intensified the debate. The losses were heavy, but Thanh held the battle to be proof that "the Southern Liberation Army is fully capable of defeating U.S. troops under any circumstance, even though they [United States troops] have absolute superiority of . . . firepower." To Giap's insistence that casualties were too high Thanh responded that the Americans had suffered 250 dead and wounded soldiers, a casualty rate that the United States would be politically unwilling to accept. Le Duan sided with Thanh. But then came the battle of the Ia Drang Valley.

The 1st Air Cavalry Division, deployed to Vietnam in September 1965, was the latest in tactical innovation. The helicopter was to airborne warfare what the tank had been to armored cavalry—a new tactical development providing mobility and firepower. The "air cav" deployed to II Corps in the Central Highlands to stop any enemy attempt to cut South Vietnam in half by driving to the South China Sea. Late in October, North Vietnamese troops attacked a United States Special Forces camp at Plei Me. Westmoreland sent in the air cav. But in mid-November, when 400 American troops went through what they thought was the unoccupied Ia Drang Valley southwest of Plei Me, the North Vietnamese 65th Regiment surprised them. Four days of fighting followed before the enemy withdrew. In the three weeks after the attack on Plei Me, American firepower buried the enemy in exploding shells: nearly 35,000 artillery rounds, more than 7,000 rounds of aerial rockets, and over 50,000 helicopter sorties. For the first time in the war, B-52 bombers flew in tactical support. When the battle ended, nearly 1,800 North Vietnamese were confirmed dead, with probably that same number wounded or soon to die. The American dead numbered 240.

In Hanoi the extent of the losses gave Vo Nguyen Giap the advantage in his debate with Nguyen Chi Thanh. To limit the effectiveness of American artillery and air power, Duan and Thanh now developed a tactic termed "clinging to the belt," engaging the Americans at close quarters under heavy jungle cover—short-range firefights, ambushes, and hand-to-hand combat—and forcing officers to call in artillery and air strikes close to their own positions or even on them. The North Vietnamese had to keep the tactical initiative by staying out of the way of American search-and-destroy operations. From July to September 1965, the United States had inflicted forty deaths for every American death. That was clearly too heavy, and by determining when and where to fight, North Vietnam reduced those figures to fifteen to one by the end of the year. While Westmoreland expected the North Vietnamese to move into what Mao Zedong called the "third phase of revolutionary warfare"—large-scale conventional battles at the battalion, regimental, and division levels—North Vietnam had returned to engagement by small units.

In Saigon, Westmoreland used Ia Drang to boost his troop requests up to 375,000 men, with the option of asking for 200,000 more. Robert McNamara was visibly shaken by the deaths of 240 Americans in one battle. He told Johnson that "U.S. killed-in-action can be expected to reach 1,000 a month and the odds are even that we will be faced in early 1967 with a 'no decision' at an even higher level." That would soon pose a colossal political problem. The war was becoming the central theme of the Johnson administration, eclipsing the Great Society domestic programs. Anticipating a hostile political reaction at home and abroad to more troop requests, McNamara suggested that "We must lay a foundation in the minds of the American public and world opinion for such an enlarged phase of the war and . . . we should give NVN [North Vietnam] a face-saving chance to stop the aggression." Johnson accepted McNamara's proposal for another pause in Rolling Thunder. On Christmas Eve 1965 the bombing stopped. But Ho Chi Minh still insisted on the unconditional withdrawal of all American troops and participation of the National Liberation Front in the South Vietnamese government. On January 31, 1966, Johnson resumed the raids.

While Johnson offered peace, the battle of the Ia Drang Valley boosted Westmoreland's morale. The deaths of 240 Americans did not startle him; he viewed those deaths in the context of a military victory. The boys had died nobly, giving the enemy a real thrashing. The foe had lost nearly half a division; attrition was working. "The death of even one man is lamentable," Westmoreland said of the Ia Drang Valley, "and those were serious losses, yet I could take comfort in the fact that in the Highlands . . . the American fighting man . . . performed without the setbacks that had sometimes marked first performances in other wars." Throughout the last half of 1965 and most of 1966 Westmoreland built the infrastructure he desired. To the jet air bases at Tan Son Nhut, Bien Hoa, and Danang he added four along with six new deep-water ports, four central supply and maintenance depots, twenty-six permanent base camps, seventy-five new tactical airstrips, and twenty-six hospitals—more than 16 million square feet of construction. He built 2,500 miles of paved roads and installed the Southeast Asia Automatic Telephone System, complete with 220 communications centers and 14,000 circuits. To supply electricity needs, he brought in 1,300 commercial generators and dozens of World War II tankers converted to floating generator barges.

For the permanent base camps Westmoreland made wooden barracks of high quality built on concrete slabs and equipped with hot showers. High-ranking officers enjoyed air-conditioned quarters in mobile trailers. Foremost Dairy and Meadowgold Dairies built fresh milk and ice cream plants at Qui Nhon and Cam Ranh Bay, and to supply troops in remote locations with fresh ice cream, Westmoreland built forty army ice cream plants. To make sure that the soldiers got three meals a day of fresh fruit, vegetables, meat, and dairy products, he built thousands of cold storage lockers throughout South Vietnam. To amuse the troops, he built the famous PXs—air-conditioned movie theaters, bowling alleys, and service clubs full of beer, Cokes, hot dogs, hamburgers, french fries, malts, sundaes, candy, and ice. No army in the history of the world had more of the amenities of home.

Of the women sent to South Vietnam as the war grew, about 11,000 were nurses. To deal with cases of sick and wounded soldiers, the Pentagon began to deploy army medical detachments in the spring of 1965. The 3rd Field Hospital went to Tan Son Nhut in April 1965, and the 58th Medical Battalion reached Long Binh in May. The 9th Field Hospital was stationed in Nha Trang in July, and it was followed by the 85th Evacuation Hospital in August, the 43rd Medical Group and the 523d Field Hospital in September, and the 1st Medical Battalion, 2nd

July 14, 1965—U.S. Army nurses Capt. Gladys E. Sepulveda, left, of Ponce, Puerto Rico, and 2nd Lt. Lois Ferrari, of Pittsburgh, Pennsylvania, rest on sandbags at Cam Ranh Bay in South Vietnam. (*Courtesy, Library of Congress.*)

Surgical Hospital, 51st Field Hospital, and 93rd Evacuation Hospital in November. Eventually, the army assigned forty-seven medical units to South Vietnam. Navy nurses worked on the USS *Repose* and the USS *Sanctuary,* hospital ships that sailed between the Demilitarized Zone and Danang off the coast of Vietnam in the South China Sea. Air force nurses worked on medevac aircraft evacuating the wounded to Japan, Okinawa, the Philippines, and the United States. There were no Marine Corps nurses.

Nursing may have been the most emotionally hazardous duty of the entire war. During the course of a tour of duty, day after day for an entire year, nurses were exposed constantly to sick and wounded young men. They frequently encountered men and boys younger than they who were suffering from massive wounds. The combination of helicopters and field hospitals allowed some soldiers to survive wounds that in any previous war would have been fatal. Sarah McGoran, an army nurse, saw wounds "so big you could put both your arms into them." Napalm and white phosphorous bombs created a new definition of burns—"fourth degree." In Kathryn Marshall's *In the Combat Zone,* published in 1987, a navy nurse speaks of burn victims who had been "essentially denuded. We used to talk about fourth-degree burns—you know, burns are labeled first, second, and third degree, but we had people who were burnt all the way through." Some wounds were so horrific that medical terminology did not exist to describe them. "Horriblectomies were when they'd had so much taken out or removed. Horridzoma meant the initial grotesque injury but also the repercussions of the injury." Rachel Smith had to numb herself "to the screams of teenaged boys whose bodies had been blown to bits, moaning for their mothers, begging for relief, praying for death. Pretty soon it just became another day's work for me. Otherwise, I would've gone nuts." Later in the war, the nurses treated soldier-addicts, young men using opium, amphetamines, cocaine, and heroin to block out the war. "Nobody told me," an army nurse recalled, "I was going to be taking care of so many strung-out motherfuckers. I mean, this was supposed to be a *war*."

Another 1,300 military women performed nonmedical jobs in Vietnam. Most were assigned to the Women's Army Corps, in which they worked as secretaries at MACV. Others were in the Army Signal Corps. Other military women were air traffic controllers, intelligence officers, decoders, or cartographers. For the most part, they were assigned to Saigon and the major bases in South Vietnam. Tens of thousands of civilian women had jobs in South Vietnam during the war. The American Red Cross sent women to Vietnam, as did such other service groups and relief organizations as the American Friends Service Committee, the Mennonite Central Committee, the Agency for International Development, Army Special Services, the USO, Supplemental Recreational Activities Overseas, Catholic Relief Services, and the Christian Missionary Alliance. Civilian women worked with the CIA's Air America and World Airways. Women came to South Vietnam with the international construction firms that had secured billions of dollars in government contracts. Among those construction firms were Brown and Root, Bechtel, and Martin Marietta.

In all, more than 50,000 American women served in Indochina in military and civilian capacities. Eight of them made the ultimate sacrifice. Seven military women died of accidents and disease; Lieutenant Sharon M. Lanz of the Army Nurse Corps died on June 8, 1969, when North Vietnamese rockets hit Chu Lai.

The widening of the ground war and bombing campaigns made infiltration of supplies from North Vietnam more difficult but did not stop it. By the early summer of 1966, 8,000 North Vietnamese Army troops a month were coming into South Vietnam. The communist troop contingent in South Vietnam reached 435,000 people: 46,300 North Vietnamese regulars, 114,000 Main Force Vietcong, 112,000 guerrillas, and more than 160,000 local militia. They did not need ice cream and bowling alleys, so the logistical requirements were simple. By 1966 they needed eight tons of supplies a day. They lived off the land and the peasants.

The supplies the communists could not get from South Vietnamese peasants came from the Soviet Union and China. During the early 1960s, when Nikita Khrushchev preached peaceful coexistence with the West, North Vietnam had gravitated toward the Chinese. But Khrushchev was ousted in 1964, and the new regime, headed by Leonid Brezhnev, was more interested in assisting North Vietnam. The Soviet Union and China were competing for leadership of the communist world, and neither could ignore the tiny ally against which the United States was conducting a major war. Moscow saw the American decision to escalate the war as an opportunity to diminish Chinese influence in Southeast Asia and augment its own. China supplied Hanoi with rice, trucks, AK-47 rifles, and 50,000 laborers; the USSR had sophisticated military technology—fighter aircraft, tanks, and surface-to-air missiles. North Vietnam exploited the Sino-Soviet split, and between 1965 and 1968 received more than $2 billion in assistance from the two powers.

The war's intensification undermined Johnson's political position and threatened his Great Society. At the end of 1965 there were 184,300 American troops in South Vietnam, with another 200,000 scheduled to arrive. Since 1959, 636 United States soldiers had died while another 6,400 were wounded, most of them in the previous two months.

The White House press corps added to Johnson's troubles. The journalists questioned everything. Throughout the 1964 election campaign Johnson had promised to avoid a land war in Asia, but the discrepancies between his promises in 1964 and his actions in 1965 were not the main reason for the growing hostility. Politicians rarely live up to election rhetoric. It was the lies that alienated reporters. Desperate to keep the war from gutting his Great Society, Johnson was trying to mislead the press. He had lied in the summer of 1964 about the incidents in the Gulf of Tonkin; in April 1965 he lied in denying that NSAM 328 had authorized offensive operations on the ground; and he lied repeatedly about the number of troops he was approving for combat in South Vietnam. On May 23, 1965, David Wise of the *New York Herald Tribune* coined the term "credibility gap," and a few days later Murray Marder of the *Washington Post* amplified it.

Theological and social liberals in the main denominations reacted to the war, forming Clergy and Laymen Concerned About Vietnam to mobilize the religious community. It attracted some conservatives and radicals and functioned as one of the first important channels for Jewish and Catholic peace activism. Adopting a moderate tone and asserting its patriotic motivation, always careful to avoid extreme arguments and tactics, the clergy and layman's organization expressed its opposition in ways that kept it on good terms with its basically white, middle-class, religiously motivated constituency.

American university faculties were fertile ground for the antiwar movement. The intellectual left, inactive in the Eisenhower era, had been unable to function as an early critic of war policy, for its connections were too close with the liberal bipartisanship in diplomacy that followed World War II. A symbiotic relationship existed between the Kennedy administration and the intelligentsia, and Johnson began his presidency with noticeable attempts to court the intellectual community. That changed when Johnson ordered 3,000 marines into Danang on March 10, 1965, the first contingent of regular combat troops sent to Vietnam. At the University of Michigan in Ann Arbor, several faculty members organized a "teach-in"—patterned after the famous 1960 civil rights sit-ins—for March 24, 1965. More than 3,500 students attended it. Similar teach-ins occurred at campuses across the country in the spring of 1965, culminating in the "National Teach-In" at 122 colleges and universities on May 15.

Students joined and went beyond faculty liberals. Johnson's lies and his calls for more troops, which disrupted or took the lives of American youths too poor to get college deferments, invaded the young on campus in another way, not lethally but devastatingly. They were the baby boomers, born in the wake of the Good War and reared in prosperity. They were better fed, better housed, and better educated than any previous generation. They thought that anything was possible, that the nation's problems—racial injustice, pockets of poverty, the cold war—would be solved. Optimism was their birthright. Johnson's war in Vietnam had no place in their world view. As the draft calls went out and the lies multiplied, they responded with anger and frustration. During the late 1950s and early 1960s a certain amount of discontent had been a rite of passage. Rock 'n' rollers rebelled against the music and the clothes of their parents; beats rebelled against materialism; college students rebelled against racism. Now rebellion took on a greater urgency still.

The most prominent of the campus antiwar organizations was the Students for a Democratic Society. SDS, founded in 1960 by a group of students politically associated with older leftists, was active in the civil rights movement. By 1964, especially after the Gulf of Tonkin incident, SDS began to organize campus demonstrations and teach-ins against the war and circulated petitions among draft-age men declaring "We Won't Go." On April 17, 1965, SDS sponsored a demonstration in Washington, D.C., which brought more than 20,000 protesters to the city. During the next year, membership grew from 2,000 to nearly 30,000. Other groups, among them the Catholic Peace Fellowship, the Emergency Citizens' Group Concerned About Vietnam, Another Mother for Peace, and the National Emergency Committee of Clergy Concerned About Vietnam, joined the opposition to the war.

Many students ventured beyond talk. Some turned in their draft cards, others burned theirs. They played "tit-for-tat" with the government. As Johnson escalated the war, they escalated theirs. Berkeley students formed a draft resistance movement. "To cooperate with conscription is to perpetuate its existence, without which the government could not wage war," announced an antiwar leader. "I choose to refuse to cooperate with the selective service," wrote Dennis Sweeney, "because it is the only honest, whole, and human response I can make to a military institution which demands the allegiance of my life."

Johnson was now facing two wars, both undeclared and both tearing at the heart of his domestic programs. Mounting casualties and the antiwar movement made the front-page news every day. To keep the political situation from worsening, Johnson decided not to call up the reserves, not to declare a national emergency, not to declare war, and not to tell the truth. When the time came to pay for the war, he chose not to raise taxes. Gordon Ackley, chairman of the Council of Economic Advisers, told him that the war was going to cost $3 billion a month in 1966. Johnson had either to reduce the war effort, to postpone Great Society domestic programs, or to raise taxes. Hoping the war would be over by the end of the year, he ignored the advice, financing the war and the Great Society with budget deficits.

Criticism intensified in Congress among liberal Democrats, whom Johnson needed to pass civil rights and antipoverty legislation. "There are limits to what we can do in helping any government surmount a Communist uprising," Senator Frank Church of Idaho had warned the president in the spring of 1965. "If the people themselves will not support the government in power, we cannot save it." The leading opponent was Senator J. William Fulbright of Arkansas. A Rhodes scholar and a former president of the University of Arkansas, Fulbright was the quintessential cerebral southerner, soft-spoken yet eloquent, politically astute but willing to take moral stands. Upon election to the Senate in 1944, Fulbright had become a close friend and ally of Lyndon Johnson, to the extent of helping the president steer the Gulf of Tonkin Resolution through the national legislature. But by 1965 Vietnam was dividing the two.

Determined to expose the administration's folly to public scrutiny, on February 1966 Fulbright convened the Senate Foreign Relations Committee for special hearings on the war. Forever after Johnson would refer to Fulbright as "Halfbright," a nickname Harry Truman had coined for him. In an effort to upstage the hearings, Johnson convened another conference in Honolulu that met for three days beginning on February 6. There he met with Nguyen Van Thieu, Nguyen Cao Ky, Henry Cabot Lodge (who had replaced Maxwell Taylor as ambassador), Maxwell Taylor, and William Westmoreland.

The Honolulu Conference did not overshadow Fulbright's hearings. Dean Rusk testified for hours spouting the administration line about external communist aggression and saving Southeast Asia. Fulbright countered that the war had really started out as "a war of liberation from colonial rule . . . [which] became a civil war between the Diem government and the Vietcong. . . . I think it is an oversimplification . . . to say that this is a clear-cut aggression by North Vietnam." Fulbright brought in James Gavin, who opposed escalation and called for the enclave strategy in place of offensive operations. Fulbright's trump card was George Kennan, the architect of the containment policy by which the Western nations had confronted communism since the late 1949s. Kennan testified that Vietnam was far away and only tangential to American strategic interests, and that the United States "should liquidate the involvement just as soon as possible."

The hearings changed few minds. Wayne Morse pushed a bill to repeal the Gulf of Tonkin Resolution, but it was voted down ninety-two to five. The Senate approved another $12 billion for the war. Westmoreland launched search-and-destroy missions in all four corps zones. More than 1,700 American troops died in the first three months of 1966, but they killed 15,000 enemy troops. Ho Chi Minh replaced each one, deploying the NVA 324B and 324C Divisions into South Vietnam. The death tolls steadily mounted in 1966, and at midyear Westmoreland asked for 100,000 more troops, hoping to have 480,000 in the field by mid-1967 and as many as 680,000 by early 1968. The joint chiefs urged Johnson to expand the Rolling Thunder raids to include petroleum storage facilities in Hanoi and Haiphong, and at the end of June 1966 he did so.

By that time the war was taking its toll within the administration. George Ball, a longtime critic, finally resigned as undersecretary of state. McGeorge Bundy, the national security adviser, decided the troop buildup had assumed ridiculous proportions. He left the White House in 1966 to head the Ford Foundation. Johnson replaced him with Walt Rostow, who still preached military victory over North Vietnam and looked to the modernization of South Vietnam. Westmoreland continued his cheery reports. But the president sensed that he was losing control of the war. One night in June 1966 he could not get to sleep. Pacing the floor and cursing, he woke up Lady Bird complaining that "victory after victory doesn't really mean victory. I can't get out. I can't finish it with what I have got. So what the hell do I do?"

7

The Mirage of Progress, 1966–1967

It lies within our grasp—the enemy's hopes are bankrupt.
With your support we will give you a success that will impact
not only on South Vietnam, but on every emerging nation in
the world.

—William Westmoreland, November 1967

For the first time in history a battlefield commander, in the middle of a war, was addressing a joint session of Congress. President Johnson had summoned Westmoreland home to discuss the latest requests for more ground troops. On April 28, 1967, his starched uniform tattooed with medals and ribbons from other wars, the general stood ramrod straight and begged for time and support. The greatest problem American boys faced in Vietnam was not enemy troops, he argued, but the will at home to continue: "These men believe in what they are doing. . . . Backed at home by resolve, confidence, patience, determination, and continued support, we will prevail in Vietnam over the Communist aggressor." The thunderous applause reminded many of Douglas Macarthur's homecoming speech with the phrase from a military song "old soldiers never die." Pivoting in a crisp about-face, Westmoreland saluted Vice President Hubert Humphrey and Speaker of the House John McCormick, made another half-spin and saluted the entire Congress, and then marched out of the House. It was great theater, "a good speech" even in the judgment of Senator J. William Fulbright. "From the military standpoint it was fine," he said. "The point is the policy that put our boys over there."

Whatever Westmoreland was saying publicly, his private comments had frightened people at the White House. In response to a question from Robert McNamara about how long it would take to achieve victory, Westmoreland said that it could be five years. The enemy was far more determined than anyone had anticipated.

At the end of October 1966 Johnson, as always thrashing about trying to find some way of explaining the war to himself and the world, had flown to Manila to meet with American military officials and the heads of state of South Vietnam, Australia, Thailand, South Korea, and the Philippines. At the end of the conference he issued the Manila Declaration calling for peace in Southeast Asia and cooperative efforts to conquer hunger, disease, and illiteracy, and provide freedom and security for everyone. On an impulse, he flew from the Philippines to the huge American base at Cam Ranh Bay, South Vietnam, where he waded into GIs shaking hands as if it were an election for county commissioner. The troops received him with so much enthusiasm that Johnson renewed his dedication to the war. He urged the GIs to keep fighting until they "nailed the coonskin to the wall." But Johnson really did not want to continue the hunt. Throughout 1966 he sent prominent American diplomats around the world with the message that he was ready to discuss "any proposals—four points or fourteen or forty; we will work for a cease-fire now or once discussions have begun." Yet Ho Chi Minh's position had not changed: End the bombing, withdraw American troops, remove Thieu and Ky from office, and establish a coalition government in South Vietnam that included the National Liberation Front. "I keep trying to get Ho to the negotiating table," the president remarked to Dean Rusk. "I try writing him, calling him, going through the Russians and the Chinese, and all I hear back is 'Fuck you, Lyndon.'" Of course Johnson's diplomatic posture had not changed either. The United States still insisted that first North Vietnam withdraw its troops from the South and stop supplying the Vietcong. Nor was Johnson willing to accept any political role for the National Liberation Front in South Vietnam. Vice President Hubert Humphrey said it "would be like putting the fox in the chicken coop." All the mediation attempts failed.

Perhaps, in time, American bombs would break the impasse. The Jason Study, commissioned by Robert McNamara in 1966, initially confirmed the effectiveness of the bombing campaigns, which encouraged administration officials in their conviction that airpower could bludgeon North Vietnam into submission. But the air war increasingly revealed itself to be a disaster.

The most stunning failure was in the bombing campaigns over the Ho Chi Minh Trail. They had little or no success in cutting off the Vietcong and North Vietnamese troops from their supply bases above the seventeenth parallel. The communists were constantly improving the transportation system into South Vietnam. In 1963 the Trail had been primitive, requiring a physically demanding, month-long march of eighteen-hour days to reach the south. But by the spring of 1964, the North Vietnamese began striking improvements in the trail. They put nearly 500,000 peasants to work full and part time, building and repairing roads. In one year the communists built hundreds of miles of all-weather roads complete with underground fuel storage tanks, hospitals, and supply warehouses. They built ten separate roads for every main transportation route. By the time the war ended, the Ho Chi Minh Trail had 12,500 miles of excellent roads, complete with pontoon bridges that could be removed by day and reinstalled at night and miles of bamboo

A truck convoy rolls along a road into Laos and the Ho Chi Minh Trail as it transports supplies to North Vietnamese troops fighting in South Vietnam. (*Courtesy, National Archives.*)

trellises covering the roads and hiding the trucks. As early as mid-1965 the North Vietnamese could move 5,000 men and 400 tons of supplies into South Vietnam every month. Robert McNamara estimated that by mid-1967 more than 12,000 trucks were winding their way up and down the trail. By 1974 the North Vietnamese would even manage to build 3,125 miles of fuel pipelines down the trail to keep their army functioning in South Vietnam. Three of the pipelines came all the way out of Laos and deep into South Vietnam without being detected.

Nor did the bombing campaigns do any militarily significant damage to North Vietnam itself. The country had an agricultural economy with few industries vital to the war effort. Anticipating an escalation of the bombing, the North Vietnamese had built enough underground tanks and dispersed them widely enough to have a survival level of gasoline, diesel fuel, and oil lubricants. In 1965 and 1966 North Vietnam began evacuating nonessential people from cities and relocating industries— machine shops, textile mills, and other businesses—to the mountains, jungles, and caves. Home manufacturing filled the modest need for consumer goods. By late 1967 Hanoi's population had dropped from one million to 250,000 people. A little planning robbed the American pilots of their effectiveness. The only targets that could not be moved were bridges, roads, and transportation centers, and almost as soon as they were bombed the North Vietnamese repaired them. They replaced steel bridges with ferries and easily mended pontoon bridges. A long history of fighting the drought and flooding in the Red River Valley was sustaining a cooperative spirit among the North Vietnamese. Political teams organized people to repair roads, help troops and supplies get across rivers, and build air-raid shelters, bunkers, tunnels, and trenches. American pilots were returning to the same places again and again to bomb the same targets. And while the bombing campaigns over North Vietnam eventually killed as many as two million people there, the effect of the air war was to stiffen the will of the North Vietnamese, deepen their resentment of the United States, and cement the power of the communist leadership. George Ball's conclusions about the limits of allied strategic bombing in Germany and Japan, and his suspicions about what a similar campaign would achieve in Vietnam, had proven disturbingly accurate.

The bombing was, to be sure, devastating. During the war the United States dropped one million tons of explosives on North Vietnam and 1.5 million tons on the Ho Chi Minh Trail. In 1967 the bombing raids killed or wounded 2,800 people in North Vietnam each month. The bombers destroyed every industrial, transportation, and communications facility built in North Vietnam since 1954, badly damaged three major cities and twelve provincial capitals, reduced agricultural output, and set the economy back a decade. Malnutrition was widespread in North Vietnam in 1967. But because North Vietnam was overwhelmingly agricultural—and subsistence agriculture at that—the bombing did not have the crushing economic effects it would have had on a centralized, industrial economy. The Soviet Union and China, moreover, gave North Vietnam a blank check, willingly replacing whatever the United States bombers had destroyed.

Weather and problems of distance also limited the air war. In 1967 the United States could keep about 300 aircraft over North Vietnam or Laos for thirty minutes or so each day. But torrential rains, thick cloud cover, and heavy fogs hampered the bombing. Trucks from North Vietnam could move when the aircraft from the carriers in the South China Sea could not.

Throughout the war the North Vietnamese steadily improved their air defense system until it was the most elaborate in the history of the world. They built 200 Soviet SA-2 surface-to-air missile sites, trained pilots to fly MiG-17s and MiG-21s, deployed 7,000 antiaircraft batteries, and distributed automatic and semiautomatic weapons to millions of people with instructions to shoot at American aircraft. The North Vietnamese air defense system hampered the air war in three ways. American pilots had to fly at higher altitudes, and that reduced their accuracy. They were busy dodging missiles, which consumed the moment they had to spend over their target and reduced the effectiveness of each sortie. And they had to spend much of their time firing at missile installations and antiaircraft guns instead of supply lines.

The full recognition of the futility of the bombing would come later in the war. In 1966, Dean Rusk and Walt Rostow had the Jason report to encourage them. The answer must be more bombing. Until May 1965, American bombing raids had been confined to targets south of the twentieth parallel. After May Johnson lifted several restrictions, though he still ordered American pilots to hit no targets within thirty miles of Hanoi or the Chinese border or within ten miles of Haiphong. In April 1966 the operational area was expanded to all of North Vietnam, and by the end of June the list of targets included petroleum storage facilities in Hanoi and Haiphong. Rolling Thunder attacks expanded in February 1967 to include factories, railroad yards, power plants, and airfields in the Hanoi area. From 25,000 sorties over North Vietnam in 1965 the number increased to 79,000 in 1966 and 108,000 in 1967. The United States stayed with the bombing campaign because it was cheaper, in dollars and lives, than ground combat and therefore more acceptable at home.

Robert McNamara was ready to try another technological tool. The only sure way of stopping infiltration across the Demilitarized Zone from North Vietnam was to station huge numbers of troops just south of the seventeenth parallel. Instead, McNamara proposed construction of an electronic barrier. Critics dubbed it "McNamara's Wall." The Third Marine Division agreed to construct the barrier—a twenty-five-mile bulldozed strip of jungle complete with acoustic sensors, land mines, infrared intrusion detectors, booby traps, and electronic wires along the northern border of South Vietnam to detect NVA infiltration. The marines constructed a bulldozed strip of land 660 yards wide and 8.2 miles long from Con Thien to the sea, but the project was weighed down by its own overambitious technology, besides lacking sufficient support from the military. The whole idea struck the North Vietnamese as silly. "What is the use of barbed wire fences and electronic barriers," said General Tran Do, "when we can penetrate even Tan Son Nhut air base outside Saigon?"

It was that kind of war. For most American combat soldiers, the Vietnam experience combined surrealistic incongruity, boredom, suffering, and danger.

At the beginning of the buildup in 1965 and early 1966, most troops arrived in South Vietnam by ship after long voyages from the United States. Their journey to war was not unlike that of their fathers, who had gone to Europe and the Pacific in large, crowded troop transports. By the end of 1966, however, most of the major military units had deployed to Vietnam, and replacement troops arrived by commercial jet. With more than one million American soldiers arriving or leaving the country each year, the military did not possess enough planes or ships to carry the load, so they contracted the job out to commercial airlines. Soldiers went to war in air-conditioned jets, drinking cocktails and beer along the way and ogling the short-skirted stewardesses. Recalling his own trip to South Vietnam via Braniff Airlines, Rob Riggan writes in *Free Fire Zone:* "We might have been over Gary, Indiana. . . . Stewardesses with polished legs and miniskirts took our pillows away from us. As we trooped out the door, they said: 'Good luck! See you in 365 days.'"

At the sixth-month point in a soldier's tour of duty, he was back on the jetliner, drinking highballs and staring at the stewardesses, now known as beautiful "round eyes from the world." The planes took the troops on "R and R"—Rest and Recreation—since the military provided a paid vacation for its men, jetting them to Honolulu, Hong Kong, Tokyo, Bangkok, Manila, Singapore, Taipei, Penang, Kuala Lumpur, and Australia, putting them up in luxury hotels and letting them do whatever they wanted. Many of the men spent the week with their wives, who were flown in, while others dissipated the time with booze and prostitutes. But at the end of the week, they left the air-conditioned hotels, climbed aboard the commercial jets, and returned to the combat zone, hoping to stay alive for six more months and to return to the world of round-eyed stewardesses.

Most of the jets landed at large American bases such as Bien Hoa and Danang. When the troops deplaned, pungent odors of burning excrement assaulted their noses. Base outhouses covered 55-gallon drums that collected the wastes. When the barrels filled, rear-echelon soldiers poured in kerosene and set them on fire, filling the air with a distinctive smell most troops would never forget. To the memory of one soldier, Vietnam smelled like "sweat, shit, jet fuel, and fish sauce all mixed together." In the thick humidity, the odors seemed to hang permanently in the air.

After several days of orientation at the big bases, the soldiers in combat groups made their way—via jeeps, trucks, or helicopters—out to their military units. More than 60 percent of the land that greeted them consisted of heavily forested mountains, hills, slopes, plateaus, and valleys, stretching from the seventeenth parallel south to within fifty miles of Saigon. Sparsely populated, the uplands provided perfect cover and staging areas for North Vietnamese regulars. The remainder of South Vietnam contained heavily populated lowlands where Vietcong guerrillas enjoyed the protection of local villages.

From base camps, combat soldiers went after enemy troops in search-and-destroy operations. They might be "inserted" into an area by helicopter and then patrol from two or three days to a month at a time. Troops often hacked their way through thick uplands vegetation, tall elephant grass, or flooded rice paddies, loaded down by 80-pound packs, heavy, armor-lined flak jacket vests, rifles, mortars, ammunition, and canteens. Infantrymen called the patrols "humping the boonies." During the monsoon season, rain fell constantly, and soldiers had to put up with perpetually wet feet and sometimes "immersion foot"—swollen, blistered, and decaying flesh. If they marched through standing water, leaches burrowed into the skin of their legs and groin. The humidity and the heat, ninety degrees and up, sapped their strength, and many troops were unable to carry enough water to keep themselves from becoming dehydrated. In heavy, canopied jungles, the air resembled a sauna. During Operation Virginia Ridge near the Demilitarized Zone in May 1969, Bravo Company of the 1st Battalion of the 3rd Marine Regiment lost 65 of its 147 men during the first three days of the operation, even though there was no contact with enemy troops. It was heat exhaustion that forced the evacuation of nearly half the company.

Land mines posed the greatest threat to patrolling American combat troops. The Vietcong placed land mines everywhere. Knowing that accidental peasant casualties would diminish Vietcong influence among the people, they taught villagers how to identify mine locations. Villagers often helped the Vietcong manufacture the land mines out of unexploded American ordnance and artillery shell casings. That so few peasants, and so many GIs, stepped on the mines convinced American soldiers that the villagers were supporting the Vietcong. Land mines caused as many as one-third of all American casualties during the war.

Despite all this effort, American soldiers had trouble locating communist troops. The tactical initiative remained with the enemy. North Vietnam's strategy was based on choosing when and where to fight. If American military pressure became too intense, the communists simply melted back into the jungles or into sanctuaries in Cambodia, Laos, and North Vietnam. Official MACV studies indicated that only one percent of all army and Marine Corps search-and-destroy sweeps into the countryside ever resulted in contact with the enemy, and that in 85 percent of all firefights the first shot was fired by enemy troops. "One of our greatest military frustrations in Vietnam," in the retrospective judgment of Robert Komer, an American pacification expert and a deputy to Westmoreland, "was . . . pinning down an elusive enemy. . . . Hanoi was able to control the rate of its own losses by hit-and-run tactics, evasion and use of sanctuaries, which led to military stalemate." Many of Westmoreland's larger operations did not find the enemy in concentrated numbers. His strategy, as the journalist Malcolm Brown described it, was "like a sledgehammer on a floating cork. Somehow the cork refused to stay down."

Worried that enemy forces were preparing to attack the major cities, Westmoreland launched Operation Attleboro in mid-September 1966. Troops probed the "Iron Triangle," or War Zone D, a sixty-square-mile area of rice paddies, dense jungle, rubber plantations, and underground tunnels twenty miles northwest of Saigon. Since late in the 1940s the Iron Triangle had been a communist stronghold. American troops encountered the Vietcong Ninth Division and the NVA 101st Regiment. When the battle was over in mid-November, Westmoreland claimed 1,106 enemy casualties, but he had not trapped and destroyed the communists. In January 1967 the 1st and 25th Infantry Divisions, the 173d Airborne Brigade, the 11th Armored Cavalry, and several ARVN units— a total of more than 35,000 troops—moved into the Iron Triangle again. They spent several weeks removing civilians before going after the Vietcong. Designating the campaign Operation Cedar Falls, they laid waste to the whole region, including the village of Ben Suc, which gained notoriety in the American press after being completely leveled. When the dust settled, another 720 Vietcong were dead and most of their tunnels, elaborately constructed over the previous twenty years, were destroyed. But given the size of the operation, the body count disappointed Westmoreland. More frustrating was its aftermath. Even as American troops were leaving the Iron Triangle, they saw Vietcong with AK-47 rifles walking back into the area.

Westmoreland followed up Operation Cedar Falls with Operation Junction City, an assault on War Zone C in Tay Ninh Province near the Cambodian border. More than 45,000 American and ARVN troops attacked in late February 1967. The operation lasted nearly three months before the Vietcong 9th Division escaped across the border. By that time the division had suffered more than 2,700 casualties. But even that number seemed paltry compared to the investment. The American attack had been unable to trap Vietcong main units. Still, the deputy MACV commander, William DePuy, claimed Junction City to be "a blow from which the VC in this area may never recover."

The communists chose to fight only when they had the advantage— a regiment against a battalion or a battalion against a company. Long before the battle, they rehearsed in scale-model exercises, hid supplies of rice, ammunition, and medicine, and camouflaged bunkers and tunnels. They moved to the battle site in small groups and then assembled for action. They preselected several withdrawal routes; the goal was always to engage the Americans and then break away before the artillery and aerial bombardment began. Soon after the battle started, they began a withdrawal that would not stop until after twelve hours of hard marching in the jungle. More often than not the Americans would be unable to find them.

To deal with that frustration, American policymakers let their faith in technology reach absurd levels. Westmoreland expanded Operation Ranch Hand. C-123 transport planes carrying several chemical agents, particularly dioxin-laced Agent Orange, sprayed suspected enemy strongholds with the herbicides. Eventually, Operation Ranch Hand dumped 19 million gallons of chemical poison on nearly 6 million acres, more than 20 percent of the entire land area of South Vietnam. Westmoreland also wanted to find some way of separating peasants from communist troops. The creation of "free fire zones" was the answer. Labeled "specified strike zones" after 1965, "free fire zones" were described by the Pentagon as "known enemy strongholds virtually uninhabited by noncombatants. They are areas which have been cleared by responsible local Vietnamese authority for firing on specific military targets." The free fire zones were an attempt to design the war along conventional military lines, with enemy forces and friendly forces occupying separate areas. The conveniently labeled "enemy areas" were then subjected to the full application of American firepower. And once more, the military called on technology to solve its problems. Isolation of enemy forces was accomplished not by combat and territorial acquisition but by computer definition. Traditional Vietcong strongholds were defined as being free of noncombatants. Anyone living there was the enemy. In places not identified as Vietcong strongholds, American and ARVN troops relocated civilians. Loudspeakers, aerial leaflet drops, and infantry unit sweeps warned inhabitants to evacuate before the killing machine arrived. Once inhabitants had been warned and evacuation attempts made, MACV declared the region a free fire zone and opened up. By 1967 the free fire zone map at Westmoreland's headquarters was so filled with designated areas outlined in red that the whole country seemed a strike zone.

When American troops went on search-and-destroy missions, they often destroyed villages suspected of harboring enemy troops. Early in August 1965, for example, marines pursued Vietcong troops into the village of Cam Ne in I Corps. Unable to find the guerrillas, the frustrated marines, using Zippo lighters, burned 150 village huts in their futile search. Morley Safer of CBS News filmed the entire event, and Walter Cronkite broadcast it on the evening news. "Zippo squads" were common during the war. Civilians who lost their homes were relocated to refugee camps.

Occasionally, the hunt for enemy troops assumed surrealistic proportions. During Operation Cedar Falls, the villagers of Ben Suc got a taste of the killing machine. A known Vietcong refuge, Ben Suc was doomed. American troops evacuated 6,100 people—no doubt Vietcong as well as civilians—and relocated them to a refugee camp at Phu Loi. A huge sign greeted them: "Welcome to the reception center for refugees fleeing communism." Engineers from the First Infantry Division brought in heavy equipment, including huge plows, and leveled the village. They destroyed every hut, every building, every piece of vegetation. They left behind twenty acres of dust and 6,100 bitter peasants. In February 1968 Vietcong troops overran Ben Tre, the capital city of Kien Hoa Province, and dug in against an awesome display of American firepower. After massive air strikes and naval bombardments, American and ARVN troops recaptured Ben Tre, but by that time the town did not exist anymore. More than 600 civilians were dead, 1,500 seriously wounded, and 4,000 homeless. The journalist Peter Arnett asked an American major about such indiscriminate use of explosives. The answer was the most famous quotation of the war: "It became necessary to destroy the town in order to save it."

The collective impact of such enormous firepower was catastrophic. Arc Light campaigns—B-52 raids inside South Vietnam—brought a level of destruction similar to what tactical nuclear weapons could accomplish. Six B-52s flying in formation at 30,000 feet could drop a bomb load that would pulverize almost everything within an area of

U.S. Air Force F-105
Thunderchief fighter-bombers
drop bombs on North Vietnam.
(*Courtesy, Library of Congress.*)

about 1.5 square miles. Often Vietnamese peasants and enemy troops did not even know the B-52s were coming. They called B-52 strikes "whispering death." The combined effect of naval shelling, B-52 Arc Light raids, 300 daily fighter-bomber sorties, helicopter gunships, howitzers, and mortars averaged out to a daily detonation of 3.5 million pounds of explosives in South Vietnam. General William DePuy summed the strategy perfectly in the spring of 1966: "The solution in Vietnam is more bombs, more shells, more napalm . . . until the other side cracks and gives up."

But civilian peasants, not the Vietcong and North Vietnamese, cracked first. Americans failed to understand that the village was the soul of Vietnamese culture, the key to the often-sought and often-labeled "hearts and minds" of the people. The village was where they were born, where the bones of their ancestors were buried, where mud and water produced the rice that fed their children. Peasants expected to spend all their lives in their villages. American forces destroyed the peasants' way of life. By the end of 1966 more than two million South Vietnamese had lost their homes in accidental bombardments or been moved out of free fire zones before soldiers intentionally destroyed their homes. The number of homeless reached three million in 1967 and almost four million in 1968.

And that was not the worst of it. Between 1965 and 1972 more than one million civilians died in South Vietnam and another one million were wounded, most from the "friendly fire" of American forces. One-third of the South Vietnamese population, and nearly 50 percent of the rural population, either lost their homes or were killed or wounded by American firepower. South Vietnamese civilian casualties reached almost two-thirds the number of Vietcong and North Vietnamese killed. In Quang Ngai Province of I Corps in 1967, the artillery and aerial bombardment was so intense that by year's end more than 300 of the province's 450 villages had been completely obliterated and the number of peasants killed or wounded from indiscriminate shelling was averaging 1,000 people a week. When the journalist Neil Sheehan asked Westmoreland whether the civilian casualties bothered him, the general replied, "Yes, Neil, it is a problem, but it does deprive the enemy of the population, doesn't it?"

In more subtle ways the American presence disrupted the social fabric of traditional Vietnamese society. The destructiveness of the war drove millions of South Vietnamese into the cities, but so did the billions of dollars being pumped into the country. The entire urban Vietnamese economy revolved around providing services to Americans. By 1967 most Vietnamese workers were either Vietcong, ARVN soldiers, or service workers for Americans. So Vietnamese employees of the United States government would have something to spend their money on, Americans brought in a cornucopia of consumer goods—transistor radios, television sets, motor scooters, and watches. Indigenous Vietnamese industries shriveled up and died; inflation skyrocketed; and corruption was rampant.

Given this level of destruction and social disruption, the idea of winning the "hearts and minds" of these peasants through pacification was absurd. Pacification became a bureaucratic backwater of the war, a hodgepodge of programs to which the United States paid lip service only. The most prominent civilian pacification program was the Agency for International Development's $500 million-a-year effort to build schools, health clinics, and agricultural stations. At the same time the CIA had its own pacification program—political action teams of trained South Vietnamese cadres whose mission was to find and eliminate the Vietcong infrastructure. Army Special Forces conducted pacification programs among Montagnard peoples. And in response to American pressure, South Vietnam launched its own pacification effort. The New Life Hamlet Program, successor to the defunct Strategic Hamlet Program, was just as unsuccessful, for it too forcibly relocated peasants and ARVN troops brutally carried out the relocations. In 1966 the New Life Hamlet Program gave way to the Ap Doi Moi Program, which translated as "Really New Life Hamlets." Like its predecessors, it was riddled with official corruption and angered peasants who did not want to leave their ancestral homelands.

The United States simply did not understand its enemy, a cardinal sin among military commanders who aspired to victory. For two thousand years, the Chinese military strategist Sun Tzu's advice had proved true again and again: "Know your enemy." The entire American political establishment had too much faith in firepower and too little an understanding of Vietnamese staying power. The other side was not about to crack and give up. Ho Chi Minh and Vo Nguyen Giap were willing to accept staggering losses—in the millions of people—in order to expel the United States and reunite the country. The pacification programs had been ineffective and counterproductive.

Westmoreland chafed at the numbers of civilians, CIA agents, and ARVN troops engaged in such disjointed pacification efforts, and he wished to bring them all under the MACV umbrella. In November 1966 Ambassador Lodge created the Office of Civil Operations to coordinate pacification, but Westmoreland kept up his demands and in May 1967 President Johnson finally gave in. He established a new agency—Civil Operations and Revolutionary Development Support (CORDS)—to control all pacification efforts. Placing CORDS under the direct control of Westmoreland and MACV militarized the pacification effort.

As director of CORDS and deputy commander to William Westmoreland Johnson named Robert Komer. Born in Chicago in 1922, Komer was a CIA veteran with a Harvard MBA who had arrived at the National Security Council in 1961 preaching the gospel of pacification. He was self-confident, pushy, and abrasive, nicknamed the "Blowtorch." According to one of Lodge's aides, Komer was "a Guildenstern at the court of Lyndon I—willing to please his President at all costs." By 1966 Komer was a special assistant to Johnson. He insisted that South Vietnam would have to win peasant loyalty before a long-term political settlement was possible. Soon there were 8,000 Americans directly engaged in pacification, and within months Komer claimed progress in winning "hearts and minds." Still again, technology was supposed to give the answers. Komer established the Hamlet Evaluation Survey, an elaborate, computerized system for measuring the number of South Vietnamese peasants living in areas "controlled" by the Saigon government. Using eighteen political, economic, and military variables, the survey classified villages into one of five categories, depending on the extent of loyalty to Saigon. At the end of 1967 Komer confidently told Johnson that approximately 67 percent of the South Vietnamese were loyal to their government. Antiwar activists dismissed the estimate. In 1963 General Paul Harkins had also declared 67 percent of the peasants loyal to Saigon. "Politically, we failed to give due weight to the popular appeal of the Viet Cong . . . or the depth of factionalism among traditional South Vietnamese elites," Komer would later confess. "We only grasped belatedly the significance of the steady attrition of GVN authority . . . in the countryside . . . which was directly linked to how the Viet Cong conducted the war."

All the pacification efforts foundered on the strategic reality of the war. For every American dollar spent on pacification, nearly one hun-

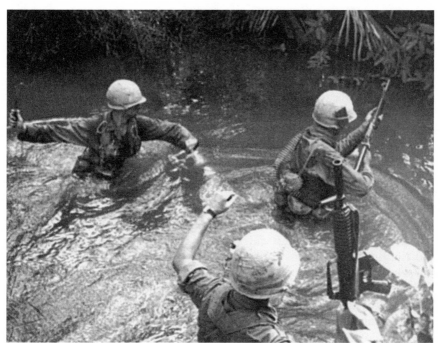

"Waist Deep in the Big Muddy" folk artist Pete Seeger sang of such scenes as this one. (*Courtesy, Library of Congress.*)

dred were spent on military operations. For every American worker engaged in land reform, health care, and education, sixty soldiers were busy blowing the country up. Neither the United States nor South Vietnam could provide villagers security from the Vietcong. During the last seven months of 1966, the Vietcong murdered or kidnapped more than 3,000 Revolutionary Development personnel. Whatever good the pacification programs achieved was undone by the indiscriminate bombardment. Four million peasants were driven from their ancestral villages. Nothing could compensate for that.

Over time, Komer worried more about the political consequences of American bombing and artillery fire in South Vietnam, especially as the number of accidental civilian deaths approached one million people. When the United States first entered South Vietnam, one of its supreme objectives had been to protect peasants from the depredations of the Vietcong. But instead of safety and security, the United States brought death, destruction, and homelessness on a wide scale, and it was easy for Vietcong and North Vietnamese propagandists to convince many peasants that their miseries came from the United States, not from the communists.

Adding to Washington's frustration over the government of Nguyen Cao Ky and Nguyen Van Thieu was their inability to reach an accommodation with the Buddhists. Both Ky and Thieu were Roman Catholics; both were drawn to the French; both were critical of Buddhist values; both were military officers. Led by Thich Tri Quang, the most prominent Buddhist monk in the country, northern Buddhists demanded a civilian government sympathetic to Buddhist culture and Vietnamese independence. The most prominent of the Buddhist dissidents was Nguyen Chanh Thi, the "Warlord of the North," a close associate of Thich Tri Quang. Thi had risen through ARVN ranks to become commander of I Corps in 1965. American marines in I Corps respected Thi for his courage and aggressiveness. In March 1966 Ky traveled to Hue for some military conferences, but Thi snubbed him, calling Ky "my little brother" and ridiculing him in public. Upon returning to Saigon seething with anger, Ky relieved Nguyen Chanh Thi of his command and put him under house arrest. It was just the signal the Buddhists had been waiting for. Thich Tri Quang organized widespread protest demonstrations throughout the northern regions of South Vietnam, claiming that the military government was capricious and dictatorial and calling for creation of a civilian, constitutional democracy. At the end of March, protesters seized the radio stations in Hue and Danang. Promising to "liberate Hue and Danang from the communists," Ky led two Vietnamese marine battalions into Danang and waited for the protests to die out. When they did not do so, he attacked Danang and had to fight his way through ARVN troops still loyal to Thi. The battle, some of it house-to-house combat in Danang, lasted more than a week. In Hue demonstrators attacked the United States Consulate, and Ky had to take military control of the city early in June.

The civil war in Danang and Hue in 1966 raised more doubts in the United States about Nguyen Cao Ky. Breaking the back of the Buddhist political movement had been expensive, especially in American public opinion. American troop levels were approaching 300,000, casualties were mounting, and now television was broadcasting images of South Vietnamese fighting South Vietnamese. Relative casualty figures were also affecting American public opinion. By the end of 1965 there were supposedly 514,000 men serving in the South Vietnamese armed forces along with 184,000 Americans. In 1966 more than 6,000 American soldiers died in Vietnam, as did nearly 12,000 South Vietnamese soldiers. But in 1967, as the pace of the war quickened, the statistics changed. American troop levels climbed to 485,000 men at the end of 1967, and ARVN forces went up to just under 800,000 soldiers. That year nearly 10,000 Americans died, compared to 12,716 South Vietnamese. In the election campaign of 1964 President Johnson had promised that "American boys shouldn't die in a war Asian boys should be fighting," but that is exactly what was happening.

On March 20 and 21, 1967, Westmoreland met with President Johnson and several other administration officials at Guam to discuss the war. The previous June, Johnson had agreed to increase American ground troops to 430,000 by mid-1967, but at Guam, Westmoreland asked for more. A week later he suggested 542,000, calling it a "Minimum Essential Force." He also let Johnson know that what he really needed was an "Optimum Force" of 678,000, which would finish off the enemy in about three years. Johnson could not give Westmoreland 678,000 troops without calling up the reserves and raising draft calls to 60,000 men a month, both of which would raise the ire of Congress and inspire more vehement antiwar protests. Westmoreland would have to make do with 542,000 men. The Vietnam War was already bigger than Korea.

And when he got back to Saigon, Westmoreland learned that MACV intelligence had estimated that Vietcong and North Vietnamese troop strength, including paramilitary and local self-defense troops, exceeded 500,000 people. The general was visibly shaken and wondered, "What am I going to tell the press? What am I going to tell Congress? What is the press going to do with this? What am I going to tell the president?" Still confident of victory, Westmoreland decided on a simple solution: Don't count the paramilitary and self-defense troops. The general did not believe they had much impact on the war anyway, but more important was that "The people in Washington were not sophisticated enough to understand and evaluate this thing and neither was the media."

The Buddhist crisis of 1966 and the inability of ARVN to fight at an acceptable level was meanwhile convincing American leaders that Ky had to go. He was too unpredictable, and he had failed to get ARVN into sustained combat. Ambassador Lodge recommended replacing Ky, and Westmoreland concurred. Nguyen Van Thieu decided to run for president in 1967. The decision caught Ky off guard. He viewed Thieu as a rival, and enjoyed baiting the chief of state by arriving at meetings early and parking his helicopter on the pad Thieu intended to use. The prospect that both of them might run for president gave the American leaders nightmares of a divided military, a civil war, or electoral victory by a weak civilian candidate. They persuaded Ky to accept the vice presidency.

The Thieu-Ky ticket ran a presidential campaign of a kind to be expected of Saigonese politics. The two arrested Buddhist leaders and denied serious rivals positions on the ballot. The election was marked by voter coercion, multiple voting by ARVN troops, fraudulent vote counts, and widespread stuffing of ballot boxes. With all that, Thieu and Ky managed to secure only 35 percent of the vote and win, while a virtually unknown Buddhist peace candidate, Truong Dinh Dzu, came in second with 17 percent. Johnson praised the elections as the "birth of democracy in Southeast Asia," but network broadcasts carried a different message: The sideshow of South Vietnamese politics had concluded another performance. Observers came to the same conclusion. Vietnamese tradition held that political authority was a mandate from heaven. Legitimate political leaders should have overwhelming support from the people, and 35 percent was hardly a heavenly mandate.

Yet American military officials in Saigon believed the Vietcong and North Vietnamese were approaching the long-awaited point at which they could not put troops in the field fast enough to replace their dead. In the first half of 1967 the body count was up to 7,316 Vietcong and North Vietnamese a month. MACV's attrition charts, which did not include local enemy militia, showed that the number of enemy troops had declined from 275,000 men in late 1966 to 242,000 in mid-1967. Westmoreland declared in August 1967 that "Enemy armed strength is falling, not spectacularly and not mathematically provable, but every indication suggests this. . . . There is evidence that we may have reached the crossover point." Victor Krulak was unimpressed. He remembered a similar claim by General Paul Harkins in 1963, a decline in Vietcong from 124,000 men to 102,000. No such decline had taken place. Then at the end of 1967 Westmoreland estimated that more than 220,000 enemy troops were dead. "Wastefully, expensively, but nonetheless indisputedly, we are winning the war," Komer proclaimed. "We are grinding the enemy down by sheer weight and mass." Krulak's pessimism was wiser. The United States was spending $2 billion per month on the war, and although the communists had taken severe casualties, Saigon and the Americans were not killing the 250,000 troops a year necessary to slow down the enemy.

Westmoreland and Komer also took cheer in the growing success of the Chieu Hoi, or Open Arms Program. Launched in 1963 by Robert Thompson, Chieu Hoi offered amnesty to Vietcong and attracted thousands of deserters by 1967—Komer claimed more than 40,000. At the end of American involvement in 1973, Americans would be estimating that 159,741 Vietcong had deserted. But critics called the program "R and R" for Communists." Most genuine defectors were low-level Vietcong who had never been enthusiastic about their commitment; the others were Vietcong plants trying to infiltrate the program. Some changed sides as many as five times during the war. William E. Colby, the pacification leader and later CIA chief, estimated that in 1969 and 1970 only 17,000 of the reported 79,000 Chieu Hoi converts were sincere. But Westmoreland and Komer were true believers.

There was other encouraging evidence, good enough at least for true believers. The Vietcong were having trouble by 1967 getting new recruits, primarily because so many millions of South Vietnamese were in refugee camps. The population of Saigon had swelled from 1.4 million in 1962 to 4 million in 1967, and it was also more difficult for the Vietcong to slip recruits out of the cities. Intelligence reports indicated that Main Force Vietcong battalions were no longer at peak strength of from 600 to 700 troops. But Hanoi was replacing the Vietcong with regular North Vietnamese troops in numbers sufficient to augment total communist strength.

While Westmoreland's confidence in military victory continued to inspire Johnson, Rusk, and Rostow, Lodge became one of an increasing number of defectors. He had decided that Westmoreland was applying World War II tactics to a modern guerrilla war and that he was incapable of incorporating political variables into his strategic thinking. In April 1967 Lodge retired to Boston. Lodge's replacement was Ellsworth Bunker. Bunker, heir to the National Sugar Refining Company fortune, was a multimillionaire who had become a Democrat during the 1930s. In the 1950s and early 1960s, he filled ambassadorial posts in India, Argentina, and Italy. A New Englander with an obsessive taste for maple syrup (he had it flown fresh to Saigon) and all the reserve of his Yankee forefathers, Bunker earned the title of "Mr. Refrigerator" from the Vietnamese in Saigon. In May 1967 Bunker was prepared to give his entire support to William Westmoreland and the war effort. Lodge's departure had deprived Johnson of his only independent point of view in Saigon.

Sir Robert Thompson, the British expert on counterinsurgency, lost faith as well. Ever since 1961 he had warned against a military solution to the political problem in Vietnam, and when he saw Westmoreland unleash the killing machine, Thompson knew immediately that the United States was on its way to failure. "American policy in South Vietnam," Thompson warned Lodge, "is stupid. It doubles the firepower and squares the error. Every artillery shell the United States fires into South Vietnam might kill a Vietcong but will surely alienate a Vietnamese peasant."

McNamara had been weakening since 1966, increasingly enduring the sickening awareness that he had been wrong, horribly wrong, and that hundreds of thousands of people were dead because of his decisions. The United States could not stop the flow of men and supplies from North Vietnam, not unless Washington was willing to unload strategic nuclear weapons on North Vietnam and Laos. In October 1966 McNamara wrote a memo warning the president that to "bomb the North sufficiently to make a radical impact on Hanoi's political, economic and social structure would require an effort which we could make but which could not be stomached either by our own people or by world opinion." As far as he was concerned, the United States had played with air power its last promising card and lost.

In May 1967 McNamara asked Johnson to stop the air war over North Vietnam, put a cap on troop levels, and seek a diplomatic settlement. The "picture of the world's greatest superpower killing or seriously injuring 1,000 noncombatants a week, while trying to pound a tiny backward nation into submission on an issue whose merits are hotly disputed," he told the president, "is not a pretty one." McNamara was now skeptical of the attrition strategy and Westmoreland's talk of the crossover. "The point," he puzzled, "is that it didn't add up. If you took the strength figures and the body count, the defections, the infiltration and what was happening to us, the whole thing . . . didn't add up. . . . How the hell the war went on year after year when we stopped the infiltration or shrunk it and when we had a very high body count. . . . It didn't add up." In June McNamara commissioned a top-secret study. With the aid of Morton Halperin, deputy assistant secretary of defense, Leslie H. Gelb of Havard set out writing what within a few years would be known as the Pentagon Papers. But at the moment McNamara was asking Gelb to get the study under way, Johnson decided to rid his administration of McNamara. By the end of the summer the president managed to position McNamara for the presidency of the World Bank. In November 1967 McNamara resigned.

Within the larger division in Washington politics, some hard-liners had strong ties to the military: Senators John C. Stennis of Mississippi, Henry Jackson of Washington, Stuart Symington of Missouri, Gale McGee of Wyoming, Russell Long of Louisiana. Long denounced all "who encourage the Communists to prolong the war. I swell with pride when I see Old Glory flying from the Capitol. . . . My prayer is that there may never be a white flag of surrender up there." The joint chiefs threatened to resign in mass if Johnson adopted McNamara's proposal for de-escalation. In August 1967 Stennis, who chaired the Senate Armed Services Committee, convened hearings on the war. After listening to a parade of military officials, the committee concluded that "civilians had consistently overruled the unanimous recommendations of military commanders and the joint chiefs of staff." At least one commander, Admiral Ulysses S. Grant Sharp, would later hold the line on paper even after it had crumbled in the real world: "We could have flattened every warmaking facility in North Vietnam. But the handwringers had center stage. . . . The most powerful country in the world did not have the willpower needed to meet the situation."

Westmoreland and Walt Rostow meanwhile worked out specific plans for increasing the pressure on the communists. In particular, they wanted to implement heavy American bombing of Vietcong and North Vietnamese sanctuaries in Laos and Cambodia. They also looked to invading Laos and Cambodia and cutting the North Vietnamese supply lines along the Ho Chi Minh Trail. Both men urged Johnson to permit Westmoreland's "hook north of the DMZ" to trap the assembled North Vietnamese troops and stop their operations in I Corps. And they wanted a massive bombing campaign against every military and industrial target in North Vietnam. Their relentless trust in battle had begun to frustrate even the president. "Bomb, bomb, bomb, that's all you know," he fumed in response to a demand by General Wheeler for a multiplication of Rolling Thunder raids. To Westmoreland's requests for more troops, he replied, "When we add divisions, can't the enemy add divisions? If so, where does it all end?"

Increasing numbers of people in the Washington establishment criticized Johnson from the other direction. Senators Wayne Morse of Oregon and Ernest Gruening of Alaska had been early critics and in 1966 and

1967 other prominent legislators joined their ranks. Senator J. William Fulbright of Arkansas, the first of the new skeptics, was soon followed by Senators Eugene McCarthy of Minnesota, Robert Kennedy of New York, George McGovern of South Dakota, George Aiken of Vermont, Edward Kennedy of Massachusetts, Frank Church of Idaho, and Mark Hatfield of Oregon. Disillusioned legislators proposed everything from a bombing halt to a troop withdrawal to peace negotiations—anything but escalation. Several retired military officers also declared their opposition to the war. David Shoup, winner of the Congressional Medal of Honor at Tarawa and commandant of the Marine Corps under Dwight Eisenhower and John Kennedy, told a college audience in May 1966, "I don't think the whole of Southeast Asia, as related to the present and future safety and freedom of the people of this country, is worth the life or limb of a single American." General Matthew Ridgway, by then retired, called for a bombing halt, insisting, "There is nothing in the present situation or in our code that requires us to bomb a small Asian nation back into the stone age." James Gavin spread the opinions he had shared with the Senate Foreign Relations Committee in 1966, that the United States should shift to an enclave strategy. A "free, neutral and independent Vietnam" he declared, "can be established, with guarantees of stability from an international body." Johnson wanted nothing of enclaves: We "can't hunker down like a jackass in a hail-storm."

In early 1965 Bess Abell, the White House social secretary, had suggested to Eric F. Goldman, the resident intellectual in the Johnson administration, that it would be nice to do something "cultural" during the spring social season. It was the sort of thing that Jack and Jackie, at their witty best fashionable and charming, had done so well at a dinner for Nobel Prize winners and the Pablo Casals concert. Johnson proposed a White House Festival of the Arts. Without thinking too much about it, he concluded that it would be a "nice thing" to do. The social secretary harbored a few reservations—"writers and artists. These people can be troublesome"—but she went along. Invitations were sent to leading artists in painting, sculpture, literature, music, dance, cinema, and photography. Goldman made certain that "no attention was given to politics, ideology, opinions or personal habits of the people chosen." The list included a former communist, a number of radicals, and a liberal sprinkling of drunks. Almost everyone who was invited accepted, and a large number of people who were not invited tried to wangle an invitation.

The trouble started when one prospective guest decided that he could not in good conscience attend. After considerable thought, the poet Robert Lowell had concluded that his attendance might serve as a form of passive support for Johnson's actions in Vietnam. In an open letter to Johnson published in the *New York Times,* Lowell wrote: "We are in danger of imperceptibly becoming an explosive and suddenly chauvinistic nation, and may even be drifting on our way to the last nuclear ruin. . . . I feel that I am serving you and our country best by not taking part in the White House Festival of the Arts."

For Johnson—who after all was simply trying to do a "nice thing"—it was proof that "these people" did not like him. He believed they certainly would not have treated Jack Kennedy in such a fashion. And that the *Times* gave front-page treatment to the letter was proof that the entire eastern establishment opposed him. Although Johnson's division between "them" and "us" was an oversimplification—most artists and intellectuals gladly accepted their invitations—it did contain a germ of truth. For "them" Johnson was the hick from the Hill Country of Texas, the cowboy who picked up puppies by the ears, proudly displayed his gall bladder scar, and held conferences while sitting on the john. The *New York Review of Books* editor Robert B. Silvers and the poet Stanley J. Kunitz drafted a public telegram to Johnson supporting Lowell's position, and eventually more than twenty influential artists, writers, and critics signed the telegram. Vietnam, not the arts, had become the issue.

Feeling betrayed, Johnson threatened not to attend the affair, but in the end he showed up for a few minutes. The event turned into a nasty political get-together. John Hersey read from his book *Hiroshima*, published in 1946, and prefaced his reading by announcing, "We can not for a moment forget the truly terminal dangers, in these times, of miscalculation, of arrogance, of accident, of reliance not on moral strength but on mere military power. Wars have a way of getting out of hand." The cultural critic Dwight Macdonald treated the festival as if it were a political rally. He offensively criticized his host, verbally assaulted guests, and worked to get signatures on a petition backing Lowell. "Having convictions doesn't mean that you have to lack elementary manners," Hollywood's Charlton Heston scolded him. "Are you really accustomed to signing petitions against your host in his own home?" Johnson, gone before the fireworks started, announced loudly enough for the press to hear that "Some of them insult me by staying away and some of them insult me by coming." At least, he added later to a friend, "nobody pissed in the punchbowl."

By 1967 the separate college-campus years of rage had long since commenced. Protesters followed government officials, obstructing their movements and interrupting speeches. In October 1966, the Socialist party leader Norman Thomas, frail and nearly blind, spoke out at Harvard against the war. "If I die before this war is ended," he said, "I will feel that my whole life's work for decency has been a failure." Students struck at symbols of the power establishment. They campaigned to abolish Reserve Officer Training Corps (ROTC) programs. Military recruiters and companies with war contracts got chased off campus. And not all the disruption occurred at the radical universities. By early 1967 even traditionally conservative Stanford had been pulled into the antiwar movement. When good-natured Vice President Hubert Humphrey spoke there, hundreds of students, in an orchestrated protest, stood up and left the auditorium halfway through his talk.

The protests swept beyond the campuses. They became part of the youth counterculture. Quick to respond to changes in the popular mood, folksingers wrote and performed antiwar songs. Phil Ochs, a handsome, angry folk artist emergent from the same Greenwich Village clubs as Bob Dylan, sang at protests across the country. As he sang, he talked— about the need to end the war and the country's reactionary government. Introducing one song, he noted, "Now, for a change of pace, here's a protest song. . . . A protest song is a song that's so specific that you cannot mistake it for bullshit. . . . Good word, bullshit . . . ought to be used more often . . . especially in Washington. . . . Speaking of bullshit . . . I'd like to dedicate this song to McGeorge Bundy." In 1967 Ochs helped to organize several rallies under the slogan "War Is Over." The songs of Phil Ochs, Joan Baez, and other troubadours of the antiwar movement combined with the voices of frustrated students. The resulting lament echoed across the country.

The stalemate in Vietnam also undermined what the historian William Turley calls "the reflexive patriotism of ordinary citizens." Some Americans opposed the war on fundamental moral grounds, while others believed Johnson was not fighting it properly. Whatever their explanations, most Americans were discouraged about Vietnam. In the summer of 1967 support for the war dropped under 50 percent for the first time. When Johnson went to Congress in August for a 10 percent income tax surcharge to pay for the war, it dropped even more. By October only 28 percent of the public said they supported Johnson. At the end of the month, more than 100,000 people gathered in Washington to protest the war; 35,000 of them showed up at the Pentagon entrance.

But it was hardly a unified movement. A. J. Muste and David Dellinger opposed all wars on moral grounds. New Left radicals like SDS leader Tom Hayden hoped to use the Vietnam War protest movement to attack racism and capitalism and build a new society. Liberal critics, among them Senator J. William Fulbright, the historian Arthur M. Schlesinger, Jr., and the economist John Kenneth Galbraith, decided that the United States was backing a corrupt regime and fighting an impossible war in a country unrelated to American national security. Protesters got to Americans who did not identify with the antiwar movement. They did so by keeping Johnson's Vietnam policies at the forefront of public debate— week after week, month after month, year after year.

In response, Johnson launched Operation Chaos, a CIA domestic surveillance campaign to spy on antiwar leaders and discover communists among them. Eventually Operation Chaos developed files on more than 7,000 Americans and accused them, without real evidence, of being communists or communist stooges directed by Hanoi. Several years later

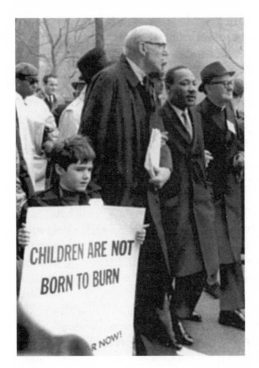

Dr. Benjamin Spock, Dr. Martin Luther King Jr., and Monsignor Charles O. Rice link arms as they march in an anti-Vietnam War rally in New York's Central Park. (*Courtesy, Library of Congress.*)

the Nixon administration would add to those files. The president also set in motion a public relations blitz to rebuild public support for the war. The program included formation of the Committee for Peace and Freedom in Vietnam, a group dedicated to inspiring the "silent center," or what Richard Nixon would later call the "silent majority." Speakers went out around the country trying to prove the war was being won. The president decided on an encore performance by General Westmoreland. The April appearance before Congress had played to such good reviews. On November 21, 1967, Westmoreland spoke before the National Press Club, claiming, "We are making progress. . . . The enemy's hopes are bankrupt."

In a further effort to calm the antiwar movement, the president in a speech in San Antonio on September 29 tried to prove his willingness to negotiate. For the first time he slightly modified American demands. Instead of insisting on an immediate withdrawal of all North Vietnamese troops, he offered to stop bombing North Vietnam if Ho Chi Minh agreed to serious negotiations and promised not to use the bombing halt to increase infiltration into South Vietnam. Johnson even hinted at allowing the National Liberation Front to participate in the South Vietnamese government. Journalists quickly dubbed the proposal the "San Antonio Formula." North Vietnam made no response, except to say that besides permitting a coalition government in Saigon that included the

NLF, the United States should stop all bombing of North Vietnam, withdraw all troops from Indochina, and remove Thieu and Ky from office. It was the same message North Vietnam had been sending for years.

While lawmakers and the nation at large debated the war, marine officials were carrying out their own war on Westmoreland and the army. Since 1965 the marines had argued that attrition was not working. Victor Krulak wrote to Robert McNamara in 1966 that the "raw figure of VC killed . . . can be a dubious index of success since, if their killing is accompanied by devastation of friendly areas, we may end up having done more harm than good." The northern five provinces of South Vietnam were thick with rain forests and rugged mountains, except along a twenty-five-mile strip between the South China Sea and the mountains, where 98 percent of the people lived. The marines wanted to spread out from bases at Chu Lai, Phu Bai, and Danang, mixing with the population, fighting the Vietcong when necessary but conducting pacification programs among peasants with combined action platoons. Campaigning in the mountains, where two percent of the population lived, was irrelevant because, as Krulak said, "there is nothing of value there."

By mid-1967 there were already 55,000 marines in I Corps, commanded by General Lewis Walt. Twice a winner of the Navy Cross in World War II, Walt had grown up on a Kansas ranch before playing football at the Colorado School of Mines and joining the Marine Corps. He had the discipline of an offensive lineman, but in I Corps he found himself in an impossible situation. On the one hand Krulak wanted him to continue the combined action platoons and wait for the Vietcong to venture down to the coast, where the killing machine could cut them to pieces. But he was under the operational command of William Westmoreland, who ordered him to head into the Annamese mountains and kill the enemy. The marine contingent would peak at 70,000 troops at the end of the year, not enough to carry out both missions. Vo Nguyen Giap understood the problem. "The marines are being stretched as taut as a bowstring," he said. The marine commandant Wallace Greene tried to make the case to the joint chiefs, but they sided with Westmoreland.

Ho Chi Minh had been watching American politics with great interest. It did not look much different from the political battles in Paris thirteen years before. Ho knew that Lyndon Johnson's political base was eroding just at the moment that American military might in South Vietnam was reaching its peak. A later remark by Vo Nguyen Giap describes the American dilemma exactly: The "Americans will lose the war on the day when their military might is at its maximum and the great machine they've put together can't move any more. . . . We'll beat them at the moment when they have the most men, the most arms, and the greatest hope of winning."

Throughout 1967 the United States and North Vietnam fought a series of battles near the Demilitarized Zone in I Corps, along the Laotian and Cambodian borders in the Central Highlands of II Corps, and in the rubber plantations and jungles in III Corps northwest of Saigon. Since 1966 the NVA 324B Division had been pushing across the Demilitarized Zone, trying to draw the marines into the jungles and hills of I Corps. Westmoreland sent the marines after them, but the North Vietnamese then pulled back across the DMZ, only to return again and again over the next several months. By October the debate over strategy between Walt and Westmoreland was finished. Walt pulled the 3rd Marine Division out of Danang and established a series of fixed positions south of the DMZ at Gio Linh and Con Thien in the east, and along Route 9 to Khe Sanh, where they could fight North Vietnamese coming across the DMZ or in from Laos. That left the 1st Marine Division stretched out from Chu Lai in the south to Danang in the north. To reinforce them Westmoreland deployed Task Force Oregon to I Corps. It was a composite unit of the 11th Infantry Brigade, the 196th Light Infantry Brigade, and the 198th Infantry Brigade. They concentrated their efforts in Quang Nam, Quang Tin, and Quang Ngai provinces. Marine pacification was over.

The first of the border battles of late 1967 took place at Con Thien. Known as the "Hill of Angels," Con Thien was actually three hills south of the DMZ in eastern Quang Tri Province. Troops from the 3rd Marine Division assumed a defensive position at Con Thien as part of McNamara's electronic barrier, hoping to interrupt NVA troop movements across the DMZ. Early in September North Vietnamese troops, equipped with Soviet artillery, began shelling the marine positions. Convinced the enemy was setting the stage for a conventional battle, Westmoreland thought he would finally have an opportunity to take the NVA 324B and 324C Divisions head-on. He launched Operation Neutralize to relieve the marines at Con Thien, and during the next month more than 4,000 B-52s and fighter-bomber sorties, along with heavy naval bombardment, struck the NVA positions. By the last week of October the United States had dumped 40,000 tons of explosives on Con Thien, and the North Vietnamese suddenly broke off the engagement, leaving behind 2,000 dead.

No sooner had the siege of Con Thien been lifted than the Vietcong and North Vietnamese struck again, far to the south near the Cambodian border. On October 27, the 88th NVA Regiment attacked Song Be in Phuoc Long Province, and two days later the Vietcong attacked at the rubber plantations of Loc Ninh in Binh Long Province. For ten days the Vietcong 273d Regiment assaulted American positions defended by the First Infantry Division. When the battle was over, the First Infantry had lost 50 men while the Vietcong sustained 2,000 casualties, half of them combat deaths. The Vietcong disengaged early in November and retreated into Cambodia. Westmoreland proclaimed another great victory. But in November the North Vietnamese staged a series of skirmishes near Dak To in Kontum Province, including an assault on the Special Forces camp there. Hoping to cut off infiltration through Laos into II Corps and relieve the attack on Dak To, Westmoreland dispatched portions of the 4th Infantry Division and the 173d Airborne Brigade. They were hunting for the 24th NVA Regiment. Throughout most of November the American troops assaulted fortified NVA positions, complete with tunnels and bunkers, along the ridge lines in the area. By November 20 the center of battle was focused on Hill 875, about twelve miles west of Dak To. Westmoreland hit the NVA positions with 300 B-52 and 2,000 fighter-bomber sorties before American troops went up the hill. By the time they got to the top, the North Vietnamese had already left. It was Thanksgiving Day. More than 1,200 North Vietnamese were dead, but so were 289 Americans. Helicopters flew in hot turkey and stuffing, mashed potatoes with gravy, candied yams, cranberry sauce, hot rolls and butter, and lots of beer, Cokes, and ice cream. "We had soundly defeated the enemy without unduly sacrificing operations in other areas," Westmoreland proclaimed. An American journalist at Hill 875 had the better judgment: "With victories like this, who needs defeats?"

But Westmoreland was never more certain that victory was at hand. By the end of 1967, the enemy death toll was more than fifteen times the 16,021 GI lives the war had taken. Nearly half of all the enemy battalions, Westmoreland claimed, were no longer combat-effective. The border battles were proof of American superiority. Enemy supply lines had been so decimated by American firepower that enemy troops had to keep close to the Laotian and Cambodian borders and the Demilitarized Zone. The communists were no longer capable, Westmoreland was convinced, of bringing the war to the heart of South Vietnam.

Johnson needed advice. Like Eisenhower and Kennedy before him, he listened to hard-liners and advocates of a scaling back, and he charted a middle course, hoping to secure the political integrity of South Vietnam without triggering a Soviet or Chinese intervention. Yet that middle course led inexorably to steady escalation. For another opinion, Johnson turned to the Wise Men.

On November 1, 1967, they assembled at the White House, the "best and the brightest" of two generations. Dean Acheson was there, as were McGeorge Bundy, Maxwell Taylor, Henry Cabot Lodge, W. Averell Harriman, and George Ball along with General Omar Bradley, World War II hero and chairman of the Joint Chiefs of Staff during the Korean War; Supreme Court Justice Abe Fortas, one of Johnson's closest advisers; Clark Clifford, another intimate of Johnson who had been a trusted Truman aide and head of the Foreign Intelligence Advisory Board during the Kennedy administration; Douglas Dillon, former secretary of the treasury under Kennedy; and Robert Murphy, a prominent career diplomat.

Johnson asked the Wise Men whether he was on the right course, and they responded as he had expected. Straight from Acheson, the old cold warrior from the Truman administration, came the opinion that "We certainly should not get out of Vietnam." McGeorge Bundy concurred, arguing that "getting out of Vietnam is as impossible as it is undesirable." While he listened to the Wise Men, Walt Rostow became exultant, urging Johnson "to have a full leadership meeting of this kind, introduced by yourself, after which you could put the whole thing on television." They all told Johnson what he wanted to hear, all except one. Former Undersecretary of State George Ball suddenly stood up and shouted: "I've been watching you across the table. You're like a flock of buzzards sitting on a fence, sending the young men off to be killed. You ought to be ashamed of yourselves."

Ball was a minority of one. Withdrawal was still out of the question if there was to be any hope for the survival of a noncommunist government in South Vietnam. Nor would Johnson's personality permit it. He was too proud, too committed to presidential greatness to give up. Bundy suggested a possibly workable course: abandoning the big-unit sweeps that brought such heavy casualties. Smaller unit operations, designed to reduce American casualties, should go with a concerted effort to transfer major combat responsibilities to ARVN. That way the American people would tolerate politically an effort that might take five or ten years to accomplish. For the first time in years, Johnson began seriously to reconsider his commitment to Westmoreland's strategy of attrition. But for the short run, he needed a big victory to salvage his administration, something akin to what the battle of Antietam had done for Abraham Lincoln in 1862 or the Normandy invasion for Franklin D. Roosevelt in 1944.

Military intelligence indicated that North Vietnam had massed nearly 40,000 troops around Khe Sanh in western Quang Tri Province, eighteen miles south of the DMZ and eight miles east of Laos. The North Vietnamese 325C Division was northwest of Khe Sanh; the 304th Division was to the southwest; and elements of the 320th and 324th Divisions were ready for reinforcement. Westmoreland thought Khe Sanh to be of great strategic significance. It could be used for covert operations into Laos and reconnaissance flights over the Ho Chi Minh Trail, and as a base to cut off infiltration along Highway 9. Perhaps a battle there would be of the conventional kind for which the military longed. Johnson hoped for Khe Sanh to provide him the victory he was seeking. He had a scale model of Khe Sanh built in the White House situation room so he could follow the battle day by day and eventually hour by hour. The press called Khe Sanh "another Dienbienphu."

Westmoreland added 6,000 marines to the force already at Khe Sanh and launched Operation Niagara to pulverize the enemy. For the next two months he sent more than 5,000 aircraft sorties against the North Vietnamese positions, detonating over 100,000 tons—200 million pounds—

of explosives on less than five square miles. On January 21, 1968, the North Vietnamese artillery bombardment began. It was just what Westmoreland had expected. As at Dienbienphu, an intense artillery attack would be followed by an infantry assault. The marines dug in and waited. Westmoreland waited. Lyndon Johnson waited. But the attack did not come. Instead, tens of thousands of Vietcong were sneaking into the cities and provincial capitals of South Vietnam. In the early morning hours of January 31, while Americans waited for the attack on Khe Sanh, the Tet offensive began.

8

Tet and the Year
of the Monkey, 1968

*If this is a failure, I hope the Viet Cong never have a major
success.*
—Senator George Aiken, February 1968

It was January 24, 1968, and in Saigon, Robert Komer offered an assessment of the war at the "five o'clock follies," when the press gathered to
hear the latest "General Blimp" reports. Komer was at his optimistic
best: "We begin 1968 in a better position than we have ever been." At the
White House, Lyndon Johnson was in his bathrobe, unable to sleep, pacing the floor as he read the cables on Khe Sanh. A Pentagon photo-
graphic analyst was on hand waiting for one of the president's requests
to explain something in an aerial photograph. A table model of Khe
Sanh, with small flags posted on the periphery, indicated the presence
of several NVA divisions. In the middle, poised on the plateau, were the
insignia of marine battalions. Khe Sanh was Johnson's obsession. "I
don't want any damn Dinbinphoo," he told Earle Wheeler.

William Westmoreland was no less obsessed. The border battles of late
1967 and early 1968 at Con Thien, Loc Ninh, Dak To, and Khe Sanh had
convinced him that the enemy shift to conventional warfare was at hand;
the invasion would begin just south of the Demilitarized Zone. For two
months Westmoreland transferred combat units north. By early January
1968 more than half of all American combat units were in I Corps.

The real target was not Khe Sanh. It was all of urban South Vietnam.

In mid-1967 North Vietnam had contemplated a major attack. American fire-power was inflicting massive casualties on communist troops,
and the Thieu-Ky government seemed to be stable. North Vietnam was
weary of the bombing and yearned for peace. United States troops controlled the cities, and the narrowness of the country, along with the
recent innovations in helicopter and air cavalry operations, allowed the
Americans to attack a wide range of targets and to do so at their pleasure. Hanoi also worried about a possible American invasion of North
Vietnam. Rapid urbanization in South Vietnam was shrinking the number of people available in the countryside for Vietcong recruitment. The
communists wanted a dramatic military event that would undermine
the Saigon regime and force out the United States.

The nature of that event was intensely debated. Nguyen Chi Thanh went to Hanoi in June 1967 to call for a massive attack on the cities of South Vietnam using local Vietcong guerrillas, Main Force Vietcong, and NVA regulars. He predicted tactical as well as strategic success. Thanh felt sure the communists could inspire a peasant uprising in South Vietnam, undermine the Thieu-Ky regime, force an ARVN surrender, secure a military foothold in the major cities and provincial capitals, and inflict enormous casualties on Americans. Thanh also wanted to bring the war home to the South Vietnamese cities. In the Politburo, Le Duan supported Thanh, but Vo Nguyen Giap opposed him. The United States was at the height of its power. If the massive attack failed and Main Force Vietcong and NVA units were destroyed, the revolution would be set back years. Giap offered an alternative. NVA troops would create diversions in border areas, drawing American combat units out of the cities, while Vietcong guerrillas, with some Main Force support, launched the general offensive. Thanh retorted that Giap was sacrificing the Vietcong, most of them southerners, while North Vietnamese regulars were safe in diversionary activities. The debate was intense until July 6, 1967, when Thanh died suddenly. Giap's view prevailed.

North Vietnam also devised a series of diplomatic diversions. In the fall the National Liberation Front initiated secret contacts with the United States embassy and mentioned the possibility of peace talks. In December 1967 Pham Van Dong announced Hanoi's intention to sit down and talk about the war once the United States stopped the bombing. The North Vietnamese were trying to drive a wedge between the United States and South Vietnam, which did not want peace talks of any kind, and to raise hopes among Americans that a negotiated settlement was near.

Late in July the Politburo voted to launch the attack early in 1968. By September the North Vietnamese were infiltrating huge volumes of supplies and hiding them near provincial capitals and major cities. More than 84,000 Vietcong troops moved into position while NVA troops distracted Westmoreland with the border battles. Tran Van Tra headed Vietcong forces in South Vietnam. He had first assumed command of Main Force Vietcong in 1963. Nguyen Chi Thanh took over in 1964. When Thanh died, Tra was back in power. As operational planner of the offensive, Tra selected Tran Do, a commander beloved by his troops because of his willingness to live in the field with them.

American intelligence realized that more supplies than ever were moving down the Ho Chi Minh Trail, but the specialists were convinced the attack would come at Khe Sanh. As the end of the year approached, the communists appealed to ARVN and MACV for a cease-fire during the Tet holiday so that Vietnamese could celebrate the new year. Believing in the sincerity of the foe, South Vietnam sent half of ARVN troops home for the holidays. That was a mistake. The Vietcong had infiltrated five armed battalions into Saigon alone. In the week before Tet they drifted into the city on foot, bicycles, and mopeds. The leadership established a central command post and a field hospital underground at the Phu Tho racetrack in Cholon.

Just after midnight on January 30, 1968, the Vietcong attacks began. In addition to assaults on thirty-six of the forty-four provincial capitals and five of six major cities, they struck the United States embassy, Tan Son Nhut air base, the presidential palace, and the South Vietnamese general staff headquarters. In I Corps they hit Quang Tri City and Tam Ky, seized Hue, raising the National Liberation Front flag over the Citadel, and attacked the marines at Chu Lai and Phu Bai. II Corps was shaken by assaults on Tuy Hoa and Phan Thiet as well as the American bases at Bong Son and An Khe. In III Corps the Vietcong went after ARVN headquarters at Bien Hoa and United States Field Force headquarters at Long Binh. The attacks in IV Corps—the Mekong Delta—were fierce. The Vietcong hit other provincial and district capitals. The extent of the surprise is caught in a comment to reporters by General John Chaisson, an aide to Westmoreland, three days after the beginning of the Tet offensive: "Well . . . the intelligence did not indicate that we were going to have any such massive attacks as this. . . . We were quite confident that something would happen around . . . Tet . . . but . . . intelligence at least never unfolded to me any panorama of attacks such as happened this week."

The most spectacular attack was on the American embassy in Saigon. At 1:30 a.m. on January 31, the Vietcong blew a hole in the embassy wall and poured through carrying explosives and automatic weapons. All night long a battle raged between guerrillas and the troops from the 101st Airborne, who helicoptered onto the embassy roof. By 9:00 a.m. the embassy was secure. Bodies littered the compound. Bloody footprints marched up the external stairway. Reporters were everywhere. Kate Webb of the UPI described the scene as "a butcher shop in Eden." Westmoreland marched into the compound at 9:20 and claimed an American victory, insisting that the communists were being slaughtered throughout the country and the attack on Saigon was only a diversion before the main attack near Khe Sanh. The journalists were dumbfounded. How could the commander claim a victory when the Vietcong had gotten into the embassy compound, supposedly the single most secure place in South Vietnam? The next day General Nguyen Ngoc Loan, head of the South Vietnamese police, saw ARVN troops escorting a Vietcong soldier down the street. Loan walked up to him, placed a revolver to his temple, and blew his brains out. Eddie Adams, an Associated Press photographer, and a Vietnamese cameraman for NBC News filmed the whole incident. Millions of Americans watched the killing in their living rooms that night or read about it the next morning. Together with clips of Westmoreland on the embassy grounds, the image of the shooting became symbolic of the Tet offensive.

February 2, 1968. ARVN Colonel Nguyen Ngoc Loan pulls out his pistol and executes the Vietcong on the spot with a single shot to the head. (*Courtesy, Library of Congress.*)

The battle to drive the Vietcong out of Saigon was bloody. More than 10,000 ARVN troops moved into Cholon in a house-to-house search. On February 3 MACV declared much of Cholon a free fire zone and told civilians to get out. The next day American and South Vietnamese aircraft conducted a massive bombing of Cholon to dislodge the enemy. After six days of bombardment, the 199th Light Infantry Brigade moved into the neighborhood, attacked the Phu Tho racetrack, and wiped out the rest of the Vietcong. Much of Cholon lay in rubble.

In Hue, where the bloodiest fighting occurred, 7,500 communist troops went on the offensive. Most of them were NVA regulars. Formerly the imperial capital of Vietnam, the center of Vietnamese cultural life, Hue was the leading symbol of Vietnamese nationalism. It was cosmopolitan and exotic, famous for its wide boulevards and pagodas. It was also difficult to defend. Isolated by the Annamese mountains and bordered by Laos to the west and the Demilitarized Zone to the north, Hue had no access to a major port. Just before 4:00 A.M. on January 30, North Vietnamese artillery began blasting away. The NVA 6th Regiment attacked MACV headquarters in Hue and the field offices of the ARVN First Division. Other NVA troops blocked Highway 1 north and south of Hue. When dawn broke, the gold-starred flag of the National Liberation Front was waving above the Citadel, the centuries-old home of the Vietnamese imperial family. Hue had fallen. The bloodbath began immediately. The communists rounded up 2,800 citizens of Hue—intellectuals, government officials, random civilians, and religious leaders—and systematically slaughtered them. Instead of leaving the bodies on public display, as they had always done in the past for political assassinations, they buried the victims in shallow graves. Another 2,000 people were never seen again. Local Vietcong cadres, not NVA regulars, carried out the massacre. Most victims had connections to the South Vietnamese army or government or worked for the American military.

Within hours elements of the 1st Air Cavalry Division, the 101st Airborne Division, the ARVN 1st Division, the 1st Marine Division, and ARVN rangers and marines began a house-to-house assault on Hue. For more than three weeks the artillery barrage continued, reducing Hue to rubble. On February 24, 1968, Westmoreland declared victory. By that time little was left. More than 10,000 civilians were dead, killed by enemy terrorism or random American bombardment. Half the buildings in the city were destroyed, and 116,000 of the city's 140,000 people were homeless. The communists suffered 5,000 combat deaths, to 216 for the United States and 384 for ARVN.

After the recapture of Hue, the Tet offensive stuttered and declined. The Vietcong started a new series of attacks beginning February 18, but they were primarily rocket and mortar bombardment. They launched "Tet II" in May and a smaller offensive in August, but American and ARVN forces easily beat them back. Giap was right. The American military had proved far more responsive than Nguyen Chi Thanh ever thought possible. When the Tet offensive was over, as many as 40,000 Vietcong were dead, compared to 1,100 Americans and approximately 2,300 South Vietnamese. The civilian toll was even worse. Up to 45,000 South Vietnamese were dead or wounded, and more than one million people had lost their homes.

The Tet offensive was a tactical disaster for the communists. They achieved none of their major objectives. The South Vietnamese did not rise up and welcome them as liberators; the government of South Vietnam did not collapse; ARVN soldiers did not surrender; and the cities did not fall under communist control. When Tet started, ARVN troops left the countryside to fight in the cities, and when they withdrew from villages, Vietcong political cadres headed into the vacuum to recruit peasants. But ARVN and American forces quickly returned to the villages, and Vietcong agents were exposed and many arrested. That process, as well as their horrendous battlefield casualties, badly debilitated the Vietcong. In fact, they never again fielded full battalions. After the Tet offensive, NVA regulars assumed a far greater role in the fighting. For South Vietnamese communists, it was about time. They resented Giap for not committing the NVA divisions to the campaign. Had Nguyen Chi Thanh lived, they believed, the offensive would have been a different story.

But tactical disaster did not mean strategic defeat. Tet was an overwhelming, if unforeseen, strategic victory for the communists. General Tran Do recognized the contradiction: "We didn't achieve our main objective, which was to spur uprisings throughout the south. . . . As for making an impact in the United States, it had not been our intention— but it turned out to be a fortunate result." Americans were in no mood for more talk about victories. Johnson's pronouncement at a press conference on February 2 that "we have known for some time that this offensive was planned by the enemy" convinced very few people.

Major battles of the Tet
offensive, January 1968

Tet stirred Capitol Hill. Senator Robert Kennedy declared that it "has finally shattered the mask of official illusion with which we have concealed our true circumstances, even from ourselves." For Senator Mike Mansfield, Tet was the disaster he had been anticipating. "From the outset," he said, the war "was not an American responsibility, and it is not now an American responsibility, to win a victory for any particular Vietnamese group, or to defeat any particular Vietnamese group." If Tet was supposed to have been a communist failure, observed Senator George Aiken of Vermont, "I hope the Viet Cong never have a major success."

Reaction in the press measures the effect of Tet. The usually conservative *Wall Street Journal* argued that "the American people should be getting ready to accept . . . the prospect that the whole Vietnam effort may be doomed." Tet, observed the *St. Louis Post-Dispatch*, had revealed "the hollowness of the Saigon government's pretensions to sovereignty . . . the fraud of our government's claims of imminent victory, and the basic untenability of the American military position." Art Buchwald parodied Westmoreland's claims of victory, titling his column, "We Have the Enemy on the Run, Says General Custer." The greatest defection was Walter Cronkite, the dean of American broadcast journalists and anchor of the CBS Evening News. His explosive response to the news of Tet—"What the hell is going on? I thought we were winning the war—" amounted to a news story in itself. After a few days, Cronkite went to Vietnam for his own look. When he returned he issued on the evening broadcast of February 27 his personal opinion: "We have been too often disappointed by the optimism of the American leaders to have faith any longer in the silver linings they find in the darkest clouds. The bloody experience of Vietnam is to end in a stalemate." There would be no military victory. Cronkite wanted peace negotiations. The president was watching the broadcast. "If I have lost Walter Cronkite," he said, "I have lost Mr. Average Citizen." Johnson and Westmoreland were victims of their own rhetoric. Ever since 1962 American leaders had predicted an enemy collapse and an imminent military victory. When the Tet offensive exposed the rhetoric, reporters knew they had a story, comparing the strength of the enemy with MACV's descriptions of its weakness. In a matter of days, Tet had turned from an American victory to a political disaster.

Johnson also had to deal with Earle Wheeler and William Westmoreland. Wheeler cabled Westmoreland on February 9 that the "United States is not prepared to accept a defeat in South Vietnam. In summary, if you need more troops, ask for them." Westmoreland came back with a request for 206,000 troops. He also asked Johnson to mobilize the reserves, permit an invasion of Laos, Cambodia, and North Vietnam, and expand the air war. His new proposal was Operation Complete Victory. So Johnson found himself dealing with the old question: whether to widen the war and raise American troop levels.

At a special meeting of his top advisers on February 9, Johnson listened to them talk about Westmoreland's proposals. Earle Wheeler, who was playing no small part in Westmoreland's troop requests, knew the war was stretching American military resources to the limit. He wanted a national mobilization, a call-up of reserves, and a declaration of war. Dean Rusk disagreed. Opposition to the war, which had prevented Johnson from even raising taxes a few years before, was more severe than ever.

By this time there was a new secretary of defense, Clark Clifford. A Kansas native and a graduate of the Washington University Law School, Clifford had been special counsel to Harry Truman in 1946 and became Truman's most trusted adviser. Tactful but tough, he headed the Foreign Intelligence Advisory Board in 1961, serving as the official watchdog over the CIA. He had a special ability to sniff out exaggeration, hyperbole, and bureaucratic dissembling. Clifford directed Lyndon Johnson's election campaign in 1964 and for several years was a leading hawk. Early in 1968 Clifford replaced Robert McNamara as secretary of defense, and within weeks he heard "Blimpies" coming out of Saigon. In the middle of Earle Wheeler's plea for more troops and fewer restrictions, Clifford voiced his concern: "There is a very strange contradiction in what we are saying. . . . I think we should give some very serious thought to how we explain saying on one hand that the enemy did not take a victory and yet [we] are in need of many more troops and possibly an emergency call-up." Johnson was quick to see Clifford's shrewdness. The press would have a fine time with the rhetoric of victory accompanied by a massive additional deployment of troops. The president asked Clifford to review the proposals and "give me the lesser of two evils." Clifford insisted that Westmoreland specifically describe what he would do with the 206,000 troops, what results he would achieve, and when he would achieve them. He asked Alain Enthoven, a senior assistant and systems analyst in the Defense Department, to evaluate American strategy. A few weeks later Enthoven presented a scathing attack on Westmoreland's notion. The troop requests would not shorten the war, and 206,000 new troops promised "no early end to the conflict, nor any success in attriting the enemy or eroding Hanoi's will to fight." And a troop buildup on that scale would completely Americanize the war and create a tremendous political backlash at home.

Enthoven proposed a new strategy. Military victory was out of the question. Westmoreland was never going to reach the crossover point. Instead Enthoven wanted to deploy American troops in areas where they could provide "population security," stop any major communist attacks, and keep the enemy off balance with limited offensive operations. In the meantime, ARVN must take the offensive and reverse the Americanization of the conflict. The proposal became known as "Vietnamization." It was actually little different from what the Eisenhower and Kennedy administrations had tried to accomplish years before. Upon its completion, the United States would seek a negotiated political settlement and withdraw, leaving South Vietnam to its own destiny.

Those were the choices Johnson faced, and none of them was really palatable. The sum of Westmoreland's tactical victories between 1965 and 1968 had been zero. "If capturing a section of the American embassy and several large cities constitutes complete failure," remarked Senator Eugene McCarthy of Minnesota, with the Democratic presidential primary in New Hampshire a few weeks ahead, "I suppose by this logic that if the Viet Cong captured the entire country, the administration would be claiming their total collapse."

Before being elected to Congress in 1948, Eugene McCarthy had been a professor of English. Ten years later he won a seat in the Senate. More mystic than politician, McCarthy seemed to belong in coffee shops discussing philosophy instead of working the halls of Congress. In the journalist Theodore White's characterization, McCarthy might "have love in his heart—but it is an abstract love, a love for youth, a love for beauty, a love for vistas and hills and song. . . . All through the year [1968] one's admiration of the man grew, but one's affection lessened." Early in 1967 McCarthy called for an end to the war. On November 30, 1967, he decided to take on Johnson in the upcoming presidential primaries. Few paid any attention until Tet. But by February thousands of college students, freshly shaved, trimmed, and dressed in shirts and ties—part of a "Get Clean for Gene" campaign—were walking door-to-door in New Hampshire garnering votes for McCarthy in the March 12 primary. The results were astonishing. McCarthy took 42 percent of the vote to 48 percent for Johnson. For the presidential incumbent and the party's nominal leader, the narrow victory was equivalent to a defeat.

Four days later Senator Robert Kennedy of New York declared for the nomination. McCarthy's supporters were outraged. Kennedy seemed a rank opportunist willing to enter the fray only after the shift in the political mood. Johnson was just as outraged. He hated Robert Kennedy. The Kennedy administration had taken the first major step in escalating the conflict in Vietnam, and Robert Kennedy, having promised in 1962 that the United States "would remain there until we win," now wanted an end to the war. McCarthy and Kennedy both opposed Lyndon Johnson on the ballot of the April 2 presidential primary in Wisconsin.

Johnson was a larger-than-life figure who personalized everything around him. On one occasion when an aide tried to direct him to one of several helicopters, saying "Mr. President, that's not your helicopter." Johnson replied, "Son, they're all my helicopters," Vietnam was his war. He brooded about it all the time. One observer described Johnson's role:

> He made appointments, approved promotions, reviewed troop requests, determined deployments, selected bombing targets, and restricted aircraft sorties. Night after night, wearing a dressing gown and carrying a flashlight, he would descend into the White House basement "situation room" to monitor the conduct of the conflict. . . . Often, too, he would doze by his bedside telephone, waiting to hear the outcome of a mission to rescue one of "my pilots" shot down over Haiphong or Vinh or Thai Nguyen. It was his war.

But if it was his war, Johnson did not want to be alone. Obsessed with consensus, he wanted agreement from everyone. Johnson was a great giver of gifts, especially presidential gifts—lighters, tie clasps, bowls, cuff links, electric toothbrushes, waterproof watches, and silk scarves, all with the presidential seal. Anyone who traveled with Johnson aboard *Air Force One* or a presidential helicopter received a certificate commemorating the event. To show his appreciation for his staff, Johnson gave "CARE" boxes filled with favorite candies. He gave and gave. Some people's gifts come with strings attached; Johnson's came with steel chains. In return he demanded gratitude, love, and, most of all, loyalty. If his gifts were not paid with the proper emotional interest, he was deeply hurt. Now, with so many people turned against him, Johnson angrily asked a friend, "How is it possible that all these people could be so ungrateful to me after I have given them so much?" His need for approval translated into a need for consensus, and seeking consensus required charting a middle course between the liberals and right-wing anticommunists. That meant that in place of seeking a victory or accepting withdrawal, Johnson would end up settling for a stalemate. And for the United States, stalemate meant defeat.

Nor did the midcourse bring any real political gain at home. On March 10 the *New York Times* released the news that Westmoreland wanted another 206,000 troops. Senator J. William Fulbright opened new hearings by the Senate Foreign Relations Committee, and 139 members of the House signed a petition asking Johnson to reevaluate Vietnam policy. On the NBC Evening News, Frank McGee told the nation that 206,000 more troops would only result in more destruction, not peace and victory. "We must decide whether it is futile," McGee said, "to destroy Vietnam in an effort to save it." By mid-March the public opinion polls indicated that only one-quarter of Americans supported Johnson's conduct of the war.

Westmoreland was not going to get the 206,000 troops, but Johnson had to decide whether to endorse the strategic proposals of Alain Enthoven and Clark Clifford. Once again he turned to the Wise Men. Just four months before, back in November 1967, all of them except George Ball had told him to stay with it and force North Vietnam to the negotiating table while turning more of the war over to ARVN. Johnson now hoped simply that they could see a way out of the quagmire, a "peace with honor." State Department officials had used the phrase for years, referring to "peace with honor" as the "number of days between the departure of the last Marine and the rape of the first nun."

On March 25, 1968, the Wise Men gathered at the State Department. It was essentially the same group that had supported Johnson back in November: Dean Acheson, Clark Clifford, Abe Fortas, McGeorge Bundy, Maxwell Taylor, Omar Bradley, Robert Murphy, Henry Cabot Lodge, Douglas Dillon, and George Ball. The retired army general Matthew Ridgway was there, as was Cyrus Vance, a former deputy secretary of defense and adviser to Johnson. The event was the Wise Men's swan song. The elaborate network of military bases, regional alliances, and global commitments they had created after World War II was stretched to the breaking point. Perhaps the United States was just not capable of stopping aggression everywhere in the world. The North Koreans had helped prove that point. On January 23, 1968, while Johnson and Westmoreland watched Khe Sanh, North Korean naval forces seized the USS *Pueblo,* a highly sophisticated intelligence-gathering ship plying the waters off the coast of North Korea. In the attack one American died and the ship and crew were taken captive. Johnson sent 350 aircraft to bases in South Korea as a show of force, but Vietnam had drawn his resources too thin. The *Pueblo* crew would languish in a North Korean prison for nearly a year. There were limits to American power, and the Wise Men were called to evaluate them.

In the first day's session, Dean Rusk, Walt Rostow, United Nations Ambassador Arthur Goldberg, and CIA director Richard Helms listened to Generals Earle Wheeler and William DePuy, together with Philip Habib of the State Department. To DePuy's announcement that 80,000 Vietcong had died during Tet, Goldberg raised his eyebrows. He wanted to know how many Vietcong were still left in the field, and DuPuy put the estimate at 230,000. Goldberg started doing a little arithmetic. "I am not a great mathematician," he responded, "but with 80,000 killed and with a wounded ratio of three to one, or 240,000, for a total of 320,000, who the hell are we fighting?" When General Wheeler argued that the United States should not seek a negotiated settlement, for "this is the worst time to negotiate," Henry Cabot Lodge leaned over to Dean Acheson and observed, "Yes, because we are in worse shape militarily than we have ever been." When Wheeler said that it might take five to ten years to win the war, Douglas Dillon thought, according to his later reconstruction: "In November, we were told that it would take us a year to win. Now it looked like five or ten years, if that. I knew the country wouldn't stand for it."

The next morning the Wise Men met alone with Johnson. Wheeler was there at the beginning of the meeting, claiming that the Pentagon was not seeking a "classic military victory in Vietnam," which prompted an incredulous Dean Acheson to ask, "Then what in the name of God do we have five hundred thousand troops out there for? Chasing girls?" Johnson waved Wheeler out of the meeting and went around the table. He received a lot of counsel but no reassurance. McGeorge Bundy then presented the collective wisdom of the group: "The majority feeling is that we can no longer do the job we set out to do in the time we have left. . . . We must begin to take steps to disengage. When we last met we saw reasons for hope. We hoped then there would be slow but steady progress. Last night and today the picture is not so hopeful." Walt Rostow "smelled a rat . . . a put-up job. . . . I thought to myself that what began in the spring of 1940 when Henry Stimson came to Washington ended tonight. The American Establishment is dead." So was Operation Complete Victory. Westmoreland would get neither his 206,000 new troops nor his invasions of Laos, Cambodia, and North Vietnam. When the meeting was over, Johnson concluded that "The establishment bastards have bailed out."

Dean Rusk had also wavered, although he would never do it publicly. His sense of loyalty ran too deep. He had pushed the war for seven years, always with the conviction that it was necessary to save the world from "a billion Chinese armed with nuclear weapons." Johnson had a deep-seated trust for Rusk, a trust born of shared rural beginnings. When Rusk urged Johnson to consider a partial bombing halt over North Vietnam as a start to a new peace initiative, Johnson listened, even though he remained skeptical. But in case there was even a glimmer of hope that Ho Chi Minh would respond, he wanted to try. "Even a blind hog," the president said, "sometimes finds the chestnut."

Lyndon Johnson was a broken man. His memoirs register that moment: "They were intelligent, experienced men. I had always regarded the majority of them as very steady and balanced. If they had been so deeply influenced by the reports of the Tet offensive, what must the average citizen be thinking?" Suddenly a president who lived to achieve consensus saw himself as a hated man. The near defeat at the hands of Eugene McCarthy in New Hampshire, the entrance of Senator Robert Kennedy into the presidential race, and his own private polls indicating defeat in the upcoming Wisconsin primary convinced him that he had to take another look at Vietnam as well as his own political career. Johnson was feeling old in the spring of 1968, tired and finished.

Johnson's health was a recurring anxiety. It was not uncommon for him to undergo physical examinations every week or call in a physician to look at him every day. His heart attack thirteen years earlier still frightened him. He had abdominal and throat surgery in 1965 and 1966, and during the course of his presidency more than forty precancerous lesions and one small malignant tumor were removed from his skin. Johnson was convinced he would not live out a second term. He even had a secret actuarial study predict his longevity: "The men in the Johnson family," he said, "have a history of dying young. . . . I figure with my history of heart trouble I'd never live . . . another four years. The American people have had enough of presidents dying in office."

Long before the Tet offensive, Johnson was giving serious consideration to retiring. Tet confirmed what his own body told him. The war was a cancer consuming his health, his political career, and his beloved Great Society. The idea of running again for president, of facing a full year of hostile crowds shouting obscenities, was unthinkable. Like few other presidents in American history, Johnson always had his nose to the political winds, and the spreading stink was undeniable. To avoid a divisive political campaign and prove his sincerity in seeking an end to the war, Johnson delivered a speech on the evening of March 31, 1968, that stunned the whole country. He told the American people that he was "reducing . . . the present level of hostilities. . . . I have concluded that I should not permit the Presidency to become involved in partisan divisions that are developing. . . . Accordingly, I will not seek, and I will not accept, the nomination of my party for . . . President."

Hanoi's leaders shouted for joy at the news. The war was over, if not militarily then certainly politically. Ho Chi Minh's prediction that the United States would not sustain the war had materialized. In an interview with a French journalist in 1968, Giap defined Tet as "the most tragic defeat for the Americans. The Tet offensive marked a turning point in this war. . . . It burst like a soap bubble the artificial optimism built up by the Pentagon. . . . Gone, and gone for good, is the hope of annihilating the Liberation forces. . . . Gone are the pacification projects. They would have to start all over from scratch." On April 1, 1968, Lyndon Johnson stopped all Rolling Thunder raids north of the nineteenth parallel, and two days later the North Vietnamese accepted the invitation to discuss the war. They were not serious, of course, any more than they had been in 1954 when they offered to talk to the French about Dienbienphu. Diplomacy was simply another tool in bringing about the final expulsion of the United States from Indochina.

But Johnson's announcements did not constitute a real change in strategy, just tactical adjustments. Along with Walt Rostow, William Westmoreland, and Earle Wheeler, he still wanted to achieve the original goal of establishing a stable, noncommunist government in Saigon. The thrashing Westmoreland had given the communists at Tet was proof of American military superiority. That ARVN had fought its Tet battles with courage and discipline was even more encouraging. The weak link in the strategy was politics at home, Johnson believed. Withdrawing from the presidential race, rejecting the requests for more troops, and limiting the bombing of North Vietnam, Johnson hoped, could buy political time for his basic policies to succeed.

William Westmoreland also had to go, another political victim of Tet and, like his predecessor General Paul Harkins, a fatality of the General-Blimp image he had self-destructively embraced. Johnson brought Westmoreland home in April 1968 and named him army chief of staff. Before he left Vietnam, Westmoreland said that the "war cannot be won in the classic sense, because of our national policy of not expanding the war . . . [but we] denied to the enemy a battlefield victory . . . and arrested the spread of communism." He returned to Washington unreconstructed. Johnson replaced him with General Creighton ("Fighting Abe") Abrams.

While limiting the air war over North Vietnam and preparing the way for negotiations in Paris, Johnson was doing everything possible to shore up the political and military situation in Saigon.

At first the center of attention was the A Shau Valley, actually a series of several valleys and mountains in Thua Thien Province. By 1968 the A Shau Valley had become one of the principal entry points into South Vietnam from the Ho Chi Minh Trail and the staging area for most enemy attacks in I Corps. More than 6,000 NVA troops were in the valley, and Westmoreland and Abrams worried that they were ready for a second offensive. Designating the attack on the A Shau Operation Delaware, Westmoreland had B-52s pound the valley for a week in mid-April before sending in elements of the 1st Cavalry (Airmobile) Division, the 101st Airborne Division, the 196th Light Infantry Brigade, and the ARVN 1st Division to attack the enemy troops, supply caches, and bunkers. The battle raged for three weeks, costing the United States more than sixty helicopters. But the campaign killed 850 North Vietnamese troops, compared to 139 Americans, drove them out of a region they had controlled for years, and captured an unprecedented number of weapons.

By the time Operation Delaware was winding down in the north, Tet II was under way farther south. With the peace talks just weeks away, enemy troops maneuvered for position. On May 5, 1968, the communists launched 119 attacks on provincial and district capitals throughout South Vietnam. They attacked Saigon and Tan Son Nhut air base and got two regiments into the northern suburbs of Saigon and back into Cholon. They also fired 122-mm rockets into Saigon for several days. The U.S. 25th Infantry Division fought back, and tactical air strikes eventually dislodged the enemy. When the fighting ended, 160,000 more civilians were homeless.

By that spring Khe Sanh was becoming an embarrassment. The Tet offensive had distracted American attention from the outpost, but Westmoreland would not back away from his prediction that it was the real communist objective. The marines repulsed NVA infantry assaults on March 16-17 and again on March 29, but Giap was already in the process of withdrawing his troops from Khe Sanh. American troops were there without an enemy to fight, and Creighton Abrams wanted to get them out of Khe Sanh for use in other battles. In Washington there was concern about the political fallout of withdrawing from Khe Sanh. Clark Clifford, sensing the mood of the nation, wondered about "all the hoopla last year, the talk of Dienbienphu, of Khe Sanh as the western anchor of American defenses in I Corps, the doorway to the Ho Chi Minh Trail. How's it going to look when we pull out?" Vo Nguyen Giap understood the dilemma: "As long as they [the Americans] stayed in Khe Sanh to defend their prestige, they said Khe Sanh was important; when they abandoned Khe Sanh, they said Khe Sanh had never been important." Still, Abrams did need the men. The marines and air cav troops left Khe Sanh on June 13, 1968. General Rathvan Tompkins described what was left of the place: "Khe Sanh was absolutely denuded. The trees were gone . . . everything was gone. Pockmarked and ruined and burnt . . . like the surface of the moon."

After Tet, Washington stressed the importance of shifting responsibility to the South Vietnamese. ARVN went from 798,000 to 850,000 troops, and Creighton Abrams conducted increasing numbers of joint American–ARVN military operations. ARVN troops received crash training programs in the latest military technology and equipment. It was not an easy task, for the South Vietnamese did not mind having the United States doing the fighting. After a visit to South Vietnam in July 1968, a frustrated Clark Clifford complained that it was still largely an American war and that "the South Vietnamese leaders seemed content to have it that way."

The pacification programs were also expanded. The Vietcong had suffered terribly during Tet and might be vulnerable to a political as well as military offensive. Robert Komer left South Vietnam later in 1968 to become ambassador to Turkey and was replaced by William E. Colby.

Colby, born in St. Paul in 1920, had graduated from Princeton in 1940 and spent World War II in the Office of Strategic Services fighting with the French resistance. After the war he earned a law degree at Columbia and in 1950 joined the CIA. In 1959 he became CIA station chief in Saigon. After three years there he returned to Washington to head the CIA's Far East Division. A devout Roman Catholic, Colby saw life as a struggle between good and evil. In the sixteenth century, as Neil Sheehan perceived him, he would have been perfect as a soldier for Christ in the Jesuit order. Now the embodiment of evil was communism, and Colby viewed himself as an anticommunist crusader, a civilian soldier fighting for a free world.

Colby's Phoenix Program put South Vietnam, with the assistance of CORDS and the CIA, to eliminating the Vietcong leadership through arrest, torture, conversion, or assassination. The South Vietnamese implemented the program aggressively, but it was soon laced with corruption and political infighting. Some South Vietnamese politicians identified political enemies as Vietcong and sent Phoenix hit men after them. The pressure to identify Vietcong led to a quota system that incorrectly labeled many innocent people as the enemy. By 1972 as many as 20,000 people, many of them Vietcong, had been assassinated. Phoenix undoubtedly hurt the Vietcong, though not nearly so much as the military campaigns during Tet and afterwards.

As the Phoenix Program was going after the Vietcong infrastructure, Colby launched the Accelerated Pacification Campaign to win over the loyalties of the 1,200 villages controlled by the communists. Using local militia to provide security and differentiate between Vietcong and nonpolitical families, the program set about land reform and economic development—clearing roads, repairing bridges, building schools, and increasing rice production. The program lasted until early 1970. By that time the Accelerated Pacification Campaign had redistributed more than 2.5 million acres of land to peasants and armed over 500,000 militia to protect villages from Vietcong attack. Those were substantial achievements, but they failed to counterbalance the destruction and dislocation that the killing machine was bringing to South Vietnamese peasants.

Back home the war was also taking its toll on American politics. It had destroyed Johnson, and was tearing up his party.

The heir to the Johnson wing of the party was Vice President Hubert Humphrey, born in South Dakota in 1911 but seasoned in the progressive Democratic politics of Minnesota. In 1944 he had become mayor of Minneapolis. He gained a national profile at the 1948 Democratic convention when he campaigned for a strong civil rights position in the party platform. Humphrey won a seat in the United States Senate in 1948 and was reelected in 1954 and 1960, firmly defining himself as a

Democratic-party liberal, an advocate of civil rights, Medicare, and labor legislation. He made an unsuccessful bid for the Democratic presidential nomination in 1960 and in 1964 accepted the vice presidential spot. The next four years were the worst in Humphrey's life. Johnson was contemptuous of him, calling him a "little boy who cries too much." Shortly after the inauguration in 1965, Winston Churchill died, and instead of sending Humphrey to the funeral, Johnson asked Chief Justice Earl Warren to go. Humphrey never forgot the insult. Humphrey worried about escalating the war, and in retaliation Johnson froze him out of policy-making discussions. Yet as a loyalist, he did not go public with his doubts, and when Johnson withdrew from the race, Humphrey stepped up.

From the beginning of the campaign for nomination, Humphrey was in trouble. For three years, despite private misgivings, he had publicly supported administration policies in Vietnam. If he continued to back the idea of military victory, he would not enjoy any support from insurgent Democrats ready to split the party in two. But if he made public his personal opposition to escalation, he risked Lyndon Johnson's wrath. Johnson no longer had the power to designate his successor, but he could veto Humphrey. In any event, as the campaign developed Humphrey would come to be defined as the surrogate for the president who had taken pleasure in despising him.

Further roiling the Democratic party were peace negotiations with the Vietnamese communists, now at last under way. The talks began in Paris on May 13, 1968. W. Averell Harriman represented the United States. North Vietnam sent Xuan Thuy. One of the earliest anti-French Vietnamese nationalists, Thuy had spent years in French prisons. Between 1963 and 1965 he served as foreign minister of North Vietnam. Nguyen Thi Binh represented the National Liberation Front, the political arm of the Vietcong. She had been a strident student nationalist, imprisoned between 1951 and 1954. She joined the National Liberation Front in 1960 and was soon traveling the world promoting Vietcong goals, a political journey that had now taken her to Paris. South Vietnam sent Vice President Nguyen Cao Ky to head its delegation.

Saigon was in no mood to compromise. Any accommodation with the communists, the South Vietnamese leaders knew, would eventually send them to labor camps or worse. The United States approached the talks believing it held the advantage in Vietnam, while the North Vietnamese were just as certain that the Americans had suffered a strategic defeat. From the beginning Johnson insisted that Harriman take the hard line: Leave the Thieu-Ky government in place, deny representation for the National Liberation Front, implement mutual withdrawal of all North Vietnamese and American troops, and exchange prisoners of war. Xuan Thuy, just as adamantly, articulated the North Vietnamese position: Cease all bombing raids over North Vietnam, withdraw all American troops from South Vietnam, remove the Thieu-Ky government, and create a coalition government in Saigon that included the National Liberation Front.

The American delegation spent the first few weeks quartered in the plush fifth floor of the Crillon Hotel, but after a few meetings with Xuan Thuy, the delegates moved down to the cheaper first floor and brought their wives from Washington. It was going to be a long stay. Throughout 1968 the impasse found expression in a debate over the size and shape of the negotiating table. Ky refused to sit at the same table with Nguyen Thi Binh, especially if her place indicated equal status with him. Binh, of course, insisted on equal status. Harriman had to think of a table design that would satisfy both. The world press corps descended on Paris to report the talks but ended up taking pictures again and again of the table. Art Buchwald observed that once they finished the six-month debate over the shape of the table, the diplomats would have all of 1969 to decide on "butcher block, Formica, or wood finish."

Harriman considered Nguyen Cao Ky an impossible, petulant hack who made the communists look like paragons. One member of the American delegation drew a laugh out of Harriman when he suggested that they solve the problem of the size and shape of the table by using "different size chairs, with the baby's high chair reserved for Ky." More than one observer noted that during debate about the table, 8,000 Americans died along with 50,000 North Vietnamese and perhaps another 50,000 South Vietnamese civilians. Throughout 1968 the Paris peace talks spent their energies in pointless procedural arguments, deepening the cynicism with which Americans viewed the war.

The presidential candidates running against the war made the most of the stalled negotiations.

Senator Robert Kennedy of Boston, Humphrey's strongest opponent, was then in his mid-forties. Kennedy had graduated from Harvard and from the University of Virginia Law School. He masterminded his brother's successful 1960 bid for the presidency and then became attorney general. Robert Kennedy was a man of intense passion and brutal honesty. Tact was not his strong suit. Joseph Kennedy, the patriarch of the family, who considered John too forgiving of other people, said of Bobby that "when he hates you, you stay hated." After his brother's assassination, Kennedy served as attorney general for a few more months, but his dislike for Lyndon Johnson was matched only by Johnson's loathing for him. Much in agreement in their domestic-policy liberalism, they were nevertheless hopelessly divided in personality, the newly genteel Irish wealth of Massachusetts against the earthy poverty of the Hill Country. Kennedy left the Justice Department in 1964 and won a United States Senate seat from New York.

After the assassination, Robert Kennedy was a different man. Well before, he had lost his cockiness and became introspective, reading deeply in philosophy, tragedy, and religion. He questioned the existence of God in a world that killed the innocent. Moved by the writings of Albert Camus, he wrote in his notebook, "Perhaps we cannot prevent this world from being a world in which children are tortured, but we can reduce the number of tortured children." By 1966 he was concluding that the war had gotten out of control, that the United States was seeking a military solution to a political problem. "I have tried in vain to alter our course in Vietnam before it further saps our spirit and our manpower, further raises the risks of a wider war, and further destroys the country and the people it was meant to save," he said on March 26, 1968, in his announcement for the presidency. His campaign was an immediate success. The Kennedy mystique was a powerful force in 1968, as were Kennedy money and ties to the party machine. Eugene McCarthy commanded the respect of the antiwar movement, but its heart was with Kennedy. Kennedy defeated McCarthy in the California primary in June, but on the night of his victory he was assassinated in Los Angeles. His death put the nomination in the hands of Humphrey, who had gathered delegates from states where the party establishment rather than the voters made the selection. The Democrats then headed for their national convention in Chicago.

The Republican campaign was also fixing on the war. Nelson Rockefeller, heir to the Standard Oil fortune and governor of New York, hoped for the GOP nomination. But Republican conservatives hated him, not only for his moderate liberalism but for his clear distaste for the nomination of Barry Goldwater in the election of 1964. Governor George Romney of Michigan, a former president of American Motors, was another liberal Republican. Although GOP conservatives rejected many of Romney's positions, they did not detest him as they did Rockefeller. But Romney made one devastating rhetorical slip. During the New Hampshire primary campaign in late February, he confessed to having been "brainwashed" by MACV during a visit to Vietnam in which he was assured of the war's progress. Politicians cannot speak of themselves with so naïve and simple an openness. Romney lost the New Hampshire primary. Out of the squabblings among the Republicans emerged Richard M. Nixon.

Between 1953 and 1961 Nixon had served as vice president under Dwight D. Eisenhower. After losing the 1960 presidential election to John F. Kennedy and suffering another loss in the 1962 California gubernatorial election, he practiced law and spoke on behalf of Republican candidates, building up a long list of political IOUs that he called in during the 1968 election. In the vaguest terms, Nixon criticized Johnson's conduct of the war and promised that he could do better. On the eve of the New Hampshire primary he made his "pledge to [the voters] that new leadership will end the war and win the peace in the Pacific." When Humphrey demanded that he spell out his peace plan, Nixon responded,

"No one with this responsibility who is seeking office should give away any of his bargaining position in advance. . . . Under no circumstances should a man say what he would do next January." The remark did not awaken the skepticism it came close to inviting. Nixon easily won the nomination.

Neither Nixon's vague peace plans nor Humphrey's equally vague promises satisfied the nation's young peace activists. For three years their calls for an end to the war had increased in stridency. Government officials and agents ignored their demands, infiltrated their organizations, and expressed contempt for their political and cultural style. For a brief time some saw a glimmer of hope in Eugene McCarthy and Bobby Kennedy. But McCarthy seemed almost determined to distance himself from the public he was soliciting, and Kennedy was dead. At his funeral Tom Hayden, a leader of SDS, wept. Across the country other students shared his grief. "As I look back on the 60s," mused Michael Harrington, whose writings a few years earlier had brought poverty back to the attention of Americans basking in the prosperity following World War II, Robert Kennedy "was the man who actually could have changed the course of American history."

The passing of Kennedy deprived young protesters of their only powerful political voice. He might have been elected president. He might have made a difference. The remaining politicians were establishment figures who cared little for the dreams of the young. To register their protests—to voice their disenchantment with the political process that was excluding them—members of various student organizations decided to go to the National Democratic Convention in Chicago. Some represented factions of the New Left. Many were committed Marxists, wedded to revolutionary change. Others were apostles of the counterculture whose politics were as nebulous as their religious beliefs. The only conviction they shared was the notion that liberal politics were moribund.

The establishment Democrats should have known what was in store. When Martin Luther King, Jr., was assassinated in April 1968, racial rebellion broke out in the nation's cities. Late in April, when Columbia University's president Grayson Kirk held a memorial service for King, the local SDS disrupted the gathering, accusing Columbia of being insensitive to the needs of black people and of supporting the Vietnam War through its membership in the Institute for Defense Analysis. As anger swept the university, students occupied several buildings on campus, including Kirk's office, and pictures of them smoking his cigars and drinking his sherry made all the wire services. The dispute went on for three weeks before New York City police forcibly cleared the campus.

The protest movement then shifted to Chicago. Orthodox urban politicians there as throughout the country cared little for the creeds of the New Left and the politically outrageous. Chicago's Mayor Richard Daley

August 28, 1968—Police squirt mace into a tightly packed crowd at an antiwar demonstration outside the Conrad Hilton hotel in Chicago. Hundreds were injured in the bloody clash. (*Courtesy, Library of Congress.*)

mobilized 12,000 police and prepared to call out national guardsmen. He denied demonstrators the right to protest or march. Short, barrel-chested, with the jowls of a big city boss, Daley promised that he would not allow any "long-haired punks" to dirty the city where he attended mass every day and decent people lived. The novelist Norman Mailer caught Daley's disdain for the eastern press and the counterculture: "No interlopers for any network of Jew-Wasp media men were going to dominate the streets of his parochial city, nor none of their crypto-accomplices with long hair, sexual liberty, drug license and unbridled mouths."

Given Daley's attitude and the determination of the protesters, violence was certain. The Youth International party, or Yippies, led by Abbie Hoffman and Jerry Rubin, urged people to "vote Pig in '68." They nominated their own candidate—"Pigasus," a fat pig they paraded through the streets. They demanded legalization of marijuana and "all other psychedelic drugs," an "end to all censorship," total disarmament of all people "beginning with the police," and abolition of money and work. "We believe," Point 15 of their manifesto stated, "that people should fuck all the time, anytime, whomever they wish." Such appeals were not part of the establishment's vision of a better nation, and it was emphatically not Mayor Daley's. Police repeatedly clashed with the demonstrators. They fired tear gas into groups of protesters. "We walked along," as Sol Lerner of the *Village Voice* would remember it, "hands outstretched, bumping into people and trees, tears dripping from our eyes and mucus smeared across our faces." The police, armed with clubs, waded into the demonstrators, one of whom "saw a cop hit a guy over the head and the club break. I turned to the left and saw another cop jab the guy right in the kidneys." Demonstrators fought back, threw rocks, overturned cars, set trash cans on fire. Reporters and photographers became victims of what was later termed a "police riot." Nicholas von Hoffman of the *Washington Post* reported police attacks on news photographers: "Pictures are unanswerable evidence in court. [The police had] taken off their badges, their name plates, even the unit patches on their shoulders to become a mob of identical, unidentifiable club swingers." But the television cameras did not blink, and the violence became entertainment in millions of homes. Disgusted by the police, Walter Cronkite told his prime-time viewers, "I want to pack my bags and get out of this city."

The violence in the streets spilled into the convention center. Several delegates were assaulted outside the convention hall. When Mike Wallace of CBS questioned the suppression of dissent, a cop slugged him on the jaw. Speaking from the podium, Senator Abraham Ribicoff of Connecticut condemned the "Gestapo tactics" of the Chicago police. His remarks brought Daley to his feet, shaking his fist and calling Ribicoff a "motherfucker." Amid all this, Hubert Humphrey—whose theme was "The Politics of Joy"—received the nomination for president.

The debacle in Chicago doomed Humphrey's chances for the election. A further complication was the candidacy of George Wallace, capable of drawing both blue-collar Democratic votes and the ballots of hard-right Republicans. Born to poor sharecroppers, Wallace was a populist who opposed civil rights legislation and called for a military victory in Vietnam. When he received no support from the regular Democratic party, Wallace created the American party. He drew substantial sympathy in the Deep South and among some white ethnic workers in the North, two constituencies Humphrey needed for victory. For his vice presidential running mate, Wallace selected Curtis LeMay, a retired air force general whose formula for the Vietnam War was quite simple. In 1967 he had argued that the United States "must be willing to continue our bombing until we have destroyed every work of man in North Vietnam if this is what it takes to win the war." At the press conference when he accepted the nomination, he was equally blunt. In response to a question about how to end the war, LeMay instantly said that he "would bomb North Vietnam back into the stone age."

Throughout most of the fall, Humphrey tried to rid himself of the Vietnam millstone without alienating Johnson. Richard Nixon kept promising an honorable end to the Vietnam War. Not until late October did Humphrey openly call for a negotiated settlement. On October 31 President Johnson, hoping to breathe some life into the peace negotiations and the Democratic candidacy, ended all Rolling Thunder bombing raids. He had little choice. Nguyen Van Thieu, suspecting that he might get better treatment from Richard Nixon as president than from Hubert Humphrey, refused to engage in serious talks in Paris. The bombing halt was too little and too late. Nixon won by a narrow margin. He received 43.4 percent of the popular vote and 302 electoral votes to 42.7 percent and 191 electoral votes for Humphrey, while Wallace gathered 13.5 percent and 45 electoral votes.

By the 1966-1967 season, as the malaise infecting politics invaded popular culture as well, television programs favoring the military lost their appeal. Americans could watch a real war every night on the six o'clock news. During 1964-1965, the Nielsen ratings had put *Combat!* in tenth place among popular television shows. Although its ratings slipped modestly in the next two seasons, the show still garnered a profitable share of the television audience. But *Combat!* was canceled at the end of the 1966 season. Several of the series' stars, including Vic Morrow, attributed its demise to the growing criticism of the war in Vietnam. By 1966, *Mona McCluskey, Convoy, McHale's Navy,* and *Wackiest Ship in the Army* were gone. *Twelve O' Clock High* disappeared the next season. When the 1968 fall season opened, only *Gomer Pyle* and *Hogan's Heroes* survived.

In the early years of the war, references to Johnson's policies occasionally appeared on the controversial *That Was the Week That Was,* which aired from January 1964 until May 1965. Other shows offered antiwar sentiments in more subtle forms, including one concerning a real-life frontier American. *Daniel Boone* aired from September 1964 through the spring of 1970. Barry Rosenzweig, supervising its writers, instructed them to portray the Revolutionary War by "making it Vietnam, with the colonials as the Vietcong and the English as the Americans." *Star Trek* consistently aired story lines condemning war and stressing the Federation command that star fleet captains avoid interfering with the internal affairs of new civilizations they encounter. Even the characters in *Mission Impossible* stopped overthrowing foreign governments and switched to more domestic missions, such as fighting organized crime.

One program, at least, was not so subtle. The Smothers Brothers were a singing-comedy team who gained national fame during the popularity explosion of folk music in the early 1960s. In a midseason attempt to steal viewers from NBC's *Bonanza,* CBS gave them their own weekly variety program on Sunday nights. Tommy and Dick Smothers soon became heroes to antiwar activists. In September 1967, they invited Pete Seeger to appear on the show. The famed activist and folk artist was scheduled to perform his antiwar song "Waist Deep in the Big Muddy," but the network cut the segment when Seeger, backed by the Smothers Brothers, refused to cut the most controversial verse. In February 1968, after a long battle with CBS, Tommy Smothers once again introduced Seeger on the show, and this time Seeger was allowed to perform the song in its entirety. The Smothers Brothers continued to battle the network and its censors, but CBS finally canceled them in 1969, even though their ratings were excellent, after they featured an interview with Joan Baez in which she made a reference to her husband's prison term for draft evasion.

Opposition to the war also found expression in a number of popular novels published in the mid-1960s. Most of the fiction portrayed Indochina as a place alien to American culture, interests, and knowledge. John Sack's *M,* published in 1967, was one of the first of the antiwar novels. It follows M Company, an army unit as it goes from basic training at Fort Dix, New Jersey, through several months of combat in Vietnam. Against the warrior idealism of Specialist 4 Demirgian, Sack sets the corruption of ARVN troops, the inability to distinguish between Vietcong and civilians, and the unbelievably poor morale among United States soldiers. The novel climaxes in a killing of a Vietnamese girl by an American grenade lobbed into a shelter to kill Vietcong.

One Very Hot Day, published by David Halberstam the same year as *M*, is a tale of several American advisers who are trying to train the South Vietnamese army. Captain Beaupre, the central character, is a veteran of World War II and Korea who has no illusions about the Vietnam War. His only objective is to stay alive in the hot, sticky, despair-ridden madness. Beaupre's second-in-command—the young, idealistic Lieutenant Anderson—has high expectations of successfully training the South Vietnamese soldiers and winning the war against communism. In the end, the South Vietnamese troops fail to fight, Beaupre manages to survive, but Anderson dies in a firefight. Beaupre is unable to find any reason for his death, any meaning for an American to be dead in a nowhere-place called Ap Than Thoi.

Incident at Muc Wa is the title of Daniel Ford's novel about the Vietnam War, which also appeared in 1967. The book centers on Corporal Stephen Courcey, a demolitions expert who has just arrived in Vietnam. Along with several other American soldiers, he establishes an outpost at Muc Wa. The novel proceeds to expose the absurdities of the war through tragicomedy. Courcey's girlfriend from the States shows up at Muc Wa as a war correspondent, but she is unable to meet him because he is off in the jungles with a visiting general and army captain who are trying to earn their Combat Infantry Badges. The novel provides a caricature of stupid officers fighting a war for the wrong reasons. In the end, the troops at Muc Wa fight off a Vietcong attack, and the Vietcong, in Ford's words, "exfiltrate" the area. In the course of this absurd episode, Courcey is killed in action.

Yet another work published in 1967, Norman Mailer's *Why Are We in Vietnam?* is actually set not in Indochina but in Texas, New York City, and the Brooks Range of Alaska. A cast of characters—D. J. Jellicoe, Rusty Jellicoe, Alice Lee Jellicoe, Medium Asshole Pete, Medium Asshole Bill, and Tex Hude—end up in the wilderness on a hunting trip. There, in a pristine and naturally savage environment, they use all the hunting technology they can muster and slaughter wolves, caribou, bighorn sheep, and bears. The carnage is extraordinary and, for Norman Mailer, symbolic of what American military technology was doing to the life and habitat of Southeast Asia.

James Crumley's novel *One Count to Cadence* and William Eastlake's *The Bamboo Red* both appeared in 1969, in the wake of the Tet offensive. *One Count to Cadence* tells of a ten-man communications detachment stationed first at Clark Air Base in the Philippines and then in Vietnam during the early stages of the war. Sergeant "Slag" Krummel is the narrator, and his foil is Joe Morning, a self-destructive loser. The novel exposes the gratuitous violence of military life—bars, brothels, fights, and profanity—as well as the futility of the war in Vietnam. The sergeant eventually betrays a best friend and buddy, and the team is decimated. The novel ends with the unit returning to the Philippines, where Joe Morning joins the communist Huk Rebellion. In *The Bamboo Red,* a surrealistic condemnation of the war, Eastlake draws on incongruous fantasies: peace-loving hippie flower children wandering aimlessly through the Indochinese jungles; helicopter pilots having sex with medevac nurses while airborne; American Rangers topped with Roman helmets and accompanied by drummer boys airlifted into French-Vietnamese villas. Like the images in *The Bamboo Red*, the Vietnam war cannot accord with any rational world.

Even comic books reflected the increasing depth of antiwar sentiment in American popular culture. Comic book readers had become too sophisticated about the Vietnam War to accept the stereotypes. Dell Comics' *Jungle War Stories,* which featured Vietnam War themes, had failed commercially in 1966, proving that the war was going to be difficult to sell to the American people. *Tales of the Green Berets* was dropped by most newspapers in 1967. In 1968 Marvel Comics abandoned cold war and Vietnam themes altogether, shifting the focus of Iron Man's exploits to such domestic issues as race relations, environmental problems, and crime.

How times had changed from the confident naivete of 1965! The treatment of the Green Berets in American popular culture captures the shift in the public mood.

During the Kennedy years, the Green Berets had been perceived as missionaries with muscle and brain. They received training that conformed to the prescription in *The Ugly American.* In theory, to be considered for the *Green Berets* Special Forces a volunteer had to be qualified as both Ranger and airborne, physically fit, and able to speak at least one foreign language. Once accepted into the outfit, he was trained to proficiency in "skills such as demolition, communications and field medicine . . . unarmed combat, SCUBA diving and mountaineering, and . . . all kinds of weapons." And he had to know his enemy. At their training center at Fort Bragg, Green Berets read the works of Mao Zedong and Vo Nguyen Giap while preparing their bodies to meet the enemy in battle. In Robin Moore's *The Green Berets* the "ugly American"—that is, the plain common sense technician as Lederer and Burdick had favorably presented him—is transformed into a bright and shining knight, a warrior for democracy. The novel was a huge financial success. Published in 1965, it rocketed onto the *New York Times* bestseller list. Although Moore upset government officials by portraying Green Berets taking part in forays into North Vietnam, his attitude toward the war was that of American officialdom. When asked why he is in Vietnam, a Green Beret replies, "First, I am a professional soldier and I take orders and do what I am told. Second, I don't want my children fighting the Communists at home." Once again the vision of toppling dominoes is conjured. And between Indochina and California, Moore posits the Green Berets, "a potent new weapon against the Communists." Describing the Green Berets in *The Best and the Brightest*, David Halberstam wrote reflectively of what these striking figures out of the Kennedy era were supposed to be: "They were all uncommon men, extraordinary physical specimens and intellectual Ph.D.s, swinging through trees, speaking Russian and Chinese, eating snake meat and other fauna, springing counter-ambushes at night on unwary Asian ambushers who had read Mao and Giap, but not Hilsman and Rostow."

Three years after the publication of Moore's work, John Wayne translated the novel onto the screen as an unabashedly direct propaganda movie for which he had bought the film rights in 1965. It is "extremely important, " Wayne wrote to President Johnson, that "not only the people of the United States but those all over the world should know why it is necessary for us to be there." Recalling the role of the film industry during World War II, he proposed that he "tell the story of our fighting men in Vietnam with reason, emotion, characterization and action. We want to do it in a manner that will inspire a patriotic attitude on the part of fellow-Americans—a feeling which we have always had in this country in the past during stress and trouble." Johnson's aide Jack Valenti advised the president that Wayne would be "saying the things we want said," and with this assurance Wayne received administration support for his project. Much of the film was shot at Fort Benning, and the army contributed Huey helicopters and technical advisers.

The result was a controversial movie that faithfully presents the administration's position. The focus of the film is the awakening of a "liberal" journalist—played by David Janssen—to the real nature of American involvement. At first the journalist is skeptical; he doubts the domino theory, the threat of communism, and the viability of the government in South Vietnam. But after following the activities of the Green Beret lieutenant colonel Michael Kirby—played by John Wayne—he reverses his earlier opinions. Nevertheless, even the journalist realizes that the liberal bias of the American press will make it difficult to tell the true story of the war in Vietnam." If I say what I feel," he informs Kirby, "I may be out of a job." In the end the film suggests that the biggest fight will be against not the North Vietnamese but the liberal establishment. In most respects *The Green Berets* was a typical John Wayne war movie. It could have been set in the Pacific during World War II or in the West during the Indian wars. The Vietnamese in the film even speak the pidgin English of the Indians in early Hollywood westerns. At one point a

South Vietnamese tells Kirby, "We build many camps, clobber many
V.C."

Unfortunately for Wayne, by the time the film was released in the
summer of 1968 most Americans no longer believed the official administration line. Critics received *The Green Berets* in the spirit of disillusion
Renata Adler expressed in the *New York Times*:

> *The Green Berets* is a film so unspeakable, so stupid, so rotten and
> false . . . that it passes through being fun, through being funny,
> through being camp, through everything and becomes an invitation
> to grieve, not for our soldiers in Vietnam or for Vietnam (the film
> could not be more false or do a greater disservice to either of them)
> but for what has happened to the fantasy-making apparatus. . . .
> Simplicities of the right, simplicities of the left, but this one is
> beyond the possible. It is vile and insane.

Even trade journals criticized the film. *The Hollywood Reporter* called it
"a cliché-ridden throwback to the battlefield potboilers of World War II,
its artifice readily exposed by the nightly actuality of TV news coverage."

At the end of 1968 there were 536,000 American troops in Vietnam,
along with another 65,000 military from South Korea, Australia, and
New Zealand. ARVN troops totaled 850,000. More than 30,000 Americans were dead. Fear, misery, dislocation, and death inflicted by both
sides to the conflict were making a wreckage of Vietnamese society. The
communists, convinced that they would always enjoy the tactical initiative and could decide when and where to engage American troops, were
waiting for the American people to tire of the war. Time for Richard
Nixon to deliver.

9

The Beginning of the End, 1969–1970

*We have to stop it with victory, or it will start all over again
in a few years.*
—Richard Nixon, 1968

As a congressman and as vice president, Richard Nixon took pride in his reputation for being the fastest dresser in the capital. It took him two and one-half minutes to put on a regular suit; formal wear took eight minutes. He was fast because there was so much to do. Other politicians doubtless were brighter than Nixon. Some certainly were better educated, better connected, and better liked. But few were better organized or willing to work as hard. For most of Nixon's career he carried a list of things to do in his suit pocket. And with an eye for the smallest detail, he did what was on the list. It was his saving grace, making up for the other graces he lacked. Unlike establishment politicians whom he hated, Nixon lacked a sense of humor, smooth social skills, and a glib style. But they lacked his drive, his willingness to do whatever it took to get the job done.

Given his background, Nixon's rise to power was swift. Born in Yorba Linda, California, in 1913, he had been raised in a poor family that, if not the embodiment of the American Dream, believed in it. His parents were hard-working, outspoken supporters of common people and critics of big business. When Nixon was nine, his father moved the family to Whittier and bought a small grocery store. He devoted his life to the small business and eventually made a success of it. Nixon also worked— in school and after school. During the early 1930s he attended Whittier College on an academic scholarship. But he continued to work at the store—waking at 4 a.m., driving into Los Angeles to pick up vegetables, setting up displays, attending classes, and studying until way past midnight. Nixon also kept the books for the store and at Whittier played football, served as president of his class and several other organizations, worked as a reporter for the school newspaper, starred in school plays, and excelled on the debating team. In a letter of recommendation for Nixon to Duke Law School, Whittier's president Walter Dexter wrote, "I cannot recommend him too highly because I believe that Nixon will become one of America's important, if not great leaders."

Yet beneath the driven young achiever lay a dark and unhappy side. As his latest biographer says: "He was sympathetic and solicitous to [a] woman who was stealing from the family store, but outraged and eager to punish those who spoke against the Constitution. He knew everyone . . . but had no real friends. He was a student leader . . . but shy around people." In every respect Nixon was a young man of action and shadows.

From Whittier College, Nixon went to Duke Law School, where he received outstanding grades but no invitations to join prestigious eastern law firms. He returned to Whittier, practiced law, married, enlisted in the navy after Pearl Harbor, and served with distinction. In 1945 a leading Republican banker in Whittier asked Nixon whether he would be interested in opposing the Democratic incumbent Jerry Voorhis in the 1946 congressional elections. Nixon was. True to form, he ran a hard race, working long hours and always planning. Aided by the conservative mood of the country—and exploiting that mood by accusing Voorhis of having communist support—Nixon won the election and then walked smack into history. A first-term congressman, he was appointed to the high-profile House Un-American Activities Committee. HUAC took its investigations on the road, conducting sensational sessions in Hollywood and other media centers seeking out communists and their hidden collaborators, and gaining a reputation for being a bit eagerly broad in its definition of subversion. Nixon's picture appeared frequently in the press. Within eighteen months he was known as a hard-working, careful congressman.

Then came the Hiss-Chambers case. The Henry Luce journalist Whittaker Chambers—overweight, rumpled, outspoken ex-communist—testified before HUAC that Alger Hiss was a communist. Hiss was a Democrat of impeccable breeding—Johns Hopkins, Harvard Law, clerk for Oliver Wendell Holmes, counsel for the Senate investigation of the arms industry, a member of the Yalta Conference team, a leader in the organization of the United Nations, and president of the Carnegie Endowment for International Peace. To accuse such a man of being a communist agent was difficult even for the conservative anti-New Dealers on HUAC to stomach. If Chambers was lying, HUAC would be embarrassed. It was Nixon who sensed that Hiss was the liar. It was Nixon who would not allow the case to die. And in the end, it was Nixon who was right and received the fame for uncovering the "New Deal" spy.

After the Hiss case, Nixon moved rapidly up. In his successful bid for the Senate against the New Deal Democrat Helen Gahagan Douglas in 1950, he employed vicious red-baiting that contrasted to his caution in the Hiss episode. In 1952 he was elected vice president of the United States. Yet for all his success, he was widely hated, among journalists and among liberals. He was thought to be sullen, abrasive, and far to the right. That in fact he was, and would remain to some extent, in the liberal wing of the Republican party went unnoticed: It was apparently beyond the imagination of his observers that anyone who radiated such brooding hostility could be a politically and socially responsible moderate. And there was the continuing memory of his nasty senatorial campaign of 1950. In 1960 Nixon ran for president, and his political luck crashed. He faced another wealthy, Ivy League, handsome easterner—John Kennedy. Nixon had more experience than Kennedy, and on paper he appeared better qualified. But Kennedy had something that could not be measured and Nixon could not duplicate. He had confidence—a deeply rooted, intrinsic confidence. Nixon's campaign went badly. He banged his kneecap into an automobile door in Greensboro, North Carolina, and when the injury became infected he spent several weeks in Walter Reed Hospital—his leg in traction, his head on a pillow, and the nation speeding toward an election. After he checked out of Walter Reed, he caught a bad chest cold. Then—tired, worried, and looking both—he had to debate a fresh, tanned Kennedy in Chicago before television cameras. Whether on the merits he lost the debate (listeners as opposed to viewers thought he had won), he looked like the loser. He also lost the election. It was a crushing defeat.

As Nixon would later truthfully say, he was no quitter. One lost election did not end a political career. In 1962 he ran for governor of California. Again he lost. Angry, frustrated, and most of all hurt, he told the press, "As I leave you I want you to just think how much you're going to be missing. You won't have Nixon to kick around anymore, because, gentlemen, this is my last press conference." At the end of the meeting Nixon exited, as one reporter commented, "snarling." It appeared that his political career was over.

Of course it was not. Nixon traversed the country, speaking out on the important issues and cultivating political contacts. And as the war in Vietnam destroyed the Johnson administration, Nixon set his sights on 1968. Soon there was talk of a "new" Nixon, a more mature, more secure, more confident Nixon. But as Tom Wicker had written in 1962: "He is, if anything, more reserved and inward, as difficult as ever to know, driven still by deep inner compulsion toward power and personal vindication, painfully conscious of slights and failures, a man who had imposed upon himself a self-control so rigid as to be all but visible." In 1968 the public need to reject Lyndon Johnson was so great that it ushered Richard Nixon into the White House.

Henry Kissinger, Nixon's selection for national security adviser, had a rotund body and a craggy face that were a cartoonist's delight. Heinz Alfred Kissinger was born in 1923 in Fürth, Germany, to a Jewish family. They fled Nazi persecution in 1938 and settled in New York City. Drafted into the army in 1943, Kissinger ended up in Germany serving as an interpreter. After the war he became one of Harvard's most brilliant undergraduates and then went on to earn his Ph.D. in 1954. By that time he was widely acknowledged, by students and professors, as a leading intellect on the campus. He joined the faculty, taking over the international relations course McGeorge Bundy had taught. Kissinger was a consultant to both the Kennedy and the Johnson administration and a foreign policy adviser to Nelson Rockefeller between 1964 and 1968. Stanley Kubrick's dark comedy film *Dr. Strangelove*, which was released in 1964, uses him as the model for the megalomaniac with a German accent and a spasmodic Nazi salute.

Kissinger possessed several powerful convictions about international politics. His doctoral dissertation, a study of the Congress of Vienna of 1815, argues that diplomacy is a complicated, interrelated balancing act among the major powers. Any significant event in the life of one power automatically affects every other major power. The achievement of absolute superiority by one power imposes absolute insecurity on every other power and destabilizes international politics. Every nation on earth has the right to legitimacy and security. Kissinger's study *Nuclear War and Foreign Policy,* published in 1957, advocates the use of tactical nuclear weapons in a total defense strategy. Kissinger disdained the intrusion of moral issues into foreign policy. Woodrow Wilson's diplomacy, he believed, had undermined the Treaty of Versailles and indirectly contributed to World War II. Kissinger was equally contemptuous of the McCarthyite form of anticommunism. Moralistic considerations, whether an idealistic anticommunism or an impassioned Marxism, prevented the United States, the Soviet Union, and China from dealing successfully with one another. Weaker nations, weaker movements could be dealt with according to the needs of the mighty, an arrangement that Kissinger believed to promote stability and therefore the well-being of the human race in general. Thus he was willing to arrange a coup replacing a leftist government in Chile with a brutal military regime. That China and the USSR professed to communism meant nothing to him; both were to be respected because they were powerful. But an upstart socialist movement in a small country in the same hemisphere as the United States: That was an impermissible insolence.

Kissinger's view of Vietnam followed logically from his more general convictions. Indochina was tangential to American national security. A conscience-driven determination to preserve freedom from communism had drawn Washington into an untenable situation. A military victory in South Vietnam was out of the question unless the United States was willing to increase its combat strength to as many as 1.3 million men, which Tet had made politically impossible. For Kissinger, the United States had no choice but disengagement. How to do that was the question. Just before Nixon's inauguration, Kissinger wrote that the United States was "so powerful that Hanoi is simply unable to defeat us militarily. . . . It must negotiate about it. Unfortunately our military strength has no political corollary; we have been unable so far to create a political structure that could survive military opposition from Hanoi." Yet it was too late to withdraw without making Washington seem unworthy of being trusted. "The commitment of 500,000 Americans has settled the issue of the importance of Vietnam. For what is involved now is the confidence of American promises."

Secretary of State Dean Rusk returned to the University of Georgia to teach, and Nixon appointed William P. Rogers to replace him. Upon graduation from Colgate and the Cornell University Law School, Rogers had enjoyed a distinguished career. He joined Richard Nixon's staff working on the Alger Hiss case in 1950, and in 1957 President Eisenhower appointed him attorney general. In 1969 President Nixon named him secretary of state. Nixon distrusted the university alumni at the State Department whose roots were deep in the eastern establishment. He viewed Rogers as one of them. And Kissinger, propelled by a giant ego and convinced that the State Department bureaucracy was inherently sluggish, insisted on making foreign policy at the White House. William Rogers was forced to explain and defend policies before Congress and the press that Nixon and Kissinger had formulated with little or no contribution from the State Department.

To replace Clark Clifford as secretary of defense, Nixon turned to Melvin R. Laird of Wisconsin. Laird had served in the House of Representatives since 1953, earning a reputation for being a tough but fair leader, a socially moderate though fiscally conservative Republican. He was a big man, an imposing figure with a bald head and piercing eyes. Nixon selected Laird for the Pentagon for the respect he had won from Democrats as well as Republicans in Congress.

Laird was eager to end the war. His opposition to further escalation was based more on political reality than on strong strategic or personal opinions. Laird knew the Congress; Nixon's honeymoon would be shortlived. Opposition to the war was endemic on Capitol Hill, by rightwingers for its restrictive rules of engagement and more recently by liberals for continuing at all. Before the inauguration Nixon had confessed to Laird his conclusion "that there's no way to win the war. But we can't say that, of course." Laird believed that if Nixon hesitated, what little political capital he had in Congress would disappear overnight. Within the administration, Laird became the voice for de-escalation.

As Nixon prepared for his inauguration in January 1969, W. Averell Harriman packed up and left the Paris hotel suite where he had spent six months arguing about the shape of the negotiating table and trying in vain to get friends in the Soviet Union to put pressure on Ho Chi Minh. Harriman returned to New York tired and disgusted. Nixon replaced him with Henry Cabot Lodge, who had seen enough of Vietnam to know that Ho Chi Minh could not be bullied.

In Saigon, General Creighton ("Fighting Abe") Abrams had replaced William Westmoreland back in 1968. At fifty-three, Abrams was everything Westmoreland was not. Shorter, rounder, and coarser, and able to curse with the lowliest private, Abrams was a hard-drinking, cigar-chomping former tank commander, one of the great combat officers of World War II with George Patton's 3rd Army. *Time* claimed that Abrams could "inspire aggression from a begonia." Yet there was complexity in this devotee of classical music who liked to retreat into the solitude of eighteenth- and nineteenth-century concertos and sonatas. He admitted that Tet had been a psychological and political and therefore strategic disaster for the United States. Abrams understood that he was working under new strategic assumptions. In 1968, 14,589 Americans died in South Vietnam. Similar casualty levels were out of the question. Abrams would not get any more troops, except for the 12,000 already scheduled to arrive. Westmoreland had tried to win the war; Abrams knew that his mission was to reduce American casualties, keep the Vietcong and North Vietnamese off guard, and get out of the country with some hope that South Vietnam was prepared to defend itself. But he did want "to kill as many of the bastards as he could."

During the last half of 1968 Abrams developed a tactical approach to fit the new strategic reality. Instead of continuing with Westmoreland's broad search-and-destroy missions, Abrams advocated smaller unit action on a more continuous basis. He liked musical analogies: "Sometimes you need to play the *1812 Overture* and now and then you have to let the violins play." It was time for the violins. The Vietcong and North Vietnamese usually found out about large-unit actions before they were even launched. "We work in small patrols," Abrams explained to a group of journalists, "because that's how the enemy moves—in groups of four or five. When he fights in squad size, so do we. When he cuts to half squad, so do we." Between May 1967 and May 1968, Westmoreland had launched more than 1,200 operations of battalion size. In 1969 Abrams reduced that number to about 700.

Abrams's tactical innovations fitted perfectly with Nixon's decision to begin withdrawing American troops. In late 1968 Secretary of Defense Clark Clifford had sanctioned Abrams's two-stage process for modernizing South Vietnamese military forces and gradually turning the war over to them. Melvin Laird resurrected Clifford's proposal and called it "Vietnamization."

The idea had a long past. In 1951 the French had called it *jaunissement* or "yellowing." France established the Vietnamese National Army, and central to the ill-fated Navarre Plan of 1953–1954 was the assumption that the Vietnamese would take on greater responsibility for combat against the Vietminh. The United States picked up where the French left off. Vice President Richard Nixon summed up American opinion about South Vietnam in April 1954 when he argued, "The Vietnamese lack the ability to conduct a war by themselves or govern themselves." J. Lawton Collins claimed that "the American mission will soon take charge of instructing the Vietnam army. . . . The aim will be . . . to build a completely autonomous Vietnamese army." During the Kennedy administration, American advisers concentrated on training ARVN officers. In October 1963 General Charles J. Timmes proudly announced, "We have completed the job of training South Vietnam's armed forces." Yet two years later the major rationale for committing United States ground forces was to buy time to build an effective South Vietnamese army and turn the fighting over to it. In a letter to Duong Van Minh on January 1, 1964, Lyndon Johnson promised that as "the forces of your government become increasingly capable of dealing with this aggression, American military personnel in South Vietnam can be progressively withdrawn." Westmoreland and the joint chiefs lost sight of that objective in their naive assumption that the killing machine would make short work of the enemy, but even then Vietnamization was in the back of their minds. In his speech to the National Press Club in November 1967, Westmoreland announced that in two years "we will be able to phase down . . . our military effort, withdraw some of our troops, with the understanding that the Vietnamese will be prepared to take over those functions that are being now performed by our troops." Vietnamization, then, had been French and American policy for twenty years. The only difference in 1969 was that as opposition to the war grew, Richard Nixon had little choice but to turn the war over to South Vietnam and begin withdrawing American troops. He took his time in doing so, not wanting to be the first American president to lose a war.

The reaction to Vietnamization was mixed. John Paul Vann enraged General Creighton Abrams with his observation that "The first 100,000 Americans to leave would be for free. They are the clerks, the laundrymen, the engineer battalions building officers' clubs throughout the country. So many extraneous things are soaking up people not essential." Others had heard it all before. Senator John C. Stennis of Mississippi argued that the United States "would be badly mistaken if we think we can depend too much upon this South Vietnamese army winning this war. . . . I don't believe they will be able to do it and I believe Hanoi knows this better than we do. . . . We'll have to stay there for ten years at best." But Nixon did not have years. He had months.

On February 22, 1969, the North Vietnamese launched that year's Tet—New Year's—offensive, and although they achieved none of the surprise of a year before, 1,140 American soldiers died in three weeks of fighting. In April the number of United States troops in South Vietnam peaked at 543,400 men, and in mid-May Nixon offered a new peace plan. But like all of the earlier proposals, it was primarily a military document, a cease-fire, rather than a comprehensive political settlement. Nixon wanted mutual, simultaneous withdrawal of all American and North Vietnamese troops from South Vietnam, release of all prisoners of war, and establishment of an international body to supervise the cease-fire. Pham Van Dong and Nguyen Van Thieu dashed Nixon's hopes for peace. In Hanoi, Pham Van Dong said that peace would come to Vietnam only after the complete withdrawal of all United States soldiers, the removal of Nguyen Van Thieu and Nguyen Cao Ky from office, and the participation of the National Liberation Front in the government of South Vietnam. Thieu reiterated what he called his "Four No's": "One, coalition government. Not negotiable. Two, territorial integrity. Not negotiable. Three, the Communist party in the Republic of South Vietnam. Not negotiable. Four, neutralism. Not negotiable." There was nothing to negotiate.

Fighting in the A Shau Valley in May 1969 brought Nixon more political problems. The North Vietnamese considered the A Shau critical to their logistical effort. Throughout 1967 and 1968 American forces had conducted search-and-destroy sweeps of the area, and in May 1969 Abrams decided to attack. Between May 10 and June 7, the 9th Marine Regiment and elements of the 101st Airborne Division carried out Operation Apache Snow. The battle captured the attention of the American press when a protracted struggle developed on Ap Bia mountain in the A Shau Valley. The North Vietnamese had elaborate bunker complexes on the mountain. Abrams called in B-52 strikes and heavy artillery bombardment to pulverize the mountain before the American assault, but just before the troops attacked on May 18, a torrential rain fell. The bombardment denuded the top of the mountain, and the mud made the attack difficult. American troops went up the mountain twelve separate times. Before taking the summit on May 20, the Americans suffered fifty-six deaths and hundreds wounded. They found 630 dead North Vietnamese troops in the bunkers. The marines titled Ap Bia "Hamburger Hill." The press loved the description and splashed it all over American newspapers and televisions at the end of May. Eventually, 241 Americans died in Operation Apache Snow.

That Hamburger Hill was a tactical success in keeping the NVA off balance mattered little to the public. When Abrams abandoned Ap Bia on May 27, just a week after the battle, a cry went up. Senator Edward Kennedy charged that "President Nixon has told us, without question, that we seek no military victory, that we seek only peace. How then can we justify sending our boys against a hill a dozen times, finally taking it, and then withdrawing a week later?" Combined with the stalled peace talks in Paris, Hamburger Hill seemed like more of the same—more firepower, more carnage, more for nothing.

As the first phase of Vietnamization, MACV upgraded ARVN firepower. During 1969 ARVN units received 700,000 M-16 rifles, 12,000 M-60 machine guns, 6,000 M-79 grenade launchers, 500,000 jeeps and trucks, 1,200 armored vehicles, and 1,000 pieces of artillery. The Vietnamese Air Force got F-5 fighters as well as 400 aircraft and 100 helicopters. The total value of American arms transfers to South Vietnam was $725 million in 1968, $925 million in 1969, and another $925 million in 1970. On June 8, 1969, Nixon flew to Midway Island for a summit meeting with Nguyen Van Thieu on Vietnamization. Out of it came Nixon's announcement: "I have decided to order the immediate redeployment from Vietnam of the divisional equivalent of approximately 25,000 men." On August 27, 1969, the United States 9th Infantry went home.

There was other progress in Vietnamization as well. The plan to get ARVN to assume more responsibility for offensive operations began to yield fruit late in 1969 and in 1970. The number of enemy troops killed in action by ARVN increased from 20 to 32 percent. Nguyen Van Thieu removed a major peasant complaint against his government in 1969 by restoring the village elections and autonomy that Ngo Dinh Diem had eliminated a decade earlier. Thieu also accelerated a land reform program and recognized titles to land given to the peasants by the Vietminh and Vietcong.

At least on the surface, still further things were going well for Saigon and the United States. The presence of 543,000 American and nearly one million ARVN troops, the Accelerated Pacification Campaign, and the Phoenix Program were preventing the Vietcong from recovering from the Tet offensive. Tran Van Tra, according to his own account, had to break up the Vietcong 320th Regiment into platoons and squads to restore the Vietcong political infrastructure: "Sending a concentrated main force unit to operate in such a dispersed manner was something we did reluctantly, but there was no alternative." The situation was serious enough that North Vietnam even flirted with the possibility of getting Chinese troops into the war. The Chinese already had 60,000 people in North Vietnam—soldiers, railway maintenance workers, storage personnel, and antiaircraft crews. But the Chinese were very cautious; they wanted to help North Vietnam, but they did not want to get into another Korea. In fact, the $525 million worth of goods North Vietnam received from China and the Soviet Union in 1968 dropped to only $200 million in 1970.

In light of both the real reformist activity on the part of Saigon and the problems of the communists, Nixon's scheduled reduction in ground forces seemed to make sense. Nixon had already scheduled the troop withdrawals. The 3rd Marine Division was supposed to leave in late November and the 3rd Brigade of the 82nd Airborne Division two weeks later. By the end of 1969, if both Nixon and Kissinger had their way, American troop levels would be down to 470,000 people. But neither the wreckage Tet had effected upon the communists nor the advances South Vietnam was making toward taking seriously its own responsibilities made enough difference. Unless Washington agreed to some tactical innovations, the North Vietnamese would take over just as soon as the last American troops left. The only substitute for American troops was increases in American firepower and a widening of the war. Arc Light raids of B-52s over South Vietnam had begun in 1965, and in the battle of Khe Sanh army and marine infantry commanders discovered just how much damage the super-bombers could do. To maximize his strength, Abrams called in saturation B-52 raids on suspected enemy strongholds before sending in his soldiers. Lifting conventional restraints was another consequence of Vietnamization. Since 1965 American military officials had requested authority to invade Laos and Cambodia in pursuit of the enemy, to cross the DMZ into North Vietnam, and to mine Haiphong harbor. During the Kennedy and Johnson administrations, policymakers avoided those alternatives for fear of triggering a Korean-like response from the Chinese. But the Cultural Revolution that disrupted China in the mid-1960s made that much less likely. Nixon and Kissinger listened to Wheeler and Westmoreland and asked them to draw up contingency plans. The White House was preparing to take the war beyond Vietnam.

In February 1969 Abrams reported that the communist Central Office for South Vietnam (COSVN) was five miles across the border in Cambodia and that there were supply dumps all along the border. The general was eager to destroy them with B-52 raids. In response, Nixon in March authorized Operation Menu to limit enemy use of those sanctuaries. Nixon also had a "madman strategy." He believed that Eisenhower's secret messages to China and North Korea in 1953 threatening nuclear weapons had brought the North Koreans to the negotiating table. Nixon aimed to convince North Vietnam's leaders that he had none of Lyndon Johnson's reservations, that he was "tougher," willing to escalate the war if necessary, perhaps by arming the raiders with nuclear weapons. Large-scale bombing of Cambodia would send a signal to Hanoi that there was a "new kid on the block who wouldn't put up with the old bullshit." Nixon wanted the North Vietnamese "to believe I've reached the point where I might do anything to stop the war. We'll just slip the word . . . that 'for God's sake, you know Nixon is obsessed about communists. We can't restrain him when he's angry—and he has his hand on the nuclear button'—and Ho Chi Minh . . . will be in Paris in two days begging for peace."

Actually, in his worst moods Nixon was precisely the unstable personality he wished the communists to think him to be. When he was under intense criticism, his lifelong demons—insecurity, resentment, and paranoia—took over. During the last days of his administration, when the pressures of Watergate became unbearable, his secretary of defense James Schlesinger was to become so alarmed about Nixon's mental condition that he issued global instructions in July 1974 to all military commanders to disregard any orders from the president that did not bear Schlesinger's countersignature.

But those days were still five years away on March 18, 1969, when

Nixon launched the B-52 raids over Cambodia. They were shrouded in secrecy. When the press picked up rumors of the bombing raids, the administration self-righteously denied them. To cover up the raids, the administration falsified military records. On May 9, 1969, however, the *New York Times* broke the story. Nixon denied it, but he was enraged at what he considered the leaking of highly classified information and authorized illegal wiretaps on the telephones of journalists and suspected collaborators. Operation Menu continued until 1973, by which time 16,527 sorties of aircraft had dropped 383,851 tons of explosives on Cambodia.

Later in 1969 the administration escalated the bombing of Laos, which had begun in 1965. Communist guerrillas—the Pathet Lao—controlled most of northern Laos, receiving substantial aid from North Vietnam. Bombing raids over the Plain of Jars were designed to assist Royal Laotian forces. The United States and South Vietnamese did not have the personnel to intervene directly in the conflict, but Nixon was intent on making life more difficult for communists in northern Laos.

The death of Ho Chi Minh on September 2, 1969, left North Vietnam grief-stricken. Ho's will decreed that neither time nor money be wasted on an elaborate funeral, and the entire proceeding took only thirty-five minutes. Sitting on a raised platform, Pham Van Dong and Vo Nguyen Giap wept openly. Westerners were accustomed to seeing unemotional, inscrutable communist leaders standing on the Kremlin balcony or in Tiananmen Square in Beijing. It dawned on many observers at that moment what had been demonstrable for decades: that Ho was beloved by his people. His death made for a collective leadership that complicated the peace process. Pham Van Dong, Le Duan, and Vo Nguyen Giap dominated the North Vietnamese Politburo. As head of the Lao Dong party, Duan presided over domestic affairs. Pham Van Dong continued to exert leadership over foreign policy, and Vo Nguyen Giap oversaw defense matters. All matters of state policy needed approval by the triumvirate, a system guaranteed to be inflexible. An intense debate raged in Hanoi throughout the summer over how best to see the war to its end. Truong Chinh, a close friend of Ho Chi Minh and chief theoretician for the Lao Dong party, argued that time was on the side of the communists and that they should be very cautious. Political reality was forcing de-escalation on the United States, and North Vietnam must avoid any military action that might give Nixon a battlefield victory. Instead North Vietnam should maintain the tactical initiative and prepare for a "long-drawn-out fight." Vo Nguyen Giap, anxious to deliver a deathblow to South Vietnam, was willing to go along with Truong Chinh's argument for a while, but within a year he would call for a new offensive against South Vietnam, which Truong Chinh thought grossly premature.

Policy quarrels roiled Hanoi, but in Washington Nixon found himself without any policy. The madman strategy was not working. North Vietnam kept insisting on its old demands: withdrawal of all American troops, removal of Nguyen Van Thieu and Nguyen Cao Ky from office, and participation of southern communists in a coalition government. Nixon and Kissinger hoped that the Soviet Union would bring pressure to bear on Hanoi. But Moscow wished desperately for a strategic arms limitation treaty, and after 1968 had started to lose interest in Vietnam; problems in Asia, the Middle East, and Europe seemed more compelling. Yet even as late as 1970 the United States still did not comprehend how independent of Chinese and Soviet control Hanoi was and had always been.

And the antiwar movement was becoming ever stronger. The trial of the "Chicago Eight" began in September 1969. The government charged them with conspiracy to riot and obstruct justice during the Democratic National Convention the year before. The trial quickly turned into a media circus. Bobby Seale, the black activist, kept up a steady series of outbursts until Judge Julius Hoffman had him gagged and chained to his seat. The Yippie leader Abbie Hoffman petitioned to have his name changed so nobody "will think I am related to this fascist judge." Jerry Rubin of the Yippies and Tom Hayden, head of the Students for a Democratic Society, draped a Vietcong and an American flag across their defense tables. The trial lasted five months. In mid-February the jury acquitted them all of conspiracy charges, and later an appellate court overturned the convictions for contempt and rioting. During the fall of 1969, the Vietnam Moratorium Committee and the New Mobilization Committee to End the War in Vietnam prepared a series of mass demonstrations. They developed a wide-reaching organization, secured endorsements from leading antiwar politicians, and placed advertisements in the major metropolitan dailies.

Millions participated in the October 15 moratorium. In Vietnam tens of thousands of American soldiers donned black armbands in support of the moratorium. More than 100,000 people gathered on the Boston Common and 250,000 marched in Washington. President Nixon reacted at once, releasing to the press a telegram from Pham Van Dong supporting the event. Then, in a television speech on November 3, Nixon made a patriotic appeal to his compatriots, most of whom, he believed, supported the war effort. In 1963 Madame Nhu had insisted that the "government of Ngo Dinh Diem is popular with a silent majority and is criticized only by a noisy minority of the population." Six years later Nixon made a similar argument with a similar phrasing: "Tonight—to you, the great silent majority of my fellow Americans—I ask for your support." The silent majority remained silent, but the antiwar activists did not. On November 15, 1969, the Vietnam Moratorium Committee staged a march that brought 500,000 people to Washington, D.C., the largest demonstration in United States history.

The antiwar movement triggered a clash of cultures in the United States. At its roots, the controversy was based on class distinctions.

A large portion of the protesters were middle- and upper-class college students who had managed to avoid the draft, for the most part through student deferments. Those deferments were supposed only to put off conscription until students graduated, and to make the point that law specified that once a student took out a deferment his time of liability would extend from twenty-six, the conventional cut-off age, to thirty-four. But at least as long as the military had no need of a vast increase in draftees, twenty-six amounted to the practical age of exemption even for students. Beyond a young man's mid-twenties, he becomes less subject to military discipline and therefore less desirable as a soldier, regardless of his beliefs. Some students, just to make sure, went on to graduate school so that they would stay out of uniform until they reached the age of thirty-four. Youth privileged by class and money could fall back on other ways of exploiting the system. Instead of relying on the routine and often perfunctory physicals performed at army induction centers, for example, a young man with money might receive a private physical and show up an induction center with certifiable proof of disqualifying ailments. And when middle-class youth did get drafted, their education level might secure them jobs in the rear areas of the military bureaucracy. Typing skills or a few business classes could be enough to keep them out of harm's way. Undoubtedly most youth in college and graduate school remained students for the honest purpose of getting an education, but the privilege that went with enrollment in school seemed, and was, an unjust entitlement by the well-to-do. Even for several years after the Vietnam-era expansion in the number of draft calls, until it was abolished and replaced with a largely egalitarian lottery, the system continued to operate on its earlier basis. Blue-collar Americans found it insufferable that college youth, protected against conscription, used their safe status to denounce working-class youth as brutes murdering innocent Vietnamese. Many working-class Americans had painfully ambivalent feelings about the war and their country. They hated the war, loved their boys, and despised the antiwar movement.

Visceral resentment against the students and antiwar activism in general exploded into the "hard hat riot" of May 8, 1970, in New York City. Construction workers had learned a few days earlier that antiwar demonstrators from New York University and Hunter College were planning a rally in the financial district. About two hundred construction workers, many of them wearing the hard hats required on the job, showed up at the rally and attacked the students, chanting "All the Way USA." They then marched to city hall and demanded that Mayor John Lindsay raise the flag, which had been at half-staff to mourn the dead students at Kent State. The workers sang the national anthem as the flag was raised. Seeing an antiwar banner over at Pace College, they broke into a building and beat up several students. Journalists called May 8 "Bloody Friday."

Two weeks later, the Building and Trades Council of Greater New York sponsored a peaceful march that attracted more than 100,000 workers. They waved flags and praised the young men in the military who were putting their lives on the line. "For three hours," *Time* magazine described the event, "100,000 members of New York's brawniest unions marched and shouted . . . in a massive display of gleeful patriotism and muscular pride. [It was] a kind of workers' Woodstock." Ralph Cole, a firefighter who had lost his son in Vietnam, caught the feeling of the workers: "You bet your goddam dollar I'm bitter. It's people like us who give up our sons for the country. The business people, they run the country and make money from it. The college types, the professors, they go to Washington and tell the government what to do. . . . But their sons, they don't end up in the swamps over there, in Vietnam. Let's face it: if you have a lot of money, or if you have the right connections, you don't end up on a firing line in the jungle." Cole's wife felt the same way: "I'm against this war, too—the way a mother is, whose sons are in the army, who has lost a son fighting in it. The world doesn't hear me, and it doesn't hear a single person I know."

Even Americans furious at the antiwar movement could be shattered by an incident that the journalist Seymour Hersh contributed to revealing, a mass rape and murder of Vietnamese civilians by American soldiers a year earlier at My Lai in Quang Ngai province. *Life* magazine published grisly color photographs taken at the massacre—twisted bodies, bloodied black pajamas, naked, mutilated babies. Ever since 1967, when Task Force Oregon deployed to I Corps in the area, the killing machine had done its job well. Throughout 1967 and again in 1968, 50,000 civilians were killed or wounded in Quang Ngai, the vast majority of them victims of indiscriminate artillery bombardment, B-52 strikes, fighter-bomber napalm raids, and gunship attacks. But the deaths at My Lai were different. Indiscriminate bombardment could at least be explained away as accidental; the killing at My Lai could not. It had been a rampage by war-maddened troops.

My Lai was a rural hamlet of approximately 700 people. On the morning of March 16, 1968, Lieutenant William Calley led an infantry platoon into My Lai. With helicopter gunships circling at 1,000 feet monitoring the operation, Calley ordered his men to round up all the civilians. Tensions ran high. The troops were frustrated with their inability to distinguish civilians from the Vietcong. Calley suddenly opened fire and ordered his men to shoot as well. They plowed through the village shooting anything that moved. When it was over, nearly 500 people were dead: children, the elderly, the able-bodied. Not one of them appeared to be a Vietcong. Calley's men spent the day in an orgy of sexual violence—sodomy, rape, and rape-murder. There were a few moments that offered a sliver of moral redemption. Some soldiers refrained from the lunacy, and a three-man American helicopter team that happened upon the scene

March 1968—Bodies of women and children lie on the road leading from the village of My Lai following the massacre of South Vietnamese civilians by American troops. (*Courtesy, Library of Congress.*)

intervened to the point of preparing to fire on the marauding troops. Several decades later, the military bestowed formal honors on the three, one of whom was no longer alive.

High-ranking officers, among them Major General Samuel Koster, commander of the Americal Division, apparently knew of the killings but made no report and attempted no investigation. For more than a year the cover-up was successful. Then Ronald Ridenhour, a former infantryman with the Americal Division, sent a letter to Congress describing the massacre. "I do not know for certain," he wrote, "but I am convinced that it was something very black indeed." The army convened a board of inquiry and decided that war crimes had occurred. The board reduced Major General Koster in rank to brigadier general; censured his assistant, Brigadier General George Young; and charged with war crimes Colonel Oran K. Henderson, commander of the 11th Infantry Brigade, along with thirteen other officers and enlisted men.

On March 29, 1971, a military tribunal convicted William Calley of the premeditated murder of at least twenty-two civilians. Two days later he was sentenced to life in prison at hard labor. The army dropped charges against all the other defendants. The conviction provoked an intense debate throughout the country. Many Americans were convinced that Calley was being made a scapegoat for the army. Nixon reviewed the case personally before the sentence was carried out. He had Calley released from a military stockade and placed under house arrest in an apartment. In August 1971 Nixon reduced the sentence to twenty years, and then to ten years. William Calley was paroled in March 1974. General William Peers, who had headed the army investigation of My Lai, summed up the absurdity of the event: "To think that out of all those men, only one, Lieutenant William Calley, was brought to justice. And now, he's practically a hero. It's a tragedy."

The troop withdrawals, the antiwar movement, and the My Lai massacre exposed serious problems in the killing machine and further undermined public support for the war. Once Nixon announced the troop withdrawals, everyone realized that the time was near when the United States would leave and the South Vietnamese would have to fight on their own. After 1969, Westmoreland's memoirs recall, "serious morale and disciplinary problems arose. That was to be expected. Men began to doubt the American purpose. Why die when the United States was pulling out?"

The war had always been confusing. Unlike soldiers in World War II, who averaged twenty-six years of age, the GIs in Vietnam had a median age of only nineteen. They knew relatively little about life or the world. They had grown up listening to the World War II recollections of their fathers, of being welcomed by the people of Europe, the Philippines, and China, and then received as heroes at home. Fresh out of high school, troops of the Vietnam conflict went to war with John Wayne on their minds, hoping to protect freedom as the Duke had done in *Flying Leathernecks, Back to Bataan,* and *The Sands of Iwo Jima.* But it was not to be. It did not take long to see that the Vietnamese loved not the GIs but, at most, only the dollars in their pockets. The Vietnamese smiled when they hustled the GIs for money and handouts, or when they worked for the military or an American company, but looked at the soldiers with silent scorn. John Ketwig, in *And a Hard Rain Fell,* speaks of a bus ride from Tan Son Nhut to Long Binh in which Vietnamese lined the road, threw garbage at the troop bus, and shouted "Go home, GI" and "Fuck you, GI." Enraged, one of the soldiers shouted back, "Hey, you fuckin' gooks. We're supposed to be here to save your fuckin' puny asses!"

Even insofar as American soldiers, at least in the early days of the widened war, believed they were there to help the South Vietnamese, they had trouble figuring out which South Vietnamese they were fighting for. It was all but impossible to distinguish Vietcong troops from simple peasants, and even the peasants wanted the Americans out. Until 1969, however, perhaps most of the young troops believed in the domino theory. They were under no illusions about preserving democracy in South Vietnam from communist assault, but they were willing to die in the jungles of Southeast Asia to protect capitalism and freedom on the other side of the world. But when Richard Nixon began withdrawing troops from South Vietnam in 1969, even the domino theory lost much of its relevancy. The United States was getting out, whether or not South Vietnam was ready to go it alone. Uncertain about the American mission in Vietnam and confused about their own role in the conflict, many combat soldiers lost faith. Survival replaced victory as the focus of their lives. They might be willing to die to protect a buddy, but there was no longer any nobility in dying for democracy. Morale plummeted.

The tour of duty reinforced the sense of frustration. Unlike World War II, when soldiers stayed away from home for years, the Vietnam conflict required only twelve months for army troops and thirteen for marines. Every few days new, green troops arrived in the field full of news about the alienation back home. Soldiers discovered that they were in a war that did not matter. "How do you feel," asked Michael Herr, "when a nineteen-year-old kid tells you from the bottom of his heart that he has gotten too old for this kind of shit?" Every six months a soldier also got an R and R leave, a week's vacation at a resort hotel in Hong Kong, Bangkok, or Honolulu. Among the troops the vacation was called "I and I"— "intoxication and intercourse." During those few days they were exposed to criticism about the war.

Soldiers lost faith in their officers. The commitment of troops to South Vietnam was so enormous that a shortage of qualified officers resulted. And the ticket punching, in which career officers insisted on a combat tour in Vietnam in order to beef up their personnel file, created an average six-month assignment with an individual unit before a new officer appeared. Six months was just not enough time for an officer to secure the loyalty of his troops or acquaint himself with the tactical situation.

One measure of the crisis in morale was the skyrocketing in the rate of desertion. The army desertion rate in 1966 had been 14.9 men per thousand. It quadrupled to 73.5 in 1971—three times higher than the worst desertion rates of the Korean War. The desertion rate for all military branches jumped from 8.43 men per thousand in 1966 to 33.9 in 1971. The AWOL rates were just as bad. In 1966 there were 57.2 AWOL incidents per thousand in the army; by 1971 that number had jumped to 176.9. Even the vaunted marines had problems. In 1967 the Marine Corps discharged 13.7 men per thousand for unfitness and misconduct; the figure in 1971 was 112.4.

Among incidents worse than desertion, AWOL, and bad conduct were epidemics of "fragging," a term soldiers used to describe the assassination of overzealous officers by their own troops. It first appeared noticeably in the Mekong Delta in 1967 when several American platoons were known for pooling their money to pay an individual for killing a hated officer or NCO, usually by throwing a fragmentation grenade into a tent, which destroyed the victim along with the weapon and leaving no evidence. To warn an officer who was too ignorantly eager about the war, troops might leave a grenade pin on his pillow or throw a smoke grenade into his tent. If he persisted, one of his men would frag him. During the Vietnam War, the army has estimated, 1,011 officers and NCOs were killed or wounded at the hands of their own men. There were 96 documented cases in 1969, 209 in 1970, and 333 confirmed and another 158 suspected incidents in 1971. In 1970 and 1971 together, when American combat deaths in South Vietnam came to 5,602, the number of confirmed fraggings was 542. After the battle of Hamburger Hill in 1969, one underground GI newspaper carried an ad offering a $10,000 reward for fragging the officers who had ordered the men up the hill.

Drug abuse soared. From the "Golden Triangle" of Laos, Burma, and Thailand, a river of heroin, marijuana, and opium flowed into South Vietnam. A steady supply of amphetamines came from the United States and from makeshift labs in Saigon. Drugs were everywhere, like candy and ice cream on the street. Inefficient and ineffective in war, South Vietnamese government officials were experts at drug dealing. A heroin addiction requiring $150 a day on the South Side of Chicago could be maintained in Saigon for $2 a day. The Pentagon estimated at the end of 1969 that nearly two of every three American soldiers in South Vietnam were using marijuana and an astonishing one out of every three or four had tried heroin. Tens of thousands of GIs returned home with a full-blown heroin addiction. Late in 1970 CBS News brought the story to the American people by broadcasting a "smoke-in" at a 1st Air Cavalry fire base in which GIs smoked marijuana through the barrel of a combat rifle.

Fragging and drug abuse were so severe that Pentagon officials began to worry about the possibility of a military rebellion or collapse. Westmoreland told the joint chiefs that "an army without discipline, morale, and pride is a menace to the country that it is sworn to defend." Reports of field units bordering on mutiny in their refusal to carry out combat operations became increasingly frequent. McGeorge Bundy recommended to the administration that "extrication from Vietnam is now the necessary precondition for the renewal of the Army as an institution." The June 1971 issue of the *Armed Forces Journal* described "The Collapse of the Armed Forces." The killing machine was turning on itself. Creighton Abrams could not believe what was happening: "What the hell is going on. I've got white shirts all over the place—psychologists, drug counselors, detox specialists, rehab people, social workers, and psychiatrists. Is this a goddamned army or a mental hospital? Officers are afraid to lead their men into battle, and the men won't follow. Jesus Christ! What happened?"

By the beginning of 1970, at least for critics of the war, the Vietnamization policy was bankrupt. Kissinger and Nixon had been running the war for a year, and although troop levels were down to 475,200 at the end of 1969, another 9,415 Americans went home dead. Bipartisan opposition to the war widened in Congress. The Senate Republican whip Hugh Scott of Pennsylvania called for "a withdrawal of American combat troops as soon as is physically possible." In full-page advertisements placed in newspapers around the country, a group of United States senators led by George McGovern, Harold Hughes, and Mark Hatfield described Vietnamization as "an invisible program to end an undeclared war backed by a silent majority."

The Paris negotiations remained stalled, Henry Cabot Lodge spending every day bickering with the North and South Vietnamese over procedural details. On February 21, 1970, Henry Kissinger began meeting secretly with Le Duc Tho, who had succeeded Xuan Thuy as the head of the North Vietnamese delegation, but Tho remained resolute in his demand that Nixon withdraw all American troops from South Vietnam, remove Thieu and Ky from power, and permit the Provisional Revolutionary Government of South Vietnam, which had superseded the National Liberation Front in 1969, to participate in the government of South Vietnam. When Kissinger suggested that the communists were experiencing setback after setback in South Vietnam, Tho replied, "Before, there were over a million U.S. and puppet troops, and you failed. How can you succeed when you let the puppet troops do the fighting now?" Thieu was just as stubborn. He would not even talk to representatives of the Provisional Revolutionary Government.

Kissinger believed that as long as American troop withdrawals proceeded as scheduled, the enemy had no reason to compromise. The 1st Infantry Division, 26th Marine Regiment, 9th Infantry Division, 4th Infantry Division, and 25th Infantry Division were all scheduled for redeployment to the United States in 1970. American troop strength would drop to 335,000 by year's end. Kissinger wanted to slow down the reductions, renew massive bombing of North Vietnam, and consider a joint American and South Vietnamese invasion of North Vietnam, all in the hope of forcing the enemy into serious negotiations. Melvin Laird criticized the proposal, telling Nixon that "such tactics have not worked in Vietnam for the last twenty years and won't work now. Moreover, Congress will not tolerate such an expansion of the war."

In January 1970 the Politburo in Hanoi had already decided to broaden the war in Indochina. It had little choice. Since early in the 1960s the Hmong army in Laos, led by Vang Pao and financed by the CIA, had steadily grown in strength and mobility. Along with as many as twenty-five battalions of troops supplied by Thailand and Royal Laotian soldiers, the Hmong had begun to threaten the Ho Chi Minh Trail by 1969. In February 1970 NVA regular troops joined with Pathet Lao guerrillas and attacked the Thai and Hmong Lao troops, driving them far to the west, away from the trail and off the Plain of Jars. That military operation secured North Vietnam's supply line to the south.

For the time being, President Nixon listened to Laird. He visited Saigon in February 1970 and he listened to Creighton Abrams's plea for an invasion of the sanctuaries in Cambodia and Laos but remained unconvinced. But that same month the bombing of Laos became public, and the political attacks started immediately. On February 19 Senator Eugene McCarthy demanded to know "under what authority . . . [are] American pilots bombing the Plain of Jars which is hundreds of miles from the Ho Chi Minh Trail and has nothing to do with the war in Vietnam?"

For years the joint chiefs had wanted to send troops into Cambodia to eliminate the sanctuaries; Lyndon Johnson and Richard Nixon refused, hoping to avoid escalating the war. But the idea of widening the war into Laos and Cambodia to compensate for the troop withdrawal gained momentum. In 1969 Nixon had opened the way for invading Laos and Cambodia by approving the expanded air strikes. At the time he viewed bombing as a compromise, something short of an invasion. The administration reacted quickly to persistent questions, denying the Cambodian raids outright and claiming that the air raids over Laos had been only at the request of the Laotian government to stop North Vietnamese aggression. At a press conference on March 6, 1970, Nixon assured reporters that there "are no American ground combat troops in Laos. . . . We have no plans for introducing ground combat forces into Laos." But two days later Captain John Bush of the United States Army was killed by North Vietnamese sappers who attacked his compound ten miles inside the Laotian border. Senator Fulbright, warning of another credibility crisis, charged that Nixon "does not have the authority, nor has Congress given him authority, to engage in combat operations in Laos, whether on the land, in the air or from the sea." When confirmation of the Laotian involvement appeared in March 1970, questions naturally arose about Cambodia. On April 2, Secretary of State Rogers told the Senate Foreign Relations Committee, "Our best policy is . . . to avoid any act which appears to violate the neutrality of Cambodia. . . . We have cautioned the South Vietnamese. . . . We think it is inadvisable to have cross-border operations." Three weeks later Rogers reassured the House Appropriations Committee, "We recognize that if we escalate and we get involved in Cambodia with our ground troops, our whole program is defeated."

Rogers had no idea what was going on. On March 27 and 28, American helicopters accompanied battalion-size ARVN forces on an invasion of Cambodia. Communist forces escaped to the west and began dumping their weapons on the Khmer Rouge, Cambodia's communist insurgents. Serious consideration of an invasion undertaken together with ARVN and American troops had been under way for months, but Prince Norodom Sihanouk, though acquiescing in Operation Menu as well as the presence of Vietcong and North Vietnamese troops in Cambodian territory, wanted to maintain at least a formal neutrality. Sihanouk was trying desperately to save his country. If he did not allow the North Vietnamese use of the sanctuaries, they would provide assistance to the Khmer Rouge, who were trying to overthrow him. When Sihanouk cooperated with Hanoi, the North Vietnamese limited their support of the Khmer Rouge. But by tacitly cooperating with Hanoi, Sihanouk risked the ire of the United States. He wavered back and forth, walking a deadly political path. MACV intelligence reports enticed Nixon, Kissinger, and Abrams with the prospects of capturing the elusive Central Office for South Vietnam. But Nixon could not invade Cambodia as long as Sihanouk was in power. It would be a violation of Cambodian sovereignty. What Nixon and Kissinger needed was a pro-American government in Phnom Penh.

Lon Nol was their man. Born in 1913 in French Cambodia and educated in French colonial schools, between 1935 and 1954 he had held a number of important posts in the French colonial administration and became close to Sihanouk. After independence in 1954, he was minister of national defense. Throughout the early 1960s Nol, a devout Buddhist and anticommunist, urged Sihanouk to side with the United States against the Vietcong, but the prince maintained Cambodian neutrality. Lon Nol started scheming. Sihanouk was a short, round man who loved Parisian suits but hated having to wear a size 48 short. Each year he took off for the Cote d'Azur in France, where he spent a couple of months in a high-class fat farm. Lon Nol knew that no matter how desperate the political situation, the prince would never forgo the trips. Late in 1969 Sihanouk had already purchased fifty new suits, all of them 44 or 42 short. He left for France in January 1970. In March, with Sihanouk in Paris, Lon Nol deposed the prince.

Lon Nol fanned political support by moving against the more than 400,000 Vietnamese living in Cambodia, where ethnic hatreds were intense. Within days of assuming power, he launched murderous attacks on the Vietnamese community, slaughtering thousands of civilians and raising ethnic rivalries to a fever. He also expressed to Richard Nixon his fears about the spread of the Vietnam War westward and the inability of Cambodian forces to handle the situation. Lon Nol doubled the size of the Cambodian army in a month and appealed to Nixon for arms. Nixon agreed.

On April 19 the president flew out to Hawaii to visit the crew of Apollo 13, who had just returned from a harrowing voyage to the moon. In Honolulu, Admiral John McCain, Jr., commander in chief of the United

States Forces in the Pacific (CINCPAC), briefed him. An Annapolis graduate and a submariner during World War II, McCain replaced Ulysses S. Grant Sharp at CINCPAC in July 1968. Known as the "Red Arrow Man," McCain was a hard-boiled anticommunist given to placing red arrows on open world maps to show communist expansion around the globe. For reporters in Hawaii and Saigon, his briefings were laughably infamous, full of gloomy descriptions of "Reds," "Commies," and "Chicoms." McCain's son was a prisoner of war in North Vietnam, which intensified the father's passion. McCain unfurled a map before Nixon, and, sure enough, there were the big red arrows, "McCain's Claws" according to the reporters. Half the country was painted red, and the claws were reaching out for Malaysia and west to Thailand. "The Cambodians need more than a few thousand rifles," McCain told the president. "If you are going to withdraw another 150,000 troops from South Vietnam this year, you must protect Saigon's western flank by an invasion of the Cambodian sanctuaries."

Developments back home upset Nixon. In April the Senate rejected both of his nominations to fill the vacancy left on the Supreme Court by Abe Fortas's resignation. The Senate turned down Clement Haynsworth for the apparent mediocrity of his credentials and G. Harrold Carswell for his hesitancy on racial change. Nixon was so angry at the sixty-one senators who had voted against his appointments that he publicly called them "vicious hypocrites." That month he watched private screenings of the film *Patton*. Nixon loved George C. Scott's portrayal of the lonely, misunderstood but tough general who had defeated the Germans at the Battle of the Bulge. Cambodia became a way for Nixon to express his toughness, to seize the political initiative back from the Senate. "Those Senators think they can push me around," Nixon told Kissinger. "But I'll show them who's tough."

On April 30, 1970, President Nixon went on television with an important national security announcement. It was vintage Richard Nixon. He wanted to sound like George C. Scott being Patton. Sweat forming on his upper lip from the camera lights, Nixon stridently warned: "We live in an age of anarchy. We see mindless attacks on all the great institutions which have been created by free civilization in the last five hundred years. . . . Small nations all over the world find themselves under attack from within and without." The president declared that "only the power of the United States deters aggression." To protect American lives and guarantee Vietnamization, he had authorized an invasion of Cambodia. "We take this action not for the purpose of expanding the war . . . but for the purpose of ending the war in Vietnam, and winning the just peace." Searching for military victory or at least a satisfactory withdrawal, the killing machine moved into Cambodia.

It was a joint "incursion," as Nixon defined it. The United States 1st Cavalry Division (Airmobile) and the 11th Armored Cavalry Regiment, along with the 1st ARVN Armored Cavalry Regiment and the 3rd ARVN Airborne Brigade, invaded the Fishhook, a region of Cambodia about fifty miles northwest of Saigon. It was the ultimate search-and-destroy mission, the hunt for COSVN. If the troops could locate and annihilate the enemy's command headquarters, they could finish off the trouble from that part of Cambodia. Melvin Laird begged Nixon not to include in his speech any reference to COSVN: "Right up to the time he gave that speech I was pleading to have that out because COSVN was never a single headquarters. . . . So again the American people were misled by not having a real understanding of what it was about. But the speech . . . was made . . . COSVN was listed as a major military target." Laird got it right. COSVN was hardly what most American officers thought of as a command headquarters. It was not a fixed installation like MACV but a small number of senior officers and staff assistants.

The reports Nixon received on the first day of the invasion were so optimistic that he ordered the Pentagon "to take out all the sanctuaries. Make whatever plans are necessary and then just do it. Knock them all out so that they can't be used against us. Ever." Two weeks later the 25th and 9th Infantry Divisions attacked the Dog's Head, a region about twenty-five miles southwest of the Fishhook, and the 4th Infantry Division invaded Cambodia west of Pleiku. Nixon renewed the bombing of North Vietnam, although he confined the strikes to areas just north of the Demilitarized Zone.

But the troops never found COSVN. Nearly 80,000 American and ARVN soldiers spent a couple of months slogging through eastern Cambodia, unloading tens of thousands of tons of explosives, but making little contact with the enemy. Communist troops were there, but the invasion actually drove them deeper—further west—into Cambodia. The destruction associated with the invasion sent a flood of refugees pouring into Phnom Penh. Creighton Abrams claimed that the invasion had resulted in more than 11,000 enemy deaths, but the CIA disputed the claim, arguing that the bombardment had been so intense that "civilians and non-combatants [were] being included in the loss figure."

Although they never found COSVN, the troops captured a wealth of enemy supplies: 15 million rounds of ammunition, 143,000 rockets, 14 million pounds of rice, 23,000 firearms, 200,000 antiaircraft rounds, 5,487 mines, and 62,000 hand grenades. They destroyed 11,700 North Vietnamese bunker complexes. Nixon announced that the captured supplies and weapons were "enough to keep the North Vietnamese going for a year. They will be crippled now." Westmoreland defended the Cambodian invasion as the event that had finally pushed North Vietnam past the elusive crossover point. But there was so little contact with the enemy that Abrams could not afford to have the United States troops on a walking tour of Cambodia. All ground operations in Cambodia by ARVN and the United States were over by the end of June. No sooner had they left than new battalions of North Vietnamese troops moved down the Ho Chi Minh Trail and back into the Fishhook, Parrot's Beak, and Dog's Head, as did the enemy soldiers driven west into Cambodia by the initial invasion. The enemy, as it had been so many times in so many places, was back.

In other ways the invasion was a disaster. Once in Cambodia, ARVN troops behaved badly, stealing everything in sight. North Vietnam gave strict orders to its troops to avoid the civilian population, and political cadres then went in behind the ARVN troops and appealed to the Khmer peasants, telling them that communism, not South Vietnam and the United States, offered the best hope for freedom. When it was over, the invasion had given the Khmer Rouge new weapons as well as a civilian population ripe for recruitment.

The administration also paid a heavy political price at home. Nixon had completely miscalculated the public reaction. On April 19 the Vietnam Moratorium Committee, sponsors of the huge, nationwide antiwar rallies in October and November 1969, announced that it would close its Washington office. The troop reductions convinced Americans that Nixon was scaling down the war. That changed on April 30, when Nixon announced the invasion of Cambodia. The incursion breathed new life into the antiwar movement. The president found himself facing one of the worst eruptions of civil disobedience in modern American history. On college campuses mass demonstrations disrupted classes. At Kent State University, National Guard troops called out by Ohio Governor James Rhodes to keep order fired into a crowd of students, killing four and creating martyrs for the antiwar movement. Similar violence occurred at the black Jackson State University in Mississippi. On May 8, some 100,000 people marched into Washington.

The extent of the protests bore deep into Nixon's paranoia. What had started out to be a military victory was turning into political disaster. In the White House, Nixon had an anxiety attack and could not sleep. After 10:30 p.m he made nearly fifty phone calls to friends and political associates, seeking reassurance and vindication. Suddenly, in the middle of the night, he ordered the limousine to drive him over to the Lincoln Memorial to visit the camped protesters. But he was not at his best. Sleepless and tired, he talked with the students but not about the war. To a group of Ohio State students, Nixon rambled on and on about Woody Hayes and times of glory. For one student from California, the evening was surrealistic: "Here we are protesting an immoral war and the president of the United States shows up in the middle of the night to tell us about baseball and how great the surfing is in California. It was unbelievable."

It was just as bad in Congress. Senators Mark Hatfield and George McGovern sponsored an amendment requiring total American withdrawal from South Vietnam by the end of 1971. Although the Hatfield-

McGovern Amendment failed to pass in the Senate, it indicated the frustration many Americans felt about the war. Senators John Sherman Cooper and Frank Church were somewhat more successful. Cooper, a Republican from Kentucky, and Church, a Democrat from Idaho, sponsored an amendment prohibiting the United States without congressional approval from sending advisers into Cambodia, providing combat air support for Cambodian troops, or financing the sending of troops into Cambodia by other nations. On June 30, 1970, the amendment passed the Senate over bitter administration opposition, fifty-eight to thirty-seven.

So in the end, the invasion of Cambodia forced Nixon to accelerate the troop withdrawals even while Henry Kissinger was arguing that those reductions weakened his hand diplomatically. The historian William Turley writes that the need to exploit mountain regions and supply routes in Laos Cambodia had long forced North Vietnam to see Indochina as "a strategic unity, a single battlefield." The Cambodian invasion showed that the United States viewed Indochina in the same way. And in the words of Senator Lee Metcalf of Montana, "With the Cambodian invasion, Nixon has made it his war."

Peace treaty = cease fire, pow exchange,
no more involvement in Laos/Cambodia
South Vietnam, North + NLF represented
in the council

negotiations were sucking b/c America
was trying to purely militarily

*Brought hatred for the Western world due to long history of foreign colonization

*Kissinger only wanted to deal w/ other super powers = his foreign policy; it isn't about morality

*S. of State Dean Rusk - American greatness

*Kissinger = "we have to recognize them as players in the game"

10

The Fall of South Vietnam, 1970–1975

*Kissinger has been secretly meeting w/ Le Duc Tho, aside from their publicly known ones

New Tet offensive, win or lose, is a great psychological win

US △ China ⎯ S.U.

> The real problem is that the enemy is willing to sacrifice in order to win, while the South Vietnamese simply aren't willing to pay that much of a price in order to avoid losing.
>
> —Richard Nixon, 1972

*Blockade = quarantine
"1 step away from invasion

Vietnam veterans against the war = vvtf
Cul for antiwar movement! Pentagon Papers → showed the public we can't trust anyone

They were probably the most influential antiwar group of all—the Vietnam Veterans against the War. Organized by six veterans in 1967, the VVAW had thousands of members by 1970. John Kerry, the VVAW spokesman, staged the Winter Soldier Investigation, and for three days between January 31 and February 2, 1971, 116 veterans testified of atrocities. Kerry argued that "the My Lai massacre was not an aberration, the isolated act of a ne'er-do-well second lieutenant gone berserk. . . . It was symbolic of a war gone berserk." With the world press focused on them, John Kerry's men testified that "at times they had personally raped, cut off ears, cut off heads, taped wires from portable telephones to human genitals and turned up the power, cut off limbs, blown up bodies, randomly shot at civilians, razed villages in fashion reminiscent of Genghis Khan, shot cattle and dogs for fun, poisoned food stocks." Their testimony was riveting, and the Nixon administration knew it. Time was running out on "peace with honor."

Nixon had to accelerate the troop withdrawals. The 3rd Brigade of the 9th Infantry Division went home in October, and in December, Abrams lost the 4th Infantry Division and the 25th. At the end of 1970 he had 335,000 troops at his disposal, and the 3rd Marine Amphibious Force, the 1st Marine Division, and the 11th Armored Cavalry were scheduled to leave in a few months. Already North Vietnam was increasing the infiltration of troops and supplies.

The Ho Chi Minh Trail had become a work of art maintained by 100,000 Vietnamese and Laotian workers. It included 12,000 miles of well-maintained trails, paved two-lane roads stretching from North Vietnam to Tchepone, just across the South Vietnamese border in Laos, and a four-inch fuel pipeline that reached all the way into the A Shau Valley. The CIA estimated that between 1966 and 1971 North Vietnam had shipped 630,000 soldiers, 100,000 tons of food, 400,000 weapons, and 50,000 tons of ammunition into South Vietnam along the Ho Chi Minh

Trail. Abrams wanted to invade Laos, cut the Ho Chi Minh Trail, and starve the North Vietnamese troops waiting in South Vietnam. But because the Cooper-Church Amendment prohibited the use of American troops outside South Vietnam, Abrams would have to rely on ARVN soldiers. During Nixon's first two years in office, nearly 15,000 American troops were killed in action.

The Nixon administration debated an invasion of Cambodia or North Vietnam, but Abrams argued forcefully for severing the enemy supply lines in Laos. Nixon, Kissinger, and Westmoreland ultimately agreed with him. While the Winter Soldier Investigation was going on in Detroit, planning for the invasion of Laos was under way. Late in 1970 the United States 101st Airborne Division and the 1st Brigade of the 5th Infantry Division reoccupied the former marine base at Khe Sanh as a staging area for the campaign. To divert enemy attention, a navy task force with the 31st Marine Amphibious Unit aboard hovered off the North Vietnamese city of Vinh, threatening an invasion. The ARVN objective was to drive west from Khe Sanh up Route 9 to Tchepone, about twenty-five miles away, cutting across the Ho Chi Minh Trail.

South Vietnam committed 21,000 troops to the effort. Supported by B-52s and fighter-bombers from the American air force and navy, they invaded Laos on February 8, 1971. The attack was code-named Lam Son 719 after a small village in Thanh Hoa Province, the birthplace of Le Loi, the Vietnamese hero who had defeated an invading Chinese army in 1428. But Laos was not Cambodia. North Vietnam was protecting its lifeline there, not isolated sanctuaries. The region surrounding Tchepone contained 36,000 NVA troops—nineteen antiaircraft battalions, twelve infantry regiments, one tank regiment, one artillery regiment, and elements of the NVA 2nd, 304th, 308th, 320th, and 324th Divisions.

For the first twelve miles, ARVN encountered only token resistance. But as heavy rains turned Route 9 to mud, the offensive fell short. The South Vietnamese troops fought well, but they were in an impossible position. ARVN air cavalry troops took Tchepone on March 6, but three days later Nguyen Van Thieu ordered a general withdrawal. It took two weeks of bitter fighting along Route 9 for the South Vietnamese to get back out of Laos, and without American air power they would not have made it at all. By the time they reached Khe Sanh, the South Vietnamese admitted to 1,200 men dead and 4,200 wounded, while MACV estimated the dead and wounded together at 9,000.

Abrams claimed publicly that Lam Son 719 had inflicted 14,000 casualties on the North Vietnamese. Back in Washington, President Nixon was even more effulgent, telling the White House press corps that "18 of 22 battalions conducted themselves with high morale, with greater confidence, and they are able to defend themselves man for man against the North Vietnamese." In a televised speech on April 7, the president proclaimed, "Tonight I can report that Vietnamization has succeeded." At the Pentagon, however, the private assessments were grim. Most of the ARVN troops had proven themselves, but in fact they suffered a major military defeat, besides having no success in severing the Ho Chi Minh Trail. The attack, as well as Vietnamization, was a failure.

Lam Son 719 had important strategic implications for both sides. For South Vietnam and the United States, it widened the field of battle and with fewer resources. For the North Vietnamese, the victory proved that they could prevail over ARVN, even the new 1-million-man ARVN backed by American technology. It was clear to both sides that ARVN was not yet prepared to go it alone. Lam Son 719 inspired another series of anti-war protests. On April 20, more than 200,000 demonstrators gathered in Washington. At John Kerry's instigation 1,000 Vietnam Veterans against the War, many of them paraplegics and amputees, joined by mothers of men killed in action, held a memorial service at the Tomb of the Unknown Soldier. Nixon secured a court order prohibiting them from camping out on the Mall and laying wreaths on graves of fallen comrades at Arlington Cemetery. That was a gift to the press. The veterans and the mothers defied the order, and the administration declined to arrest them. Over police barricades on the Capitol steps, on April 23 nearly 2,000 veterans threw away medals they had won in Vietnam. They wanted to help the nation understand, Kerry explained, "the moral agony of America's Vietnam war generation—whether to kill on military orders and be a criminal, or to refuse to kill and be a criminal."

In the case of one governmental figure, the Winter Soldier Investigation sharpened an agony already close to unbearable: Daniel Ellsberg, born of Jewish converts to Christian Science and blessed, and like everyone with a conscience cursed, with a moral passion and a sense of personal responsibility.

After graduation from Harvard in 1952, Ellsberg had spent a year at Cambridge University doing graduate work, and then joined the Marine Corps. He wanted to serve his country. When his marine tour ended in 1957, Ellsberg returned to Harvard for doctoral work. He left Harvard in 1959 for a job with the Rand Corporation, a civilian think tank. Ellsberg received the highest security clearances. When John Kennedy won the White House in 1960, Ellsberg got a leave of absence from Rand to serve on McGeorge Bundy's staff, and in 1964 he became special assistant to John McNaughton, deputy for foreign affairs at the Pentagon.

Despondent about the breakup of his marriage in 1965, Ellsberg volunteered for the Marine Corps again. When the marines turned him down, he secured a spot on Edward Lansdale's pacification team. He came back to the Defense Department convinced that success in Vietnam would require massive social and political changes, not just military victories. When Robert McNamara commissioned a study in 1967 of the history of American policy in Vietnam, Ellsberg was one of the senior researchers. A few months at the task convinced him that American policy in Vietnam was a disaster born of a political fact: "no American President, Republican or Democrat, wanted to be the President who lost the war. . . . That fear was sustained by years of duplicity, lies, exaggerations, and cover-ups."

By 1968 Ellsberg suffered from a profound guilt about his own role in formulating Vietnam policy. Throughout 1968 he called for a bombing halt and wrote policy papers for Senator Robert Kennedy and then Senator George McGovern. When Richard Nixon was elected in November, Ellsberg sank into a deep depression, and early in 1969 he began photocopying the secret Pentagon study and carrying it page by page to his Washington apartment. He covertly delivered documents to Senator J. William Fulbright so "that the truths that changed me could help Americans free themselves and other victims from our longest war."

The Winter Soldier Investigation deepened Ellsberg's sense of personal responsibility for the war. When he learned of the invasion of Laos later that month, he decided to hand over the secret documents to the *New York Times*. On June 13, the *Times* began publishing them, now known as the Pentagon Papers. Nixon was incensed. He ordered the wiretapping of dozens of administration officials to make sure no similar leaks of classified information would occur. The Justice Department secured a court order stopping the *New York Times* from publishing the documents, but the *Boston Globe* and the *Washington Post* continued to make them public. On June 29, 1971, Ellsberg was indicted for conspiracy, theft, violation of the Espionage Act, and converting government property to his personal use. The next day the Supreme Court, by a vote of six to three, overturned the injunction against publishing the Pentagon Papers, citing the First Amendment freedoms of speech and the press. The Pentagon Papers dramatized what the press had long spoken of as the credibility gap, a recognition that the public could not believe anything the government declared.

South Vietnamese politics deepened disillusionment within the portion of the public that followed events with any attentiveness. President Nguyen Van Thieu was still embarrassed about the election of 1967, when he won office with only 35 percent of the total vote. The debacle in Laos in February and March increased his need for an overwhelming political victory in the October elections. In March 1971 he exempted all civil servants and ARVN from paying income taxes, and the CIA provided him with funds to bribe members of the National Assembly. He secured a bill requiring presidential candidates to receive nominations from forty legislators or 100 of the country's 554 city and provincial counselors. Thieu then eliminated all of Nguyen Cao Ky's supporters from the cabinet. When Ky submitted the nominations in July, the Supreme Court of South Vietnam disallowed them. In August several American newspapers revealed that Thieu already had elaborate plans for stuffing ballot boxes and jailing opposition leaders. On election day, 6.3 million people voted and gave Nguyen Van Thieu, the only candidate, a 94.3 percent plurality. Thieu finally had his "mandate from heaven."

While the antiwar protests, the controversy over the Pentagon Papers, and the South Vietnamese election were going on, American troops were leaving South Vietnam. In April 1971 the 1st Cavalry Division (Airmobile), the 1st Marine Division, and the 11th Armored Cavalry Regiment departed. American troop levels were down to 240,000 men. Three months later the 1st Brigade of the 5th Infantry Division and the 173rd Airborne Brigade departed. The Americal Division left in November, just as President Nixon announced that all remaining American combat operations would be exclusively defensive in nature. On New Year's Day 1972, Creighton Abrams had only 157,000 troops left. If the United States was going to get out of the war with any grace, it would not happen on the battlefield. Richard Nixon and Henry Kissinger had to find another way.

"They're just a bunch of shits. Tawdry, filthy shits," exploded Kissinger in frustration to Nixon. In encounters during the cumbersome negotions, Kissinger found Le Duc Tho to be impossible. Tho was rigid and doctrinaire, his hatred of Western imperialism embedded in his psyche by years in French colonial prisons. He was also antiforeign to the point of xenophobia and fiercely patriotic, a "Vietnamese chauvinist" in the words of William Turley. Back in February 1971, at a small house on the Rue Darthe in the Paris suburb of Choisy-le-Roi, Kissinger held the first of many secret meetings with Le Duc Tho. But meetings at the house on Rue Darthe were as disappointing as the formal talks at the Hotel Majestic. The United States was still approaching the negotiations on exclusively military terms, proposing a ceasefire, mutual withdrawal of American and North Vietnamese troops from South Vietnam, and an exchange of prisoners of war. Le Duc Tho insisted on a comprehensive political settlement: total withdrawal of all American troops, removal of Nguyen Van Thieu from office, immediate participation of the Provisional Revolutionary Government in the government of South Vietnam, exchanges of prisoners of war, and a cessation of hostilities—in that order. Four years of talking and fighting had not yielded a thing.

Well, they achieved one thing. By early 1972 the negotiators in Paris were in agreement on the shape of the table: a circular table twenty-six feet in diameter, without name plates, place settings, flags, or identifying markings of any kind, where the chief negotiators would sit, and two rectangular tables, three by four and one-half feet each, placed eighteen inches from the circular table and at opposite sides. Nguyen Cao Ky has left a comment on the table debate: "Oh! that table . . . it was of fundamental importance to us. There was no way we were prepared to negotiate with the NLF, who in our view were traitors, and therefore we

North Vietnam's Lo Duc Tho and U.S. negotiator Henry Kissinger meet in secret at Saint-Nom-La-Broteche near Paris to seek agreement on a ceasefire in Vietnam. (*Courtesy, Library of Congress.*)

insisted that the agreement not to distinguish the NLF as a separate party to the talks must be carried out to the letter—and this meant not sitting down 'officially' with them at the same table."

Le Duc Tho had a long memory. In 1954 the Vietminh had accepted a military settlement at Geneva and agreed to postpone the political issues—the nebulous promise of free elections two years down the road. The elections never took place. On his deathbed in 1969, Ho Chi Minh warned Pham Van Don and Le Duc Tho not to make the same mistake. It had cost them fifteen years and nearly two million deaths. None of the superpowers—the Soviet Union, France, the United States, and the People's Republic of China—could be trusted. "Don't sign the next agreement," Ho Chi Minh insisted, "until we're certain of the political outcome."

The whole messy business of Vietnam was for Kissinger a distraction from his grand design for a new relationship among the superpowers. By 1971 the Chinese were more afraid of the Soviet Union than of the Americans, and Kissinger thought the time was right for the United States to seek a rapprochement. As an increasingly powerful Vietnamese military spread along China's southern border in Indochina, and huge Soviet forces arrayed themselves at its northern frontier, Chinese leaders might be ready to talk. They were. Kissinger met secretly with Chinese representatives several times in 1971, and the talks were productive. Kissinger further realized that improving relations between Washington and Beijing would alarm the Soviet leaders, increasing their willingness to negotiate in good faith, particularly on such critical issues as the Strategic Arms Limitation Talks then going on at Geneva. A unique opportunity to play the USSR off against the Chinese and improve the American diplomatic position vis-à-vis both was at hand. Kissinger called the new diplomatic initiative "détente," a mutual, morality-free process of cooperation and accommodation among the superpowers. Throughout 1971 and early 1972 Kissinger planned summit meetings in Moscow and Beijing so that Richard Nixon, the old militant anticommunist, could reshape modern international politics. Nixon began that process in February 1972 with a triumphant visit to Beijing. The summit with the Soviet Union was scheduled for May.

Between Kissinger and destiny stood Vietnam. If the United States lost the war, the political repercussions back home would be severe. The right wing might rise up in self-righteous indignation and set off another McCarthy era, wrecking any hopes Kissinger had of implementing a new relationship with the USSR and the Chinese. If the United States withdrew without achieving "peace with honor," its reduced credibility would abort détente because neither the Soviet leaders nor the Chinese would take the United States seriously. Kissinger needed an acceptable settlement of the war in Vietnam.

Nixon worried constantly that the public would interpret endless negotiations as a sign of weakness. He was in his tough mood, as if George C. Scott's version of George S. Patton had become his alter ego. He was up for reelection and needed to do something to prove himself, to show the public that his "secret plan" of 1968 to end the war was more than campaign rhetoric. But at the end of 1971, Vietnamization was playing into Le Duc Tho's hands. In just a short while, there would be no American troops to cope with. As far as Nixon was concerned, Kissinger had a weak hand to play in Paris. The only military option left to the president was bombing, and he was ready to use it. "I'm going to show the bastards," he told Kissinger in the spring. "Unless they deal with us I'm going to bomb the hell out of them." Nixon was in an anxious mood; the madman device was turning from strategy to psychological condition.

In the spring of 1972 the North Vietnamese tested the madman. The huge reduction in American forces and the failure of ARVN during the Lam Son invasion made possible the thought of winning. Combined with the increasing confidence in success was a new urgency about seeking it. The improvement in relations between China and the United States threatened to pull Vietnam's northern neighbor away from its commitment to Hanoi. That danger was confirmed in late 1971 when the Chinese intimated that Vietnamese reunification might be a matter of years, not months. A major figure behind the determination to act quickly was Vo Nguyen Giap, who guaranteed "a great victory over the Americans and their Saigon puppets." The Politburo in 1971 decided on "a decisive victory" to force "the United States to end the war by negotiating from a position of defeat."

Abrams was expecting an attack. Since 1968 the North Vietnamese had used the Tet holidays for offensives, and as early as October 1971

MACV was warning ARVN to get ready. February 1, 1972, came and went, with no attack. ARVN maintained an alert status throughout most of February, but the American warnings grew stale. ARVN commanders relaxed, and Giap traded the Vietnamese New Year holiday for the American Easter celebrations.

The North Vietnamese offensive began on Good Friday, March 30. By that time there were 95,000 American troops still in South Vietnam, only 6,000 of them combat forces. Under a heavy, advanced artillery barrage, more than 30,000 North Vietnamese, accompanied by 200 Soviet tanks, crossed the Demilitarized Zone and attacked Quang Tri Province in I Corps. Giap had moved long-range 130-mm artillery just north of the Hieu Giang River, bringing under bombardment Quang Tri City and an area five miles south. Heavy cloud cover limited the effectiveness of American tactical air strikes. The NVA troops kept up the artillery assault on ARVN posts, and on April 27 they attacked Quang Tri City. Thousands of South Vietnamese refugees fled the city for the protection of Hue, but the North Vietnamese targeted the 130-mm artillery on Highway 1, exacting a heavy toll on the refugees. The ARVN 3rd Division was caught off guard and began falling back along Highway 1. On May 1, the 304th North Vietnamese Division took control of Quang Tri City.

Giap hoped to inspire a deployment of American and ARVN troops north into I Corps while he prepared for three other attacks. Another 35,000-man contingent of North Vietnamese troops, the now-reinforced remnants of the units attacked in Cambodia in 1970 and Laos in 1971, assembled in Cambodia for an assault on Saigon, while 35,000 more soldiers prepared for a campaign against Dak To in the Central Highlands. Giap hoped the battle in the north would distract ARVN forces, increasing the possibility of success in the scheduled attacks in the Central Highlands and on Saigon. On April 2 North Vietnamese troops moved out of Cambodia, employing tanks and armored personnel carriers. They moved down Highway 13, seized Loc Ninh, surrounded An Loc, and severed the route to Saigon. One week later North Vietnam attacked Dak To with the objective of taking Kontum. As the commanders planned it, if Kontum fell they would drive toward the South China Sea and cut South Vietnam in half. To prepare for that possibility, two North Vietnamese divisions invaded Binh Dinh Province and took control of several districts along the South China Sea, cutting Highway 1 and the link between Hue and Saigon. The combined total of Vietcong and North Vietnamese troops committed to the offensive was 200,000.

The Eastertide offensive could not have come at a worse time for the Nixon administration. On April 2, Ambassador Ellsworth Bunker cabled Kissinger and Nixon that "ARVN forces are on the verge of collapse in I Corps." Back in his more naive days of 1969, Kissinger had told several of his aides, "I can't believe that a fourth-rate power like North Vietnam doesn't have a breaking point." Now a military offensive led by North

Vietnam threatened to derail everything. If the Eastertide offensive succeeded, even partially, Kissinger would lose bargaining power with Le Duc Tho. Massive bombings, which Nixon had already indicated his willingness to pursue, now looked to be the only way out of disaster.

Kissinger had scheduled a summit meeting for May between the president and the Soviet leadership. If the United States launched a full-scale bombing campaign over North Vietnam, the Soviet Union might cancel the summit and destroy Kissinger's hopes for détente and the signing of a treaty limiting nuclear arms. Yet in the absence of American bombs, the Eastertide offensive would overrun South Vietnam, inflict a military defeat on ARVN, and compromise the strategic position of the United States throughout the world. Kissinger was walking a very narrow path.

Nixon and Kissinger decided to unleash the B-52s. On April 6, 1972, they met in the White House with General John W. Vogt, new commander of the Seventh Air Force. Nixon told Vogt "to get down there and use whatever air you need to turn this thing around. . . . Stop this offensive." Code-named Operation Linebacker, the bombing began later that day, the first sustained raids over North Vietnam since 1969. The president confined the attacks to targets within sixty miles of the Demilitarized Zone, but on April 10 he extended the radius and by midmonth B-52s were attacking targets within a few miles of Hanoi and Haiphong. The raids elated the joint chiefs. Admiral Thomas Moorer, who had replaced Earle Wheeler as chairman of the joint chiefs in 1970, remarked, "Finally we will be able to win the war."

On May 2 Kissinger met once again at the house on the Rue Darthe in Paris with Le Duc Tho. Kissinger tried to achieve some movement in the negotiations. But Le Duc Tho would not budge. Quang Tri City had fallen to NVA troops, Hue was threatened, Loc Ninh was taken, An Loc was under siege, and Saigon was bracing for an attack; and in the Central Highlands the NVA troops were preparing for a breakthrough that would carry them to the South China Sea. Le Duc Tho had one message for Kissinger on May 2, 1970: "What difference is all this talk going to make? The end is in sight." Kissinger was upset, his anger no doubt deepened by what seemed Le Duc Tho's arrogance. That night, when he got back to Washington, he met with Nixon. His restraint was gone. "It's time," he told Nixon, "to send them an undeniable message, to deliver a shock, to let them know that things might get out of hand if the offensive doesn't stop." Nixon was ready, too. "The bastards have never been bombed like they're going to be bombed this time." Two days later, on May 4, Nixon suspended the Paris peace talks after their 149th session.

On May 8 Nixon announced that Operation Linebacker would continue indefinitely and the navy would mine the North Vietnamese ports of Haiphong, Cam Pha, Hon Gai, and Thanh Hoa and impose a naval blockade of the entire coast—all to cut the flow of supplies to North Vietnamese troops fighting in the South and to protect the lives of American forces still in Vietnam. Nixon hoped the raids would pressure North Vietnam into taking the Paris negotiations seriously. Privately, he wanted the B-52s to do what ARVN could not: stop the Eastertide offensive. Kissinger's concern was that the raids not disrupt the upcoming Moscow summit.

Both Nixon and Kissinger got their wishes. Nixon shifted more than 100 B-52s from the Strategic Air Command and assigned them to tactical strikes over South Vietnam and strategic air raids over North Vietnam. The size of the Seventh Fleet nearly doubled, including the addition of four aircraft carriers and hundreds of fighter-bombers. By the end of May the United States was flying more than 2,200 sorties a month, up from only 700 in March, and most of the raids were concentrated on Quang Tri, Kontum, Dak To, An Loc, and Loc Ninh, and over selected strategic targets in North Vietnam. At An Loc and Quang Tri the B-52s struck every forty-five minutes, twenty-four hours a day, for weeks on end, pounding the North Vietnamese. They took a fearsome toll. On June 18 the NVA troops began pulling out of An Loc; the fighting petered out near Kontum, which ended North Vietnam's hopes of driving to the South China Sea; and up north, the ARVN Airborne Division, 1st Division, and marines began a counterattack that lasted throughout the summer and eventually recaptured Quang Tri City. Eastertide was over. And to Kissinger's pleasure, the Soviet leaders acted with restraint. They offered only the most tepid protest against the bombing and mining campaigns, decided not to challenge the naval blockade, and did not withdraw their invitation for Nixon to come to Moscow. The Chinese were equally circumspect, issuing a mild protest but also calling for a negotiated settlement. Pham Van Dong felt betrayed: He condemned both Moscow and the Chinese for abandoning the "world revolutionary movement and acquiescing in the brutal violence of the American imperialists." Later in the month Nixon went to Moscow, drank champagne with a smiling Leonid Brezhnev, and signed the coveted Strategic Arms Limitation Treaty.

In Hanoi the Eastertide fiasco was a humiliating defeat for Vo Nguyen Giap. He had also fallen victim to Hodgkin's disease, a cancer of the lymphatic system, which prevented him from taking an active role in the government. Pham Van Dong began looking to General Van Tien Dung as his military chief. Dung, born in Tonkin in 1917 to a peasant family, had joined the revolutionary movement in 1936 and fought against the French and then the Japanese. Shrewd and fearless, he exuded confidence, but his perpetually smiling countenance hid an all-consuming passion for Vietnamese independence. In the early 1950s Dung performed brilliantly as a Vietminh battalion commander, and Giap trained him in logistics and maneuvers. In 1953 Giap named him chief of staff, gave him command of the 320th Division, and charged him with logistical planning at Dienbienphu. For the next eighteen years Dung was Giap's closest associate.

When Dung assumed control of the North Vietnamese army, he faced a complicated military situation. On August 23, 1972, the last American combat battalion—3rd Battalion of the 21st Infantry—left South Vietnam. ARVN troop strength had reached nearly 1.1 million troops, the highest since the beginning of the war, and with military equipment transfers from the United States, South Vietnam had a state-of-the-art fighting force. It had the fourth largest army in the world, its navy was the world's fifth largest, possessing nearly 1,500 ships, and at more than 2,000 craft, Saigon had the fourth largest air force. Because during Eastertide Giap had persisted in making repeated frontal assaults into fortified ARVN bunkers protected by massive American air support, fully half of the NVA combat divisions were devastated. More than 100,000 of North Vietnam's best troops were dead, and Dung estimated it could take three years to restore the army to fighting strength. It was obvious to Dung that North Vietnam would not be able to contemplate a major offensive against South Vietnam anytime soon.

The political situation in the United States did not bode well either. Pham Van Dong and Le Duc Tho had been hoping ever since the Cambodian invasion in 1970 that the antiwar movement would sweep Richard Nixon from office and bring a Democrat to power who would be anxious to complete the American disengagement. They took heart when the Democrats nominated Senator George McGovern of South Dakota as their presidential candidate. A leading political figure in the antiwar movement since 1965, McGovern campaigned for an immediate, unilateral American withdrawal. For their purposes the North Vietnamese could not imagine a better American president. But the McGovern campaign self-destructed. When the press found out that Senator Thomas Eagleton of Missouri, McGovern's vice-presidential running mate, had once been hospitalized for mental illness and treated by electric shock therapy, the Democrats dumped him from the ticket and replaced him with Sargent Shriver. That, though, made the party look incompetent. And the Republicans were able to portray McGovern as representative of the radical cultural forces that Americans had come to associate with the antiwar movement. At some point, surely, Pham Van Dong and Le Duc Tho came to know that Richard Nixon would be reelected in November.

The military situation in South Vietnam and the political climate in the United States left North Vietnam with only one option: Negotiate a settlement to the war. Van Tien Dung had a central role in convincing the Politburo to return to the talks. Pham Van Dong and Le Duc Tho were more stubborn. Operation Linebacker, like the earlier Rolling Thunder bombing campaigns, fed on their resentment toward the United States. They did not want to give in to what they considered technological terrorism. But Dung saw no point in digging in. He could not launch an invasion of South Vietnam anyway, and no dramatic change appeared in American politics. Why not reopen the talks, secure an end to the Linebacker attacks, rebuild the logistical network, and prepare for the final assault on South Vietnam?

Dung's logic was compelling, and in August, Kissinger resumed private talks with Le Duc Tho. Both sides wished for an accommodation. North Vietnam wanted an end to the Linebacker raids, and Nixon was looking ahead to the election, hoping to sign a peace treaty before November. In Paris at the end of September, Kissinger agreed to a complete withdrawal of American troops while allowing North Vietnamese soldiers to remain in place in South Vietnam, a major concession to Le Duc Tho. Kissinger had little choice. Ten years of war and the greatest expenditure of firepower in history had not dislodged the enemy. "We could not make it [NVA troop withdrawal] a condition for a final settlement. We had long since passed that threshold." Le Duc Tho dropped the long-standing North Vietnamese demand that Nguyen Van Thieu resign and a coalition government be created. By the end of September the outlines of a peace treaty had emerged: a mutual cease-fire and an end to American bombing; complete withdrawal of American troops; exchanges of prisoners of war; agreement to allow Vietcong, North Vietnamese, and South Vietnamese troops to remain in place; recognition of the Provisional Revolutionary Government of South Vietnam and the government of Nguyen Van Thieu as legitimate political entities in South Vietnam; and creation of a "council of national reconciliation" to work out the remaining problems.

The settlement was the easy part. Kissinger encountered opposition from the State Department, typical bureaucratic intransigence that, in his opinion, so often foiled modern diplomacy. When several State Department and National Security Council staff officials argued that the United States had caved in to the North Vietnamese position, Kissinger reacted violently, shouting at them in a White House briefing session: "I want to meet their terms. I want to reach an agreement. I want to end this war before the election. It can be done and it will be done. What do you want us to do? Stay there forever?" In Saigon, President Nguyen Van Thieu too perceived a sellout. He was apoplectic in his opposition to the treaty. Leaving fourteen divisions of North Vietnamese troops in South Vietnam and extending political recognition to the Provisional Revolutionary Government were unthinkable. When Kissinger met with Thieu in Saigon in mid-October, the South Vietnamese flatly rejected the proposals, insisting on withdrawal of all North Vietnamese soldiers, recognition of the Demilitarized Zone as a sovereign international boundary, and a public American repudiation of the Provisional Revolutionary Government's legitimacy. When Kissinger termed the demands "insane and absurd," Thieu went mute with rage.

When Kissinger returned to Washington with the news that Thieu was going to sabotage the deal, Nixon flew into one of his own rages, ordering Kissinger to fly to Saigon and "tell that little son of a bitch to sign or else." Kissinger demurred and Nixon reconsidered, hoping that there was some way of finessing Thieu into agreement. On October 22 the United States, which had staged more than 41,000 bombing sorties over North Vietnam since April 1, scaled back the Linebacker raids to targets south of the twentieth parallel. In a press conference on October 24 Thieu denounced the bombing halt and the draft treaty, calling on South Vietnam to "wipe out the Vietcong and North Vietnamese invaders quickly and mercilessly." Nixon was also hesitating. With the election just two weeks away, he did not want the settlement to appear politically contrived, and he thought that Thieu's demands might give the United States more bargaining power. Kissinger began another round of talks, which made Hanoi very suspicious. In a political dance inspired by the presidential election and fear of losing the settlement outright, Kissinger promised a group of journalists that "peace is at hand. We believe that an agreement is within sight."

It was not, not quite yet. On November 7 Nixon won a landslide victory in the election. When Kissinger renewed negotiations with Le Duc Tho after the elections, he presented to the North Vietnamese sixty-nine proposed changes in the treaty, all of them demanded by Nguyen Van Thieu. The North Vietnamese found the proposals unacceptable, and later in the month they began introducing changes of their own. The agreement, which had seemed so close back in October, was disintegrating.

Toward South Vietnam Nixon switched from stick to carrot, promising Thieu that if "North Vietnam violates the agreement and stages offensive operations against you, the United States will take swift and severe retaliatory action." Thieu knew better than anyone that South Vietnamese survival depended on that retaliation. Only massive American bombing had stopped the Eastertide offensive. Without American air support and military assistance, South Vietnam would not survive another attack. Yet Thieu still would not budge. Pham Van Dong saw the feud between the United States and South Vietnam as an opportunity. If he could stall the talks, raise more procedural issues, and delay a final settlement, North Vietnam might be able to strengthen the air defenses around Hanoi and Haiphong, repair the rail lines to China, and adjust its supply routing to compensate for the American blockade. On December 13 Le Duc Tho suspended the negotiations and returned to Hanoi "for consultations."

The next day Nixon gave Pham Van Dong an ultimatum: "Resume serious negotiations within seventy-two hours or suffer the consequences." Nixon was reaching the end of his emotional rope. He wanted a signed peace treaty before the inauguration on January 20, 1973. He was even more blunt to Admiral Thomas Moorer, instructing him to develop immediate plans for massive bombing of North Vietnam: "I don't want any more of this crap about the fact that we couldn't hit this target or that one. This is your chance to use military power to win this war, and if you don't, I'll hold you responsible." On December 18, 1972, Moorer followed orders and launched Operation Linebacker II, a final eleven-day bombing campaign that evolved into one of the heaviest aerial assaults of the war. B-52s, F-105s, F-4s, and F-111s flew nearly 2,000 sorties over North Vietnam, employing highly accurate laser-guided, television-targeted bombs—"Christmas bombs"—to strike rail yards, power plants, communications, air defense radar sites, bridges, highways, docks and shipping facilities, petroleum stores, ammunition supply depots, air bases, military installations, and means of transportation.

Early in January 1973 Le Duc Tho indicated a willingness to resume the negotiations. Van Tien Dung had been right all along. It was best to wait for a better opportunity to carry out the final offensive. The only roadblock to a settlement was Nguyen Van Thieu, but Richard Nixon was not about to let a peace treaty slip through his hands again. On January 5, 1973, he secretly communicated with Thieu, sending him a threat and a promise:

> Gravest consequences would then ensue if [you] . . . reject the agreement. . . . It is imperative for our common objectives that your government take no further actions . . . that make more difficult the acceptance of the settlement by all parties. . . . Should you decide . . . to go with us, you have my assurance of continued assistance in the post-settlement period and that we will respond with full force should the settlement be violated by North Vietnam.

Thieu got the message. With or without him, Nixon was going to sign a treaty. Refusal to cooperate would mean an end to American military assistance and certain defeat. Stone-faced, his teeth tightly clenched, Thieu told Ambassador Ellsworth Bunker that he would sign. On January 8 Kissinger met with Le Duc Tho in Paris; a week later Nixon halted all military operations against North Vietnam; and on January 27 all four parties—the United States, North Vietnam, South Vietnam, and the Provisional Revolutionary Government of South Vietnam—signed the treaty. The document provided for release of all American prisoners of war and withdrawal of all United States military personnel within sixty days; a cease-fire to be monitored by a four-nation International Commission of Control and Supervision; cessation of all foreign military activity in Laos and Cambodia; American provision of replacement military aid and unlimited economic assistance to South Vietnam; and formation of a Council of National Reconciliation and Concord, composed of representatives from the Saigon regime, the Provisional Revolutionary Government of South Vietnam, and a neutral body, to resolve outstanding political questions and organize elections in South Vietnam.

The settlement came none too soon. When Congress convened in January, the Democratic caucuses of both houses voted overwhelmingly to eliminate all funds for military operations in Indochina, and polls of the new Congress indicated huge majorities for the end of American involvement in the region. There were only 24,000 American troops still in South Vietnam. Political support for the war in the United States had completely evaporated. Nixon had no choice but to get the treaty signed and sealed. In a national television address, he announced that within sixty days all American troops would be out of South Vietnam and the prisoners of war would be home. "South Vietnam," he said, "has gained the right to determine its own future. . . . Let us be proud that America did not settle for a peace that would have betrayed our ally." The speech repelled Nguyen Cao Ky, "so nauseating was its hypocrisy and self-delusion. . . . This is an enormous step toward the total domination of Vietnam and there is no reason why they [the Communists] should stop now. . . . I give them a couple of years before they invade the South."

There were a few good months before it all started to unravel. On February 12, 1973, the first of 591 American prisoners of war returned home, and the rest were in the United States by the end of March. Nixon and Kissinger hosted them at the White House, and the soldiers paid homage to the president who had ended the war. On February 21 the Royal Laotian government signed a cease-fire with the communist Pathet Lao guerrillas. The International Commission of Control and Supervision, composed of Canada, Indonesia, Hungary, and Poland, went into operation in March. A relieved Henry Kissinger remarked to the press, "It should be clear by now that no one in the war has had a monopoly of anguish and that no one has a monopoly of insight. Together with healing the wounds in Indochina, we can begin to heal the wounds in America."

But those wounds continued to fester, and the Nixon administration was unable to deliver on its promise to rescue South Vietnam if Hanoi broke the agreement. Richard Nixon's insecurities and paranoia, his resentment of the press and the eastern establishment, were about to catch up with him. The Watergate scandal enveloped him, and when the final North Vietnamese offensive came in 1975, he would be living in exile in San Clemente.

During the election campaign of 1972, operatives connected with the White House had conducted a series of illegal and unethical programs, all directed at undermining the political efforts of liberal Democrats. On June 22, 1972, police caught several men attempting to wiretap Democratic Party National Headquarters in the Watergate Building in Washington. A few days later, when it was clear that a number of top administration officials were involved in planning and financing the break-in, Nixon ordered a cover-up of the entire affair. Two enterprising reporters from the *Washington* Post—Robert Woodward and Carl Bernstein— eventually exposed the whole story.

Two of the president's closest advisers, John Ehrlichman and H. R. Haldeman, resigned on April 30, 1973, when they were implicated in the cover-up, and on May 11 a federal judge dismissed charges against Daniel Ellsberg when he learned that the Justice Department had illegally wiretapped his phone, and a rogue group believing itself to be acting on behalf of the government had burglarized the files of Ellsberg's psychiatrist to "find some dirt" about him. Senator Sam Ervin of North Carolina headed up a Select Committee on Presidential Campaign Activities, and the televised hearings dominated the news for the next six months. The testimony indicated that despite his self-righteous denials, Nixon had been personally involved in the cover-up from the very beginning, It was separately discovered that he had tape-recorded most of his White House conversations. The tapings were not in themselves illegitimate: They were a practice the presidency had instituted to provide for history a record of how the executive branch made policy. But it would have been wise of Nixon to remember that they were also catching him in some very damaging moments. Throughout 1973 and much of 1974 Congress, the press, and the special Justice Department prosecutor demanded copies of those tapes, which the administration refused to provide. Late in 1973 the House Judiciary Committee began impeachment proceedings against the president, and when the Supreme Court forced Nixon to hand over the tapes, and the tapes clearly implicated him in the cover-up, he resigned from office. On August 9, 1974, Gerald Ford became the thirty-eighth president of the United States.

During the Watergate controversy, Nixon's presidential authority had steadily eroded, and he was unable to keep control over Southeast Asia policy. Late in June 1973 Congress attached a rider to a supplemental appropriations bill cutting off funds for American bombing in Cambodia. Nixon vetoed the bill on June 27, but when it became clear that an override was a distinct possibility, he compromised, guaranteeing to Congress that all American military activity in Cambodia would be over by August 15. Congress passed legislation ending all American combat activities in Indochina by that day. Nixon signed the bill on July 1.

By that time there were already signs that the peace agreement was not working. The ending of American bombing of Cambodia and Laos freed North Vietnam to initiate massive increases in the infiltration of troops and supplies, and to provide matériel to the Khmer Rouge guerrillas in Cambodia and the Pathet Lao in Laos. The Soviet Union increased shipments of weapons and financial assistance to North Vietnam by 400 percent. To counter Moscow's generosity toward Hanoi, the United States funneled $3.2 billion in military aid to South Vietnam.

When it became clear in August 1973 that North Vietnam had no intention of abiding by the Treaty of Paris, Canada withdrew from the International Commission of Control and Supervision. Iran became the fourth member nation. The Council of National Reconciliation and Concord was stillborn.

In Laos and Cambodia the prospects were equally dismal. The Khmer Rouge gained ground in Cambodia, and the Lon Nol government seemed impotent. By 1974 the Pathet Lao controlled most of northern Laos. Prince Souvanna Phouma tried to maintain a neutralist government, but the North Vietnamese were making it difficult. He was skeptical of their willingness to keep their cease-fire agreement, entered on February 21, to withdraw their troops from Laos. "If pressure is kept on the North Vietnamese to understand the risk they run from violating the Agreement," the prince said in an appeal to Kissinger, "then perhaps they will respect the Agreement. . . . Therefore we must count on our great friends the Americans to help us survive. We hope, we dream, that this wish will be granted." It was a futile plea. Kissinger met with Le Duc Tho in Hanoi on February 10 and learned that North Vietnam would withdraw after a political settlement in Laos between the government and the Pathet Lao, not before. There was nothing Kissinger could do about it.

The continuing fighting in Indochina triggered a movement in Congress to restrict the authority of the White House. In July, Congress began debating a joint resolution requiring the president to report to Congress within forty-eight hours if he committed American forces to a foreign conflict or "substantially" increased the number of combat troops anywhere abroad. Unless Congress approved the deployment within sixty days, the president would have to end it. At the insistence of the Senate, a modification was inserted allowing the deadline to be extended another thirty days if the president certified that more time was necessary to complete the evacuation of American forces. Congress could also order an immediate withdrawal within the sixty- or ninety-day period by passing a concurrent resolution, which could not be vetoed. Congress passed the War Powers Resolution at the end of October. Nixon vetoed it, but on November 7, Congress overrode the veto and the measure became law.

The North Vietnamese were watching Washington politics very closely. The Canadians were right. North Vietnam had no intention of abandoning the dream of unification and independence. Pham Van Dong and Le Duc Tho were cautious about the next offensive. They knew that the Nixon administration was weakening under the pressures of Watergate, but they did not underestimate the president. Le Duc Tho in particular was certain that if Nixon had a chance, he would unleash the B-52s again. Van Tien Dung did not want another Eastertide. He could not afford the casualties. The North Vietnamese leadership watched with interest the political debates in Congress. In mid-1974 the legislature limited aid to Vietnam to $1.1 billion, down from $3.2 billion the year before, and the funding for fiscal 1975 was cut to only $700 million, which included shipping costs to South Vietnam. A major American intervention seemed unlikely.

South Vietnam was also facing severe economic problems. Ever since the early 1960s the economy had been driven by massive American aid and the spending power of hundreds of thousands of United States soldiers. Army construction projects alone employed 100,000 South Vietnamese workers. The withdrawal of the troops and the decline in American aid sent the economy fluttering out of control. Inflation hit 65 percent, and urban unemployment reached 40 percent. That the government kept an army of 1.1 million people worsened the economic situation. President Thieu's support within the general population, never really very high, dropped even further.

The war had forever transformed Saigon. In less than a decade its population had swelled from 1 to nearly 4 million, without any real improvements in housing or city services. People came to the city for homes or jobs, for access to the tide of American money, for the security that was absent in the countryside. It was now a city of prostitutes, pimps, black marketeers, petty thieves, drug dealers, assassins, orphans, refugees, deserters, Vietcong, terrorists, and opportunists. The GIs said they could get anything in Saigon—"laid and way-laid, diarrhea and gonorrhea, drugs and slugs." For more traditional Vietnamese, especially Buddhists, the worldliness of Saigon was an abomination.

In Saigon the regime of Nguyen Van Thieu became even more authoritarian. In 1971 Thieu abolished village elections and raised Buddhist ire. He established the Dan Chu (Democracy) party in March 1973 and then promptly did the most undemocratic things—forcing all civil servants to join, manipulating the National Assembly elections, abolishing rival political parties, closing down newspapers, and maintaining a state of martial law. A variety of protest movements emerged in 1973 and 1974, the most influential of which was led by Father Tran Huu Thanh, a Roman Catholic priest who accused Thieu of subverting anticommunism in order to line his own pockets. Late in 1974 Thieu tried to deal with Thanh's increasing power by firing several hundred patently corrupt military and civilian officials, but it was only a token attempt at reform. The regime remained an authoritarian, single-party state.

Le Duan decided the time had come for the final offensive. The United States was out of Vietnam for good. The Arab oil embargo of 1973 had triggered higher unemployment and inflation in the United States. And the Watergate scandal, the corruption in Saigon, the increasing power of the Pathet Lao in Laos and the Khmer Rouge in Cambodia, and the intense congressional opposition to continuing involvement in Indochina guaranteed, as far as Le Duan could judge, that the United States would not be able to save South Vietnam. Planning for the offensive accelerated.

General Van Tien Dung began the campaign, predicting that it could take years to succeed, particularly if the United States intervened with air power. By the end of 1974 he had in place in South Vietnam twenty-two fully equipped infantry divisions, complete with hundreds of tanks and thousands of artillery pieces. Improvements in the Ho Chi Minh Trail gave the North Vietnamese army more mobility than ever before. But rather than an all-out offensive, Dung decided to attack Phuoc Long, a sparsely populated province that bordered Cambodia on the west and at its southern tip was only forty miles from Saigon. Such an offensive would yield two important pieces of information: Was ARVN prepared for serious resistance, and would the United States intervene? If ARVN collapsed, the United States did not intervene, and Phuoc Long fell, North Vietnam would gain a critically important psychological and logistical victory. North Vietnamese troop movements would be unimpeded all the way from Hanoi to within forty miles of Saigon.

Thieu believed that North Vietnam was still too weak in 1975 to launch a full offensive. But Van Tien Dung had already moved the NVA 3rd and 7th Divisions into position. The NVA artillery bombardment began on December 26, 1974. On January 5, the North Vietnamese attacked with two full divisions, T-54 tanks, and 130-mm field-gun batteries. Thieu sent in only one ARVN battalion to defend Phuoc Long, and it was woefully inadequate. Most important was that the dreaded B-52s did not appear over Phuoc Long. Le Duan summed it up in a speech to the Politburo in Hanoi: "Never have we had military and political conditions so perfect or a strategic advantage so great as we have now."

As a beginning to their next objective, cutting South Vietnam in half by a thrust from the Central Highlands to the South China Sea, Van Tien Dung, Le Duc Tho, and Pham Van Dong planned to attack Ban Me Thuot from their new base at Phuoc Long. Dung spent the next two months moving his troops, tanks, artillery, and supplies into place, and on March 9, 1975, the NVA 316th, Tenth, and 320th Divisions struck. Assuming that North Vietnam would not attack unless as a diversion, ARVN defenders at Ban Me Thuot were unprepared, and the NVA took the city on March 12. Once again, there had been no B-52s overhead or American fighter-bombers from the South China Sea.

The fall of Ban Me Thuot had immediate consequences. Over the opposition of all of his senior military advisers, on March 14 Thieu made the fateful decision to abandon the Central Highlands and redeploy ARVN forces to the major cities—an enclave strategy designed to protect the major population centers. On the same day, General Van Tien Dung resolved to attack up Route 14 and seize Pleiku and Kontum. In the process he encountered hundreds of thousands of South Vietnamese refugees fleeing the Central Highlands and tens of thousands of ARVN troops withdrawing. He cut them to pieces with heavy artillery. More than 100,000 civilians and 15,000 ARVN troops died in the wholesale flight out of the highlands.

In Cambodia the Khmer Rouge pushed toward victory. By the end of 1974, the Lon Nol government was dying. The Khmer Rouge guerrillas sealed off the Mekong River as a source of commerce for Phnom Penh, and they surrounded the capital, tightening the noose day by day. They controlled 80 percent of the country. No ground transportation routes into the capital remained open. More than 2.7 million Cambodians crowded into Phnom Penh, and there was no way of supplying them. The American ambassador John Gunther Dean reported that Cambodia was finished. Events in Laos were just as bad. On March 27, the Pathet Lao launched an offensive against the Souvanna Phouma government, attacking Vang Pao and Sala Phou Khoun and then driving south along Route 13 toward the capital city of Vientiane. During the offensive anti-government demonstrations and riots erupted in Vientiane, and Souvanna Phouma was unable to suppress them. Similar insurgency broke out in other towns and cities throughout the country. The Pathet Lao also infiltrated guerrilla soldiers into Vientiane and towns along the border with Thailand, among them Pakse, Savannakhet, and Thakhek. Like the Khmer Rouge and the North Vietnamese, the Pathet Lao could smell victory.

A week after the ARVN debacle in the Central Highlands, Van Tien Dung surprised South Vietnam again with a major offensive in I Corps. The NVA 341st Division attacked out of Quang Tri Province and headed South along Route 1 toward Hue, while the NVA 324B and 325C Divisions came east out of the mountains of Quang Nam Province and drove to the South China Sea, cutting off Route 1 and isolating Hue. On March 20, 1975, Thieu abandoned Hue, hoping to hold the line at Danang. North Vietnam took Hue on March 24. But no sooner had Hue fallen than the NVA 2nd Division seized Tam Ky on Route 1, isolating Danang. The NVA 711th and 304th Divisions then moved on the city. The South Vietnamese Air Force and Navy evacuated 50,000 refugees and 16,000 ARVN troops before Danang fell on March 29. Left behind were more than 2 million civilians and 25,000 ARVN soldiers, who surrendered. To make sure that the few Americans still in the city got away, North Vietnamese troops refrained from reaching the docks at Danang until March 30. Van Tien Dung was taking no chances on baiting the United States into intervention.

The collapse of South Vietnamese forces in the Central Highlands and in I Corps was speeding the war toward a quicker end than Washington had expected. President Ford and Henry Kissinger, who had replaced William P. Rogers as secretary of state in 1973, went to Congress for emergency assistance. In January they had unsuccessfully lobbied Congress for $300 million for South Vietnam and $222 million for Cambodia, but early in February Ford returned with a request for $1.3 billion for South Vietnam and $497 million for Cambodia. Senate Majority Leader Mike Mansfield reacted angrily to the request: He was "sick and tired of pictures of Indochinese men, women, and children being slaughtered by American guns with American ammunition in countries in which we have no vital interests." Ford failed. He tried again in April with a new request for $722 million, but he received only $300 million, and it was confined to humanitarian assistance and funds to help evacuate Americans if necessary. South Vietnam, Cambodia, and Laos were on their own.

South Vietnam was imploding. For years the United States had trained ARVN to fight a conventional war with the support of enormous firepower, a strategy that, although incapable of achieving military victory, had at least staved off defeat. But Vietnamization took American troops out of the strategic formula, and opposition to the war in the United States gradually eliminated the firepower. Only the B-52s had stopped the Eastertide offensive in 1972. In 1975 the South Vietnamese did not have that backing. They no longer had much American money. And between 1970 and 1975, when ARVN lost its American support, the war expanded all across Indochina, increasing the field of battle and stretching ARVN's resources to the breaking point. Those strategic factors, combined with a crumbling economy and an isolated political regime, guaranteed defeat.

On March 31, 1975, Le Duan cabled Van Tien Dung with orders to take Saigon. He called it a "once in a thousand years opportunity to liberate Saigon before the rainy season." The offensives in I Corps and the Central Highlands had decimated ARVN forces. South Vietnam lost 150,000 troops to death, capture, or desertion, along with more than $1 billion in military equipment. President Thieu had isolated himself in the presidential palace, and the Joint General Staff was doing nothing to get ready for the North Vietnamese attack. Le Duan was right. Van Tien Dung had a "once in a thousand years opportunity."

On April 3, 1975, Ambassador John Gunther Dean asked President Gerald Ford for permission to evacuate all Americans from Phnom Penh. The 1.7 million people in the city were starving. The Khmer Rouge had cut off all routes into the city, including the Mekong River, and the airlift of supplies was becoming precarious, for the guerrillas were closing in on Pochentong Airport. The communists poured 107-mm rockets into the city. Lon Nol had abdicated two days before to a military coalition and left the city for Indonesia, on his way to Hawaii. Hoping to work out a last-minute arrangement for the return of Prince Norodom Sihanouk to power, Kissinger delayed the American evacuation. On April 1 the Khmer Rouge were on the outskirts of Phnom Penh. President Ford then implemented Operation Eagle Pull. Naval helicopters from the Seventh Fleet landed on the embassy grounds and evacuated 276 Cambodian and American embassy personnel and their families, with Ambassador John Gunther Dean the last to leave, carrying the United States embassy flag, neatly folded in a plastic bag, at his side. Six days later the Khmer Rouge swept through the streets of Phnom Penh.

By that time the North Vietnamese were ready for a final assault of their own. Le Duc Tho was so excited that he came down the Ho Chi Minh Trail to stay in Loc Ninh at Dung's headquarters. During late March and early April, Dung moved eighteen NVA divisions into place within a forty-mile radius of Saigon. Poised due east of the city were the 3rd, 304th, 325th, and 342B Divisions, charged with taking out the ARVN 1st Airborne Brigade at Ba Ria and the 951st ARVN Ranger Group and the 4th Airborne Brigade near Long Thanh. Northeast of Saigon, Dung placed the 6th, 7th, and 314th Divisions, ordering them to hit Bien Hoa. To the north, the 320B, 312th, and 338th Divisions were assigned the conquest of the ARVN 5th Division at Ben Cat and the ARVN Ninth Ranger Brigade at Lai Thieu. Northwest of Saigon, Dung had the 7th, 316th, 320th, and 968th Divisions ready to pounce on the ARVN 25th Division at Trang Bang and Cu Chi. In the west, the 3rd, 5th, 9th, and 16th divisions were poised to attack the ARVN 22nd Division at Tan An and Ben Luc and the 7th and 8th Ranger Brigades just outside of Saigon. To the southwest, the NVA 8th Division prepared to attack the ARVN 7th Division at My Tho.

On April 21, President Thieu resigned. Duong Van ("Big") Minh, Thieu's longtime rival, assumed the presidency. Graham Martin, the United States ambassador to South Vietnam who had replaced Ellsworth Bunker in 1973, cabled Henry Kissinger two days later telling him that Operation Frequent Wind, the American evacuation of Saigon, was only a few days away. Martin complained to Kissinger that "the only person whose ass isn't covered is me." Kissinger cabled back: "My ass isn't covered. I can assure you it will be hanging several yards higher than you when this is all over."

The end came eleven days later. On April 26, 1975, Dung launched the Ho Chi Minh Campaign, and ARVN immediately collapsed in toward Saigon. With television cameras broadcasting the events throughout the world, the North Vietnamese moved in on the city. President Ford implemented Operation Frequent Wind on April 29, and in the next several days American helicopters airlifted 7,100 American and South Vietnamese military and civilian personnel out of Saigon, many of them from the roof of the United States embassy, while naval ships ferried more than 70,000 South Vietnamese to American vessels in the South China Sea. On April 29 Duong Van Minh surrendered unconditionally. Graham Martin left the embassy on April 30. The NVA 325th, 471st, and 968th Divisions then headed for Laos, in further assurance of the Pathet Lao

April 1, 1975—A U.S. civilian pilot in the aircraft doorway tries to maintain order as panicking South Vietmamese civilians scramble to get aboard. Thousands of civilians and South Vietnamese soldiers fought for space. (*Courtesy, Library of Congress.*)

victory several months later. Twenty-one years after the Geneva Convention of 1954, Indochina had fallen to the communists.

On the afternoon of April 30, 1975, after Graham Martin and the last Americans were out of Saigon, a column of North Vietnamese tanks appeared on Thong Nhut Avenue and rumbled across Cong Ly Boulevard toward Independence Palace. The tank column crashed through the gates of the palace and lined up on the lawn. A soldier, bearing the blue and red flag with the yellow star of the Provisional Revolutionary Government, emerged from the belly of the lead tank and waved the banner from the palace steps. Neil Davis, a war correspondent from Reuters, went up to the young man and asked his name. "Nguyen Van Thieu," the soldier replied. The Vietnam War was over.

Although the design of the Vietnam Veterans Memorial triggered a storm of protest in the United States, the "wall" eventually became a secred shrine to millions of people who visited it. (*Courtesy, Library of Congress.*)

11

Distorted Images,
Missed Opportunities,
1975–1995

No more Vietnams.

—Richard Nixon, 1985

It was not at all like the Iwo Jima monument. On that point nearly everyone agreed. The Iwo Jima statue stands proud in Arlington, Virginia, an eloquent reminder of a simpler, more straightforward war. Frozen in bronze are the five marines thrusting the American flag into the soil on top of Mount Surabachi. Its style is heroic realism, a faithful attempt to reproduce the award-winning photograph. It trafficks in uncomplex emotions: the "good war," John Wayne in the Pacific, go get'em boys, "I shall return." Not far from the Iwo Jima monument, across the Potomac River, broods the Vietnam War Memorial. It rises out of a depression in the ground, shifts direction a bit, and then descends back into the ground. Its surface is polished black granite, an inscrutable veneer that reflects the image of the viewer and the landscape that faces it. Cut into the granite are the names of the more than 58,000 American men and women who died in the war. What did they die for? What caused the war? What was the nature of the conflict? If you look for the answers in the silent black stone, all you will see is yourself.

From its inception the memorial generated controversy. It was too vague, some said, too abstract, not heroic enough. Others complained loudly and bitterly about the architect, Maya Ying Lin, a student at Yale. The war had been against Asians. Students had been the most outspoken opponents of the war. Should an Asian-American student memorialize the war? Many veterans answered no. The memorial, meant to commemorate sacrifice, quickened old pains that the years had turned dull. The questions about the meaning of the war returned with fresh force. In response to opponents of the Wall, another sculpture was commissioned. This one, the work of Frederick Hart, is a realistic rendition of soldiers. Both memorials were dedicated on November 13, 1982.

The controversy died quickly. The polished black stone has taken its place near the other stones—some polished, some not—that memorialize other events and other wars and other men. Tourists dutifully visit it along with the others. Most are pleased by what they see. In some very special way, the memorial is like the war itself—so misunderstood and complex and even abstract. Americans went to a land few understood. They fought a war. And then they returned home. And within a short time Vietnam left the news shows and the news magazines, replaced by other stories.

During the war 11,000 women nurses had treated 153,000 wounded soldiers. Within months of the dedication of the Vietnam War Memorial, woman veterans began to campaign for recognition of their role in Indochina. In 1983 Diane Carlson Evans, who had served in Vietnam in 1968 and 1969 as an army nurse, was thinking of a memorial to the war's women. For years she struggled to secure the necessary congressional approval and to raise $2.5 million. By 1991 she had the money and the authorization, and Glenna Goodacre received the commission to design the memorial. She produced a bronze sculpture, larger than life, of three women cradling a wounded GI. The memorial was unveiled and dedicated on Veterans' Day in 1993.

The struggle of Americans to come to terms with the Vietnam War has been largely outside the corridors of power. Politicians, diplomats, and military leaders, their credit spent in the years of conflict, lost their chance to influence popular opinion. They gave way to intellectuals and artists and media executives, a diverse collection of historians, writers, and film and television producers. It was now their turn to explain the war and its impact on American society. The time to ask, "What should we do?" had passed. Now the questions took many forms. What had we done? Why did we do it? How did Vietnam change its veterans? Could they peacefully return to American society? How did their experiences scar them? What did the war accomplish? How did it change American culture and politics? Why did the United States lose? Who or what was to blame?

It was not the first American war to pile up civilian deaths, and not the first to deserve to be called unjust; it was far more just, for example, than the Mexican War, which stole half of Mexico to the intended benefit of slaveholders. Nor was the United States defeated in battle. Yet defeat it was, foreseen by many Americans even during the war, and that amounted to saying that every life lost or taken by the Americans was for a cause unredeemed by achievement.

Very quickly the Vietnam veteran himself became an issue. Often he was seen as a person not to pity or hate or love but to fear, for he was a ticking time bomb, waiting to plant his lethal self somewhere at home.

The psychotic or maladjusted Vietnam War veteran was portrayed as a product of the war and the war alone. In most cases, he is a man without a background, without a home or parents or life before his service in Vietnam. It is as if he were bred in the country's steamy jungles and fertile rice fields. All he knows is war, and when he returns to the United States he continues to ply his trade.

The Vietnam Women's Memorial, dedicated in 1993, commemorates the service and sacrifice of tens of thousands of American women who spent part of their lives in Vietnam. (*Courtesy, Library of Congress.*)

Sometimes he joins an outlaw motorcycle gang in which violence is a way of life and a reason for being. Such B-movies as *Angels from Hell*, issued in 1968, next year's *Satan s Sadists*, and in 1971 *Chrome and Hot Leather* together with *The Losers* transport the veteran from a helicopter to a Harley. In other films the veteran remains a loner, violence seething within him. In *Taxi Driver*, released in 1976, Travis Bickle (Robert De Niro) ticks quietly in New York City. He has no past and no future; he seems to invent both out of emptiness. His letters to his parents are a cluster of lies, and a viewer of the film can suspect that his parents themselves are part of his fantasy life. The only reality in his life is the war that he cannot articulate while it drives him toward violence as surely as he drives his taxi. As Seth Cagin and Philip Dray observe: "Travis Bickle is the prototypical movie vet: In ways we can only imagine, the horror of the war unhinged him. He's lost contact with other human beings, he doesn't hear them quite properly, and his speaking rhythms are off. He's edgy; he can't sleep at night, not even with the help of pills, so he takes a job as a taxi driver on the night shift." And he waits to explode. That in the end he kills a pimp, for reasons that on the surface seem driven by virtue, is irrelevant. He might just as easily have killed a politician or anyone else, including himself. His violence knows no reason. It is not directed toward society or politicians or any particular person. It just is. In Karel Reisz's *Who'll Stop the Rain*, a movie rendering in 1978 of Robert Stone's novel *Dog Soldiers*, published four years earlier, a veteran is involved in smuggling a shipment of heroin into the United States. Not only does he bring the corruption of Saigon back home with him—for the heroin will ruin civilians just as it did soldiers—but violence and death follow in his wake. As in the other films, the ultimate threat of the veterans is the Vietnamization of the United States. Tommy Lee Jones's character in *Between Heaven and Earth* and Kevin Costner's in *The War*, both issued in 1994, carry debilitating psychological baggage back from Vietnam.

Tracks, a low-budget film directed by Henry Jaglom and screened in 1976, gives violence greater direction and logic. An army sergeant, played by Dennis Hopper, escorts home the body of a friend killed in Vietnam. On the cross-country train trip he tries to tell his fellow passengers about the dead soldier, a black hero who saved his life. He asks the civilians about the war and wonders why the United States was in Vietnam. Most of the other passengers are not interested in the sergeant, his dead comrade, or his questions; some are hostile, a few embarrassed. His war is not their war; his sufferings are not their sufferings. The film ends with the burial. Alone, the sergeant watches the coffin being lowered into the ground. Then he jumps in after it. When he emerges from the hole, he is dressed for battle and fully armed. "You want to go to Nam?" he cries out. "I'll take you there."

A film marking a transition in the image of the Vietnam veteran is *Coming Home*, directed by Hal Ashby and released in 1978. Ashby's *Shampoo*, which appeared three years earlier, features a collection of wealthy southern Californians during the 1968 presidential election. As the characters get ready for a Nixon victory party, news of the horrors of Vietnam comes at them from radios and televisions. But they pay no mind; it is not their war, not their concern. *Coming Home*, to the contrary, brings the war to southern California. Its central characters are Luke Martin (Jon Voight), a bitter paraplegic, and Sally Hyde (Jane Fonda), the wife of a marine captain (Bruce Dern) serving a tour in Vietnam. During the course of the film the conservative, sexually repressed Sally flowers into a liberated woman. She puts on Levis, allows her hair to follow its natural frizzy disposition, and with Luke experiences an orgasm for the first time in her life. Luke too is transformed. Bitter and angry at the start of the film, he becomes introspective and gentle. *Coming Home* suggests that love can cure the trauma of Vietnam, that understanding can erase the pain of bad memories.

Viewed in retrospect, *Coming Home* is sentimental and pat. But in 1978, it was a bold film. Frank Rich of *Time* magazine called it "one long, low howl of pain," and other reviewers agreed that it was an important statement. It also showed Hollywood that a film about the Vietnam War could be political and profitable. At the same time it contributed to the rehabilitation of the popular image of the Vietnam veteran. Influenced by Ron Kovic's autobiographical *Born on the Fourth of July*, published two years earlier, *Coming Home* portrays the veteran as not only in need of healing but capable of being a healer. Luke is not a loner; he is not a ticking bomb; he is not a threat to society. His anger flows from the unwillingness of the nation to recognize his plight. "When people look they don't see me," Luke tells Sally. His crippled body is an important legacy of Vietnam. Toward the end of the film he tells a group of high school students, "There was a lot of shit over there I find fucking hard to live with. But I don't feel sorry for myself. I'm just saying that there's a choice to be made." And that choice is as present in the United States as it was in Vietnam. Choosing not to live consumed by bitterness but to use his pain to help others, Luke is reintegrated into society.

The Deer Hunter, which appeared the same year as *Coming Home*, tells of a similar redemption. Directed by Michael Cimino, the film shows how the war changed the lives of three men from a western Pennsylvania steel town. Of the three, the most important is Michael (Robert De Niro). He begins the film as a loner, and violence seems an integral part of his character. Yet in Vietnam, it seems, surrounded by death and terror, he finds compassion. He saves his life and that of his two companions, and when one of them, Nicky (Christopher Walken), becomes addicted to heroin and Russian roulette, Michael risks his own life in an attempt to reach him. "I love you," he says just before Nicky's luck runs out and he loses his final game of Russian roulette. Vietnam purges Michael of his aggression and anger. He is at peace with himself and his surroundings. The film ends on a note of affirmation. After Nicky's funeral, Michael joins his other friends—women as well as men—in singing "God Bless America." He is finally a whole person, reconciled with himself, his community, and his country. That same theme comes through in Oliver Stone's 1990 film *Born on the Fourth of July,* in which Tom Cruise portrays Ron Kovic, a paraplegic Vietnam veteran who finally comes to his separate peace. The book and movie are not fiction: They tell of Kovic's actual experiences.

After 1980 the popular image of the Vietnam veteran began to change on television. Like Michael in *The Deer Hunter* and Luke in *Coming Home,* the veteran was transformed into a figure of compassion and imbued with a sense of justice. Rather than threaten society, the new television veteran defends society, upholds justice, and restores order. In Vietnam he learned how to fight, use sophisticated weapons, and function in a tight-knit group The very same virtues that led him to Vietnam or were instilled there now compel him to battle evil and injustice in the United States. Television depicted this new veteran in such shows as *Magnum, P.I., The A-Team, Riptide,* and *Air Wolf.* Most of the heroes of these shows are unmarried, but their bachelorhood is not viewed as a hostility to women, family, and children. The group functions as their family, and they display a healthy attraction to women that is amply reciprocated. Nor are they scarred emotionally or physically by their service in Vietnam. No guilt troubles their thoughts, no injuries plague their days.

It is especially notable, as a reflection of how Vietnam changed public views, that these new heroes no longer act on behalf of the government. Crippled by red tape and bureaucratic lethargy, the modern state is presumed unable to act with speed and justice. The veteran heroes are part of the private sector—the United States of Ronald Reagan. As the viewer is told each week at the beginning of *The A-Team,* "If you have a problem, if no one else can help, and if you can find them . . . you can hire the A-Team." But while these veteran heroes act outside the government, they fight for their country. Often they combat external threats—drug smuggling, terrorism, and spying—and on some occasions they operate beyond the national borders. Their cause is always just and on television ends justify means. Perhaps, as Lisa M. Heilbronn writes, they "represent a desire on the part of the public to see our control secured beyond the boundaries of the United States."

The transformation of the Vietnam veteran on television since 1980 is part of the more general rehabilitation of the popular image of the United States military. During the 1970s films and television portrayed the military as a corrupt, bloodthirsty institution. While enlisted men were occasionally presented as decent people, officers were invariably pictured as incompetent, self-serving, and destructive. "The bullshit piled up so fast in Vietnam you needed wings to stay above it," Captain Willard remarks in *Apocalypse Now,* which came out in 1979. And in the same movie, Lieutenant Colonel Kilgore orders his men into battle to secure a strip of beach that offers him good surfing. In films released from 1980 through 1982—*Private Benjamin, Taps, Stripes, An Officer and a Gentleman,* and *Lords of Discipline*— Hollywood revitalized the military. It is not a machine for killing boys; it turns boys into men, or in the case of *Private Benjamin,* remakes a spoiled girl as an independent woman.

In part, the promilitary films reflect the economy of the late 1970s and early 1980s. High-paying jobs in heavy industry were becoming scarce, and there was little glamour or money in flipping hamburgers at McDonald's. For many young Americans the military became a desirable alternative. Enlistments in the armed forces jumped in the 1980s, and enrollment in ROTC programs doubled. The mood of Reagan's era, its overt patriotism and promise of restored greatness, contributed to the popularity of the films. It contrasted especially with the malaise and perceived impotency of the Carter years. Americans yearned for a return to greatness. They wanted a military with teeth, equipped to act and fortified by a commitment to a higher code.

As Americans reappraised the Vietnam veteran and the military, they also attempted to understand the war itself. Aided by the illegally released Pentagon Papers, they searched for its causes.

During the 1960s and most of the 1970s two schools of thought emerged. One held that the war, in Arthur Schlesinger, Jr.'s words, was a "tragedy without villains." It resulted from unfortunate decisions made by well-meaning officials. The other judged the war to be more deliberately malign, the result of an imperialistic American foreign policy. William Appleman Williams, Walter LaFeber, and Gabriel Kolko presented the nation's past as a history of expansion and domination and argued that at least since the turn of the century it had been establishing its hegemony over the Pacific. The Vietnam War marked a setback in this policy of expansion, but the decision to fight in Vietnam was very much a part of it.

During the 1980s a third school of historical thought gained ascendancy. It maintained that the war was an honest and straightforward expression of American commitment to democracy and liberty. And the military could have won the war. "The sense of guilt created by the Vietnam War in the minds of many Americans," declares Guenter Lewy's *America in Vietnam*, published in 1978, "is not warranted and the charges of officially condoned illegal and grossly immoral conduct are without substance." The loss of Vietnam was not the fault of the troops. Civilians back home, both inside and outside the government, had failed to understand what the war was about and refused to live up to their country's honorable commitment to South Vietnam. Of course, this perception reflected the changing political face of the United States. By 1980 politicians were once again talking about falling dominoes and the obligations the United States had to countries struggling to stay free. In 1980 Ronald Reagan proclaimed that the nation had "an inescapable duty to act as the tutor and protector of the free world."

Some neoconservatives have argued that a full use of conventional weapons and tactics would have brought victory. This view requires two assumptions that LBJ in the 1960s had been unwilling to make: that the Chinese, involved in their own cultural revolution and possessing a weak economy, would never have invaded Vietnam as they had Korea and that neither they nor the Soviet Union would have employed atomic weapons in South Vietnam. These quite accurate conclusions are clearer today, however, than they were in the mid-1960s when the world was caught in the grip of cold war determinism. Only a decade before the United States had buried some 50,000 Americans killed in Korea. Harry G. Summers in his work *On Strategy*, published in 1982, argues, with some degree of persuasiveness if military questions alone are to be considered, that the United States had weakened the Vietcong guerrillas by 1968 and that the mistake of the allies was to fail to cut off the sources of supplies for the communists in the south. This would have involved, among other tactics, a naval blockade of the port of Haiphong—and not "let a grain of rice nor a single bullet" enter the country on a Chinese or Soviet ship—and an occupation of southern parts of North Vietnam. In answer, partisans of the antiwar movement observe that Summers ignores a main point of the military strategist General Karl von Clausewitz, in his classic *Principles of War*, to whom he appeals: that wars are ultimately political. Certainly the anticommunist effort was a political disaster within both the Vietnamese and ultimately the American public. Critics claim that Summers overlooks the persistence with which the Vietnamese over the centuries have resisted foreign occupation, and the advantage the communists possessed of choosing at every moment where to attack and how extensively. They also recount a conversation Summers himself had conducted with a North Vietnamese officer. "You know, you never beat us on the battlefield," Summers said. Responded Colonel Tu: "but it is . . . irrelevant." Nor does Summers take into account the strategic advantage Hanoi and the insurgents enjoyed of being able to chose when and where to engage the Americans, and their ability to rely on the discomfort of the public at home about supporting a lengthy and badly explained war.

In ideology, too, defenders and critics of the Vietnam War miss the point. The behavior of American troops was admirable, for the most part, under difficult circumstances. But the anticommunist cause, which included the commendable belief that freedom and pluralism are superior to totalitarianism, came up against an equally commendable belief on the part of the communists that Vietnam required a massive redistribution of power and wealth. Would an anticommunist victory have brought a regime of constitutional liberty? Did the communists achieve economic democracy? The reasonable answer in both cases would have to be pessimistic. In the end, about the only generalizations on the American intervention are that it was based in Cold War thinking that had made much sense in the early days after the end of World War II, and that it never addressed the social and political realities of Vietnam.

In the public at large, where a search for comprehension of the Vietnam War continued as it did in academia, many of the novelists who wrote about the war had served in Vietnam, and for them the whole business was a moral, practical, and intellectual swamp. Raised on World War II films that ooze moral certainty and enshrine a sporting ethos and the notion of fair play, these writers confront in Vietnam a world of shadows and moral ambiguities. Their schoolboy rules belonged to a distant continent. "It was the dawn of creation in the Indochina bush," declared Philip Caputo in 1977 in A *Rumor of War*, "an ethical as well as a geographical wilderness. Out there, lacking restraints, sanctioned to kill, confronted by a hostile country and a relentless enemy, we sank into a brutish state." The same sense is expressed in Tim O'Brien's *Going after Cacciato*, which he published in 1978. His protagonist doesn't know who is right, or what is right; he doesn't know whether it is a war of self-determination or an institutionalized madness of self-destruction, outright aggression or national liberation; he doesn't know which speeches to believe, which books, which politicians; he doesn't know whether nations will topple like dominoes or stand separate like trees; he doesn't know who started the war, or why, or when, or with what motives; he doesn't know whether it matters.

Francis Ford Coppola's *Apocalypse Now* attempted to translate that confusion into a narrative film. "The most important thing I wanted to do in the making of *Apocalypse Now*," Coppola wrote in the program notes for the film, "was to create a film experience that would give the audience a sense of the horror, the madness, the sensuousness, and the moral dilemma of the Vietnam War." Captain Willard's voyage up the river into the "heart of darkness"—the film draws on Joseph Conrad's great story of a man, named "Kurtz" like Marlon Brando's character, who has traveled into his own heart of darkness—is as much a quest for answers as it is a mission of death. In trying to understand the sanity behind Colonel Kurtz's insanity, Willard is attempting to fathom the logic of the illogical conflict. Everywhere there is madness. The coldly unemotional military and civilian officials who tell Willard that Kurtz's mentally disordered command must be "terminated with extreme prejudice" are mad. They speak the language of madness; the meanings of their words cannot be found in a dictionary. Kilgore is mad. He attacks the enemy not to win the war but to secure a good surfing beach. "After seeing the way Kilgore fought the war," remarks Willard, "I began to wonder what they had against Kurtz." And Kurtz, well, he is quite mad. He is like a computer fallen into Alice's Wonderland and fed bits of incoherent data. His response to his environment is to become insane, for as the film demonstrates, only the insane survive.

Apocalypse Now may be the best film about the war, and its theme of madness is unquestionably accurate on a psychological level, but it does not help the viewer understand how or why the United States became involved in the war. It does not deal with what the war accomplished or how it changed the country. Its major political criticism is aimed not at the war itself but at its management. Willard describes his superior officers as "a bunch of four star clowns who are giving the whole circus away." He openly sympathizes with the outlaw Kurtz: "Charging someone with murder in a place like this is like handing out speeding tickets at the Indianapolis 500."

Of all filmmakers in the decades since the end of the war, Oliver Stone has been the most committed to a full understanding of the conflict, the American Homer of the Vietnam War. Michael Cimino and Francis Ford Coppola made a film about the war and then moved on to other subjects. Stone has brooded over the conflict, seeking to get inside the war and its political and cultural origins. A veteran of the war who experienced combat, he understood that the war was a complex reflection of American society that defied easy understanding and glib definitions.

Stone's *Platoon*, released in 1986, explores the physical nature of the war. From the dust and heat to the ants and the mosquitoes, Vietnam is a land of creeping, crawling, biting, stinging insects, a place where long stretches of boredom and sudden outbursts of violence go hand in hand. *Born on the Forth of July* details the martial culture in the United States that embraced the war. From John Wayne movies to competitive sports, Stone suggests, American males were conditioned to follow orders and go to war. In *JFK*, which appeared in 1991, and *Nixon* four years later, Stone moved from cultural anthropologist to historian. In both films he delves into the political roots of the war. Embracing popular conspiracy theories and speculations on the order of what-if, he argues that the worst of the war could have been prevented—would have been prevented—if a combination of politicians and industrialists had not been bent on power and profits. His *Heaven and Earth*, released in 1993, traces the physical and psychological impact of the war on Vietnam and the United States. Wars, he suggests, don't end when peace treaties are signed. The leave scars, deep and raw, that require decades to heal, if they heal at all.

It is in dealing with the fact of defeat that filmmakers become most perplexed. Most of the films depict a thoroughly corrupt or stupid officer corps. But beyond this limited explanation of failure few producers have been willing to go. Part of the reason is financial; industry leaders have feared that Americans would not pay to watch a film about their country's losing a war. During the 1970s amid a mood of self-criticism in the country, few films about the war were made. And when producers turned to the subject of the war, the age of self-criticism had passed. The Reagan years affirmed patriotic values. Heroes dominated popular culture. The rock star Bruce Springsteen, at a concert in Dallas, expressed frustration that his anti-Vietnam megahit "Born in the U.S.A." had actually become, in the popular mind, a patriotic anthem.

The best expression of this new mood is Sylvester Stallone's films *First Blood*, which appeared in 1982, and *Rambo: First Blood II*, screened three years later. In the earlier film John Rambo is an ex-Green Beret mistaken for a hippie. By nature a loner and even a peaceful man, he is forced by a series of inept government officials to defend his freedom in the wilds of the Pacific Northwest. The movie suggests that men like John Rambo did not lose the war; politicians back home did. In the climactic scene Rambo tells his former Special Forces commanding officer: "Nothing is over, nothing! You just don't turn it off. It wasn't my war— you asked me, I didn't ask you . . . and I did what I had to do to win— but somebody wouldn't let us win." Yet there is no examination of just what "winning" in the context of the war in Vietnam means. It is enough for Rambo and his audience that the war could have been won. In the second film Rambo returns to Vietnam to find and rescue Americans missing in action from Vietnam—a popular scenario in the mid-1980s that was central to films released during the decade. But Rambo was really returning to Vietnam to win the war. When Colonel Trautman (Richard Crenna), his former commander, tells him, "The old war's dead, John," Rambo replies, "I'm alive. It's still alive." And later Rambo asks, "Do we get to win this time?" Trautman answers, "This time it's up to you." And since winning is again never defined, Rambo rewrites history. He wins.

Complete redemption of the American military did not really occur until the outbreak of the Gulf War. On August 2, 1990, Saddam Hussein sent Iraqi troops into the tiny, oil-rich nation of Kuwait. The invasion threatened Saudi Arabia and the vital sea lanes of the Persian Gulf, through which most of Japan's and the Western world's oil flowed. President George H. W. Bush carefully constructed a coalition backed by the United Nations and ordered Iraqi forces out of Kuwait. When Saddam Hussein refused to withdraw, the president ordered a massive military buildup. On January 17, 1991, after giving the Iraqis another chance to retreat, Bush unleashed Operation Desert Storm. Allied bombers pounded Iraq, and Iraq forces in Kuwait, for more than five weeks, and on February 24 the ground offensive began. The war was over four days later—a stunning victory for the military.

General Norman Schwarzkopf, the field commander of Allied forces, had conducted a brilliant military campaign, crushing Iraqi forces and achieving a public relations tour de force. Americans watched navy and air force pilots carrying out pin-point bombing campaigns using laser-guided "smart bombs," marines storming Persian Gulf beaches, and armored divisions sweeping across the deserts of the Middle East. When the war was over, the GIs returned triumphant to a grateful nation. Whatever images of an incompetent military still lingered in American popular culture were rapidly put to rest. And in the victory parades that took place across the country in 1991 and 1992, thousands of Vietnam veterans spontaneously joined the marchers down Main Street, getting the attention they had deserved, but never received, during the Vietnam War era.

While American filmmakers Ramboized the conflict, Vietnam labored to construct a nation out of the rubble of war. American bombing had destroyed the infrastructure of Vietnam. Roads and bridges, power plants and factories lay in ruins. Ports suffered from damage and neglect. For a generation the resources of Vietnam had been used to fuel the war machines. Conversion to a peacetime economy presented difficult, at times almost insurmountable, problems. Raw materials were scarce, and investment capital had left with the Americans. Machines imported from the United States broke down, and spare parts were impossible to obtain. Along with hope, peace brought the specter of economic ruin.

Vietnamese communism smothered the country with a stifling bureaucracy. The communists tried to implement Ho Chi Minh's dream:

political reunification of the two Vietnams and imposition of a socialist economic order. North Vietnamese cadres and Vietcong took control of South Vietnam, seized private property, collectivized plantations and farms, squeezed out small businesses, and hunted down South Vietnamese political and military officials. The government forcibly moved nearly one million civilians from Ho Chi Minh City, Hue, Danang, and Nha Trang to "New Economic Zones" in abandoned sections of South Vietnam. Blessed with a strategic location, a huge capacity for producing rice, and an enterprising people, the SRV declined into Third World poverty complete with high unemployment, crippling food shortages, and starvation. Along with the direct results of the war—hundreds of thousands of orphans, paraplegics, and amputees, and the physical destruction wrought by the American military—the ideology of communism rendered as a system of massive control at the hands of a party bureaucracy transformed Vietnam into one of the poorest countries in the world. The average worker made the equivalent of 300 dong a month in 1980. That same year a pair of cotton trousers cost 400 dong and a new bicycle 20,000 dong. Malnutrition became a normal condition. As one Soviet professor in Vietnam privately confided, "How much poverty in Vietnam? We have nothing like this in Moscow. Their party has made so many mistakes." The SRV also failed in its attempt to de-Westernize the country, replacing capitalist with socialist habits. A number of critics even contended that southerners "Westernized" northerners. The official party newspaper *Nhan Dan* warned that the "new-colonial culture" of the south was "expanding to the north" and threatened to "spoil our younger generation and wreck our revolution." French food, American beer, and Western ideas became blackmarket commodities. Governmental corruption, always a staple in the south, wound its way north. As one loyal northerner admitted, "I've been a Communist all my life. But now, for the first time, I have seen the realities of Communism. It is a failure—mismanagement, corruption, privilege, repression. My ideals are gone." The worst of capitalism, it appears, had mated with the worst of collectivism.

As conditions in Vietnam worsened, hundreds of thousands of Vietnamese fled the food and electricity rationing, de-Westernization, grinding poverty, and countless other daily hardships. Ethnic Chinese, the business leaders and merchants in Ho Chi Minh City, left the country in droves. The "boat people" risked the dangers of the South China Sea to find a new home. Tens of thousands drowned when their rickety ships sank, and thousands more were killed by pirates. Tens of thousands were caught by Vietnamese authorities before they had gone very far. Indonesia and Malaysia frequently rejected them when they did make landfall. Although exact statistics are difficult to obtain, as many as 250,000 Vietnamese boat people died during their escape attempt.

Diplomatic woes compounded domestic unrest. In 1977 President

Jimmy Carter cautiously approached the SRV. Determined to improve the image of the United States among Third World countries, soon after his election Carter announced that he "would be perfectly glad to support the admission of Vietnam to the United Nations and to normalize relations with Vietnam." That autumn he made good on his promise, and the two countries allowed academic and other cultural exchanges. At that moment what the SRV most needed were the investment capital and technological expertise of the United States. But in 1978 the SRV committed several critical mistakes, the most important of which was to demand reparations as a precondition for normalization. That prompted a quick reaction in Congress, opening still fresh psychological wounds. Carter's decision to pardon all Americans who had fled to Canada during the war to avoid the draft and to extend that pardon to all who had deserted from the armed forces had a similar effect. Carter's initiatives—Vietnam's best hope of recovery and economic stability—died on the floor of Congress. In 1978 the SRV made another decision that, however justifiable, brought further disaster. It invaded the newly named Kampuchea (formerly Cambodia).

In comparison with the wretchedness of Kampuchea, Vietnam's problems seemed insignificant. "Everybody, Cambodians and foreigners alike," the *New York Times* correspondent Sydney H. Schanberg would recall of the mid-1970s, "looked with hopeful relief to the collapse of the city, for they felt that when the Communists came and the war finally ended, at least the suffering would be over. All of us were wrong." When Pol Pot and the Khmer Rouge roared into downtown Phnom Penh in armored personnel carriers and trucks in April 1975, they brought a demanding, ruthless ideology with them. They began emptying the cities of Cambodia, forcing people into the countryside for reeducation. For Pol Pot it was the beginning of a new age—"Year Zero" for the new country of Kampuchea. Dreaming of a preindustrial, agricultural utopia, he launched an assault on cities, teachers, intellectuals, professionals, and the middle class. He completely evacuated Phnom Penh, turning the city of three million people into a ghost town. He ordered the destruction of libraries, temples, schools, colleges, businesses, and whole cities. He transformed Kampuchea into a concentration camp, a huge "killing field" where two million Kampucheans lost their lives.

The Vietnamese watched the horrors with growing anxiety. A revolt in eastern Kampuchea in 1977 sent hundreds of thousands of frightened Kampucheans fleeing across the border into Vietnam. By 1978 the SRV had witnessed enough of Pol Pot's megalomania. Vietnamese troops invaded Kampuchea, drove Pol Pot and the Khmer Rouge into the jungles, and established the People's Republic of Kampuchea. But the invasion did not end the suffering. Coming as it did during the planting season, it deprived peasants of their rice crop, and widespread starvation resulted. Pol Pot regrouped his forces and with 35,000 troops began a guerrilla action against the invasion. The Khmer People's National Liberation Front, supplied by the United States, fielded 15,000 of its own guerrillas, and another guerrilla army, 9,000 strong, was loyal to Prince Norodom Sihanouk. The three groups fought guerrilla wars against one another and the Vietnamese. With the Vietnamese in Kampuchea, the premeditated killing of civilians stopped, but once again war was sweeping across Indochina.

The centuries-old animosities between Vietnamese and Khmer stirred other ancient hatreds and fears. China did not want to see the SRV extend its influence. On February 17, 1979, Deng Xiaoping sent the People's Liberation Army across the border into Tonkin. The war lasted less than one month, but it took the lives of 35,000 people. On their way out of Tonkin, the Chinese destroyed several towns, blew up vital railway links, and obliterated important power plants and a phosphate mine responsible for most of Vietnam's fertilizer.

The border war against China and the guerrilla war against Kampuchea further strained the Vietnamese economy. Before the two wars the SRV had been attempting to secure desperately needed loans from China, Japan, and several Western countries. As the fighting became hotter, the international financial community became colder. The SRV had the added cost of maintaining a standing army of more than one million men and stationing 140,000 troops in Kampuchea. By the mid-1980s the SRV had become one of the poorest nations in the world, but its army was the world's fourth largest. The American war in Vietnam was over. The ancient wars, pitting Vietnamese against Khmer and Chinese, continued.

For the money needed to keep its country solvent, Vietnam turned to the Soviet Union. The loans the Soviet Union provided—$1.5 billion annually—carried strings that stretched back to Moscow. To many people inside and outside of Vietnam, it soon appeared that Soviet domination had simply replaced American domination, Soviet advisers and experts flocking to Vietnam as the Americans had done twenty years later. "Americans without dollars," the Vietnamese called them.

By the mid-1980s the SRV was at its lowest point. Economic reorganization had failed. Emigrants—many of them valuable professionals whom the country needed—continued to leave. The guerrilla war in Kampuchea dragged on. And Soviet advisers worked to turn the SRV into Cuba East. Finally, in 1986 the SRV committed itself to a radical change. At the Sixth Communist Party Congress, party leaders admitted that their experiment in communism had failed. The old guard retired and a new set of leaders, led by Nguyen Van Linh, took office. Linh, born in Hanoi but resident for most of his life in the south, symbolized the desire for true national unification. He realized that the economic and foreign policies of Pham Van Dong were bankrupt. Boldly, and with a firm sense of resolve, he once again looked West.

Undoubtedly influenced by the ideas and actions of Mikhail Gorbachev, Linh opened Vietnam to increasing amounts of democracy and capitalism. He permitted politicians to contest for assembly seats, and he released political prisoners. He sanctioned limited free enterprise and trimmed the glutted governmental bureaucracy. He even opened up Vietnam to Western goods. The historian Terry H. Anderson noted Western T-shirts and Madonna tapes on the streets of Hanoi. A few years earlier the SRV had frightened away Western investment capital; now it courted Western bankers and industrialists by enacting a liberal foreign investment code. An "underdeveloped nation such as Vietnam," Linh emphasized, "needs even more to look to the capitalist world for lessons."

Vietnam had little choice but to turn to the West. In spite of Mikhail Gorbachev's *glasnost* and *perestroika* reforms, throughout the 1980s the economy of the Soviet Union continued its downward spiral. Ever since the early 1960s, infusions of financial aid from the Soviet Union had kept the North Vietnamese economy afloat, and after 1975, the process of rebuilding Vietnam required even more money. The influx of Russian rubles that for a decade had at least partially masked the economic disaster Vietnamese communists were bringing to their country the Soviet Union had to cut further. (In response to an appeal for loans, so went a story among the Vietnamese, Moscow sends a cable: "Tighten your belts." Vietnam replies: "Send belts.") The USSR could no longer prop up the economies of its satellites, for its own economy was imploding. Nor could it politically control them. With stunning rapidity beginning in 1989, the Soviet bloc in Central and Eastern Europe disintegrated. Poland, East Germany, Czechoslovakia, and Hungary went their separate ways. A rebellion succeeded in overthrowing the communist government of Romania, an especially brutal regime that had kept itself independent of Moscow. Yugoslavia broke up into petty warring states. And in 1991 the Soviet Union itself collapsed and ceased to exist. The river, or creek, of rubles dried up. Vietnam's choice was simple: Turn to the West and liberalize its economy or face economic collapse and political ruin.

The emergence of new forms in popular culture reflected Vietnam's political and economic changes. Such American films as *Platoon* played to crowded houses in Ho Chi Minh City and Hanoi. And the Vietnamese film industry started to make films that showed the emotional complexity of the war. In *Ahn va em* (Brothers and Relations, issued in 1986) a veteran returns from war to find a changed Vietnamese society. Hanoi is wallowing in consumerism, his family has betrayed the ideas of socialism, and government corruption hampers efforts to reconstruct Vietnam. The veteran questions why he fought. In the end of the film, he turns away from the modern Vietnam and withdraws to the traditional, "unprogressive" life of the rural village. Recent films also revise the image of Americans. American soldiers are portrayed as victims of a senseless and unjust war: confused, frustrated, and angry but not evil. *Free Fire Zone*, which appeared in 1979, assigns evil not to the soldiers but to the machines of war. The filmmaker anthropomorphizes helicopters, endowing them with malevolence. They drop from the sky like prehistoric birds of prey. They, not their pilots, are blamed for the destruction. In the last scene of the film the Vietnamese shoot down a helicopter. In the wreckage they discover a dead pilot. "It is a sad moment," notes the film critic Karen Jaehne, made "all the sadder for a photo of the pilot's family carried away from the carnage on the wind."

Altogether the films signal a shift in Vietnam's attitude toward the United States. Since 1986 the SRV has promoted cultural exchanges with the United States by liberalizing its visa policy and allowing American writers and journalists greater access to Vietnam. American tourists can now visit Hue, Dienbienphu, and the Cu Chi tunnels. The government has allowed Vietnamese Amerasian children to emigrate to the United States to reunite with their parents. Through actions and words, the SRV has conveyed the simple message that the war is over and the time to forgive is at hand.

The message, however, was at odds with American foreign policy in the 1980s. During his two presidential terms, Ronald Reagan consistently ignored Vietnamese efforts to normalize relations between the two countries. Rather than emphasize points of agreement, he stressed fields of discord. Reagan focused on two issues: Vietnam's continued occupation of Kampuchea and the POW-MIA controversy.

On the matter of their invasion of their neighbor, the Vietnamese began accommodating Washington even before the end of Reagan's presidency, expressing a willingness to withdraw their troops; in 1988 they actually began to pull back. This was not an especially good thing. Given the centuries of hostilities between the Vietnamese and the Khmer, the SRV was not anxious to see the Khmer Rouge return to power. And other nations feared that a reinstalled Pol Pot (which to the great benefit of the Khmer people did not happen) would resume his genocidal war against all Western influences within Kampuchea. Nevertheless, the Vietnamese completed their withdrawal from Kampuchea in 1989.

The POW-MIA issue was largely imaginary. Fueled by a series of POW-MIA movies and the incendiary rhetoric of the Reagan administration, a large portion of the American public became convinced that thousands of prisoners of war and other American soldiers listed as missing in action were still alive in Vietnam. This emotionally charged issue blocked talks between the United States and the Socialist Republic of Vietnam for almost a decade. It also defied logic and impartial investigation. Of the Reagan administration's intractability, Terry H. Anderson observes:

Technically, it is impossible for any Vietnamese government to find "all recoverable remains" under fifteen years of jungle growth. . . . Also MIAs are not just an American problem. The French still have 20,000 MIAs from their war in Indochina, and the Vietnamese list over 200,000. Furthermore, the United States still has 80,000 MIAs from World War II and 8,000 from the Korean War, figures that represent 20 and 15 percent, respectively, of the confirmed dead in those conflicts; the percentage is 4 percent for the Vietnam War. . . . The real "noble cause" for [the Reagan] administration is not the former war but its emotional and impossible crusade to retrieve "all recoverable remains."

Yet in its effort to improve its foreign relations, Vietnam coupled with its withdrawal from Kampuchea an attempt to address the POW-MIA charges. High-level contacts between Washington and Hanoi increased in number and significance late in the Reagan administration. In September 1988, the two countries agreed to joint field investigations in Vietnam to identify the remains of American MIAs. In April 1992 President George Bush eased the American trade embargo in Vietnam by allowing the sales of products for humanitarian needs, primarily grain and medicines. At the end of 1992, Bush agreed to permit American companies to open offices in Vietnam, sign business contracts, and begin feasibility studies.

During the first year of the Clinton administration, the president dropped American opposition to settlement of Vietnam's debts with the International Monetary Fund. The move toward normalization of relations, however, ran into trouble late in 1993 when circumstantial evidence from former Soviet archives and Vietnamese defectors indicated that several hundred American prisoners of war remained in Indochina after the return of the 591 POWs in 1973. Pentagon officials immediately went to work trying to confirm the stories, but they were unable to find any evidence corroborating the charges. Few politicians, however, were willing to risk promoting normalization until Vietnam became more cooperative, whatever an increased cooperation in regard to an issue so deliberately murky might mean. Bob Smith, a New Hampshire Republican who visited Vietnam frequently to investigate the issue, remarked late in 1993: "I don't know if anyone is alive today, but I do know that we don't have all the facts."

Eager to get on the good side of administration officials in Washington, D.C., Vietnamese leaders early in 1994 began releasing more and more information about American soldiers missing in action and worked more diligently at returning the remains of MIAs. To acknowledge the Vietnamese effort and to encourage Hanoi to be even more forthcoming, in February 1994 President Clinton lifted the trade embargo, opening Vietnam and most of Indochina to American business.

Only one step remained in the normalization process: diplomatic recognition of the Socialist Republic of Vietnam.

Early in 1995, the Clinton administration began leaking stories to the press about possible diplomatic recognition. Many Vietnamese-Americans opposed normalization, insisting that the United States should withhold recognition until the communist regime collapsed. The potential Republican presidential candidates Robert Dole of Kansas and Phil Gramm of Texas voiced opposition as well. So did POW-MIA advocacy groups, among them the National League of Families of Vietnam POWs and MIAs. Clinton lined up some heavy hitters of his own. Senator John McCain, an Arizona Republican and former POW, backed the idea of recognition, as did Senator John Kerry, a Massachusetts Democrat and Vietnam veteran, and Senator Bob Kerrey, a Nebraska Democrat who had lost a leg in Vietnam.

While the Clinton administration was moving toward recognition, the Vietnamese were preparing for the twentieth anniversary of the fall of Saigon, planning parades, parties, and solemn observances through-out the country. They wanted to make the most of history, to remember better days when a Third World nation had humbled the greatest superpower. Images of the North Vietnamese Army's triumphant march toward the United States embassy in Saigon still stirred the hearts of tens of thousands of Vietnamese; Vo Nguyen Giap was a military genius and living icon; and Ho Chi Minh had become a demigod to his country. But the celebrations demanded tact. Vietnam, desperately impoverished, needed good relations with the United States. And in 1995 Vietnamese under the age of twenty-five, a majority of the country's population and carrying no memories of the war or few, yearned for a better life, which millions of them thought to see in the wealth and culture of the United States. The Vietnamese leadership was not about to let any raucous, self-righteous twentieth-anniversary celebrations anger influential Americans. Vietnam moved forward with the anniversary preparations, but the Politburo made sure to keep them subdued.

What stoked the still burning embers of the Vietnam War in the spring of 1995 and postponed normalization efforts was not anything perpetrated by the Vietnamese, but a publishing event in the United States.

To coincide with the twentieth anniversary of the fall of South Vietnam, Random House issued *In Retrospect,* the memoirs of former Secretary of Defense Robert McNamara. For twenty-eight years after leaving the Johnson administration, McNamara had kept his peace, refusing to answer any questions about the Vietnam War. To most antiwar activists, he was *persona non grata*, the arrogantly intellectual architect of an unnecessary war that killed three million Vietnamese and nearly 60,000 Americans, a war that had polarized the country and created a nation of cynics. Random House hyped the book as McNamara's *mea culpa,* the confessions of a troubled man who wanted to come clean. The publisher booked him on every talk show in every major media market, and he responded to questions directly, his voice sometimes cracking and his eyes welling up in tears. In conducting the Vietnam War, he admitted, the Kennedy and Johnson administrations had mistakenly seen a communist Vietnam as a grave threat to national security, underestimated the power of Vietnamese nationalism, overestimated the influence of communism, and tried to find a military solution to what was essentially a political problem. In short, he acceded to every major criticism the antiwar movement had offered in the 1960s. "It seems beyond understanding, incredible that we did not force ourselves to confront such issues head-on. But then, it is very hard, today, to recapture the innocence and confidence with which we approached Vietnam in the early days. . . . We were wrong, terribly wrong."

The book rocketed to the top of the bestseller lists, not because Americans accepted McNamara's confession or endorsed his ideas, but because its publication drew hostility from across the public spectrum: liberals as well as conservatives, antiwar protesters as well as veterans. Anger drew readers to the book, and its reading as like as not deepened the anger. Skeptics charged that the man who had sent millions of boys to Vietnam and brought hundreds of thousands home in body bags or on hospital gurneys, meanwhile devastating the Vietnamese land and people, was just as arrogant as ever, and greedy as well, poised to make millions off the book. Former critics of the war wondered about the length of his silence, if indeed ever since 1966 he had realized his mistakes. McNamara's disclaimer about not speaking up earlier—"I didn't know any way to do it. At that point my voice wouldn't have made any difference"—went nowhere. "It's the same McNamara as ever," one former antiwar activist fumed. "He still thinks he's one of the best and the brightest. Those are crocodile tears he sheds." Veterans' groups joined in the fury though not in the reasons for it. The Gulf War had resurrected the reputation of American soldiers, and the luster of Vietnam veterans was brighter than ever. Just when the country was finally taking note of their sacrifice, the architect of the war was disparaging the American effort there and, as far as many veterans were concerned, tarnishing the men who had fought. "That no good son-of-a-bitch," remarked Wendell Johnson, a purple-hearted marine who had lost part of his foot near Chu Lai. "He's making a couple of million now, going to the bank with his blood money. You would think he'd at least have the good sense to donate the profits to some handicapped veterans he sent off to war. Hell, I'd be satisfied if he gave the money to wounded Vietnamese. Anything but keep it himself. Has he no sense of decency?"

The Clinton administration was forced to postpone temporarily its plans for diplomatic recognition. The president had to wait for the Vietnamese victory celebrations, tame as they were, to be off the news, and

McNamara to be off the television screens. But opinion polls indicated that most Americans supported normalization. On July 11, 1995, at a brief White House ceremony, the president extended diplomatic recognition to Vietnam. "This moment," Clinton said in a prepared statement, "offers us the opportunity to bind up our own wounds. They have resisted time for so long. We can now move on to common ground."

A generation after the fall of Saigon in 1975, the American people wondered how it had happened, how the Vietnam War had gone out of control, how the richest country in the world could sacrifice hundreds of billions of dollars and tens of thousands of young men and women in a military effort that seemed, in the end, to have so little significance. Vietnam, Laos, and Cambodia had fallen to communism, but the rest of Asia survived. Only three dominoes went down. During the 1970s and 1980s the victorious Socialist Republic of Vietnam slipped into stupefying poverty, while the United States recovered from its malaise and enjoyed a period of unprecedented growth and prosperity. Communism had taken over Indochina in the end, and the United States was just fine anyway.

Back in the late 1940s, when the American confrontation of communism began, it had all seemed so simple, so clear, the threat so real and the sacrifice so necessary. Communism was on the march—in Europe and in Asia—and it appeared to be enjoying great success. Much of Eastern Europe was under Soviet domination, and in 1949 China fell to Mao Zedong's cadres. Communism threatened to do the same to Vietnam, Laos, and Cambodia. The United States adopted a policy of containment and looked to apply it all around the world. Because Southeast Asia seemed crucial to the economic recovery of Japan and Western Europe, American policymakers committed themselves to the survival of the French empire. Given a choice between colonialism and communism, they chose colonialism. And when outright colonialism under the French collapsed, the United States went to the support of its remnant in the form of South Vietnam.

Standing up to Ho Chi Minh, then, meant upholding a tiny elite in South Vietnam—an urban, Roman Catholic minority that had nothing in common with the masses of rural Buddhist and Confucian peasants. The government of South Vietnam, distant and corrupt, was never able to win the loyalties of its own people, and great numbers of them gravitated instead to the Vietcong. The American attempt to win the war militarily by bludgeoning the Vietcong and North Vietnamese with massive firepower brought inordinately large numbers of civilian casualties, and the problem of winning political loyalty deepened.

Throughout most of the war, however, the United States did not worry much about peasant loyalties. The Kennedy and Johnson administrations decided to fight a war of attrition, to kill so many enemy troops and inflict so much damage on North Vietnam that continuation of the war would be impossible. Long before the conversion of the peasantry to democracy, so Johnson's advisers believed, the war would be over, the communists bandaging their wounds and retreating back across the seventeenth parallel. What the Americans did not know was the extent of the communists' dedication to reunification and independence at whatever expense. The American resolve fell far short of that, for however passionately the American public and its government embraced freedom and democracy, neither could become entirely convinced that democracy and freedom were dependent on the continuation of a corrupt regime in a small country an ocean away, and achievable only by the military trashing of much of the country. The Vietcong and North Vietnamese were willing to wait until the American public reached its political and economic limit.

So the United States found itself getting deeper and deeper into the war, not out of any forthright determination to achieve military victory in this year or that but by doses of military power carefully measured: frustrating, the liberal managers of the war thought, both to Neanderthals who wanted to bomb the enemy into rubble and to the weak-kneed pacifists who wanted out at any cost. Each escalation of the conflict was undertaken as a compromise, and each step was taken with the conviction that just a little more firepower would win the day. But the sum of dozens of small escalations was the dreaded land war in Asia. And what Washington considered to be cautious and prudent increases in force the Vietnamese experienced as total, indiscriminate war against their society and their lives.

Even when American policymakers began to see Vietnam for the quagmire it was, disengagement was excruciatingly difficult. Presidents Eisenhower, Kennedy, Johnson, and Nixon all expressed the fear of becoming the first American president to lose a war. Each of them remembered the political abuse Harry Truman had taken from the Republican right wing over the "loss" of China to the Reds, and none of them wanted to be the target of similar abuse for losing Vietnam. Domestic politics, as much as the perceived need to stop communism in Vietnam, kept the United States in the war against the better judgment of much of its political and intellectual leadership. Even in the early 1970s, when the war had become an albatross to the Nixon administration, blanket withdrawal was rejected for threatening American credibility around the world. What had begun as a genuinely idealistic venture to save the world from communism ended in the 1970s as a face-saving game to get out of an impossible mess without looking too bad.

And the end of the Vietnam War is a black wall in Washington with 58,175 names, an epitaph to a loss that is every American's.

12
'Nam, Islam, and the American Future

On September 11, 2001, when a team of Islamic fundamentalists brought down the World Trade Center, the United States suffered a Pearl Harbor worthy of the twenty-first century. But startling though 9/11 was, its ingredients had been simmering for years. Within a five-hundred mile radius of Mecca in Saudi Arabia rests half the world's petroleum reserves, which Americans gulp with the thirst of a man lost in the Middle East's vast deserts. The conflict between Israelis and Arabs—rooted in a full measure of legitimate grievances and illegitimate bigotry on both sides—frustrated the world's finest diplomats, and Washington's unwavering support of Israel drove a wide wedge between the United States and Islam. The desperate economic plight of Middle East peoples, shamelessly exploited at the hands of their own corrupt regimes, contrasted to American wealth and widened the alienation. And as a superpower with modern, secular values, the United States seemed a threat to Islam's future, its spoiled luxury an affront to sobriety and virtue.

In 1979, only four years after the fall of Saigon, the Ayatollah Khomeini had risen to power in Iran. His followers seized the United States embassy in Tehran and held State Department employees hostage for more than a year. Bewildered Americans sitting in front of television sets watched hundreds of thousands of Muslims fill the streets and condemn the United States as "the great Satan." The mantra of hate astonished Americans, who considered their country a beacon of freedom in a dark, despotic world. Three years later, anti-American rhetoric turned bloody in Beirut, Lebanon. As part of a peace-keeping mission to stop a deadly civil war between Christians and Muslims, 241 marines died when a suicide truck bomber, in the name of *jihad*, exploded 2,500 pounds of TNT in front of their barracks.

The Gulf War of 1990 and 1991 provided a more direct ground for global *jihad*. Home to the Wahhabis, Islam's most revolutionary, anti-American sect, Saudi Arabia teetered on the edge of a dangerous political precipice. Wahhabi hate for the Saudi royal family ran almost as deep as the sect's loathing of the United States. For two generations, the

Saudis had enjoyed a virtual military alliance with Washington, supplying Americans with a river of petroleum in return for protection and an ocean of dollars. When Iraq invaded Kuwait, the royal family panicked. Convinced that Saddam Hussein hungered for Riyadh, Mecca, and Medina as well as Kuwait City, the Saudis agreed to let their land serve as the staging area for a counterattack led by the United States. American troops soon occupied military bases in Saudi Arabia. The presence of so many infidels so close to Islam's most holy shrines convulsed the Wahhabis in rage. The United States made short work of Iraq, but the easy victory, combined with cable television broadcasts of Iraqi soldiers surrendering by the tens of thousands and pleading for mercy, embarrassed Arabs and deepened their resentments. More than ever, the American economy depended on Saudi oil, but Saudi Arabia had become, in the words of the former CIA operative Robert Baer, "more and more an irrational state—a place that spawns global terrorism even as it succumbs to an ancient and deeply seated isolationism, a kingdom led by a royal family that can't get out of the way of its own greed. Is this the fulcrum we want the global economy to balance on?"

Throughout the 1990s, that question assumed increasing urgency. Osama bin-Laden, a wealthy Wahabbi, and his al-Qaeda network began to finance what became a global guerrilla war against American interests. Porous borders and a powerful respect for civil liberties made the United States especially vulnerable, as was demonstrated vividly on February 26, 1993, when a van loaded with TNT detonated in a parking garage of the World Trade Center, blasting out a crater 150 feet in diameter and giving President Bill Clinton, only one month in office, a rude introduction to the new world. So soon after the sun set on the Soviet Union and the cold war, a new war of civilizations and ideologies had dawned.

The terrorist affinity for ambushes, kidnapping, car bombs, suicides, booby traps, and assassinations suggested, though not to the notice of Americans at the time, a Vietnam sprawled across the world. Because American interests could be defined so broadly—military bases, corporate offices, government agencies, hotels, university campuses, and even individual tourists—guerrilla attacks might occur anywhere. On August 7, 1998, al-Qaeda proved as much, bombing the embassies of the United States in Nairobi, Kenya, and Dar es Salaam, Tanzania, and killing twelve Americans together with 245 Kenyans and Tanzanians. Secretary of State Madeline Albright, Secretary of Defense William Cohen, and President Bill Clinton all condemned the bombings: "Neither time, nor distance, can bend or break our resolve," said Secretary Albright, "to bring to justice those who have committed these unspeakable acts of cowardice and horror. We will never retreat from this mission." Two years later, al-Qaeda suicide bombers blew a huge hole in the USS *Cole,* an American destroyer getting resupplied in Yemen, and killed seventeen sailors. Again President Clinton employed the language of an earlier era, when John F. Kennedy and Lyndon B. Johnson accused North Vietnam and the Vietcong of such vices as "cowardice and deceit" and vowed that "America [would] not be intimidated."

Conventional military engagements in the Islamic world also bedeviled the United States, repeatedly confronting policymakers with the dreaded Vietnam syndrome. To protect sea lanes at the Horn of Africa and rescue hundreds of thousands of people from anarchy, President George Bush in 1992 dispatched troops to Somalia, a Muslim nation gripped by civil war. Their mission poorly defined, the troops were soon caught among tribes and clans more interested in ritual vengeance and butchering one another than in peace and getting food supplies to the interior, a major objective at a time of more than usual misery inland. President Clinton inherited the problem. When Black Hawk helicopters crashed and American soldiers died in the streets of Mogadishu, surrounded by jeering mobs as unfamiliar with democracy as they were with a good meal, many Americans wondered whether another president had forgotten the lessons of Vietnam. The Massachusetts Democrat and former Speaker of the House "Tip" O'Neill warned the White House that "Somalia could become a big problem for us unless we're careful. We don't have a clue what those people are like or what they want. They don't even know. Remember Vietnam." In 2000 President Clinton, as part of a multinational United Nations force, ordered soldiers to the Balkans. Ethnic cleansing there had brought the systematic slaughter of Muslims in Bosnia and Kosovo. Muslim-American civil rights groups and many Muslim clerics had accused President Clinton of ignoring genocide in the Balkans, and Clinton's intervention spoke to that criticism. But pundits reminded him that World War I had started in the Balkans, where politics historically sinks to blood feuds among people whose loyalties barely extend beyond first cousins. The Balkans, they warned, might become another Vietnam. Senator Strom Thurmond, Republican of South Carolina, a bit condescendingly challenged President Clinton to "read some history and remember the war you personally protested." Senator Paul Wellstone of Minnesota, Clinton's fellow Democrat, asked the president "to keep Vietnam in mind when pressures to escalate come, as they almost most certainly will." Vietnam had become the yardstick by which every United States foreign policy initiative was measured.

Serbia, Kosovo, and Somalia did not become new Vietnams. President Clinton withdrew the troops from Somalia with relatively little loss of American life, leaving Somalis to their own barbaric devices. In Bosnia and Kosovo, the military intervention stopped a reign of massacre and ethnic cleansing without ever remotely resembling Vietnam. But relatively few in the Muslim world noted that the United States had stopped the twenty-first century's first state-sanctioned genocide. In the minds of tens of millions of people, the United States, Israel, and oil had long ago melted into an evil, sticky blob.

When the World Trade Center imploded on September 11, 2001, President George W. Bush described the attack as the opening salvo in "the first war of the twenty-first century." For a full generation, Americans had struggled with the legacy of Vietnam, exhibiting a guilt, paranoia, and self-absorption that permeated foreign policy, domestic politics, and popular culture. In a country that treated victory as an entitlement, defeat had exacted a special toll. Americans knew that the attack on the World Trade Center could not be ignored, but they also feared the prospects of sinking into foreign adventures that would, in the end, spend the lives of a new generation of soldiers without really addressing the threat of terrorism. The Vietnam bogeyman was aprowl.

George W Bush did not share their concerns. Emboldened by the work of conservative revisionists like Harry G. Summers, Jr. and Guenter Lewy, the defense establishment was now convinced that the United States had lost in Vietnam only by refusing to employ a full range of conventional weapons and tactics, not because the war was inherently unwinnable. Nor was Vietnam the "wrong war in the wrong place at the wrong time" or the deaths of 58,175 American soldiers futile. In *The Necessary War,* published in 2000 and carefully examined by Republican conservatives, Michael Lind proposes that Vietnam was a painful but virtuous battle in the Cold War, fought not so much over Indochina but to hammer additional nails into what would become the Soviet Union's coffin. Rather than a colossal blunder, Vietnam was a "necessary war," critical in the struggle against communism. Because Vietnam really did not matter and was irrelevant to American or Soviet strategic interests, it was the perfect war to lose, a defeat without a downside. Better yet is that Vietnam encouraged the Soviet Union to undertake a series of disastrous foreign adventures, overextending itself in Afghanistan and assuming global responsibilities it could not sustain, all in the illusion that since it had championed the successful cause of one Third-World country it could do so for others. In the jungles of Indochina, the United States lost the Vietnam War but won the Cold War. The book's arguments stretched far.

Not given to self-doubt, second-guessing, or even much contemplation, and free of the specter of Vietnam, President Bush responded aggressively to the new Islamic threat. He sent military advisors to the Philippines to train the Filipino army in battling Abu Sayyaf radicals and the Moro Islamic Liberation Front. To Afghanistan, where the Taliban government harbored Osama bin Laden and had imposed a radical, Islamic state inspired by the Wahhabi, the president deployed 130,000 American troops. Opponents reminded him that Afghanistan

had long been a death trap for foreign armies. Of Great Britain's imperial wars, a poem by Rudyard Kipling declares:

> And the end of the fight is a tombstone white with
> the name of the late deceased,
> In the epitaph drear: "A fool lies here who tried
> to hustle the East."

In 1979, the Soviet Union had tried to hustle the East, only to limp out
ten years later, poor and broken, leaving behind more than 13,000 of its
troops and its reputation for being a superpower. "We will defend ourselves without regard to losses," warned Wakhil Ahmed Mutawakil, the
Taliban foreign minister. "We won against the English and Russians,
the Americans will lose too. . . . If they march into our country, they will
suffer great losses. Afghanistan will become a graveyard for the US military." The Taliban fell, however, in a matter of months, overthrown by
insurgents reinforced by American and other forces, and by December
2003, American troop levels were settling down to 8,000 soldiers. Fifty-
three American soldiers had died. Afghanistan was as yet neither a vast
cemetery for Americans nor another Vietnam.

Vietnam crowded its way into the national consciousness again in
March 2003, when President Bush went to war with Iraq. Without sanc-
tion on the part of the United Nations and with little support from traditional allies, the United States and Britain were joined by several
other nations in a full-scale invasion, accusing Saddam Hussein of con-
spiring with terrorists and developing weapons of mass destruction.
Opponents of the war predicted disaster, warning of heavy death tolls
in combat house-to-house, hand-to-hand. But in a textbook invasion
that would have won accolades from Sun Tzu and Karl von Clausewitz,
a coalition composed predominantly of American and British soldiers
quickly toppled the Iraqi government. When the alleged weapons of
mass destruction could not be located, when no evidence of nuclear research could be presented, and when no tie between 9/11 and Saddam
Hussein could be demonstrated, critics charged the president with deceit. The administration soon switched the subject, justifying the invasion as a humanitarian mission to save Iraqis from a vicious regime and
as a strategy for handicapping al-Qaeda terrorists.

In Afghanistan and Iraq, military victory did not translate immediately into political success. Fashioning a stable, democratic government
out of Afghanistan's cauldron of tribes and warlords came to be far more
daunting than overthrowing the Taliban, as did establishing a government capable of serving Iraq's Sunnis, Shiites, Turks, Kurds, Arabs,
Hazaras, Pushtuns, and Ishmailis. Antiwar activists could not resist
Vietnam analogies. Back in 1954, when trying to find a leader for the
newly-established government of South Vietnam, the United States had

come up with Ngo Dinh Diem, a hapless megalomaniac. In 2003 and 2004, as the United States scoured Baghdad, Kabul, and the rest of the world for Iraqis and Afghans ready to assume power, apparitions of Diem flashed regularly in the media. Professor Edward Said of Columbia University, a severe critic of American policy in the Middle East, predicted that "It will not be long before the Bush administration and the rest of the country will remember Vietnam with nostalgia."

As the United States and British military forces in Iraq faced an insurgency gaining momentum and organization, GIs kept dying in a combat that was supposedly over. Throughout 2003, journalists had tracked the number of Americans killed during the actual invasion and the number killed after the end of formal hostilities, searching for a crossover point when casualties from the partisans, Iraqi and foreign, outnumbered the count sustained in conventional operations, as if to gauge when Iraq would cease to be a conventional battlefield conflict and deteriorate into another Vietnam. As of December 2003, 440 American troops had died in the war, more than half killed at the hands of guerrilla insurgents. At those rates, critics insisted, Iraq could indeed become another Vietnam.

Civilian casualties raised additional concern. Indiscriminate use of military firepower in Vietnam had squandered any hope of winning "hearts and minds." So many peasants were killed, wounded, or made homeless—a calculus of suffering numbering in the millions—that building a government friendly to the United States became impossible. In Afghanistan and Iraq, journalists with long memories of My Lai, "friendly fire," strategic hamlets, and "free fire zones" searched the landscape for dead and wounded noncombatants. Accurate estimates of civilian casualties became difficult to come by. The Bush administration treated civilian casualty figures like state secrets but argued that no country in the history of war had been more sensitive to noncombatants. The antiwar Project on Defense Alternatives in Cambridge, Massachusetts, estimated that by November 2003 nearly 25,000 Afghan and Iraqi civilians had died in warfare engaged by the United States, and twice that many were seriously injured. The Bush administration treated the claims as statistical fantasy. "We regret any loss of civilian life," remarked a State Department official, "but remind the world of Saddam Hussein's butchery. Over the years, he has seen to the slaughter of hundreds of thousands of his own people. Iraq today is a far safer place for its citizens than it has been in decades."

And as in 1968, an election approached that was bound to be a referendum on the war or at least its management. While the conflict in Iraq slogged on without a clear sign of success or even a definition of what success might look like, a host of Democratic presidential candidates cranked up their criticisms of the president. But they did so carefully. American voters can be fickle about wars. Any attack on the war that also maligned the troops would constitute political suicide. So Democrats raised issues oblique to the fighting. They accused the president of inventing the issue of weapons of mass destruction, as LBJ had manufactured the Gulf of Tonkin incident in 1964; of hurtling into war without the support of allies, as had Johnson in 1965; and of manufacturing a credibility gap that would have made Lyndon B. Johnson and Richard M. Nixon blush. Senator Kerry likened the president to Theodore Roosevelt, except that Bush was a "bully without a pulpit."

Demonstrations against the wars in Afghanistan and Iraq erupted in major cities around the world, providing perfect sound- and video-bites for cable and network television and generating a media frenzy not seen since the 1960s. In the Vietnam years, firefight tapes had reached American living rooms quickly; for the wars after 9/11 the scenes were still fresher. Civil libertarians meanwhile accused the Bush administration of violating the First, Fourth, Fifth, and Sixth Amendment rights of suspected terrorists, and a federal circuit court held against the Bush administration. The case was expected to reach the Supreme Court. Supporters of the war charged antiwar demonstrators with treason, aiding and abetting the enemy. In the war on terror and the confrontation with radical Islam, Vietnam lurked everywhere.

So did Richard Nixon. In 1989, fourteen years after the fall of South Vietnam and twelve years before 9/11, he had published *No More Vietnams,* a defense of his own policies in Indochina but today bridging some of the distance between Vietnam, Afghanistan, and Iraq. "The most violent and dangerous forces in the Mid-east," he warned, "are not Communist revolutionaries taking orders from Moscow but Moslem fundamentalist revolutionaries." When fundamentalism becomes fanaticism and fanaticism terrorism, the threat to the world "is insidious . . . and deadly. . . . State-supported and sponsored terrorism is one of the most dangerous threats to peace in the world." Nixon offered a blunt antidote. "Swift, timely retaliation," he promised, "even if there is some risk to innocent people, will mean that other terrorists will be less likely to threaten and kill innocent people in the future. Repeated threats to retaliate that are not followed up by action are counterproductive. A president of the United States should warn only once." Our objective, the former president concluded, "should always be to use force as a last resort. But the capability and the will to use force as a first resort, when our interests are threatened, reduces the possibility of having to use force as a last resort, when the risks of casualties would be far greater." Insofar as the military mindset of President Bush can be likened to that of Nixon, the outcome of Vietnam does not offer a promising forecast of the result. George W Bush's wars may deal a deathblow to al-Qaeda and alter the balance of power in the Middle East, or Afghanistan could still become Rudyard Kipling's cemetery and Iraq another Vietnam.

Saddam Hussein's capture on December13, 2003, encouraged the ad-

Soldiers from the U.S. Army's 4th Infantry Division lift the cover that concealed the entrance to the chamber where Saddam Hussein was caught. (*Courtesy, Library of Congress.*)

ministration and improved the morale of American troops. But its long-term effects remained as dark as the tiny bunker where American troops found the dictator. Near the underground hideout were Mars bars and Spam, not cell phones, which leaves unanswered the question about Saddam's role in the anti-American insurgency. His unkempt appearance suggested that perhaps he was simply a man constantly in flight. So many questions were left unanswered. Had the Bush admin-

Saddam Hussein as he appeared after his capture on December 13, 2003. (*Courtesy, Library of Congress.*)

istration, as Shakespeare put it, busied its citizens' "giddied minds with foreign quarrels" so that he could press a range of domestic and international policies? Would the administration be able to reconstruct Iraq and plant democracy there, even with the $166 billion budgeted to date and additional sums to come? How long would Iraqi Muslims tolerate an uninvited foreign military presence on Islamic soil? Would the war in Iraq help bring the United States a victory in the war on terror? And as the most important question of all: Would the United States ever recover its old role, self-appointed but at times plausible, of beacon of freedom and justice?

Possibly the war on terrorism will finally relegate Vietnam to the history books. "We are seeing," wrote the *New York Times* columnist Thomas L. Friedman, "from Bali to Istanbul, the birth of a virulent, nihilistic form of terrorism that seeks to kill any advocates of modernism and pluralism, be they Muslims, Christians, or Jews. This terrorism started even before 9/11 and is growing in the darkest corners of the Muslim world. It is the most serious threat to open societies." Should the war on terrorism eventually expand into a full conflict of civilizations, with more 9/11s at home and battles on fronts throughout the Muslim world, Americans will put Vietnam to rest, though its slumber will provide little repose. "In general," writes Robert Wright in *Nonzero,* "too few who opposed the war [on terror] understand the gravity of the terrorism problem, and too few who favored it understand the subtlety of the problem." The war on terror will write its own rules and generate its own legacies, as did Vietnam, and its leaders will need to pick their battles carefully, for as Frederick the Great so long ago warned: "He who defends everything defends nothing."

Bibliography

Writing about Vietnam continues in high gear as the year 2006 dawns. Some of the best or most useful recent books include David Mariness on the pre-Tet Offensive time, *They Marched into Sunlight: War and Peace, Vietnam and America October 1967* (2002); see also George B. Smith, *The Siege at Hue* (1999). An important study of the usefulness of tactical air support for ground troops is Craig Hannah's *Striving for Air Superiority: The Tactical Air Command in Vietnam* (2002). A new account of the war that stretches even neoconservative imaginations is Michael Lind, *The Necessary War* (2000); consult also the more balanced Lewis Sorley: *A Better War: The Unexamined Victories and Final Tragedy of America's Years in Vietnam* (1999). Henry Kissinger had revived debate about Nixon's attempts to extricate himself from Vietnam in *Ending the Vietnam War: A History of American's Involvement and Extrication from the Vietnam War* (2003); see also Larry Berman, *No Peace No Honor: Nixon, Kissinger, and Betrayal in Vietnam* (2001) and Jeffrey P. Kimball's *Nixon's Vietnam War* (1998). A surprisingly and perhaps deservedly generous account of President John F. Kennedy's misgivings about the course of the war, and his willingness to explore its de-escalation and even withdrawal, may be found in Robert Dallek's *An Unfinished Life: John F Kennedy, 1917–1963* (2002).

William Duiker's *Ho Chi Minh* (2000) will long be the standard biography of the Vietnamese leader; see also Peter G. McDonald, *Giap* (1993). Recent books that retrace but expand previous studies include William Head, ed., *The Tet Offensive* (1996) and James J. Wirtz, *The Tet Offensive: Intelligence Failure in War* (1991). The Vietnamese insurgency continues to attract historians. Robert Mann's *A Grand Delusion: America's Descent into Vietnam* (2001) holds to the consensus that the war was a misguided blunder. See also Ken Post, *Revolution, Socialism and Nationalism in Vietnam* (1989); William Duker, *Sacred War: Nationalism, Intervention, and the Lessons of Vietnam* (1966), and Military History Institute of Vietnam, *Victory in Vietnam: The Official History of the People's Army of Vietnam, 1946–1975* (2002). The critical junction of 1963 to 1965, when United States policymakers grappled with the challenges of Vietnam and ultimately decided on a military solution, continues to fascinate historians. See H. R. McMaster, *Dereliction of Duty: Lyndon Johnson, Robert McNamara, the Joint Chiefs of Staff, and the Lies that Led to Vietnam* (1977), Frederick Legevall, *Choosing War: The Lost Chance for Peace and the Escalation of War in Vietnam* (1999), and David E. Kaiser's pro-Kennedy *American Tragedy: Kennedy, Johnson, and the Origins of the Vietnam War* (2000). The antiwar movement of the 1960s and 1970s dominated much of the political era, and historians are still examining its effect and meaning. See Tom Wells, *The War Within: America's Battle Over Vietnam* (1966) and Rhodri Jeffrey Jones, *Peace Now! American Society and the Ending of the Vietnam War* (1999). A new compendium on Vietnam is Spencer C. Tucker, ed. *The Encyclopedia of the Vietnam War: A Political, Social, & Military History* (2000), and see the interesting Dana Sachs, *The House on Dream Street: Memoirs of an American Woman in Vietnam* (2000). Texas Tech University in Lubbock, Texas, has in recent years developed one of the country's best archives devoted to the Vietnam War.

Among the most recent monographs on Vietnam are Robert Buzzanco, *Masters of Deceit* (1997), Marita Sturkan, *Tangled Memories* (1997), Arnold A. Isaacs, *Vietnam Shadows: The War, Its Ghosts, and Its Legacy* (1997), Fred Turner, *Echoes of Combat: The Vietnam War in American Memory* (1996), Karen

Gottschang Turner with Phan Tham Hao, *Even the Women Must Fight* (1998), Keith Beattie, *The Scar that Binds: American Culture and the Vietnam War* (1998), and Jerry Lembeke, *The Spitting Image: Image, Memory and the Legacy of Vietnam* (1998).

Long before Americans ever heard of Vietnam—indeed long before the United States even existed—the people of Indochina had been struggling to secure their place in the world. Keith Weller Taylor's *The Birth of Vietnam* (1983) surveys the ancient period. For general surveys, see Joseph Buttinger, *The Smaller Dragon: A Political History of Vietnam* (1958) and George Coedes, *The Making of Southeast Asia* (1964). The nineteenth-century presence of China in Vietnam is the subject of Henry McAleavy's *Black Flags in Vietnam: The Story of the Chinese Intervention* (1968). Van-Kiem Thai's *Viet Nam Past and Present* (1956) provides a Vietnamese perspective. An excellent bibliography is Richard Dean Burns and Milton Leitenberg, *The Wars in Vietnam, Cambodia, and Laos, 1945–1982* (1983). Two useful encyclopedias are James S. Olson, ed., *Dictionary of the Vietnam War* (1988) and Harry G. Summers, Jr., *Vietnam War Almanac* (1985).

There are a number of important works on Vietnamese culture. A good survey is F. Raymond Iredell, *Vietnam: The Country and the People* (1966). Danny J. Whitfield's *Historical and Cultural Dictionary of Vietnam* (1976) is an encyclopedia of Vietnamese historical figures, geography, and customs. For a discussion of religion in Vietnam, see Gustave Dumoutier, *Annamese Religions* (1955) and Pierro Gheddo, *The Cross and the Bo-Tree: Catholics and Buddhists in Vietnam* (1970). The best work on the Montagnard people is Gerald C. Hickey's *Free in the Forest: An Ethnohistory of the Vietnamese Central Highlands, 1954–1976* (1982) and his *Sons of the Mountains: Ethnohistory of the Vietnamese Central Highlands to 1954* (1982).

The seminal event in the nineteenth century is the arrival of the French. John Cady's *The Roots of French Imperialism in Asia* (1954) looks at the early penetration of Indochina by French missionaries and entrepreneurs. Milton E. Osborne, *The French Presence in Cochinchina and Cambodia: Rule and Response 1859–1905* (1969) looks at the nineteenth century. Raymond F. Betts's *Assimilation and Association in French Colonial Theory* (1961) analyzes the policy implications of French racial attitudes. For an indigenous look at French imperialism, see Ngo Vinh Long, *Before the Revolution: The Vietnamese Peasants under the French* (1973). Nguyen Khac Vien's *Tradition and Revolution in Vietnam* (1974) shows that Vietnamese nationalism long predated the arrival of the French, although French rule sharpened it. Joseph Buttinger's *Vietnam: A Dragon Embattled,* volume 1, *From Colonialism to Vietminh* (1967) is a masterful survey of French colonialism and the Vietnamese reaction to it. Ellen J. Hammer's *The Struggle for Indochina* (1954) *is* a good supplement. David G. Marr's *Vietnamese Anticolonialism 1885–1925* (1971) and *Vietnamese Tradition on Trial 1920–1945* (1981) describe the political resistance to the French among the Vietnamese. Also see William Duiker, *The Rise of Nationalism in Vietnam, 1900–1941* (1976). For a Marxist perspective on Vietnamese nationalism, see Thomas Hodgkin, *Vietnam: The Revolutionary Path* (1981).

The leading Vietnamese nationalist was, of course, Ho Chi Minh. Charles Fenn's *Ho Chi Minh: A Biographical Introduction (1973) is* the memoirs of an OSS officer who knew Ho Chi Minh during World War II. For two highly readable biographies, see Jean Lacouture, *Ho Chi Minh: A Political Biography* (1968) and David Halberstam, *Ho* (1971). For Lacouture's recollections, see *Ho Chi Minh and His Followers: A Personal Memoir* (1968). Also see William Warbey, *Ho Chi Minh and the Struggle for an Independent Vietnam* (1972). Some of Ho Chi Minh's own writings are also illuminating, especially *Selected Works* (1960–

1962) and *Prison Diary* (1966). For descriptions of other Vietnamese leaders, see Bernard B. Fall, *The Viet-Minh Regime* (1956) and Huynh Kim Khanh, *Vietnamese Communism 1925–1945* (1982). Joseph Buttinger's portraits can be found in *Vietnam: A Dragon Embattled,* volume 2, *Vietnam at War* (1967). Two good but not very accessible reference works are the CIA's *Who's Who in Vietnam* (1969) and the U.S. State Department's *Who's Who in North Vietnam* (1972). Also see Robert J. O'Neill, *General Giap: Politician and Strategist* (1969). Truong Chinh's *Primer for Revolt: The Communist Takeover in Vietnam* (1963) is an excellent first-hand account. A good deal can also be learned from Tran Van Dinh, *This Nation and Socialism Are One: Selected Writings of Le Duan* (1977).

Anti-French nationalism culminated in the first Indochina War. For the history of French politics, see Alexander Werth, *France 1940–1954* (1956). Ellen Hammer's *The Struggle for Indochina* (1954) and Donald Lancaster's *The Emancipation of French Indochina* (1961) are both useful surveys. So is Robert F. Turner's *Vietnamese Communism: Its Origins and Developments* (1975). Bernard Fall, a leading journalist who observed the first Indochina War and died in the second, describes Vietnamese insurgency in *Street Without Joy: Insurgency in Vietnam, 1946–1963* (1963). David G. Marr's *Vietnamese Tradition on Trial* explains how the Vietminh displaced the other Vietnamese nationalist groups. Vo Nguyen Giap's *People's War, People's Army* (1962) is an anthology of his writings about the French war. Lucien Bodard's *The Quicksand War* (1967) provides a good description of the war from 1946 to 1950. The best account of the war is Giap's *Unforgettable Days* (1978). On the battle at Dienbienphu, see Jules Roy, *The Battle of Dien Bien Phu* (1965) and Bernard Fall, *Hell in a Very Small Place: The Siege of Dien Bien Phu* (1966). For the Geneva Conference, see Robert F. Randle, *Geneva 1954* (1969) and Philippe Devillers and Jean Lacouture, *End of a War: Indochina 1954* (1969).

The best writing on Vietnam remains the property of journalists, not historians. Stanley Karnow, who spent years in Vietnam as a reporter, wrote *Vietnam: A History* in 1983. It is full of anecdotal material about the leading figures in the war. David Halberstam, who won a Pulitzer Prize for his early reporting of the war, subsequently wrote *The Making of a Quagmire* (1964), a book that proved prophetic in its prediction of the outcome of the war. Halberstam's *The Best and the Brightest* (1972) is outstanding in its description of leading American policymakers. The best book of all is Neil Sheehan's *The Bright and Shining Lie: John Paul Vann and America in Vietnam* (1988), a devastating critique of United States policy. Peter Arnett, a former AP reporter in Vietnam, and Michael Maclear wrote *The Ten Thousand Day War* (1981).

There are also a number of general works by historians. One of the most recent is George Donelson Moss, *Vietnam: An American Ordeal* (1989). Also see Philip Davidson, *Vietnam at War: The History, 1945– 1975* (1988). An early history which romanticizes the communists is Frances FitzGerald's *Fire in the Lake* (1972). Chester Cooper's *The Last Crusade: America in Vietnam* (1970) is well-informed by its author's policy-making role in the war, as is Paul Kattenburg's *The Vietnam Trauma in American Foreign Policy, 1945–1975* (1980). Guenter Lewy's *America in Vietnam* (1978) is a revisionary work which seeks to justify the United States involvement. Norman Podhoretz's *Why We Were in Vietnam* (1982) follows a similar vein. Two of the best surveys are George C. Herring's *America's Longest War: The United States and Vietnam, 1950–1975* (1986) and William S. Turley's *The Second Indochina War: A Short Political and Military History, 1954–1975* (1986). Turley is especially good in his discussion of Vietcong and North Vietnamese politics. Also see William J. Duiker's *Sacred War* (1995).

The reasons behind the American commitment to Southeast Asia have been the focus of intense debate. President Franklin D. Roosevelt flirted with the idea of trusteeship for Indochina, but he was merely expressing a concern rather than developing a policy; see Christopher Thorne, *Allies of a Kind: The United States, Britain, and the War Against Japan, 1941–1945* (1978) and William Roger Louis, *Imperialism at Bay: The United States and the Decolonization of the British Empire* (1978). One school argues that the United States became involved because of its fear of Soviet expansionism in Europe. For that point of view, see George C. Herring, "The Truman Administration and the Restoration of French Sovereignty in Indochina," *Diplomatic History* 1 (1977), 97–117. Richard J. Barnet's *Roots of War* (1972) argues that the United States simply defined its national interests too broadly. Leslie H. Gelb and Richard K. Betts, in *The Irony of Vietnam: The System Worked (1978),* claim that American politicians were unable, because of the realities of domestic politics, to withdraw without committing political suicide. A more recent argument attempts to integrate complex economic and political factors in Europe, Japan, and Southeast Asia. See Robert M. Blum, *Drawing the Line: The Origin of the American Containment Policy in East Asia* (1982); Andrew J. Rotter, *The Path to Vietnam: Origins of the American Commitment to Southeast Asia* (1987); and Gabriel Kolko, *Anatomy of a War* (1985).

For information on the growing commitment in the 1950s, see Stephen E. Ambrose, *Eisenhower,* volume 2, *President and Elder Statesman, 1952–1969* (1984) and Townsend Hoopes, *The Devil and John Foster Dulles* (1973). Also see Stephen Jurika, Jr., ed., *From Pearl Harbor to Vietnam: The Memoirs of Admiral Arthur W. Radford* (1980). The decision whether or not to intervene at Dienbienphu in 1954 is the subject of John Prados's *The Sky Would Fall: Operation Vulture: The U.S. Bombing Mission in Indochina, 1954* (1983) and Matthew B. Ridgway, *Soldier: The Memoirs of Matthew B. Ridgway* (1956). Robert Shaplen's *The Lost Revolution* (1966) *is* an especially good survey of the period.

For discussions of events inside South Vietnam during the 1950s, see Edward G. Lansdale, *In the Midst of Wars* (1972) and J. Lawton Collins, *Lightning Joe: An Autobiography* (1979). The early role played by the United States military is described in J. Lawton Collins, *The Development and Training of the South Vietnamese Army, 1950–1972* (1975); Robert H. Whitlow, *U.S. Marines in Vietnam: The Advisory and Combat Assistance Era, 1954–1964* (1976); Ronald H. Spector, *United States Army in Vietnam: Advice and Support: The Early Years* (1985); and Edwin Hooper et al., *The United States Navy and the Vietnam Conflict: The Setting of the Stage to 1959* (1976). Denis Warner's *The Last Confucian* (1963) and Anthony Bouscaren's *The Last of the Mandarins: Diem of Vietnam* (1965) describe the Diem regime.

Good general surveys on communist insurgency can be found in Frances FitzGerald's *Fire in the Lake* and in the second volume of Joseph Buttinger's *Vietnam.* For the connection between North Vietnam and the southern communists, see P. J. Honey, *Communism in North Vietnam* (1963). Also see King C. Chen's "Hanoi's Three Decisions and the Escalation of the Vietnam War," *Political Science Quarterly* 90 (1975). One of the earliest scholarly works on the insurgency was Douglas Pike's *Viet Cong* (1966). Also see Pike's *The Viet Cong Strategy of Terror* (1970). William Henderson's *Why the Vietcong Fought: A Study of Motivation and Control in a Modern Army* (1979) is a psychological portrait of the guerrillas. William Duiker's *The Communist Road to Power* is first-rate. A number of books look at insurgency on the local level. See William R. Andrews, *The Village War: Vietnamese Communist Revolutionary Activities in Dinh Tuong Province, 1960–1964* (1973); Stuart Herrington, *Silence Was a Weapon* (1982); and Jeffrey Race, *War Comes to Long An: Revolutionary Conflict in a Vietnamese Village* (1972). For Vietcong memoirs, see Nguyen Thi Dinh, *No*

Other Road to Take (1976) and Truong Nhu Tang, *A Vietcong Memoir* (1985). An outstanding oral history is David Chanoff and Doan Van Toai, *Portrait of the Enemy (1986)*. Also see Kate Webb, *On the Other Side: 23 Days with the Viet Cong* (1972).

For an even-handed history of the Kennedy years, see Herbert Parmet's *JFK: The Presidency of John F. Kennedy* (1983). Bruce Miroff's *Pragmatic Illusions: The Presidential Politics of John F. Kennedy* (1976) is a New Left critique. Two works that specialize on Kennedy and Vietnam are R. B. Smith, *An International History of the Vietnam War*, volume 2, *The Kennedy Strategy* (1985) and William J. Rust, *Kennedy in Vietnam* (1985). Among the books by administration officials, see George T. Ball, *The Past Has Another Pattern* (1982) and Roger Hilsman, *To Move a Nation: The Politics of Foreign Policy in the Administration of John F. Kennedy* (1967). Also see Walt W. Rostow, *The Diffusion of Power, 1957–1972* (1972); Henry Cabot Lodge, Jr., *The Storm Has Many Eyes: A Personal Narrative* (1973); and Maxwell D. Taylor, *Swords and Ploughshares* (1972). Warren Cohen's *Dean Rusk (1980)* looks at the secretary of state. For the events in South Vietnam during the Kennedy years, see Mieczyslaw Maneli, *War of the Vanquished* (1971) and John Mecklin, *Mission in Torment: An Intimate Account of the US. Role in Vietnam* (1974). Joseph Buttinger's second *Vietnam* volume is also good, as is David Halberstam's *The Making of a Quagmire*. Frederick Nolting, the United States ambassador to South Vietnam in the early 1960s, wrote *From Triumph to Tragedy: The Political Memoirs of Frederick Nolting* (1988). For the events leading up to Diem's assassination, see Ellen J. Hammer, *A Death in November: America in Vietnam, 1963* (1987). Also see John Newman, *John F. Kennedy and Vietnam* (1992).

A number of books look at counterinsurgency. The best survey is Larry E. Cable, *Conflict of Myths: The Development of American Counterinsurgency Doctrine and the Vietnam War* (1986). Douglas S. Blauburg's *The Counterinsurgency Era: U.S. Doctrine and Performance 1950 to the Present* (1977) is also excellent. Robert W. Komer discusses how badly the United States underestimated the insurgency in *Bureaucracy Does Its Thing* (1972). Milton E. Osborne's *Strategic Hamlets in South Vietnam* (1965) is an early study of that disaster. Sir Robert Thompson discusses his role in *Defeating Communist Insurgency* (1966) and *Peace Is Not at Hand* (1974). For a look at the Marine Corps pacification programs, see Michael E. Petersen's *The Combined Action Platoons: The U.S. Marines' Other War in Vietnam* (1989). Shelby L. Stanton's *Green Berets at War* (1985) and Charles M. Simpson III's *Inside the Green Berets: The First Thirty Years* (1983) provide descriptions of Special Forces pacification efforts. Andrew F. Krepinevich's *The Army and Vietnam* (1986) has an excellent chapter on army counterinsurgency.

Lyndon B. Johnson's decision to escalate the war, of course, enjoys a voluminous literature. Although flawed by a self-serving defensiveness, Johnson's *The Vantage Point: Perspectives of the Presidency, 1963–1969* (1971) is a necessary starting point. Vaughn Robert's *The Presidency of Lyndon B. Johnson* (1983) is the best history of the administration. For a revealing portrait of Johnson, see Doris Kearns, *Lyndon Johnson and the American Dream* (1976). Robert Caro's *The Years of Lyndon Johnson: The Path to Power* (1982) and *The Years of Lyndon Johnson: Means of Ascent* (1990) are a savage critique. For the events surrounding the Gulf of Tonkin incident, see John Galloway, *The Gulf of Tonkin Resolution* (1970) and Eugene C. Windchy, *Tonkin Gulf* (1971). There are several excellent books that describe the decision-making process in Washington. Especially good are Henry Graff's interviews with administration officials, published as *The Tuesday Cabinet: Deliberation and Decision on Peace and War under Lyndon B. Johnson* (1970). Equally good are two books by Larry Berman—

Planning a Tragedy: The Americanization of the War in Vietnam (1982) and *Lyndon Johnson's War: The Road to Stalemate in Vietnam* (1989). Also see Henry Brandon, *Anatomy of Error: The Inside Story of the Asian War on the Potomac, 1954–1969* (1969). There is no really good biography on McNamara, but see Henry L. Trewhitt, *McNamara: His Ordeal in the Pentagon* (1971). Alain Enthoven and K. Wayne Smith provide an inside look at McNamara in *How Much Is Enough? Shaping the Defense Program, 1961–1969* (1971). Gregory Palmer's *The McNamara Strategy and the Vietnam War: Program Budgeting in the Pentagon, 1960–1968* (1978) is highly critical of the secretary of defense. For the role played by such elder statesmen as Dean Acheson and W. Averell Harriman, see Walter Isaacson and Evan Thomas, *The Wise Men: Six Friends and the World They Made* (1986). David Di Leo's *George Ball, Vietnam, and the Rethinking of Containment* (1991) is excellent. Also see Robert McNamara, *In Retrospect: The Tragedy and Lessons of Vietnam* (1995).

The question of strategy remains highly controversial. David Richard Palmer's *Summons for a Trumpet* (1978) argues that the attrition strategy was hopelessly inadequate, while Guenter Lewy's *America in Vietnam* claims that the United States should have focused on pacification.

Andrew F. Krepinevich argues in *The Army and Vietnam* that United States military policy should have focused on light infantry formations, firepower restraint, and solving political and social problems, not conventional warfare. The best survey of the army effort is Shelby L. Stanton, *The Rise and Fall of an American Army: U.S. Ground Forces in Vietnam, 1965–1973* (1985). For arguments that the American command and control function during the war was badly designed, see Robert L. Gallucci, *Neither Peace Nor Honor: The Politics of American Military Policy in Vietnam* (1975) and George S. Eckhart, *Command and Control, 1950–1969* (1974). Another school of thought argues that the United States should have isolated North Vietnam from South Vietnam. See Harry G. Summers, Jr., *On Strategy: The Vietnam War in Context* (1981) and Bruce Palmer, Jr., *The 25-Year War: America's Military Role in Vietnam* (1984). Finally, some argue that the United States did not apply enough firepower. This point of view is clearly expressed in two memoirs: William Westmoreland, *A Soldier Reports* (1976) and Ulysses S. Grant Sharp, *Strategy for Defeat: Vietnam in Retrospect* (1978). Also see William Colby and Alexander Burnham, *Lost Victory* (1990). Wilbur Morrison summarizes this argument in *Vietnam: The Winnable War* (1990). Also see H. G. Moore and Joseph Galloway, *We Were Soldiers Once and Young* (1992); Christian Appy, *Working-Class War* (1993); and Eric Bergerud, *Red Thunder, Tropic Lightning: The World of a Combat Division in Vietnam* (1993).

The literature on American women in Vietnam is just beginning to grow. For a look at the role played by nurses in the war, see Dan Freedman and Jacqueline Rhoads, *Nurses in Vietnam: The Forgotten Veterans* (1987) and Elizabeth Norman, *Women at War* (1990). Also see Lynda Van Devanter, *Home before Morning: The Story of an Army Nurse in Vietnam* (1983). The best oral history is Kathryn Marshall's *In the Combat Zone: An Oral History of American Women in Vietnam, 1965–1975* (1987). Also see Shelley Saywell, *Women in War* (1985); Keith Walker, *A Piece of My Heart: The Stories of 26 American Women Who Served in Vietnam* (1985); and Patricia Walsh, *Forever Sad the Hearts* (1982). For a more recent description of American women in Vietnam, see Winnie Smith, *American Daughters Gone to War* (1992).

The effectiveness of the air war over Vietnam is quite controversial. For general surveys see Raphael Littauer and Norman Uphoff, eds., *The Air War in Indochina* (1972) and Bernard C. Nalty et al., *The Air War over Vietnam* (1971).

William Momyer's *Air Power in Three Wars* praises the air force from an insider's perspective. In a similar vein is John B. Nichols and Barrett Tillman, *On Yankee Station: The Naval Air War over Vietnam* (1987). William A. Buckingham, Jr.'s *Operation Ranch Hand: The United States Air Force and Herbicides in Southeast Asia, 1961– 1971* (1982) *is* important reading. Criticisms of the air war can be found in James Clay Thompson, *Rolling Thunder: Undertaking Policy and Program Failure* (1980) and Mark Clodfelter, *The Limits of Air Power: The American Bombing of North Vietnam* (1989).

For the Vietnamese perspective on the American military effort, there are a number of valuable works. Jon M. Van Dyke's *North Vietnam's Strategy for Survival* (1972) describes how North Vietnam adjusted to the strategy of attrition. Also see Patrick J. McGarvey, ed., *Visions of Victory: Selected Vietnamese Communist Military Writings, 1964–1968* (1969), which describes North Vietnamese debates over military strategy. William Duiker's *The Communist Road to Power in Vietnam is* excellent. North Vietnam's official history of the conflict is entitled *The Anti-U.S. Resistance for National Salvation 1954–1975* (1980). For discussions of communist strategy, see Vo Nguyen Giap's *Big Victory, Big Task* and *Banner of People's War: The Party's Military Line* (1970). Tran Van Tra's *Ending the Thirty Years War* (1982) is also revealing. Douglas Pike's *PAVN: People's Army of Vietnam* (1986) *is* an outstanding portrait of the North Vietnamese army. An excellent survey of the war from the communist perspective is Nguyen Khac Vien, *The Long Resistance 1958–1974* (1975). Nguyen Thi Dinh's *No Other Road to Take* (1976) describes the efforts of the People's Liberation Army of Vietnam. For descriptions of South Vietnamese politics, see Charles A. Joiner, *The Politics of Massacre* (1974) and Allen E. Goodman, *Politics in War* (1973). The best survey of South Vietnam is the book by Anthony James Joes, *The War for South Viet Nam, 1954–1975* (1989). The best series of oral histories collected from ordinary people in South Vietnam is Don Luce and John Sommer, *Vietnam: The Unheard Voices* (1969). For Vietnamese recollections, see Cao Van Vien and Dong Van Khuyen, *Reflections on the Vietnam War* (1980); Hoang Ngoc Lung, *The General Offensives of 1968–69* (1981); Tran Van Don, *Our Endless War* (1978); and Nguyen Cao Ky, *Twenty Years and Twenty Days* (1976).

The watershed event in the war was the Tet offensive of 1968. Don Oberdorfer's *Tet!* (1971) is a highly readable account by a journalist who was there. Also see his *Tet: The Turning Point of the War* (1983). Walter Isaacson and Evan Thomas in *The Wise Men* provide excellent descriptions of the frustration in Washington. For the political implications of Tet, see Herbert Y. Schandler, *The Unmaking of a President: Lyndon Johnson and Vietnam* (1977). Peter Baestrup's *Big Story* (1977) criticizes the press for its reporting of Tet. For histories of two key battles, see Keith W. Nolan, *Battle for Hue: Tet, 1968* (1983) and Robert Pisor, *The End of the Line: The Siege of Khe Sanh* (1982). In *The Viet Cong Tet Offensive* (1969), Pham Von Son and Le Van Duong provide a local perspective. Ronald H. Spector's *After Tet* (1993) is especially illuminating.

For a survey of the antiwar movement, see Nancy Zaroulis and Gerald Sullivan, *Who Spoke Up? American Protest Against the War in Vietnam, 1963–1975* (1984). Also see Thomas Powers's two books, *The War at Home: Vietnam and the American People* (1973) and *Vietnam, the War at Home: The Antiwar Movement, 1964–1968* (1984). On the issue of draft resistance, see Lawrence M. Baskir and William A. Strauss, *Chance and Circumstance: The Draft, the War, and the Vietnam Generation* (1978) and David S. Surrey, *Choice of Conscience: Vietnam Era Military and Draft Resisters in Canada* (1982). For two recent books on the antiwar movement, see Kenneth Heineman, *Campus Wars* (1993) and Tom Wells, *The War Within: America's Battle over Vietnam* (1994).

The available sources on the Nixon administration are more limited than for Eisenhower, Kennedy, and Johnson. For Richard Nixon's perspective, see his memoirs, *RN: The Memoirs of Richard Nixon* (1978) and *In the Arena* (1990). Also see his *No More Vietnams (1985)*. Kissinger's point of view is expressed in his memoirs, *White House Years* (1979) and *Years of Upheaval* (1983). Also see William Safire, *Before the Fall* (1975); U. Alexis Johnson, *The Right Hand of Power* (1984); John Ehrlichman, *Witness to Power* (1982); and H. R. Haldeman, *The Ends of Power* (1978). For an evenhanded version of Nixon's early years, see Stephen E. Ambrose *Nixon: The Education of a Politician, 1913–1962* (1987). Nixon's approach to foreign policy is explained in C. L. Sulzberger, *The World and Richard Nixon* (1987) and Robert S. Litwack, *Detente and the Nixon Doctrine: American Foreign Policy and the Pursuit of Stability, 1969–1976* (1984). For a highly sympathetic view of Henry Kissinger, see Marvin Kalb and Bernard Kalb, *Kissinger* (1974). Contrast it with Seymour M. Hersh, *The Price of Power: Kissinger in the Nixon White House* (1983). Also see Robert D. Schulzinger, *Henry Kissinger: Doctor of Diplomacy* (1989); Roger Morris, *An Uncertain Greatness: Henry Kissinger and American Foreign Policy* (1977); and John Stoessinger, *Kissinger: The Anguish of Power* (1976).

Vietnam as an international issue is surveyed in R. B. Smith, *An International History of the Vietnam War,* volume 1, *Revolution versus Containment, 1955–61* (1983) and volume 2, *The Kennedy Strategy (1985)*. Also see Paul M. Kattenburg's *The Vietnam Trauma in American Foreign Policy.* Douglas Pike's *Vietnam and the Soviet Union: Anatomy of an Alliance* (1987) analyzes Soviet foreign policy, as does Leif Rosenberger's *The Soviet Union and Vietnam* (1986). For the impact of the Vietnam War on China, see Robert G. Sutter, *Chinese Foreign Policy after the Cultural Revolution: 1966–1977* (1978) and Ray Hemen, *China's Vietnam War* (1983). Also see Daniel S. Papp, *Vietnam: The View from Moscow, Peking, and Washington* (1981). Two books deal with Canada: Douglas A. Ross, *In the Interests of Peace: Canada and Vietnam, 1954–1973* (1984) and Charles Taylor, *Snow Job: Canada, the United States and Vietnam, 1954–1973* (1984). For the Japanese perspective, see Thomas R. H. Havens, *Fire across the Sea: The Vietnam War and Japan 1965–1975* (1987). On the British, see George Rosie, *The British in Vietnam* (1970). For the Australians, see Peter King, *Australia's Vietnam* (1983). Also see Robert Larsen and James Lawton Collins, Jr., *Allied Participation in Vietnam* (1975).

A number of books deal with the end of the war. For negotiations leading to the Paris agreements of 1974, see the memoirs of Nixon and Kissinger as well as Gareth Porter's *A Peace Denied: The United States, Vietnam, and the Paris Agreement* (1975). Allan Goodman's *The Lost Peace* (1978) is critical of the treaty. On the Christmas bombing of 1972, see Mark Clodfelter, *The Limits of Air Power,* as well as Martin F. Herz, *The Prestige Press and the Christmas Bombing* (1980). For the offensive that inspired the bombing campaign, see G. H. Turley, *The Easter Offensive: Vietnam, 1972* (1985). Ngo Quang Truong, *The Easter Offensive of 1972* (1980) provides a Vietnamese perspective. Also see A.J.C. Lavelle, ed., *Airpower and the 1972 Spring Invasion* (1976).

P. Edward Haley's *Congress and the Fall of South Vietnam and Cambodia* argues that Congress severely limited the effectiveness of Presidents Nixon and Ford. Two works highly critical of the settlement are William F. LaGro, *Vietnam from Cease-Fire to Capitulation* (1981) and Stuart A. Herrington, *Peace with Honor?* (1983). A.J.C. Lavelle's *Last Flight from Saigon* (1978) describes the hectic final hours at the end of April 1975. John Pilzer's *The Last Day* (1976) is highly readable. For a scathing attack on Ambassador Graham Martin's failure to anticipate the communists' final offensive, see Frank Snepp, *Decent Interval: An Insider's Account of Saigon's Indecent End* (1977). Three books deal with the spring 1975 offensive: Alan Dawson, *55 Days: The Fall of South Vietnam* (1977); Tiziano Terzani, *Giai Phong! The Fall and Liberation of South Vietnam* (1977); and David Butler, *The Fall of Saigon* (1985). Stephen T. Hosmer's *The Fall of South Vietnam* (1980) consists of interviews with former South Vietnamese officials. See Cao Van Vien's *The Final Collapse* (1982) for another South Vietnamese account. Tran Van Tra's *Ending the Thirty Years War* and Van Tien Dung's *Our Great Spring Victory* (1977) give the communist view.

Laos and Cambodia have also received considerable attention. Charles Stevenson offers a highly critical account in *The End of Nowhere: American Policy Toward Laos Since 1954* (1973). For histories of the 1971 invasion of Laos, see Nguyen Duy Hinh, *Lam Son 719* (1981) and Keith William Nolan, *Into Laos: The Story of Dewey Canyon/Lam Son 719* (1986). An outstanding look at communist insurgency in Laos is MacAlister Brown and Joseph J. Zasloff, *Apprentice Revolutionaries: The Communist Movement in Laos, 1930–1985* (1986). Perala Ratnam's *Laos and the Super Powers* (1980) summarizes the diplomatic issues. The catastrophe in Cambodia is the subject of David P. Chandler's *A History of Cambodia* (1983). For the background to the struggle, see Wilfred Burchet, *The China-Cambodia-Vietnam Triangle* (1982) and Michael Leifer, *Cambodia: The Search for Security* (1967). The 1970 invasion is covered in Shelby L. Stanton's *The Rise and Fall of an American Army* and Tran Dinh Tho, *The Cambodian Incursion* (1979). Arnold Isaacs deals with the fall of Cambodia to the Khmer Rouge in *Without Honor,* as does Craig Etcheson in *The Rise and Demise of Democratic Kampuchea* (1984). Also see Michael Vickery, *Cambodia, 1975–1982* (1984). For a critique of American policy, see William Shawcross, *Sideshow: Kissinger, Nixon, and the Destruction of Cambodia* (1979). Several books deal with the Khmer Rouge's genocidal assault on Cambodia in the late 1970s. See William Shawcross, *The Quality of Mercy: Cambodia, Holocaust, and the Modern Conscience* (1984); George Hildebrand and Gareth Porter, *Cambodia: Starvation and Revolution* (1976); and Francois Ponchaud, *Cambodia: Year Zero* (1978). For the most recent books on the holocaust in Cambodia, see Usha Welarafua, *Beyond the Killing Fields* (1993) and David A. Chandler, *Brother Number One: A Biography of Pol Pot* (1992).

The steady decline of Vietnam after the final victory is the subject of Nguyen Van Canh's *Vietnam under Communism, 1975–1982* (1983) and Nguyen Long's *After Saigon Fell* (1981). William Duiker describes the state of Vietnam in the late 1970s in *Since the Fall of Saigon* (1980). For post–1975 conflict in Indochina, see Ray Hemen, *China's Vietnam War.* Also see David P. Elliott, ed., *The Third Indochina Conflict* (1981). The best general survey is Nayan Chanda, *Brother Enemy: The War after the War* (1986).

The legacy of the Vietnam War for Americans continues to generate interest and debate. One survey of the topic is James F. Veninga and Harry A. Wilmer, eds., *Vietnam in Remission* (1985). Several books deal with the impact of the war on American culture. See Philip D. Beidler, *American Literature and the Experience of Vietnam* (1982) and John Hellman, *American Myth and the Legacy of Vietnam* (1986) for the part played by Vietnam in recent literature. Also see W. D. Ehrhart, ed., *Carrying the Darkness: American Poetry of the Vietnam War* (1985) and Timothy J. Lomperis, *Reading the Wind: The Literature of the Vietnam War* (1986). James C. Wilson's *Vietnam in Prose and Film* (1982) surveys the films of the 1970s. Also see Andrew V. Martin, "Critical Approaches to American Cultural Studies: The Vietnam War in History, Literature, and Film," Ph.D. dissertation, University of Iowa, 1987. For the war's impact on foreign policy, see Anthony Lake, ed., *The Legacy of Vietnam: The War, American Society and the Future of American Foreign Policy* (1976). Also see Earl C. Ravenal, *Never Again: Learning from America's Foreign Policy Failures* (1978) and Ole R.

Holsti and James N. Rosenau, *American Leadership in World Affairs: Vietnam and the Breakdown of Consensus* (1984). Several books deal with the question of American identity. See Walter H. Capps, *The Unfinished War: Vietnam and the American Conscience* (1982) and Myra MacPherson, *Long Time Passing* (1984).

Finally, there is an increasing volume of documentary source material becoming available to scholars. The starting place, of course, is the Pentagon Papers. Neil Sheehan and several other scholars and journalists wrote an early introduction to the papers which is still useful; see *The Pentagon Papers as Published by the New York Times* (1971). The best edition of the papers is U.S. Congress, Senate, Subcommittee on Public Buildings and Grounds, *The Pentagon Papers,* The Senator Gravel Edition, 4 vols. (1971). Also see George H. Herring, ed., *The Secret Diplomacy of the Vietnam War: The Negotiating Volumes of the Pentagon Papers* (1983). Gareth Porter's two-volume documents collection—*Vietnam: The Definitive Documentation of Human Decisions* (1979)—is very useful. Less useful, because of how it is organized, is the 12-volume *Department of Defense, U.S.–Vietnam Relations, 1945–1967* (1971). During the last several years the State Department, National Security Council, and CIA have released a series of research reports and classified reports through the "Indochinese Research Collections" of University Publications of America. For the U.S. military side of the conflict, scholars should consult Records Group 338 (Vietnam War: MACV/USARV Records) at the Washington National Records Center in Suitland, Maryland. There is also a valuable oral history collection called the Senior Officer Oral History Program, at the U.S. Army Military History Institute, Carlisle Barracks, Pennsylvania, which contains the reminiscences of major American army officers.

For those individuals interested in the policy debates taking place in the Kennedy and Johnson administrations, there are invaluable resources at the John F. Kennedy Presidential Library in Boston, Massachusetts and the Lyndon B. Johnson Presidential Library in Austin, Texas. At the JFK Library, scholars should look at the Presidential Office Files, particularly the sections on Counterinsurgency, on Vietnam, and on Vietnam Security. They should also see the National Security Files, especially the Vietnam section. At the LBJ Library, the most revealing materials on the policy debates can be found in the National Security File and the White House Central Files. There are also oral histories at the LBJ Library by William Bundy, George Christian, Clark Clifford, Chester Cooper, Alain Enthoven, W. Averell Harriman, Lyndon B. Johnson, Cyrus Vance, Paul Warnke, and William Westmoreland.

Documentary sources for the communists are far more limited. Cornell University maintains a microfilmed *Catalog of Viet Cong Documents,* while the Library of Congress has on microfilm a series of *Communist Vietnamese Publications.* At the Center for Research Libraries in Chicago, there is a very useful *Documents of the National Liberation Front of South Vietnam* on microfilm. Finally, there is the State Department's *Working Paper of North Viet-Nam's Role in the War in South Viet-Nam* (1968).

A Vietnam War Chronology

1945

    Sept. 2 Ho Chi Minh proclaims the Democratic Republic of Vietnam.

        26 A. Peter Dewey, head of the OSS mission in Saigon, is shot by Vietminh troops, becoming the first American to die in the Vietnam War.

1946

    Mar. 6 Franco-Vietnamese Accords signed.

    June 1 The Fontainebleau Conference convenes.

    Dec. 19 The Vietminh attack French forces in Tonkin, formally beginning the first Indochina War.

1948

    June 5 The French name Bao Dai head of state of Vietnam.

1949

    Mar. 8 Elysée Agreement signed.

    Oct. 1 Mao Zedong proclaims the People's Republic of China.

1950

    Jan. 14 Ho Chi Minh again proclaims establishment of the Democratic Republic of Vietnam.

    June 27 President Harry S. Truman announces increased U.S. military assistance to Vietnam.

    Aug. 3 United States Military Assistance and Advisory Group arrives in Saigon.

    Dec. 30 United States signs a Mutual Defense Assistance Agreement with France, Vietnam, Cambodia, and Laos.

1952

    Nov. 4 Dwight D. Eisenhower is elected president.

1953

    July 27 Korean War armistice is signed.

1954

    Mar. 13 Vietminh attack the French fortress at Dienbienphu.

        20 Admiral Arthur Radford proposes Operation Vulture to assist the French in defending Dienbienphu.

    Apr. 7 President Dwight D. Eisenhower uses the domino analogy to explain the political significance of Indochina.

        25 Winston Churchill and the British refuse to participate in Operation Vulture.

        29 President Eisenhower announces that the United States will not provide air support to the French garrison at Dienbienphu.

    May 7 The Vietminh conquer Dienbienphu.

        8 The Geneva Conference opens.

    July 20 France signs a cease-fire ending hostilities in Indochina.

    Aug. 1 The first of nearly 1 million refugees from North Vietnam cross into South Vietnam.

    Sept. 8 United States signs the Manila Treaty forming the Southeast Asia Treaty Organization.

1955

Mar. 28 Ngo Dinh Diem attacks the Binh Xuyen.

June 5 Ngo Dinh Diem attacks the Hoa Hao.

July 6 Ngo Dinh Diem repudiates the Geneva Agreements and refuses to plan for open elections throughout the country.

Oct. 26 Ngo Dinh Diem proclaims the Republic of Vietnam with himself as president.

1957

May 5–19 Ngo Dinh Diem visits the United States.

1959

Apr. 4 President Eisenhower makes his first commitment to maintain South Vietnam as a separate nation.

22 Christian A. Herter replaces John Foster Dulles as secretary of state.

July 1 General Lyman Lemnitzer replaces General Maxwell Taylor as chief of staff, U.S. Army.

8 First American servicemen (Major Dale Bius and Master Sergeant Chester Ovnard) killed by Vietcong attack at Bien Hoa.

Dec. 1 Thomas S. Gates, Jr., replaces Neil H. McElroy as secretary of defense.

31 Approximately 760 U.S. military personnel in Vietnam.

1960

Oct. 1 General George Decker replaces General Lyman Lemnitzer as chief of staff, U.S. Army.

Dec. 20 National Liberation Front established.

31 Approximately 900 U.S. military personnel in Vietnam.

1961

Jan. 21 John F. Kennedy succeeds Dwight D. Eisenhower as president. Dean Rusk succeeds Christian A. Herter as secretary of state. Robert S. McNamara succeeds Thomas S. Gates, Jr., as secretary of defense. McGeorge Bundy succeeds Gordon Gray as national security adviser.

28 Kennedy approves a Vietnam counterinsurgency plan. Mar. 23 Kennedy insists that a Laotian ceasefire must precede negotiations to establish a neutral Laos.

May 9–15 Vice President Lyndon Johnson visits South Vietnam and recommends a strong American commitment there. Geneva Conference on Laos opens.

June 9 President Ngo Dinh Diem asks for U.S. military advisers to train the South Vietnamese Army.

July 1 General Maxwell Taylor is appointed military adviser to President John F. Kennedy.

Nov. 3 General Maxwell Taylor concludes that U.S. military, financial, and political aid will bring victory without a U.S. takeover of the war. He advises Kennedy to send 8,000 U.S. combat troops to Vietnam.

Dec. 15 Kennedy restates U.S. commitment to an independent South Vietnam.

31 U.S. military personnel in Vietnam now number 3,205.

1962

Feb. 6 MACV (U.S. Military Assistance Command, Vietnam) established in Saigon under the command of General Paul Harkins. The major buildup of American forces begins.

14 Kennedy authorizes U.S. military advisers in Vietnam to return fire if fired upon.

Mar. 22   United States launches the Strategic Hamlet (rural pacification) Program.

July 23   Geneva Accords on Laos signed.

Oct. 1   General Earle Wheeler replaces General George Decker as chief of staff, U.S. Army. General Maxwell Taylor replaces General Lyman Lemnitzer as chairman, Joint Chiefs of Staff.

Dec. 31   U.S. military personnel in Vietnam now number 11,300.

1963

Aug. 21   South Vietnamese troops attack Buddhist pagodas.

22   Henry Cabot Lodge replaces Frederick Nolting as U.S. ambassador to Vietnam.

Nov. 1   Military coup overthrows the government of President Ngo Dinh Diem.

2   Diem and his brother Ngo Dinh Nhu assassinated.

22   President John F. Kennedy assassinated.

Dec. 31   U.S. military personnel in Vietnam now number 16,300.

1964

Feb. 7   Johnson removes American dependents from South Vietnam.

June 20   General William Westmoreland replaces General Paul Harkins as head of MACV.

23   General Maxwell Taylor replaces Henry Cabot Lodge as U.S. ambassador to South Vietnam.

30   Admiral Ulysses S. Grant Sharp replaces Admiral Harry D. Felt as CINCPAC.

July 3   General Harold Johnson replaces General Earle Wheeler as chief of staff, U.S. Army.

Aug. 2   U.S. destroyer *Maddox* allegedly attacked by North Vietnamese patrol boats in the Gulf of Tonkin.

4   U.S. destroyer *Turner Joy* claims attack by North Vietnamese patrol boats.

7   U.S. Congress passes Gulf of Tonkin Resolution.

Oct. 1   U.S. Army Fifth Special Forces Group arrives in Vietnam.

Nov. 1   Vietcong attack Bien Hoa Air Base. Six U.S. B-57 bombers destroyed; five American service personnel killed.

2   Johnson defeats Senator Barry Goldwater in presidential election.

Dec. 24   Vietcong kill two U.S. soldiers in an attack on the Brinks Hotel in Saigon.

31   U.S. military personnel in Vietnam now number 23,300.

1965

Feb. 7   Vietcong launch a widespread attack on American military installations in South Vietnam.

Mar. 2   Operation Rolling Thunder begins.

8   First American combat troops (U.S. Third Marine regiment) arrive in Vietnam to defend Danang.

24   First teach-in held at the University of Michigan.

Apr. 6   Johnson permits U.S. ground combat troops to conduct offensive operations in South Vietnam.

17   Students for a Democratic Society hold antiwar rally in Washington, D.C.

May 15   National Teach-In held throughout the country.

June 8   State Department reports that Johnson has authorized the use of U.S. troops in direct combat if the South Vietnamese Army requests assistance.

July 8   Henry Cabot Lodge succeeds Maxwell Taylor as U.S. ambassador to South Vietnam.

Oct. 15–16   Antiwar protests in forty American cities.

Nov. 14–16   Battle of the Ia Drang Valley.

Dec. 25   Johnson suspends bombing of North Vietnam (Operation Rolling Thunder) and invites North Vietnam to negotiate.

31   U.S. military personnel in Vietnam now number 184,300; 636 U.S. military personnel killed in action to date; 22,420 Allied troops in Vietnam.

1966

Jan. 31   Bombing of North Vietnam (Operation Rolling Thunder) resumes.

Feb. 4   Senate Foreign Relations Committee opens televised hearings on the Vietnam War.

6   President Lyndon Johnson convenes the Honolulu Conference.

Mar. 1   Senate refuses to repeal the Gulf of Tonkin Resolution.

20   President Lyndon Johnson convenes the Guam Conference.

Apr. 1   Walt Rostow replaces McGeorge Bundy as national security adviser.

7   President Lyndon Johnson offers the Johns Hopkins Speech. May 1 U.S. forces bombard Vietcong targets in Cambodia.

June 29   United States bombs oil facilities in Haiphong and Hanoi.

Oct. 26   Johnson visits U.S. troops in Vietnam.

Dec. 31   U.S. military personnel in Vietnam now number 385,300; 6,644 U.S. military personnel killed in action to date; 52,500 Allied military personnel in Vietnam.

1967

Jan. 8   Operation Cedar Falls begins.

26   Operation Cedar Falls ends.

Feb. 22   Operation Junction City begins.

Apr. 15   One hundred thousand antiwar protesters rally in New York.

May 1   Ellsworth Bunker replaces Henry Cabot Lodge as U.S. ambassador to South Vietnam.

9   Robert Komer appointed deputy to the MACV commander.

14   Operation Junction City ends.

19   U.S. planes bomb a power plant in Hanoi.

July 7   Congressional Joint Economic committee estimates the war will cost $4 billion to $6 billion more in 1967 than the $20.3 billion requested by Johnson.

Sept. 3   Nguyen Van Thieu elected president of South Vietnam.

29   Johnson offers to stop bombing of North Vietnam if they will immediately come to the negotiating table (San Antonio Formula).

Oct. 21   Fifty thousand antiwar activists protest at the Pentagon.

Dec. 31   U.S. military personnel in Vietnam now number 485,600; 16,021 U.S. military personnel killed in action to date.

1968

Jan. 3   Senator Eugene McCarthy announces his decision to seek the Democratic presidential nomination.

21   NVA siege of Khe Sanh begins.

30   Tet offensive begins.

31   Vietcong and NVA capture Hue.
      General Leonard F. Chapman replaces General Wallace M. Greene as Marine Corps commandant.

Feb. 1   Richard M. Nixon announces his candidacy for the presidency.

25 ARVN and U.S. troops reconquer Hue.

27 Westmoreland requests 206,000 more troops. CBS anchorman Walter Cronkite predicts over the evening news that the war cannot be won.

Mar. 12 Eugene McCarthy almost defeats Lyndon Johnson in the New Hampshire Democratic presidential primary.

16 Senator Robert Kennedy announces his decision to seek the Democratic presidential nomination.

My Lai massacre takes place.

25–26 Senior Advisory Group on Vietnam recommends de-escalation of the American commitment in Vietnam.

31 Lyndon Johnson announces his decision not to run for reelection.

Apr. 23 Columbia University demonstrations begin.

26 Two hundred thousand people in New York City demonstrate against the war.

27 Vice President Hubert Humphrey announces his decision to seek the Democratic presidential nomination.

May 3 Johnson announces that formal peace talks will take place in Paris.

12 Vietnam peace talks open in Paris.

June 6 Robert Kennedy is assassinated.

July 1 General Creighton Abrams replaces General William Westmoreland as head of MACV.

3 General William Westmoreland replaces General Harold Johnson as chief of staff, U.S. Army.

31 Admiral John McCain replaces Admiral U.S. Grant Sharp as CINCPAC.

Aug. 28 Antiwar protests and riots in Chicago during the Democratic National Convention.

Oct. 31 Johnson announces end of bombing of North Vietnam. Operation Rolling Thunder ends.

Nov. 5 Richard Nixon defeats Hubert Humphrey in the 1968 presidential election.

Dec. 31 U.S. military personnel in Vietnam now number 536,000; 30,610 U.S. military personnel killed in action to date; 65,600 Allied troops in Vietnam.

1969

Jan. 22 Operation Dewey Canyon begins.

Richard Nixon inaugurated as president.

William Rogers becomes secretary of state.

Melvin Laird becomes secretary of defense.

Henry Kissinger becomes national security adviser.

Mar. 18 Operation Dewey Canyon ends. Operation Menu begins.

26 Women Strike for Peace demonstration in Washington, D.C.

Apr. 30 The number of U.S. military personnel in Vietnam reaches 543,300.

May 10 Operation Apache Snow begins.

14 Nixon proposes peace plan for Vietnam involving mutual troop withdrawal.

June 7 Operation Apache Snow ends.

8 Nixon announces the removal of 25,000 troops from Vietnam.

July 25 Richard Nixon proclaims the Nixon Doctrine.

Aug. 27 U.S. Ninth Infantry Division withdraws from Vietnam.

Sept. 3 Ho Chi Minh dies.

Oct. 15 National Moratorium antiwar demonstrations staged throughout the United States.

Nov. 15 The New Mobilization Committee to End the War in Vietnam sponsors a demonstration of 250,000 in Washington, D.C.

16 My Lai massacre described in the press.

30 U.S. Third Division withdraws from Vietnam.

Dec. 11 U.S. Third Brigade, Eighty-second Airborne Division, withdraws from Vietnam.

31 U.S. military personnel strength in Vietnam declines to 475,200; 40,024 U.S. military personnel killed in action to date. Allied military personnel in Vietnam totals 70,300.

1970

Feb. 20 Henry Kissinger opens secret peace negotiations in Paris.

Mar. 18 Prince Norodom Sihanouk of Cambodia deposed by General Lon Nol.

Apr. 15 U.S. First Infantry Division withdraws from Vietnam.

29 Operations in Cambodia begin.

30 United States invades Cambodia.

May 4 National Guard troops kill four students at Kent State University during demonstrations against the Cambodian invasion.

June 30 Operations in Cambodia end.

Oct. 11 U.S. Third Brigade, Ninth Infantry Division, leaves Vietnam.

Nov. 21 Unsuccessful raid on the Son Tay Prison in North Vietnam.

Dec. 7 U.S. Fourth Infantry Division leaves Vietnam.

8 U.S. Twenty-fifth Infantry Division withdraws from Vietnam.

22 U.S. Congress prohibits U.S. combat forces or advisers in Cambodia and Laos.

31 U.S. military personnel strength in Vietnam declines to 334,600; 44,245 U.S. military personnel killed in action to date. Allied military personnel declines to 67,700.

1971

Jan. 30 Operation Lam Son 719 begins.

31 Winter Soldier Investigation begins in Detroit.

Mar. 3 U.S. Fifth Special Forces Group leaves Vietnam.

5 U.S. Eleventh Armored Cavalry Regiment withdraws from Vietnam.

29 Lieutenant William L. Calley, Jr., found guilty of murder.

Apr. 6 Operation Lam Son 719 ends.

14 U.S. III Marine Amphibious Force withdraws from Vietnam. 20 Demonstrators in Washington, D.C., and San Francisco call for an end to the war.

29 U.S. First Cavalry Division withdraws from Vietnam.

30 U.S. Second Brigade, Twenty-fifth Infantry Division, withdraws from Vietnam.

May 3–5 People's Coalition for Peace and Justice demonstrates against the war in Washington, D.C.

June 13 *New York Times* starts publishing the Pentagon Papers.

30 Supreme Court allows publication of the Pentagon Papers.

Aug. 25 U.S. 173d Airborne Brigade withdraws from Vietnam.

27 U.S. First Brigade, Fifth Infantry Division, withdraws from Vietnam.

31 Royal Thai Army withdraws from Vietnam.

Nov. 12 Nixon confines U.S. ground forces to a defensive role.

Dec. 26 Nixon orders resumption of bombing of North Vietnam.

31 U.S. military personnel strength declines to 156,800; 45,626 U.S. military personnel killed in action to date. Allied military personnel in Vietnam declines to 53,900.

1972

Feb. 21 Nixon seeks détente with the People's Republic of China by visiting Beijing.

Mar. 10 U.S. 101st Airborne Division leaves Vietnam.

23 United States suspends Paris peace talks until North Vietnam and the NLF enter into "serious discussions."

30 Eastertide Offensive begins.

Apr. 7 Battle of An Loc begins.

15 U.S. bombing of Hanoi begins again.

15–20 Widespread antiwar demonstrations across the United States.

27 Paris peace talks resume.

May 1 North Vietnamese conquer Quang Tri.

4 United States suspends the Paris peace talks.

8 U.S. Navy mines North Vietnamese ports.

June 18 NVA forces an end to the battle of An Loc.

22 Watergate break-in and arrests.

26 U.S. Third Brigade, 1st Cavalry Division, withdraws from Vietnam.

29 U.S. 196th Infantry Brigade withdraws from Vietnam.

July 1 General Bruce Palmer, Jr., becomes acting chief of staff, U.S. Army.

13 Paris peace talks resume after ten weeks.

Aug. 23 U.S. Third Battalion, Twenty-first Infantry, withdraws from Vietnam.

Sept. 15 ARVN forces recapture Quang Tri.

26–27 Henry Kissinger conducts secret talks with North Vietnamese diplomats in Paris.

Oct. 16 General Creighton Abrams becomes chief of staff, U.S. Army.

17 Peace talks begin in Laos.

19–20 Kissinger meets with President Nguyen Van Thieu in Saigon to secure South Vietnamese support for the pending Paris Peace Accords.

Nov. 7 Nixon is reelected president in a landslide over Senator George McGovern.

20–21 Kissinger and Le Duc Tho put finishing touches on the Paris Peace Accords.

Dec. 13 Paris peace talks stall.

18–29 Operation Linebacker II conducted.

31 U.S. military personnel strength declines to 24,000; 45,926 U.S. military personnel killed in action to date.
Allied military personnel drops to 35,500. SVNAF personnel killed in action to date numbers 195,847.

1973

Jan. 8–12 Kissinger and Le Duc Tho convene more private negotiations.

15 Nixon halts all U.S. offensive action against North Vietnam.

27 Peace pact signed in Paris by the United States, South Vietnam, North Vietnam, and the National Liberation Front.

30 Elliot L. Richardson becomes secretary of defense.

Feb. 12 First of American POWs released by North Vietnam.

21 Peace agreement signed in Laos.

Mar. 16 ROK Capital Division and Ninth Infantry Division withdraw from Vietnam.

29 MACV headquarters removed.
Last of American POWs released by North Vietnam.

June 13 Implementation accord signed in Paris by the United States, South Vietnam, North Vietnam, and the National Liberation Front.

24 Graham Martin becomes U.S. ambassador to South Vietnam. Congress prohibits all bombing in Cambodia after August 15.

July 2 James Schlesinger becomes secretary of defense.

Aug. 14 All direct American military operations end in all of Indochina.

Sept. 22 Henry Kissinger becomes secretary of state.

Nov. 7 War Powers Resolution becomes law despite a presidential veto.

Dec. 31 U.S. military personnel in South Vietnam drops to 50. To date, 46,163 U.S. military personnel killed in action. No Allied military personnel remain in Vietnam.

1974

Aug. 9 Nixon resigns the presidency.
Gerald Ford is inaugurated as president of the United States.

20 Congress reduces aid to South Vietnam from $1 billion to $700 million.

Sept. 4 General Creighton Abrams dies.

16 Ford offers clemency to draft evaders and military deserters.

Oct. 3 General Frederick Weyand becomes chief of staff, U.S. Army.

Dec. 13 Combat between NVA and ARVN is conducted in Phuoc Long Province.

31 U.S. military personnel in Vietnam remains at 50.

1975

Jan. 6 NVA troops take control of Phuoc Long Province.

8 North Vietnam decides on a massive invasion of South Vietnam.

Mar. 10 NVA captures Ban Me Thuot.

14 President Nguyen Van Thieu withdraws ARVN forces from Central Highlands.

19 NVA captures Quang Tri Province.

26 Hue falls to the NVA.

30 Danang falls to the NVA.

Apr. 1 Cambodian President Lon Nol flees Cambodia in face of Khmer Rouge invasion. South Vietnam abandons the northern half of the country to North Vietnam.

8–20 Battle of Xuan Loc.

11–13 Operation Eagle Pull removes U.S. embassy personnel from Phnom Penh, Cambodia.

12 President Nguyen Van Thieu resigns.

17 Cambodia falls to Khmer Rouge troops.

29–30 Operation Frequent Wind evacuates all American personnel and some South Vietnamese from Vietnam.
NVA captures Saigon.

30 Vietnam War ends.

May 12 *Mayaguez* seized in Kampuchean waters.

Glossary and Guide to Acronyms

AID: Agency for International Development.

Airborne: People or material delivered by helicopter.

Amtrack: An amphibious vehicle, equipped with armor , primarlily used by the Marine Corps to transport troops and material.

ARVN: Army of the Republic of Vietnam.

Base Area: An area of installations, defensive fortifications, or other physical structures used by the enemy.

Base Camp: A semipermanent field headquarters and center for a given unit, usually within the unit's tactical area of responsibility.

Battalion Days in the Field: Days when battalions are patrolling in the field. It was a standard measure of battalion productivity.

Body Bags: Plastic bags used for retrieval of bodies in the field.

Charlie, Charles, Chuck: Nickname used by American troops for the Vietcong.

Chieu Hoi: An amnesty program offered to the Vietcong by the government of the Republic of Vietnam.

CIA: Central Intelligence Agency.

CIDG: Civilian Irregular Defense Group.

CINCPAC: Commander in Chief, Pacific (U.S. Navy).

Clear and Hold: An American military tactic in which U.S. troops tried to capture and permanently hold an area.

CORDS: Civil Operations and Revolutionary Development Support.

COSVN: Central Office of South Vietnam.

DeSoto: U.S. Navy destroyer patrols in the South China Sea.

DMZ: Demilitarized Zone.

DRV: Democratic Republic of Vietnam (North Vietnam).

Firebase: A temporary artillery firing position, often secured by infantry.

Firefight: An exchange of small-arms fire between opposing units.

I Corps: Northernmost military region in South Vietnam.

IV Corps: Southernmost military region in South Vietnam, located in the Mekong Delta.

Frag: To kill or attempt to kill one's own officers or sergeants.

Free Fire Zone: Any area in which permission was not required prior to firing on targets.

Gooks: Slang term, brought to Vietnam by Korean War veterans, for anyone of Asian descent.

Green Berets: U.S. Special Forces troops.

Guerrilla Warfare: Military operations conducted in hostile territory by irregular, primarily indigenous forces.

GVN: Government of Vietnam (South Vietnam).

Hedgehogs: Isolated outposts in which the French high command concentrated troops.

Hot Pursuit: Policy allowing American troops to chase Vietcong and NVA soldiers across the border into Cambodia.

JCS: Joint Chiefs of Staff.

Khmer Rouge: Cambodian communists.

Light at the End of the Tunnel: Term used to describe the imminent demise of the Vietcong and North Vietnamese.

MAAG: Military Assistance and Advisory Group.

MACV: Military Assistance Command, Vietnam (Mac-Vee)

Main Force: Vietcong and North Vietnamese military units.

M-16: The standard American rifle used in Vietnam after 1966.

Napalm: An incendiary used by French and Americans as a defoliant and as an antipersonnel weapon.

NLF: National Leberation Front (the political organization of the Vietcong until 1969).

NVA: North Vietnamese Army.

Pacification: Several programs of the South Vietnamese and the US. governments to destroy the Vietcong in the villages, gain civilian support for the Republic of South Vietnam and stablize the countryside.

Pathet Lao: Laotian communists.

PAVN: People's Army of Vietnam (North Vietnamese Army, NVA).

PLVN: People's Liberation Army of Vietnam (Vietcong troops).

PRGVN: Provisional Revolutionary Government of South Vietnam (the political organization of the Vietcong after 1969).

Punji Stake: A razor-sharp bamboo stake sometimes coated with poison or feces and usually hidden under water, along trails, at ambush sites, or in deep pits.

ROKs: Troops from the Republic of Korea.

Ruff-Puffs: South Vietnamese Regional Forces and Popular Forces; paramilitary forces usually of squad or platoon size recruited and utilized in a hamlet or village.

RVN: Republic of Vietnam (South Vietnam).

SAM: Soviet-made surface-to-air missiles.

Sappers: North Vietnamese or Vietcong demolition commandos.

Search and Destroy: Offensive operations designed to find and destroy enemy forces rathern than establish permanent government control.

II Corps: Central Highlands military region in South Vietnam.

Seventeenth Parallel: Temporary division line between North and South Vietnam.

Sortie: One aircraft making one takeoff and landing to conduct a mission for which it was scheduled.

Special Forces: U.S. soldiers, populary known as Green Berets, trained in techniques of guerrilla warfare.

SRV: Socialist Republic of Vietnam.

Tet: Vietnamese Lunar New Year holiday period.

III Corps: Military region between Saigon and the Central Highlands. **Vietcong:** Communist forces fighting in South Vietnam.

Vietminh: Communist forces fighting the French before 1954.

Vietnamization: President Nixon's program to gradually turn the war over to the South Vietnamese while phasing out American troops.

Index